THE LIONS' DEN

SUSIE LINFIELD

The Lions' Den

ZIONISM AND THE LEFT

FROM HANNAH ARENDT

TO NOAM CHOMSKY

Yale UNIVERSITY PRESS   NEW HAVEN AND LONDON

Published with assistance from the foundation established in memory of Calvin Chapin of the Class of 1788, Yale College.

Yale University Press books may be purchased in quantity for educational, business, or promotional use. For information, please e-mail sales.press@yale.edu (U.S. office) or sales@yaleup.co.uk (U.K. office).

Set in Scala type by IDS Infotech, Ltd., Chandigarh, India.
Printed in the United States of America.

Library of Congress Control Number: 2018954877
ISBN 978-0-300-22298-2 (hardcover : alk. paper)

A catalogue record for this book is available from the British Library.

This paper meets the requirements of ANSI/NISO Z39.48-1992 (Permanence of Paper).

10 9 8 7 6 5 4 3 2

In memory of my father

We are interested in history because therein are hidden the small experiences of the human race. . . . Within the historical failures, there is still concealed a power that can seek its correction.

—*Gershom Scholem*

Jews and Arabs have a special reverence for the past. But they are also fatally trapped in its lies.

—*Shlomo Ben-Ami*

It is hard to be a prophet in the land of prophets. There are too many.

—*Amos Oz*

· Do you know why we Palestinians are famous? Because you are our enemy. . . . Yes, the interest is in you, not me! . . . We are lucky that Israel is our enemy, because the Jews are the center of the world. . . . I do not have any illusions. The international interest in the Palestinian question is only a reflection of the interest in the Jewish question.

—*Mahmoud Darwish*

CONTENTS

Introduction: A Double Grief, and a Hope   1

THE LIONS' DEN

Introduction

A DOUBLE GRIEF, AND A HOPE

THIS BOOK GREW OUT OF SEVERAL EXPERIENCES that were simultaneously emotional and intellectual. Here are two of the most salient and painful.

New York City, 2011: I am at a dinner party with my partner and his friends, who are mostly left-wing intellectuals at the university where he teaches. These are highly informed, sophisticated, accomplished people: philosophers, anthropologists, a humanitarian-aid worker. We share a worldview, a moral sensibility, a pride in holding certain values, and a great deal of warmth.

In the course of our dinner, the name of a well-known journalist—acclaimed for his writings on genocide in Africa—comes up. "Oh, he's a *Zionist!*" one person says disparagingly, and the others dutifully shake their heads in condescension and dismay. There is a pause, during which I debate the pros and cons of disturbing this amicable gathering, and then I say, with a slight gulp, "Well, so am I." A frozen, stunned silence ensues. I explain: "I believe in a state for the Jewish people, along with a Palestinian one." The silence continues; no one addresses or looks at me, though they shoot pitying glances at my partner. (How, they seem to wonder, has he ended up with such a reactionary?) Finally, because we are all friends, we turn, abruptly and with embarrassment, to more congenial topics.

1

Hebron, West Bank, 2012: I am visiting Israel with an American group called Partners for Progressive Israel, which supports a two-state solution, works against the Occupation and the Likud, and is aligned with Meretz, the left-wing Israeli party. We have traveled to Hebron, a Palestinian city of about 200,000 inhabitants, in which a few hundred ultra-nationalist Israeli settlers have established themselves. Rather than representing Zionist values, as they claim, they have re-created the despised, endangered, and ghettoized position of the Jews that Zionism was designed to eradicate. Talk about the return of the repressed! Because of these few but fanatical settlers, Hebron is now divided. The Arab sector of the city is off-limits to us; my colleagues and I walk down a designated Israeli street. We Americans are surrounded by, "protected" by, Israeli soldiers who, I am pretty sure, would rather be anywhere but here. Palestinian boys scamper beside us, but are prevented from crossing over to our side of the street from theirs. The scene is bizarre, ludicrous, mortifying; a progressive Israel seems very far away. I am ashamed to be a Jew.

How has it come to this? How has "Zionist," sometimes shortened to the disparaging "Zio," become the dirtiest word to the international Left— akin, say, to racist, pedophile, or rapist? How is it that anti-Israel activists in London scream at, and assault, an Israeli speaker, though he is one of the leading architects of the joint Palestinian-Israeli Geneva Initiative, which would ensure a Palestinian state? How is it that signs proclaiming "We Are All Hezbollah" are brandished at supposedly left-wing demon-strations in London and New York? This is not the lunatic fringe. On the contrary: A highly respected American academic has praised Hezbollah and Hamas as "progressive" social movements that are part of the "global left," while the leader of Britain's Labour Party—the Labour Party!—has described these groups as "friends"; Labour has recently issued a forty-one-page report on its internal problems with anti-Semitism.[1] An acclaimed British psychoanalyst diagnoses Zionism as "a form of collec-tive insanity" that is dogmatic, ruthless, and irrational.[2] A leading women's-rights activist in the United States proclaims that feminism and Zionism are irreconcilable—though this might be news to the hundreds of women who took to the streets of Tel Aviv, Jerusalem, and Haifa in the summer of 2017 to protest gender violence.[3]

On the other side: How did Israel, through the ruinous settlements project, come to recreate itself as a ghettoized minority amongst a hostile population? How did it come to deny the national rights of a neighboring people and to violently suppress them—not for a year or two, but for over a half century? How did it come to impose closures, checkpoints, house demolitions, imprisonment without trial, land thefts, torture, and murder in the Occupied Territories?

The usual answer is that the first development (antipathy to Israel) is a response to the second (its Occupation). But this is too perfunctory and at best incomplete. For many on the left are repelled not only by Israel's oppression of the Palestinians; they are repelled by the existence of Israel itself. Hence the idealization, or at least acceptance, of fundamentalist Islamist groups dedicated to its eradication. Furthermore, for the past half century or so, those who define themselves as progressive have shown a startling ability to support regimes far more repressive and violent, and far less egalitarian and politically open, than Israel—even the Israel of the Occupation. (There are multiple ironies here: In the 1960s, when Israel had two above-ground Communist parties and the Baathists were torturing Iraqi Communists to death, the Left castigated Israel as "fascist" and celebrated Iraq as "revolutionary." Today, in the midst of Syria's savage civil war, there are self-proclaimed leftists who are more sympathetic to Bashar al-Assad's right to rule Syria than to Israel's right to exist.) So there must be more to the story than this—more, that is, to the well-known story of the Left's break with Israel after the latter's 1967 victory and subsequent occupation of the West Bank and Gaza. There is something here that does not compute.

In the course of writing my first book, *The Cruel Radiance: Photography and Political Violence*, I delved into the lives of Robert Capa, David Seymour (Chim), and their colleagues. I was struck by how passionately pro-Israel the Left of Capa's time was, both in the 1947–48 Arab-Israeli wars and afterwards; this was true of photographers, journalists, writers, and ordinary Left activists.[4] (Capa himself thought of settling in Israel.) Not only that: Leftists of the time reviled Britain—not Israel—as the imperialist power of the Middle East; in equal measure, they abhorred the retrograde Arab regimes arrayed against the new Jewish state. Capa and his comrades represented the Left that emerged just after the end of the Russian Revolution and World War I; grew to maturity in the Weimar

Republic and France's Popular Front; fought fascism in Spain; and trekked through the rubble of a continent, and through the remnants of the death camps, at the end of the Second World War. For them, the creation of the State of Israel and the fight for its independence were a seamless continuation of their previous struggles; they compared the Haganah to the Loyalists in Spain.

After completing *The Cruel Radiance,* I found myself wondering about the positions of various other Left intellectuals and about more general shifts in Left politics since Capa's era. That led to this book, in which I probe how eight mid-twentieth- (and early twenty-first-) century writers of the American and European Left viewed Zionism before 1948 and, subsequently, the Israeli-Arab conflict. In the course of my research, I discovered much that surprised and pained me, and I was forced to examine—and reevaluate—my own views as well.

Researching this book led me to question whether the Left's changing attitudes toward Israel—from firm though never unanimous support to angry repudiation—was mainly the result of the brutal Israeli Occupation. Undoubtedly, that is a major factor. But I came to conclude that another factor in that shift, of perhaps even greater importance, was the transformation of the Left itself. Starting in the second half of the twentieth century, the Left moved from defining itself as anti-fascist to defining itself as anti-imperialist, and to an identification of the formerly colonized peoples of the Third World as the main agents of social justice. This was not a particularly Marxist position—he did not believe that socialism would or could be founded in the colonized world—but never mind. (Here I should clarify that my definition of the Left is ecumenical: It includes anti-fascists and anti-colonialists, social democrats, Marxists of the Old Left, anti-imperialists of the New Left, avatars of Third World revolution, and the more recent term "progressives." Though I often use the term "the Left," I am aware that there are many Lefts and many kinds of leftists; I am interested in major trends. There are, also, many kinds of Zionists; unless otherwise noted, I generally take this to mean those who support a democratic state for the Jewish people.)

These changes in Left theory and practice had their roots in the 1950s, beginning with the Algerian and Tunisian revolutions, the anti-colonial movements in the wider Arab and African worlds, and the confused responses to them by the European Left. A 1958 essay by British

Marxist Harry Hanson in the *New Reasoner*, which defined itself as "A Quarterly Journal of Socialist Humanism," illustrates the problem. Addressing what he called the Arab nationalist movement, Hanson explained: "Despite its disorderliness, its confusion of objectives, its superficially farcical features, its exaggerated xenophobia, its apparent resemblance, in certain of its aspects, to Fascism or Nazism, and—most serious of all—its vitriolic hatred of the State of Israel, it is fundamentally and essentially a progressive movement."[5] Such convolutions were a foretaste of the future.

The new orientation came to fruition in the 1960s, partly as a result of deep disappointment with the failed revolutions of 1968. Despite triumphalist rhetoric at the time and since, 1968 heralded a series of defeats for the Left: These included the crushing of the Prague Spring and the student protests in Poland, accompanied by anti-Semitic purges; the violent repression of the Mexican student movement; the election of conservative governments in France and the United States; and the escalation of the U.S.'s war in Vietnam. This was Richard Nixon's year of victory—not, as the title of one book puts it, *Year of the Heroic Guerrilla*. Most devastating of all, no worldwide student-worker revolution broke out. These defeats led the Left to look for new revolutionary heroes, preferably outside the developed West and those associated with it.

In a fateful historic conjunction, these frustrations, and the search they inspired, were directly preceded by Israel's stunning victory in the Six-Day War. Israel was almost instantly transformed into the colonialist-racist-imperialist-fascist oppressor, while the Palestinians were anointed as revolutionary-socialist-Marxist-Leninist-anti-imperialist freedom fighters. Two months after the war, the esteemed civil rights organization SNCC (Student Nonviolent Coordinating Committee) accused Israelis of "imitating their Nazi oppressors."[6] SNCC linked "Jews who are exploiting black people in the ghettos" with "the oppression of the Arabs by the Israelis," charged that Jews "control much of Africa's mineral wealth," and accused Israel of having "sabotaged African liberation movements." In September 1967, the National Conference for New Politics, a meeting of major black and white New Left groups held in Chicago, excoriated the "imperialist Zionist war"; such denunciations soon became de rigueur.[7] The Black Panthers would endorse Fatah's program, which explicitly called for the liquidation—its word—of Israel.

After the Six-Day War, the anti-Israel phenomenon became worldwide, and it moved with speed. In Germany, an older Left, represented by people like Günter Grass, defended Israel, but the New Left immediately tagged Israel as an imperialist and—irony of ironies—fascist state. "Within a remarkably short space of time," political analyst Hans Kundnani writes, the "view of the Arab-Israeli conflict would be virtually turned on its head." For the German New Left, the Palestinian struggle "would replace the war in Vietnam as its *cause célèbre* and become an obsession." German New Left militants became enthusiastic proponents of—and, sometimes, participants in—Palestinian terror attacks. (As the chairman of Germany's Socialist German Students League explained a few days after the war, "We don't have any anti-Semitism to overcome.")[8] For much of the French New Left, Palestinians became the new Algerians (though Jean-Paul Sartre—again, representative of an older generation— disagreed). None of this was a reaction to the Occupation and the settlements, which didn't yet exist. At the same time, Israel, too, would embark on a radically new direction—a rightward direction—albeit not nearly so quickly. The story of Israel and the Left in the late 1960s is thus the story of a perfect, or rather perfectly disastrous, storm. It is one that has never receded.

In my view, Israel became, and still functions as, the prism through which changes in Left values can be most clearly seen and have been most clearly acted out. Israel is the Rorschach test of the Left. And, for a number of reasons that I will discuss in the following chapters, hostility toward Zionism—the political self-determination of the Jewish people—became the Left's "answer," albeit a contorted and dishonest one, to one of the Left's fundamental postwar questions: How can we maintain our traditional universalist values in light of the nationalist movements sweeping the formerly colonized world? The Left's vitriol toward Zionism—its turning of Israel, as the socialist-Zionist Simcha Flapan wrote shortly after the 1967 war, into "the new Shylock of the non-aligned world"—has enabled it to avoid looking at its own contradictions, shortcomings, and failures.[9] More important, it has occluded the complex nature of the Israeli-Palestinian conflict.

Rather than being viewed in a clear and multifaceted light, Israel is often reduced to a metaphor (as in, Israel = South Africa). The problem with metaphors—with seeing one thing as another—is that, when it comes to politics as opposed to literature, they are often wildly misleading and hide more than they reveal. Historian Enzo Traverso put it well (though his views on Israel are different than mine), and what he wrote applies to Israelis and Palestinians alike: "The temptation to interpret new phenomena in old categories is ever-present. Basically, when the insurmountable traumas bequeathed by the past are projected onto the present, debate slips into polemics that are both virulent and sterile."[10] The Arab world, too, has used Israel as a reflecting pool; as historian Fouad Ajami wrote, "From the time of Israel's birth as a state, talking about Israel has been, in part, a way that Arabs talk about their own world."[11]

The Western Left has, rightly, supported the just national and human aspirations of the Palestinians. This is, and continues to be, a major political and moral accomplishment. But the accomplishment has exacted a heavy price: the idealization, misrepresentation, and distortion of the Palestinian national movement and the evasion, if not defense, of its most antihuman acts. As some of the writers discussed in this book argue, in the Left's keen focus on anti-imperialism and its animus to Israel, it twisted itself into supporting some of the world's most sadistic modes of terrorism and most fearsomely repressive regimes—regimes that many leftists had little interest in *except* as symbols of anti-Zionist "resistance."

It is in the case of Israel that these new, anti-imperialist values were realized to the most extreme degree. For only in the case of Israel is the eradication of an extant nation—a nasty wolf sometimes hidden in the gentle sheep's clothing of a "one-state solution," a "democratic secular Palestine," or the "right of return"—considered a progressive demand. Only in the case of Israel is a nation's right to exist questioned—a question that, if applied to any other state, would be considered an expression of ethnocide or politicide. Only in the case of Israel is a bloody birth considered an argument for infanticide—or, even better, for a preventive abortion.

Today, the disputes over Israel have become woefully reductive, debased, and venomous; my students often tell me they are afraid to broach the subject. There is no other issue, either domestic or foreign, that is debated in such rancid tones. Today's debate is also a remarkably ignorant one; many people will confidently tell you their *opinions* of the Israeli-Palestinian conflict despite lacking any grasp of its history. In fact, a major theme of this book is the glib pseudo-history that is endlessly regurgitated from author to author, generation to generation—and then used as the foundation on which to justify political positions.

Here, for instance, is a line from an April 2016 press release from my university's graduate student union after it voted to endorse the Boycott, Divestment, Sanctions (BDS) movement: "In 1948, Zionist militias established a Jewish-only state." This is a false claim that even a modicum of uncontested research could have corrected. (At the end of hostilities in 1949, Israel's population consisted of 750,000 Jews and 160,000 Arabs, all citizens.) The problem here is BDS's political, not numerical, ignorance. That this statement was signed by many history students, who are presumably the professors of tomorrow, is not a good sign.

Unfortunately, they learn this anti-history from their elders such as Traverso. He is an often brilliant, admirably nondidactic historian, which makes the numerous errors in his recent book, titled *The End of Jewish Modernity*, so perplexing. Contrary to his claims, Israeli citizenship was not (and is not) bequeathed on "strictly religious and ethnic grounds"; Israel is not "a state reserved for Jews alone"; Arab atrocities in 1948 (and, presumably, 1947) were not "essentially reactive"; and the Haganah did not practice "the collective rape of women." Traverso praises the work of Ilan Pappé, an anti-Zionist Israeli historian, who "has chosen to place his research in the service of the Palestinian cause."[12] But shouldn't a scholar place his research, as have Israel's New Historians, in the service of the truth?

This dearth of historical knowledge and this false history—which in the Trump era have been defended by the Orwellian phrase "alternative facts"—have not always been so widespread. In looking at the eight writers discussed here, I have been impressed by how much deeper, better informed, and more nuanced their discussions were when compared to ours. These public intellectuals approached Israel with great intensity: with admiration and wrath, tenderness and hostility, hope and despair. But they also approached it with complex questions, intellectual maturity, and a hard-won understanding of tragedy.

Yet what is most conspicuous is how these writers, who often agreed about so many vital things—especially the virtues of socialism and the evils of colonialism—disagreed so radically about Israel. There is something about the particular ideology of Zionism and the particular State of Israel that have always confounded and polarized the Left. The Left has spent a lot of time and intellectual energy trying to solve the Jewish Problem—but it also has one.

The Lions' Den is not a general survey of the Left's relationship to Zionism or of the relationship of Jews to the Left. It does not propose a solution to the Israeli-Palestinian conflict, because I do not have one. Instead, it is an interrelated series of portraits through which I seek to uncover a rich, fraught, sometimes buried intellectual history. It examines writers who engaged what we might call "the Zionist Question" with fearless intellectual energy and, sometimes, far more perception and knowledge than exists in similar debates today.

Still, I am struck by the presuppositions and illusions that some leftists, even in previous periods, foisted upon the Zionist enterprise and the Jewish state. Israel, and the Arab-Israeli conflict, are templates upon which the Left has projected all sorts of inapt ideologies, hopes, anxieties, and fears. Too often, when these writers talked about Israel they talked about everything *other than* Israel itself; the same is true today. Inevitably, this has prevented the emergence of clear analyses and attainable solutions.

And so this book is, in large part, about the dangers of fantasy, symbol, metaphor, and theory overtaking reality and history. This book's heroes, if I can use that term, are those who allowed history *to matter:* those who, like Albert Memmi and Fred Halliday, based their political positions on history rather than vice versa. Necessarily, their positions were far from static, for history—and our understandings of it—are nothing if not fluid. Conversely, I am most critical of those who viewed Israelis and Arabs as projects on which to impose their a priori concepts. This is what links Hannah Arendt, my first subject, with Noam Chomsky, my last, though their ideas are so starkly dissimilar in other ways. If this book is a plea for anything, then, it is for honoring the demands of the reality principle over those of ideologies (however clever) and of wishes (however well-meaning). Caring about history is the only way we can care about politics—especially in a conflict that is, to a great extent, *about* history.

It is necessary, for instance, to document, and condemn, Zionist atrocities during the 1948 Arab-Israeli war. But there is no use in evading the fact that the war was instigated by five Arab states, which invaded Israel—an evasion practiced by such Left cultural critics and historians as

Stanley Aronowitz and Perry Anderson.[13] (Would these writers be so reluctant to name the aggressors in the 2003 invasion of Iraq?) There is no use
in pretending, as many accounts imply if not assume, that the Palestinians
or the Arab states were fighting for a binational or democratic entity—in
fact, in the areas where the Arab forces prevailed, all Jews were expelled or
killed; or that the neo-feudal Arab monarchies and their allies were a revolutionary force. (At the time, the *Daily Worker*, Britain's Communist newspaper, described the Arab detachments as a kind of mutant International
Brigade: They included Iraqi fascists, German Nazis, and Yugoslav
Royalists.) There is no use in pretending that the Arab Legion, which was
formed, financed, and led by the British, was anti-imperialist, or that
Palestinian society had no role in its own collapse. The problem with this
ersatz history, which is enormously widespread, is not that it is biased or
unfair (though it is). The problem is that it cannot lead us to an understanding of the past and, therefore, to what is either achievable or just in
the future. It is hard to learn from history when you use it primarily as a
cudgel or when a sliver of truth substitutes for the whole.

All the thinkers I examine here were influential in their time; many
still are, though sometimes for the wrong reasons. Each presented ideas
that, in my view, are eminently worthy of attention and discussion,
though I came to strongly disagree with some and was at times disappointed, frustrated, and angered by them. And though each wrote from a
particular viewpoint, determined by an individual mix of intellectual and
personal factors, various topics recur in their writings—topics that have
defined global, not just Israeli, politics in the twentieth century. The idea
of a state for the Jewish people, even before its founding, has been the
focal point of the most exigent questions: about democracy, nationalism,
socialism, the morality of violence, racism, anti-Semitism, secularism,
colonialism, self-determination, and justice. And so when we study the
history of the Left and Israel, we study the twentieth century's knottiest
dilemmas. When we talk about Israel, we talk about the very nature of
modernity and the often catastrophic history of the past century, which
continue to define our world. The stakes in this debate have always been
high—not just intellectually but emotionally too.

In "Part One: Europeans," I examine two thinkers whose lives and ideas
were formed by the rise of fascism in the 1930s. Chapter 1 analyzes

Hannah Arendt's long, extremely complicated relationship to Zionism and, then, to Israel. I also discuss how the subject of *Eichmann in Jerusalem* is Zionism (and Israel) as much as it is Nazism (and Germany). Arendt is often lauded by anti-Zionists for her presumed hostility to Israel and presumed prescience about the Arab-Israeli conflict. In fact, she was often the opposite of hostile, and she was not particularly prescient.

Or, rather, her prescience, which was confined to the question of Arab antipathy to Jewish settlement in Palestine, was hardly singular. The old chestnut about "a land without a people for a people without a land" is frequently hauled out to prove the Zionists' callous obliviousness to Palestine's native population. There was considerable truth to this, especially in the early years—though the blindness and contempt were mutual. (The Arab mayor of Jerusalem greeted the Balfour Declaration by observing of the Jews, "In all the countries where they are [living] at present they are not wanted . . . because they always arrive to suck the blood of everybody.")[14] Yet this analysis misses the central point.

The pre-state Zionists were nothing if not pragmatic—they had to be—and most realized, long before 1948, that the Arab inhabitants of Palestine were there, were a majority, and were opposed to the Jewish presence. This realization was shared by liberals like Ahad Ha'am, leftists like Chaim Arlosoroff and David Ben-Gurion, and rightists like Vladimir Jabotinsky. In fact, it was precisely this knowledge—this comprehension of Arab nationalism, which the 1936–39 Arab Revolt made unmistakably visible—that led the Zionists to organize in anticipation of the coming military conflict. As historian and diplomat Shlomo Ben-Ami wrote, "What became patently clear with the Arab Revolt was that it was now a struggle to the death, a war for individual and national survival between two antagonistic national communities."[15] Had the Yishuv ignored or underestimated the Palestinian Arabs, it would have been unprepared for the 1947–48 war. But it wasn't. Some Arabs, within Palestine and outside it, also realized the national meaning of the conflict. Others, however, clung to the delusion that the Yishuv was a flimsy colonial transplant that would either crumble of its own accord or be swiftly eradicated—a delusion for which they paid dearly.

It was Arendt, not the Zionists, who stubbornly denied the cruelly existential nature of the conflict and who retreated into the imaginary. Far from excelling in foresight, her writings on Zionism and Israel raise a fascinating—and troubling—question: How and why did a thinker who scorned abstraction and blind ideologies fall into these very traps when analyzing the Israeli-Palestinian conflict, especially in its most crucial periods?

Arthur Koestler, the subject of Chapter 2, was in some ways the iconic twentieth-century man: a refugee who traveled between different nations and was at home in none. He enthusiastically adhered to, and then violently rejected, the century's most important ideologies, including Communism and Zionism, though even as an anti-Communist he maintained a basically Stalinist mind-set that brooked no opposition, allowed no ambiguities, and admitted no errors. And even at his most fervently Zionist, his scorn for what he viewed as the defining Jewish qualities—in his view, neurosis and cowardice—was unrelenting. Koestler loved Zionism, when he did love Zionism, precisely because he thought it was *un-Jewish* in its militancy and self-reliance. Koestler's writings therefore raise the question: Can a movement for national liberation be based on self-contempt?

The subjects of "Part Two: Socialists" are four interconnected writers: Maxime Rodinson, Isaac Deutscher, Albert Memmi, and Fred Halliday. Two were classical Marxists (one a Stalinist, one an admirer of Trotsky), one a neo-Marxist. One was active in Tunisia's anti-colonial movement, another in Britain's anti-imperialist New Left. Three were European, while one was born and raised in an Arab country. Three were Jewish; two had parents slaughtered in the Shoah. One spoke Yiddish, three spoke Hebrew, three spoke Arabic. None lived in Israel, though three traveled there, and three had a deep knowledge of the Arab world.

Yet despite certain shared basic values—anti-capitalism, anti-colonialism, staunch secularism—they viewed Israel, and the Israeli-Arab conflict, in starkly different ways. I can think of no other political issue where this is so: no other issue, that is, which has been so bitterly divisive among leftists. As the British socialist (and former Communist) Mervyn Jones wrote in 1970: "One cannot easily recall another problem over which Socialists of good faith have disagreed so much—disagreed in their sympathies, disagreed over possible solutions, disagreed in finding a way to apply basic Socialist principles, disagreed in analysis of the very nature of the problem. . . . The maxim of 'Tell me where my enemies stand, and I'll know where I stand'—however useful in other situations—will not guide Socialists through this labyrinth."[16] His words ring true today.

In "Part Three: Americans," I turn to I. F. Stone and Noam Chomsky. Stone remains America's outstanding leftist journalist of the twentieth century, admired as a fearless foe of McCarthyism and of the Vietnam War. Along with Capa, he eagerly traveled to Palestine to cover Israel's War of Independence, which he celebrated as an anti-imperialist struggle against British oppression and as the long-awaited rejuvenation of the Jewish people. Yet he became a severe, sometimes tormented critic of Israeli policies. His writings on Israel were often perceptive; on the Arab world, much less so. That, too, is another theme of this book: the impossibility of analyzing the Arab-Israeli conflict when a major aspect of it is swathed in idealization or ignorance. A conflict is a dialectic; to shield oneself from part of it is to miss the meaning of the whole.

Noam Chomsky, the subject of my last chapter, is a different case from the other writers in this book. First, unlike most of those I discuss, he is alive and prolifically publishing as I write. More important, I chose to include him primarily because of the vast influence he has had on debates over Israel-Palestine and the reverence he inspires among so many. But of all the writers discussed in his book, he is the one whose strict adherence to ideology has most severely handicapped him and who has promulgated a palpably erroneous history of the Arab-Israeli conflict. Yet Chomsky clearly self-identifies as a member of the Jewish people; in no sense is he an anti-Semite. The great paradox, I believe, is that some of his most deeply flawed ideas about Israel stem from his fears about its survival.

This book is born out of a double grief. First, I am grieved by the contemporary Left's blanket hatred of Israel, which has done a tremendous amount to injure not just Israelis but Palestinians too; the glib, often uncritical "solidarity" offered to the latter has been a toxic gift. Second, I am grieved by the trajectory of contemporary Israel, by which I mean the decades-long Occupation; the denial of Palestinian rights to land, suffrage, the rule of law, and sovereignty; and the violence that the Occupation's maintenance has inevitably dictated. I am equally grieved by the Occupation's noxious offspring within Israel itself: chauvinism, religious fundamentalism, intolerance, attacks on democratic freedoms, and sheer racism.

One might ask: Why study the Left and Israel at a time when the Left itself is in decline—in Israel, as elsewhere? (As I write, right-wing parties are making gains in Germany, Poland, Austria, Hungary, and parts of

Latin America; the Likud alliance retains its firm grip on power; and—the true astonishment—Donald Trump is America's president.) One answer is that the relationship between Jews and the Left, and Israel and the Left, is essential to an understanding of either. Jews and the Left have been so intimately entwined throughout the modern era that it is impossible to discuss the Jewish people without considering their tremendous impact, as theorists and activists, on Left movements. It is equally impossible to understand Israel's history without comprehending how it came out of, and was nurtured by, the Left. But it is also true that, perhaps like all intimate relations, this one has encompassed anger, scorn, disappointment, rejection, even hatred. The Left has been Israel's indispensable lover and resolute enemy. Each party accuses the other of betrayal.

Of course, conservative and right-wing thinkers have their own ideas about Israel. Their notions of what it means to be "pro-Israel" are the opposite of mine. I do not discuss them here because, to paraphrase Albert Memmi, they are not my people.

Along with grief, this book is born in hope—as, I think, every book must be. Perhaps in engaging the ideas of the eight writers profiled here, we will be able to foster a better, more productive dialogue about the Arab-Israeli conflict than the one that exists today. By "better" I mean morally realistic, intellectually honest, and dialectical. In the Conclusion, I offer my thoughts on what that might mean.

August 2018
Brooklyn, New York

PART ONE EUROPEANS

CHAPTER ONE

Hannah Arendt

LEFT, RIGHT, OR WRONG?

IT'S A PLEASANT DAY IN THE SUMMER OF 2013, and I sit with a Jewish-Israeli intellectual in a lively Tel Aviv café. She is a member of the far Left who advocates a one-state solution and is adamantly anti-Zionist. (She has since emigrated from Israel.) She asks me what I've been reading lately, and I mention Hannah Arendt. "Oh, she *hated* Zionism!" my companion responds with gusto.

This is a commonly held belief on the left—and, as it turns out, on the right. Arendt's writings on Zionism and Israel are cited with increasing frequency by leftist advocates of a "non-Zionist" or binational state, who hail her presumably prophetic vision regarding the Israeli-Palestinian conflict and regard her as an authority on it. Accolades like "impressively accurate," "remarkably prescient," and "trenchant" are heaped upon her; she is praised for her brave denunciations of "the follies and crimes of Zionism."[1] From the opposite end of the spectrum, conservative supporters of Israel heartily agree that Arendt was a concerted enemy of Israel and the mother of "Israelophobia."[2] Depending on one's politics, Arendt is saint or sinner, prophet or traitor, goddess or devil.

In fact, she was none of the above. The attempts to use Arendt—uses that are always highly selective—to support contemporary positions vis-à-vis Israel almost always get her wrong. And yet to parse her views on Zionism is important. Most of the things she cared (and worried) about—nationalism, sovereignty, resistance, collaboration, freedom, justice, judgment—are entwined with her writings on Zionism, the Shoah, and Israel.

Arendt wrestled with Zionism, and then with Israel, for over three decades: with force and passion, respect and scorn. She wrote hundreds of thousands of words, scores of articles and essays, and, most famously, the book *Eichmann in Jerusalem*. She derided Jewish political sovereignty yet argued fervently for a Jewish army and Jewish self-defense, the Jewish right to Palestine, and the creation of a specifically Jewish politics and a specifically Jewish world. ("A people can be a minority somewhere only if they are a majority elsewhere," she observed.)[3] Arendt was a scathing opponent of assimilation and an ardent admirer of Zionist accomplishments—economic, political, intellectual, and social—in Palestine and, later, in Israel, though she also expressed disgust at actually-existing Zionism. She opposed the partition of Palestine and became a critic of Israel after the state was founded, though she unambiguously supported Israel in the 1967 and 1973 wars. In short, her attitudes toward Zionism oscillated: not only between months or years or decades, but within them. These attitudes cannot be whittled down to "pro" or "anti," despite the efforts of reductionists to do so. Arendt was sometimes right but, in my estimation, more often wrong, both in her analyses and in her predictions. Yet this is the least important aspect of her views.

The reason to read Arendt on this topic is not to victoriously cherry-pick particular lines: "She said this! No, she said that!" Nor can one plausibly argue that there was always an overriding logic to her views on Zionism. On the contrary: It is precisely the extreme contradictions in her writings—evidence, I believe, of a genuine effort to tackle what she saw as the most crucial issues—that can act as a sober antidote to the coarse simplicities to which current debates on Israel have descended. The reason to read Arendt on Zionism is to bring home to us the nettlesome difficulties that have always confronted the establishment of a state for the Jewish people. Equally important, Arendt's writings on Israel are a warning—though not against Zionism or the nation-state, as she thought and as her contemporary admirers believe. Her writings are a warning against imposing abstract political theories, even brilliant ones, on a distinct political problem.

Hannah Arendt has aptly been described as "a political theorist with a flair for grand historical generalization."[4] Arendt was born in 1906 in

Hanover, Germany, to a secular but not assimilated Jewish family. A brilliant student, she was mentored by Martin Heidegger, with whom she
had an affair and who became a Nazi, and Karl Jaspers, an anti-Nazi
philosopher and lifelong friend. (Historian Richard Wolin considers her
one of Heidegger's philosophical "children.") Arendt completed her PhD
at the University of Heidelberg in 1928; its subject was the concept of love
in the work of Saint Augustine. She escaped Nazi Germany and, arriving
in America in 1941, embarked on a prolific writing and teaching career
and became one of the country's leading public intellectuals. It is safe to
say that Arendt's 1951 book *The Origins of Totalitarianism* changed the
ways we think about twentieth-century history and politics as much as, if
not more than, any other single work. She died in 1975 in New York City.

Arendt came to politics through Zionism and to Zionism through
Hitler. In contrast to friends such as Walter Benjamin and the philosopher Hans Jonas, she was largely untouched by the tumultuous political
confrontations of the Weimar Republic, and she had little interest in
public affairs, much less Jewish issues, before 1933. "I was interested
neither in history nor in politics when I was young," she recalled years
later; by her own account, she "found the so-called Jewish question
boring."[5] Hers was, therefore, a kind of defensive Zionism—the Zionism
of catastrophe—spurred by anti-Semitism; this is one, though certainly
not the only, form that Zionism can take and inspiration that it can have.
(There is also positive Zionism, whose goal is the flourishing of Hebrew
culture and of Jewish independence as valuable in themselves.) But if
Arendt was slow to come to politics, she was a fast learner. With the
burning of the Reichstag in 1933, she began working with Zionist organizations in Berlin.

Deranged anti-Semitism as the fulcrum of Nazi theory and practice is
blindingly clear now. But it wasn't at the time, even, or especially, to some
on the left. As late as 1939, Max Horkheimer tried to rationalize anti-
Semitism as the by-product of a decaying capitalist order—"The Jews are
stripped of power as agents of circulation"—and insist, all evidence to the
contrary, that "the workers in Germany, schooled in revolutionary teach-
ings, watched the [Nazi] pogroms with disgust."[6] Arendt, who was never
a Marxist, saw the situation more clearly. She later remembered the
sudden, transformative impact of 1933: "I arrived at the conclusion . . .
'When one is attacked as a Jew, one must defend oneself *as a Jew.*' Not as

a German, not as a world-citizen, not as an upholder of the Rights of Man."7 Anti-Nazi Zionist activity led to her arrest that year. But quickly, and perhaps miraculously, she was released by a friendly policeman. (There were, apparently, policemen who were still friendly to Jews in the Berlin of 1933.) She fled to Prague, Geneva, and then Paris, where she worked with Youth Aliyah, a group that brought Jewish teenagers to Palestine, which she visited in 1935. This period of Zionist activity was one of the few times in Arendt's life when she engaged in concrete political action; another, ironically, would be her work against the establishment of a Jewish state.

In 1940, Arendt escaped from Gurs, the French internment camp where she had been imprisoned as an enemy alien; the following year, she arrived in New York with her second husband, Heinrich Blücher, who had been a street-fighting Spartacist. In America, her identification as a Jew remained strong. She worked as an editor for the Jewish publisher Schocken and wrote for Jewish publications like *Menorah Journal, Jewish Frontier*, and the German-language *Aufbau*. Arendt's writings of the 1930s and early 1940s—the years of the Nuremberg Laws, the spread of fascism, the war, the ghettoes, the camps, and, eventually, the growing awareness of the genocide—are those not just of a Zionist but of a militant one; some of her views, especially on Jewish self-defense, would not be out of place among various right-wing parties in Israel today. The Arendt of those years desperately wanted the Jewish people to move into history, by which she meant into militant action, autonomy, and political self-determination: into battle, figurative and literal. She wanted, above all, for her fellow Jews to abandon the delusion that a disavowal of their Jewishness or the goodwill of other peoples would somehow save them. She repeatedly castigated what she called Jewish "worldlessness," which she defined as a propensity to suffer from history rather than make it, an aversion to political power, and a reliance on God, fate, the Messiah, or kind strangers.

Though Arendt's attitudes toward Zionism were spurred by the rise of the Nazis and the Jewish reaction to it, she argued that the disease of worldlessness had crippled the Jewish people for most of its history. How much Jewish history Arendt actually knew is, however, questionable; she fixated on figures like Sabbatai Zevi, the false Messiah of the seventeenth century, and ignored or generalized about much else. Indeed, she prophesized that the establishment of a Jewish state would result in a Zevi-like catastrophe for the Jewish people. Hans Jonas would observe, "I was shocked . . . at Hannah's ignorance when it came to things Jewish. . . . For her, the history of the Jews . . . basically began toward the end of the eighteenth century. Everything before that was surrounded by a general fog."[8] Arendt was apparently unaware of major works which argued that Judaism's prime characteristic is the spirit of revolt and that Judaism, and even Jewish messianism, is inherently public and political. This was the understanding of the nineteenth-century socialist-Zionist Bernard Lazare, one of Arendt's (few) heroes. Revolt and agitation, he wrote, are "the very essence of the Hebrew spirit," which places human rather than divine justice at its core. Because of this, Lazare argued, "The role played by the Jews in the political and social upheavals of history has been one of capital importance. . . . The Jew . . . belongs to both those who prepare the way for revolution through the activity of the mind, and those who translate thought into action."[9] Heinrich Graetz, the influential nineteenth-century German-Jewish historian, argued that Judaism is "a constitution for the body politic" that "has produced, in addition to a passive history of severe trial and martyrdom also an active history which gives the most striking evidence of infinite vitality and flexible energy."[10] Graetz viewed revolt as Judaism's key characteristic. Ironically, Arendt's emphasis on Jewish passivity implied a kind of mysticism, though she was the least mystical of thinkers. As the historian David Biale noted, "Without an appreciation of the political acumen of the Jews in earlier times, their long history can only appear to be a miraculous accomplishment."[11]

Arendt did not discern any political acumen. "Jewish history offers the extraordinary spectacle of a people . . . [who] avoided all political action for two thousand years," she claimed. "The result was that the political history of the Jewish people became even more dependent upon unforeseen, accidental factors than the history of other nations, so that the Jews stumbled from one role to the other and accepted responsibility for none."[12] (This disparaging view of Diaspora Jewry was shared by Zionists such as David Ben-Gurion, whom Arendt would bitterly oppose.) She argued that the Jews were uniquely stunted: "What they needed was not only a guide to reality, but reality itself; not simply a key to history, but the experience itself of history."[13]

It is typical of Arendt that there is something right, and something dubiously selective, about this view. The shadow of the Shoah hangs over these observations, and it is true that most Jews, from the educated cosmopolitans of Berlin to the immiserated shtetl-dwellers of Poland, were unable to understand, much less resist, the murderous assault that the Nazis and their supporters unleashed; it is true that most Jews "avoided all political action" until too late. Some German Jews viewed the Nazi regime as a temporary aberration and believed that Germany offered a viable future even after the propagation of the Nuremberg Laws.

Still, it is awfully hard to know how any people—especially one that was scattered over a vast continent and that lacked a land, a state, a government, an army, and recognition by the international community—could prepare for, and fight against, an onslaught that in Arendt's own estimation was unprecedented. And it is strange to hear Arendt accuse the Jews of being monotonously apolitical throughout their history, which spans thousands of years. Arendt's critique was apt in describing certain periods of Jewish history, but it is particularly weak when applied to the modern era, which is the only one she cared about. It was Jewish culture and the Jewish people, after all, who brought the world Karl Marx and Ferdinand Lassalle, Rosa Luxemburg and Emma Goldman, Leon Trotsky and Grigory Zinoviev, Paul Levi and Béla Kun, Léon Blum and Georg Lukács, Karl Radek and Rudolph Slansky (and, later, Joe Slovo and Albie Sachs), not to mention millions of rank-and-file union organizers, social democrats, socialists, anarchists, and Communists. Arendt herself would note that Marx's "fanatical zeal for justice" had "carried on the Jewish tradition."[14]

In short, the Jewish tradition can be, and often has been, the basis for courageous political struggle; to define Jews primarily as cowardly escapists misses an awful lot. Of course, Arendt might have argued that these revolutionaries were not struggling for liberation *as* Jews. But this argument, too, is seriously flawed, for it ignores Zionists, socialist-Zionists, and anti-Zionist but expressly Jewish groups like the Bund. An alternative view—as extreme as Arendt's, but in my view more accurate—recognizes the Jewish people as a moving force of modern politics, history, and culture rather than simply its passive victims or feckless observers. The historian Yuri Slezkine argues, "The Modern Age is the Jewish Age, and the twentieth century, in particular, is the Jewish Century. Modernization is about everyone becoming urban, mobile, literate, articulate, intellectually intricate. . . . Modernization, in other words, is about everyone becoming Jewish." Slezkine observes that the most influential ideologies of modernity—Marxism, psychoanalysis, Zionism, and fascism/Nazism—were all "solutions to the Jewish predicament."[15] In their own demented way, anti-Semites have intuited the Jewish propensity for modernist transformation and radical politics; thus Hitler's obsession with "Judeo-Bolshevism" and Hamas's complaint, expressed in its charter, that Jews have "stood behind the French and Communist Revolutions" as well as many others.

The fatalism that Arendt abhorred (and feared) is certainly part of the Jewish tradition. But she consistently insisted that apolitical worldlessness was the *defining* Jewish characteristic. And its antidote was Zionism. Of her political awakening, she recalled, "Zionists . . . were the only ones who were ready [to oppose Nazism]. It would have been pointless to join those who had assimilated. . . . I wanted to go into practical work, exclusively and only Jewish work."[16] To counter worldlessness, every people needed to ground itself in "a place in the world," by which Arendt meant not just a physical location but a sphere of freely chosen political action. Zionism was the one movement that offered this possibility to the Jews; Arendt described it as "the *only* political answer Jews have *ever* found to antisemitism and the *only* ideology in which they have *ever* taken seriously a hostility that would place them in the center of world events."[17] (The emphases are mine, but the absolutism is typically Arendtian.) Zionism was also the only movement to reject what she called the "spurious selflessness" of left-wing internationalists, who believed that the Jewish Question would be solved as an organic by-product of socialist revolution.

In sum: Beginning in 1933 and for the next fifteen years, Arendt viewed Zionism as "the Jewish liberation movement" and the sole "truly political organization" of the Jewish people.[18]

Throughout the 1930s and 1940s, Arendt extolled Zionist accomplishments in Palestine. She was literally a labor Zionist: It was work, not great-power declarations and certainly not God, which justified Jewish settlement there (although she never forgot, as she put it in a letter to Blücher, that "whichever way you look at it, that land is unavoidably bound with our past").[19] In 1942, she wrote that the Zionist movement "must base its argument on the realities we have created in Palestine and on the determination of its people to be free. . . . The right of the Jewish people in Palestine is the same right every human being has to the fruits of his work." Zionism had created a new, and in her view vastly improved, Jew. She praised in particular the builders of the "magnificent" kibbutzim and proudly noted that Jews in Palestine "live as Jews, just as other peoples live, . . . without covering their nakedness with the fig leaf of a different nationality."[20]

The Zionists had not only constructed a physical world—schools, businesses, hospitals, farms, factories, cities—but an inclusive place of belonging. In 1942, Arendt observed that war requires the willingness to die, but that "you can be ready to die only when you know for certain why you are fighting, and only when you are a full-fledged citizen of the community that embodies that 'why.' " Palestinian Jews, she wrote, knew the answer to that "why," for they had forged such a community. Even in the midst of harshly criticizing Zionist leaders and the Zionist movement, she would write that the Zionist project in Palestine "constitute[s] today the great hope and the great pride of Jews all over the world."[21] It is significant that Arendt wrote this in May 1948—during the War of Independence for the Israeli state, whose establishment she opposed.

In the winter of 2017, I heard Michael Sfard, one of Israel's foremost human rights lawyers, address an audience at the New School, the left-wing university in New York that served as a "university in exile" for intellectuals fleeing Hitler. Several students in the audience accused Israel of being a "colonialist" entity (Sfard answered their questions with patience and an impressive lack of defensiveness). Arendt taught at the New School and is closely identified with it; she is revered by its students and faculty alike. Those students might have been surprised to learn that Arendt's analysis of Zionism directly contradicted theirs: She insisted that Jewish settlement in Palestine was not remotely comparable to, much less synonymous with, colonialism or imperialism. "The realities of Jewish achievement in Palestine were unique in many respects," she wrote in 1948. "What happened in Palestine was not easy to judge and evaluate: it was extraordinarily different from anything that had happened in the past."[22]

She delineated the extraordinary differences. The Zionists came to Palestine not to steal its rich natural resources—in fact there were none—but to develop a desolate land with their own labor; not to oppress others, but to save themselves; not to extract labor power from peasants or proletarians, but to transform themselves *into* peasants and proletarians. (Jews who were interested in economic well-being emigrated to the United

States, where the streets were paved with gold, not to dilapidated Palestine.) "The building of a Jewish national home was not a colonial enterprise in which Europeans came to exploit foreign riches . . . at the expense of native labor," Arendt observed. "Palestine was and is a poor country and whatever riches it possesses are exclusively the product of Jewish labor. . . . Exploitation or robbery, so characteristic of the 'original accumulation' in all imperialist enterprises, were either completely absent or played an insignificant role." The Zionists had created something new, something that "could not possibly fit into the political scheme of imperialism because it was neither a master nor a subject nation." Arendt never suggested that Zionism did not harm Palestinian Arabs. On the contrary, she well understood how and why "the Arabs considered the whole Jewish venture a strange interlude out of a fairy tale at best, and, at worst, an illegal enterprise which one day would be fair game for looting and robbery."²³ But she insisted that the straitjacket of European colonialism could not be imposed on the Zionist body.

Arendt also took up the charge of inauthenticity, which is lodged against Israel to this day, and turned it on its head. Zionism, she admitted, was not native to Palestine. That was one of its virtues. "The development of the soil, the erection of a Hebrew University, the establishment of great health centers, were all 'artificial' developments, . . . initiated by a spirit of enterprise which paid no heed to calculations of profit and loss."²⁴ For Arendt, there was nothing particularly good or admirable about the so-called natural world. It is the worlds that men and women consciously *build*—it is culture and civilization—that constitute achievement and moral progress. Only culture and civilization can be judged; only they are normative and, therefore, worth defending.

Arendt was obsessed with Jewish shame, Jewish honor, and Jewish dignity, which suggests that this proud woman harbored a deep sense of humiliation. Shame, and its negation, were a major impulse behind Zionism, as they have been for so many projects of national liberation. (And for some reactionary ones too, such as German fascism.) However, unlike movements that glorify the supposedly great accomplishments of their people, Zionists tended to be the harshest critics of Diaspora Jewry; as the Israeli historian Zeev Sternhell noted, the early Zionists' characterizations of their people "at times resembled those of the most rabid anti-Semites."²⁵ Bernard

Lazare, for instance, observed that after "centuries of oppression," the Jewish people's "spirit and soul have become debased. The stiff-necked tribe has become a tribe of slaves." And though this was especially true of poor Jews, the Jewish bourgeoisie was no better: Lazare described it as "our garbage, our rubbish."²⁶ Agrarian Zionist A. D. Gordon agreed. The Jews, he wrote, were "broken and crushed . . . sick and diseased in body and soul."²⁷ As we'll see in the next chapter, Arthur Koestler was a major exponent of this view.

The vanquishing of shame was, I suspect, one of Zionism's major attractions for Arendt. But her writings show that it is a perilously short leap from humiliation to contempt. "We [Jews] actually glory only in being victims, innocent victims," she wrote in 1944, a year in which there were many Jewish victims—who were, in fact, innocent—though it is extremely doubtful that any gloried in their agony. The image of Jews as despicably supine appears repeatedly in Arendt's writings, as when she notes, in the midst of the Shoah, that "a people that no longer defends itself against its enemies is not a people but a living corpse."²⁸

It is the "living" part of this phrase that bothered Arendt most. In her view, the Jewish people's shame derived in large part from its will to survive. In the ancient world, the Jews had insisted on enduring as a people even after losing their political base; for Arendt, who regarded the political realm as the essence of freedom, this was the Jews' original sin. (To the Biblical injunction, "choose life," she would essentially counterpose, "choose politics.") In the modern world, she charged, the survival instinct had turned the Jews into groveling victims. "Death begins his reign of terror precisely when life becomes the highest good," she warned in 1942. "No one is more easily murdered than a slave." This oft-repeated theme led to some of Arendt's least charitable writings. In 1941, she complained, "The Jewish nation has begun to resemble an old man," one who "renounces life and dedicates himself to survival; he lives from one birthday to the next and rejoices in that one day of the year on which he can proclaim to relatives who are not entirely well-wishers, You see, I've done it again."²⁹ Arendt was not, of course, the only Jew who yearned for her people to rise up and who felt shame—along with shock, bewilderment, terror, guilt, and rage—about the catastrophe that was unfolding in Europe. I admire her pride and her urgency.

Yet, as so often with Arendt's writings, there is something here that is profoundly unsettling, something that simply feels wrong. It is deeply off-putting, if not obnoxious, for a lucky émigré in New York to chastise her brethren—trapped in the ghettoes, the camps, the occupied countries, or on the Eastern Front—for their determination to survive. Determination? Perhaps that is too strong and noble a word to describe people exhausted by physical pain, psychic anguish, and sheer terror. Better to say that many maintained a hope against hope: of being rescued by the Russians or the Americans or God, of outliving the madness, of saving a child or two.

Years later, the high price of survival would become a theme of the Eichmann trial—especially for Arendt. She was no expert on this topic; as she admitted to Karl Jaspers in 1960, "Don't forget how early I left Germany and how little of all this I really experienced directly."[30] But regardless of her personal knowledge—or perhaps because of its absence—it was resistance that held her interest. The annihilation of European Jewry offered too little of that.

Given her worldview and psychological makeup, it is unsurprising that, as the world war intensified, Arendt became an impassioned advocate of a Jewish army that would fight "as Jews, in Jewish battle formations under a Jewish flag." At times she composed almost Fanonesque paeans to violent self-defense. Of the Jewish partisans, she promised, "These guerrilla fighters will present us with an entirely new type of Jewish mentality. . . . To the extent that the Jew is disappearing, Jews have come to life: organizing, fighting." One can understand, indeed readily share, the emotional appeal of this stance; it is stirring to read Arendt insist that "we want to fight; we do not want mercy, but justice."[31] Still, one wonders, didn't the victims need even a bit of mercy, too? What of the many millions who could not fight?

And while a Jewish army might have boosted Jewish self-esteem, it is hard to find a historian who thinks it would have made a practical difference to the war effort. Even the presumed psychic benefits are debatable; as the Israeli philosopher Elhanan Yakira wrote, "It is doubtful that such an army could even have restored the Jews' lost honor, while what was really at stake was not their honor but their lives."[32] Nor did Arendt seem to understand that an armed force that does not represent a sovereign state is regarded by other nations as, at best, a freelance militia—think of al-Qaeda or Hamas—rather than as an army with internationally recognized protections. Her claim that a Jewish army would have "forced [the

Nazis] to grant European Jews the status of enemy aliens, which would have been tantamount to saving them" was pure fantasy.[33]

Nonetheless, Arendt repeatedly insisted that an army was the sine qua non of Jewish dignity—and was justified by Zionist settlement in Palestine: "The right to take up the sword . . . can be denied to no one who has put his hand to the plow or trowel."[34] In a 1941 essay called "The Jewish Army—The Beginning of Jewish Politics?," she argued that Jews must, "by the hundreds of thousands with weapons in hand . . . fight for their freedom and the right to live as a people."[35] The revealing but problematic title of this article is indicative of her belief that an anti-Nazi Jewish army would be central to a political settlement in Palestine *after* the war. Without such an army, Arendt was sure, the Jewish people's loathsome dependence on others would persist: "All that is left . . . is something purely negative: perhaps other nations can be prevented from exterminating us."[36] In Palestine, Ben-Gurion and his comrades had a different strategy and, frankly, a better grasp of the situation than she. They knew that politics, Jewish or otherwise, require the building of a viable state, not just the training of an army; the latter is meaningless without the former. It is not clear whether Arendt knew that the other main advocate of a pre-state army was the Revisionist leader Vladimir Jabotinsky, whose movement she regarded as fascist and whose ultra-nationalism horrified her.

Arendt's writings on the Jewish Question, even before the Shoah, leave the distinct impression that she had never recovered from the Jewish defeat at the hands of the Romans almost two thousand years before. Emotionally speaking, she was a Zealot: Fighting and death were preferable to surrender and life. Thus, in 1947, she wrote glowingly of the "genuine change in the so-called national character" that Zionism had wrought: "Large segments of the people . . . reject survival as the goal . . . and are prepared to die."[37] Yet in 1948, when the Haganah broke the ancient Jewish bond between resistance and Thanatos—when it showed that Jews could fight and *live*—Arendt was one of its most vociferous opponents. The puzzle is why.

Arendt's polemics extolling Jewish settlement in Palestine, independent Jewish politics, and Jewish self-defense can only be termed Zionist. Despite this, she was a scathing critic of the Zionist movement and

Zionist politics, which she deemed insufficiently revolutionary and overly fixated on statehood.

Arendt relentlessly assailed Theodor Herzl, whom she described as "a crackpot" and possibly "insane."[38] She lambasted his elitist politics from above, his dealings with the imperialist powers, his nationalism, and his Eurocentrism. (Arendt's own Eurocentrism was a major factor in her antipathy to Israel, which turned out to be not as European as she had hoped.) She particularly scorned Herzl's emphasis on statehood, arguing that he sought Jewish independence just as "the whole concept of national sovereignty had become a mockery": a serious misunderstanding, on Arendt's part, of twentieth-century politics. Herzl fared particularly badly when compared to Lazare, whom Arendt praised for considering "the territorial question" as "secondary"; she thus ignored the painfully large differences between the France of the Dreyfus Affair and the France of Drancy.[39] In any case, by the late 1930s Arendt was ready to toss the mainstream Zionist movement into the dustbin of history, deriding it as a "bourgeois" failure.

And if the Zionists were bad at politics, they were bad historians too. In a long essay on anti-Semitism written in 1938–39, Arendt ridiculed the Zionists' "utterly unhistorical theory" (she would later call it "utterly stupid"), which posited that anti-Semitism is eternal—though this was never a tenet of all or even most Zionists.[40] Against this, she argued that the late nineteenth and early twentieth centuries had incubated a new kind of secular anti-Semitism, which reviled Jews not as religious infidels but as bearers of modernity and strangers to the *Volk*.

Though the historic trajectory Arendt traced was valid, she downplayed the ways that anti-Semitism could transcend the realms of economics, traditional politics, and reason itself. (Her view in *The Origins of Totalitarianism* was much more expansive.) And her field of vision at this time was narrow. She did not grasp that while political anti-Semitism might flourish in Germany and Western Europe, the old, religious kind was alive and well in Poland, Russia, and the rest of Eastern Europe, where the majority of Jews resided. Contrary to what Arendt implied, there was no sharp rupture between old and new anti-Semitisms; Jews in Poland, for instance, were killed for the old bad reasons (as Christ-killers) and for the new bad reasons (as Communists). Indeed, anti-Semitism's ability to incorporate the modern and medieval, the intellect and the emotions, the secular and the religious—and to embrace Left and Right—remains impressively robust, as even a cursory glance at the contemporary Middle East will show. Arendt may have been right to scoff at the idea of eternal anti-Semitism, but this form of hatred *has* proved capable of thriving in radically different contexts and eras. Nor did she understand that the Arab rejection of a Jewish presence in Palestine was, and would continue to be, simultaneously political and economic, cultural and religious.[41]

In looking at Palestine, Arendt did see one thing clearly. It was phenomenally important, and it is the main reason her writings on Zionism are remembered today, at least by leftists. That one thing was, in the words of the time, the Arab Question. Yet, ironically, her sensitivity to this issue would blind her to everything else and lead her to advocate increasingly insular, reckless positions. Many of Arendt's admirers see her writings on the Israeli-Palestinian conflict as her most perceptive and prophetic. I see them as her weakest.

Arendt liked to disparagingly quote the Zionist maxim describing Palestine as "a land without a people for a people without a land." Yet by the 1940s (and some would say by 1929 or 1936), few in the Yishuv, from Jabotinsky's right-wing Revisionists to the Marxists of Hashomer Hatzair, believed this. Indeed, in the nineteenth century, Ahad Ha'am, the influential founder of cultural Zionism, had warned Zionists against ignoring Palestine's Arab majority or underestimating its political intelligence. By Arendt's time, the disagreements, and they were enormous, within the Jewish community in Palestine centered on if, and how, competing Arab and Jewish rights and claims could be resolved. But few ignored the fact of a national, or at least communal, conflict.

Beginning in the early twentieth century, there were numerous attempts by Arabs (who were not, at the time, called Palestinians) and Jews to forge some sort of agreement in Palestine. Some of these attempts were cynical, others heartfelt. But in either case, world events pushed the parties further apart as the century progressed. With the rise of Hitler and, then, the beginning of the genocide, the main Zionist demand became unrestricted Jewish immigration to Palestine. This was utterly necessary for the Jews and, for understandable reasons, utterly anathema to the Arabs. (And, it would turn out, to the British.) This was a clash of basic needs that could not be fudged, evaded, or philosophized away. Even today, or perhaps especially today, critics of Israel refuse to recognize this stubborn, unhappy fact and indulge in the wooziest of retroactive fantasies. British literary critic Jacqueline Rose, for instance, believes that a wonderful binational moment was missed in the pre-state period, when "Zionism might have created a form of nationhood that would slash away politics, face its own dark beast . . . [Zionism] had the opportunity to forge a model of nation-hood" that would be "ambivalent, uncertain, obscure . . ."[42] The historian Neil Caplan's multi-volume work on Arab-Jewish negotiations is closer to reality; it is titled, sadly but accurately, *Futile Diplomacy.*

Still, there is no doubt that Arendt saw the long-term problems of the Arab-Jewish conflict more clearly than some others, and that she insisted they were of central rather than peripheral importance. The heart of the issue was not that Zionism was imperialist or colonialist; Arendt regarded it as neither. Nor did she sentimentalize Palestinian culture or try to blur the vast differences that separated it from the Yishuv. In fact, Arendt's writings on this topic would sound harsh and politically incorrect today. She contrasted what she called the advanced culture and economy of the Zionists to the "hopeless misery and sterility," "backwardness and ineffi-ciency," and "disease-stricken poverty" of Palestinian Arabs. She believed that Palestine could flourish only with the skills and knowledge the Zionists had brought. She was not a cultural relativist: "The Arabs had 1,500 years to turn a stony desert into fertile land, whereas the Jews have had not even forty, and the difference is quite remarkable." And she was hardly a fan of the nascent Palestinian national movement, which had "sold itself to German and Italian imperialism" and was "thoroughly fascist-infiltrated."[43]

What Arendt did perceive was the inability of Palestinian Arabs and Jews to see each other's reality—or even to see that the other *was* real. "In hope or in hate both peoples have focused their attention so exclusively upon the British that they practically ignored each other: the Jews forgot that the Arabs, not the English, were the permanent reality in Near Eastern policies and the Arabs that Jewish settlers, and not British troops, intended to stay permanently in Palestine," she wrote in 1948.[44] These mutual miscomprehensions and antipathies were not momentary blips, she warned, but would define the Jewish state. Without an accommoda-tion between Jews and Arabs, Israel would always be imperiled.

In her eyes, however, security didn't mean statehood. Arendt vociferously opposed the demand of the Zionists' Biltmore Conference of 1942—a demand put forth by her nemesis, Ben-Gurion—that "Palestine be established as a Jewish commonwealth integrated into the structure of the new democratic world." (Typically contrarian, she also opposed the binational proposal of Judah Magnes, with whom she would soon work; in fact, she opposed *all* of the conference's suggested planks.) No surprise, then, that she opposed the World Zionist Organization's more radical resolution, adopted unanimously at an Atlantic City conference two years later, which stated that a "free and democratic Jewish commonwealth . . . shall embrace the whole of Palestine, undivided and undiminished." She argued—correctly, I think—that this would leave Palestinian Arabs with only two choices: "minority status . . . or voluntary emigration."[45] From an ethical standpoint, that would be grossly unjust; from a political standpoint, it was extraordinarily dangerous.

One would think, then, that when the Zionists dropped their maximalist program and agreed to the partition of Palestine into independent Jewish and Arab states, Arendt—the great proponent of Jewish "national emancipation"—would have been among their heartiest supporters. Here, finally, was the opportunity to solidify the Jewish world that she had so passionately advocated. Here, finally, was the chance to move from pariahdom to politics, from helplessness to self-reliance, from worldlessness to sovereignty. Here, finally, was the opportunity for Jews to forge relations of equality with other nations, upon which she set great store. And here, finally, was a way to honor the validity of Palestinian-Arab national claims (though, obviously, not maximal claims). Here was a plan that offered possibilities *other than* minority status or forced expulsion for either Arabs or Jews.

Instead, as 1947 rolled into 1948, Arendt became increasingly vitriolic in her opposition to partition and Jewish sovereignty, even as the nascent Israeli state, and her beloved kibbutzim and Hebrew University, were under siege and attack by Palestinian militias and, then, five Arab armies. Arendt's writings from this time show how one shaft of insight can morph into sightlessness when the part is allowed to substitute for, and blot out, the whole. Almost all the judgments she made during this crucial period proved deeply, radically, *perplexingly* wrong. It was here that she entered what George Lichtheim would characterize, in a different context, as "[Arendt's] twilight zone where it no longer seems to matter whether we are dealing with actual events."[46] Faced with escalating violence and then outright war between Jews and Arabs, Arendt put forth, with certitude for herself and scorn for others, a series of increasingly impossible, unworkable, and deeply undemocratic solutions. At the crucial historic moment—the moment of existential crisis—Arendt retreated from the worlds of judgment, history, and reality: the worlds she held most dear.

In place of independent states for Jews and Arabs, what did Arendt offer? In the years between 1943 and 1948 her answers to this question varied. The sole consistency was opposition to Jewish statehood, which she regarded as impossible and unjust.

In the late 1940s, Arendt worked closely with Magnes, an American founder of the Ihud ("Union"), to lobby against Israeli statehood and U.S. recognition of it. Ihud had been preceded in the 1920s by Brit Shalom ("Covenant of Peace"); both were tiny groups that advocated a binational Jewish-Arab state and were supported mainly by German-born intellectuals such as Martin Buber, Gershom Scholem, and Albert Einstein. Contemporary leftist critics of Israel spend a lot of energy lauding these organizations, which they view with hazy wistfulness. Brit Shalom followers *were* genuine humanists. But they were not necessarily sharp political thinkers; a sympathetic biographer of Scholem describes them as "dreamy academics whose knowledge of the Arab people was derived primarily from books and chats with their gardeners."[47] Especially after the bloody clashes of 1929 and 1936 and the escalating internecine violence of the late 1940s, Jewish support for such groups was minuscule; according to historian Benny Morris, Ihud had all of ninety-seven members in 1943. (The Jewish community in Palestine was small, but not that small.) On the Arab side, the prospects for binationalism were even worse. The concept "had no Arab suppport," the historian John B. Judis bluntly wrote, a statement with which historians of diverse political tendencies concur.[48] In short, there was nothing binational about binationalism. It was an exclusively Jewish initiative, no less than the mainstream Zionist movement it opposed.

In parsing Arendt's writings on this subject, one finds that she proposed, alternately, a Palestinian Arab-Jewish federation, a United

Nations protectorate, a pan-Arab-Israel commonwealth, a Mediterranean commonwealth, a British commonwealth, and a European commonwealth incorporating Israel and the Arab countries. (Contrary to popular belief, Arendt actually criticized the idea of a binational state per se.) Virtually any configuration was preferable to either Jewish sovereignty or to separate Arab and Jewish states. This was not mere stubbornness on Arendt's part. By the time of these writings she believed, and would continue to believe, in the council system, the federation, and the commonwealth as preferable to—that is, more democratic than—the state. The problem is that, in the context of Palestine, this led her to proposals that were ludicrously chimerical and to solutions that were shockingly heedless of history, culture, and political realities. Thus, in an article titled "Can the Jewish-Arab Question be Solved?," written at the end of 1943, Arendt argued for a Jewish-Arab federation in Palestine that would be integrated within a new British Commonwealth, which would presumably serve as its protector. "Without requiring a national state of their own, the Jews would have the same political status as all other members of the Commonwealth"; eventually, this federation could "of course" embrace a larger European federation that would include North Africa, thus ensuring that "the Arabs would be brought into union with European peoples."[49]

The problems with this strategy were—"of course"—so large, and its distance from reality so great, that no hindsight is needed to detect them. Arendt never explained how the federation of two such culturally and politically dissimilar communities would formulate a foreign policy, an educational and legal system, political and military institutions, or a concept of rights. And if common ground on such basic issues could not be found, on what basis would a federation rest, and why would it be superior to independent states? More surprising, Arendt was peculiarly oblivious to the fact that most Zionists—and, certainly, most Arabs—did not aspire to membership in a European federation or a British Commonwealth. (This may have been their one point of agreement.) And if anything, Britain desired this even less; by the end of the Mandate the British were "sickened by their duties, revolted by the Jews, and disappointed in the Arabs," as one historian succinctly put it.[50]

Furthermore, Arendt never explained how Britain would protect the Jewish homeland within this commonwealth; under the Mandate, it had proved noticeably unable to prevent Jews and Arabs from killing each other despite the presence of 100,000 British troops. Nor did she apprehend that the British Commonwealth in which she placed so much confidence would soon be shattered; she had not, it seems, noticed that the Indian National Congress's "Quit India" campaign was already in full swing. In the postwar world, "a national state of their own" is *precisely* what the anti-colonial movements that swept Asia, the Caribbean, the Middle East, and Africa would demand—and win.

Arendt prophesied the end of the national state just before a tsunami of national liberation movements swept through the Third World, transforming the lives of millions of people and changing global politics forever. One can argue, I suppose, that all those movements were mistaken, and that many of those states—including the multiethnic and multicultural ones—turned out badly. Still, to follow Arendt's logic, one would have to imagine how those colonies and protectorates could have emerged into self-determination with an alternative, non-state strategy, and why that would have turned out well. This is counterfactual history on a very large scale. The salient point is that, much like the Bolsheviks of 1917 prophesizing an imminent, worldwide socialist revolution, Arendt based her analysis of the Jewish-Arab conflict on her unshakable belief that an anti-national, anti-sovereign world was just around the corner. Like the Russian revolutionaries, she staked everything on this faith; like them, she proved to be stunningly wrong.

Arendt composed a major essay, "Zionism Reconsidered," in October 1944—one of the deadliest years in Jewish history—in furious reaction to the aforementioned maximalist program adopted in Atlantic City. She warned, rightly, of the dangers that a tiny Jewish state facing an Arab sea of hostility would encounter—dangers that, obviously, persist. It is the rest of Arendt's essay that is so problematic; she fails to put forth either a cogent analysis of Zionism or a viable alternative to partition. This essay has been effusively hailed by latter-day writers; one calls it "breathtaking" in its "political perspicacity."[51] That is perplexing, because virtually every claim Arendt makes is wrong.

As part of her reconsideration, Arendt denounces Zionism and socialism as "living ghosts amid the ruins of our times" that have "outlived their political conditions." (Four years later, the State of Israel would come into being; five years later, the Communist revolutionaries in China would come to power; the list of living ghosts is long.) In one of the essay's strangest sections, she accuses the Zionist movement of "depriv[ing] the Jewish people of . . . what we generally call Western culture"—this at a time when the Yishuv's residents came almost entirely from Europe and when the movement was denounced by Arabs as an *extension* of Western culture. Palestine, Arendt avers, has "always belonged to the European continent," a claim that would have surprised Palestine's Jews and enraged its Arab inhabitants. (Talk about Eurocentrism!) And she definitively proclaims "the decline of the national state and of nationalism."[52]

Strangely, Arendt also indicts the Zionists for harboring "a fundamentally unpolitical attitude." It is difficult to square this with her admiring admission that, under the Mandate, the Zionists had erected a state within a state that "in some respects was more modern than the most advanced governments of the Western world." She noted, "All sorts of functions, such as administration, immigration, defense, education, health, social services, public works, communications, and so forth, were developed. . . . This explains the miraculous fact that a mere proclamation of Jewish self-government eventually sufficed to bring a state machine into being."[53] Miraculous, no; but if this sort of state-building isn't political, what is? Arendt's charge can only be understood within the peculiar linguistic world that she created, wherein "politics" was defined solely as the public discourse of free citizens and divorced from economic, social, and cultural concerns as well as from questions of justice and equality. But this definition is so idiosyncratic, especially in the context of Palestine, that it loses all meaning; Arendt was essentially writing in an idiolect. One can argue that the Zionist movement created the wrong *kind* of politics, but not that it failed to create a political world or present a political solution to the crisis of the Jewish people.

Perhaps most ill-informed was Arendt's attack on the kibbutzniks. She had previously praised these new, improved Jews in almost gushing terms. In "Zionism Reconsidered," however, these formerly virile heroes are transformed into persnickety schlemiels and selfish narcissists. Now the communal farmers are "concerned only with the personal realization of lofty ideals"; they are "too decent for politics" and guilty, therefore, of a "tragic abdication of political leadership."[54] Their admirably soil-stained hands have been regrettably scrubbed clean.

Nothing in this description was true. Far from creating "small islands of perfection," as Arendt charged, the socialist communes served as underground arms factories, and their military resistance would prove crucial in the independence war.[55] They would supply a disproportionately large number of military leaders, and soldiers for the elite military units, in the 1948 war and subsequently. More important, for the next three to four decades the kibbutzim nurtured the political leadership for the dominant left-wing political parties and the Histadrut labor federation, the crucial state institution. In short, the kibbutzim produced much of Israel's elite: social, military, political, and moral. Arendt's misunderstanding of this fundamental fact of Israeli life has, alas, been repeated almost verbatim by subsequent writers.[56]

The odd thing about Arendt's thinking at this time is that as Jewish-Arab violence in Palestine intensified, she clung to her ideas ever more tenaciously. The day after the United Nations partition vote, Palestinian militias attacked the Yishuv. The subsequent fighting would be characterized by massacres, mutilations, sieges, starvation, and terror attacks; no side emerged with clean hands. None of this led Arendt to alter, or even question, her intercommunal prescriptions. Nor did she seem to notice that as Palestine descended into bloody destruction in late 1947, both the Palestinian and Jewish communities regarded the British as an oppressive imperialist power rather than a benign protector.

To argue for binationalism or Arab-Jewish federation before 1948 was, in my view, a wrong position but not a crazy one. But Arendt's writings make the least informed and therefore least convincing arguments for it, for they were based on her ideological antipathy to sovereignty rather than on the political situation in Palestine. It was something entirely different, however, to oppose a Jewish state *during* the 1948 war—when its very existence was at stake—and to urge President Harry S. Truman to oppose partition and withhold recognition of Israel. These were Arendt's positions.

Commentary magazine published Arendt's misleadingly titled article "To Save the Jewish Homeland" in May 1948, the month that Israel declared independence and was invaded. She again affirmed the absolute centrality of the Zionist project. The destruction of the Yishuv, she wrote, would be "another catastrophe . . . almost beyond imagining." Yet she insisted, once more, that Jewish political independence would lead to just that and should be replaced by "mixed Jewish-Arab municipal and rural councils." Arendt must have known that no such councils existed, or ever had, and that there was no possibility of forming them in the midst of what Jews and Palestinians alike now perceived as a zero-sum war for survival. But Arendt *had* been reading the newspapers, and she admitted to "the Arab refusal of any compromise" on the question of partition, Jewish statehood, and a Jewish presence in Palestine. "It is obvious," she wrote, that the Arabs "have decided to expend in time and numbers whatever it may take to win a decisive victory."[57] The military commander Abd al-Qadir al-Husseini explained the Palestinian position clearly: "It is inconceivable that Palestine will be for the Arabs and the Zionists together—it's us or them."[58]

Yet nothing shook Arendt's insistence on joint ventures. How to form such councils in the midst of what Arab League leader Azzam Bey promised would be a "war of extermination" against the Jews?[59] Arendt never answered this troublesome but obviously crucial question.

Instead, she insisted again that a non-sovereign Jewish "homeland" could somehow thrive under a United Nations protectorate. Unfortunately, many of the UN's key nations, including Britain, France, and the Soviet Union, were in ruins at the end of the war. Jewish protection, like Jewish immigration, was hardly a priority for them, and East-West tensions were already dividing the UN. And by 1948 most Zionists, and certainly most of the Jewish survivors languishing in displaced persons camps, were hardly inclined to place their hopes of survival in the nascent global organization or the so-called international community. Every Jew knew that the world's nations had, with striking near-unanimity, abandoned the Jewish people during the genocide; this was a betrayal that Arendt herself had bitterly decried as "the complete breakdown of international solidarity." She would later describe this, even more eloquently, as "the nightmare of absolute helplessness and abandonment—as though the whole world was a jungle" and the Jews "its prey."[60]

But the nightmare was apparently over and the whole world had changed. In a stark reversal of her previous stance, Arendt now insisted, in the midst of war, that the Jewish people's best bet, indeed sole bet, was protection by others; in fact, she equated Israeli sovereignty with suicide. Here we encounter something strange: The woman who had demanded an imaginary Jewish army now opposed the actual one; the woman who had denounced Jewish submissiveness now opposed Jewish self-determination; the woman who insisted on the creation of a specifically Jewish political world now opposed the creation of a state to protect that world. It was inconceivable to Arendt that Jews could fight and win; it was inconceivable that they could sustain an independent political presence, on terms of equality, within the league of nations.

Arendt was never shy about assessing the political situation in Palestine and dictating what should happen there. How she obtained the information on which her views were based is, however, unclear. She did not visit Palestine between 1935 and 1955. She could not read the Hebrew or Arabic newspapers, and though she was in touch, via letters, with some of her old Zionist friends from Germany, I can find no evidence that she ever spoke to more mainstream Zionists or to any Palestinian Arabs. This disconnection is glaringly evident in her writings of the 1940s. In "To Save the Jewish Homeland," for instance, she complains that the terrorist Irgun and Ben-Gurion's Haganah are in cahoots and "about to conclude an agreement," which proved that "political initiative is already in terrorist hands."[61] It is true that the Haganah and the Irgun had cooperated in attacks against the British, but it was well known that this alliance had ended two years before Arendt wrote this piece. In fact, one month after her essay appeared, the Haganah would fight, and kill, Irgunists who were smuggling arms into Israel via the *Altalena*. The Haganah would thus permanently establish the state's monopoly on force—the "one gun" principle—and the terrorist groups were militarily (and politically) vanquished; so much for an agreement. Arendt was no Cassandra, though this is no sin; she cannot be faulted for failing to see the future. But she can be faulted for failing to see the present.

It is precisely as a prophet, however, that Arendt is now praised; the word "prescient," sometimes preceded by adverbs like "remarkably," "amazingly," and "eerily," attaches itself to her with ease.[62] And while her warnings about the centrality of the Arab-Israeli conflict were correct, her predictions regarding what would happen *after* independence proved wide of the mark. Even if Israel won its (first) war, Arendt averred, the Yishuv's achievements would quickly collapse. Its economic, intellectual, and cultural life would shrivel into nothing; it would "degenerate into one of those small warrior tribes," isolated from the world and from the Jewish Diaspora. These assumptions led Arendt to her counter-intuitive claim that "a Jewish state can only be erected at the price of the Jewish homeland."[63] The exact opposite proved true. Virtually every historian agrees that an Israeli loss in 1948 would have led to the crushing of the Yishuv's institutions and the expulsion or mass murder of its inhabitants. (To imagine, as Arendt implied, that a victorious Arab regime would have protected either the Jews or their institutions is chimerical.) Arendt was right about the persistence of the Arab-Israeli conflict. But she did not grasp what has turned out to be the central paradox of Israel. Israelis have created a thriving polity *without* attaining what they most need: peace.

If binationalism was unpopular among Palestinian Jews and virtually anathema to Palestinian Arabs before 1948, it was dead once the Arab-Israeli war began. Arendt conceded this, but it seemed to only stiffen her resolve. In 1948, she suggested that representatives of the tiny Ihud and various "non-Zionists" should negotiate—it is not clear on what basis or with what power—with "Arab individuals" who were "sincere believers in Arab-Jewish cooperation."[64] These sincere believers remained unnamed, for good reason. Very few Arab leaders were willing to enter into talks with Jews, much less discuss joint councils, federation, or binationalism. (At the 1939 London Conference on the Future of Palestine, the Palestinian delegation had refused to sit in the same room with Jews, much less discuss a shared entity.) And an alarmingly high number of the few who broached agreement were assassinated by other Arabs; see, for instance, the unhappy fates of Fawzi Darwish Hussaini, Sami Taha, Fakhri Bey Nashashibi, and, later, King Abdullah of Transjordan. Even aside from its implausibility, Arendt's prescription is extraordinary in light of her heated criticisms of the Zionist movement for its undemo-cratic, top-down tendencies. She was essentially arguing that *her* ideas—unrepresentative, unsupported, unreal—should be imposed (by whom?) on Palestine regardless of the political realities and the political will of virtually all its inhabitants. Arendt is known, indeed hailed, as an advo-cate of spontaneous democratic political action from below. Yet there was no political program less spontaneous, less organic, or less popularly based than the one she proposed for Palestine.

Arendt's last major article directly addressing Zionism was titled "Peace or Armistice in the Near East?" It was written in 1948 and published in 1950. In the intervening two years, important events had transformed the political landscape of the Middle East and, therefore, the world. These included the partition of Palestine, the first Arab-Israeli war, the Israeli victory, the expansion of the Israeli state, massive immigration to Israel of Shoah survivors and Jews from the Arab countries, the creation of the Palestinian refugees, growing nationalist movements in the Arab states, and the emergence of a pan-Arab rejectionist front opposing Israel. Yet I can find no evidence that Arendt saw a need to rewrite, or even reconsider, her original essay. She did not admit that her major forecast—the destruction, or auto-destruction, of the Yishuv—had not materialized. Nor did she entertain the possibility that her proposals would have led to precisely the catastrophes that she prophesied. Indeed, in what can only be read as a kind of wish fulfillment, she *continued* to predict ceaseless disasters for Israel: a possible military dictatorship, "cultural and political sterility," and the near-certainty of domination by the Soviet Union.[65] None of this came to pass.

What *had* been confirmed was unrelenting Arab hostility to any Jewish state or, even, any Jewish presence in Palestine; and it is here, once again, that Arendt proved perceptive. "It is remarkable how little the accomplished fact of a state of Israel and Jewish victories over Arab armies have influenced Arab politics," she wrote. "It seems as though the *one* argument the Arabs are incapable of understanding is force. . . . Defeats seem to confirm the Arabs' attitude as much as victories do that of the Jews." Her prediction that Israeli "chauvinism . . . could use the religious concept of the chosen people and allow its meaning to degenerate into hopeless vulgarity" has, alas, also been fulfilled.[66]

Arendt acknowledged that the creation of a state for the Jewish people was "a turning point in Jewish history."[67] But in her thinking and her prescriptions, everything remained unchanged. In *On Revolution,* she would criticize Lenin for failing to "reorient his thought" between the revolutions of 1905 and 1917—for failing, that is, to learn from the "direct impact of the events themselves."[68] The same was true of Arendt. She remained ever alert to the dangers of Arab hostility and ever oblivious to the substantially greater dangers that statelessness posed. She deplored the left-wing parties' support for partition but failed to understand that their reluctant abandonment of binationalism was an acknowledgment of reality, not a betrayal of principle; nor did she ever consider that, as residents of Palestine, their assessment of the situation might be more informed than hers. She continued to maintain that "the Near Eastern peoples"—presumably Israel, Arab Palestine, Egypt, Lebanon, Syria, Iraq, and Transjordan—could find "lasting agreement . . . on questions of defense, foreign policy, and economic development"; one can imagine what a merry federation that would have been, given that these countries often hated one another almost as much as they hated Israel.[69] (The only "lasting agreement" they found was opposition to the Jewish state.) Arendt had accused the kibbutzniks of overlooking the political realities of the Middle East. But, as with her criticism of Lenin, this was an accusation she could have leveled at herself.

"National sovereignty, which so long had been the very symbol of free national development, has become the greatest danger to national survival for small nations," Arendt proclaimed in 1948.[70] The greatest? It is unlikely that one could find many Vietnamese, Tunisians, Sri Lankans, Finns, Bangladeshis, East Timorese, Kosovars, Lithuanians—or, especially, Palestinians—who would subsequently agree. It was this kind of obtuseness that led the political philosopher Judith Shklar to describe Arendt's ideas on nationalism as "immune to evidence."[71]

And evidence is awfully important to imperiled peoples, as Bosnians, Rwandans, and Kurds can attest; they cannot afford the fantasies that more fortunate bystanders impose upon them. Thus, in January 1946, Arendt's old friend Gershom Scholem wrote an angry, disappointed letter to her. Scholem had moved from Germany to Palestine in 1923 and was originally a follower of Brit Shalom, though he had abandoned binationalism because, he explained, "The Arabs have not agreed to a single solution that includes Jewish immigration, whether it be federal, national, or binational." His correspondence with Arendt was prompted by his belated reading of "Zionism Reconsidered," which he described as "political balderdash."[72]

"Your article has nothing to do with Zionism," Scholem charged. "The structure of your arguments is extremely odd, and the whole displays such inconsistency of scale and perspective that I can make sense of it only by viewing it as an assemblage pieced together by someone who wishes to disavow the 'reactionary' concerns of Zionism." He zeroed in on the catch-22 that Arendt repeatedly set up: "You denounce Jews in Palestine for maintaining an otherworldly separation from the rest of mankind, but when these same Jews make efforts to fend for themselves, . . . you react with . . . derision." He sensed, and resented, the arrogant purism that permeated Arendt's thinking. Zionism, he wrote, "has created a situation full of despair, doubt, and compromise—precisely because it takes place on earth, not on the moon. . . . The Zionist movement shares this dialectical experience of the Real (and all its catastrophic possibilities) with all other movements that have taken it upon themselves to change something in the real world."[73] Arendt's insistence that the Zionists have no truck with the imperialist powers—that they remain too pure for what Scholem would have called "real" power politics—was, in my view, her secular version of Jewish "chosenness" and an example of the very worldlessness that she decried.

Scholem also hinted at what I consider one of the most morally troubling aspects of Arendt's writings on Zionism, especially during the war of 1948. This lies in what we might call her "armchair politics": her propensity to dictate policies and prescriptions in the midst of a life-threatening crisis about which she had little tangible knowledge and for which she would pay no personal price—unlike critics of Zionist policies such as Buber and Scholem, who remained in Israel as oppositional Zionists. "The cynicism with which you used lofty and progressive arguments against something that is for the Jewish people of life-or-death importance is unlikely to persuade me to abandon the [Zionist] sect," Scholem wrote. "I never dreamed that it would be easier for me to agree with Ben Gurion than with you! But after reading your essay, I have no doubt about this. I consider Ben Gurion's political line disastrous, but at the same time it's much more noble—or a lesser evil—than the one we would have if we followed your advice."[74] In quoting (and agreeing with) this critique, I do not mean to suggest that only insiders, or those on the ground, have a monopoly on insight or the standing to suggest solutions; sometimes observers perceive what combatants cannot. But the fact remains that Arendt repeatedly and strenuously advocated a policy of non-sovereignty that was equivalent to surrender. And surrender would not have "saved" the Jewish homeland; as Scholem and everyone else in the Yishuv knew, it would have meant, quite simply, the death of Israel and of Israelis. Arendt's failure to realize this is incomprehensible. After all, it was she who had argued, time and again, that the "traditional Jewish aversion against military organization" had proved ruinous to the Jewish people throughout its history.[75]

Again, the question is: Why? Arendt valued the capacity for judgment above all else. Judging, she wrote, is the ultimate act of political freedom and "one, if not the most, important activity in which . . . sharing-the-world-with-others comes to pass."[76] Why, then, was *her* judgment so bad? She insisted on the importance of living "in the world as it happened to be, without illusions," and warned that political theorists risk devolving into useless abstraction "if we lose the ground of experience."[77] Why, then, was she so heedless of the actual situation in Palestine? Arendt scoffed at political romantics and reserved her highest praise for people such as Bertolt Brecht because, in her view, his "intelligence was uncommonly close to reality."[78] In fact, it is difficult to overstate Arendt's emphasis on the reality principle and her derision of those who abandoned it; this theme recurs so often in her writings that it verged on obsession. Yet confronted with the Arab-Jewish collision, she retreated into political sentimentality and magical constructs. Conservatives often explain Arendt's essays in this period as manifestations of anti-Zionism, anti-Semitism, or Jewish self-hatred. But these terms simply don't describe Arendt; there is too much in her writings and her life that belies them. Such explanations do nothing to illuminate this chapter in her thought. And so we must look elsewhere.

A major source of Arendt's failures can be found, I believe, in the tension between her fear of the state and her fear of statelessness. It was a tension that was never resolved, for good reason. Both the state *and* its absence had proved deadly to vulnerable populations in the prelude to the Second World War; the result was deportation and, eventually, mass death. (A parallel condundrum exists today, when grotesque human rights abuses are committed by centralized states that are too strong—North Korea, Eritrea, Iran—and in collapsed states like Somalia and Congo.) And it was Zionism, far more than any other political movement, which would highlight these contradictory impulses in Arendt's thought, especially in the crisis years of the 1940s.

Arendt was one of the great chroniclers of statelessness, which she understood as a psychic and political calamity. In her 1943 essay "We Refugees," she explored the desperation of the stateless—even those who, like she, had been relatively fortunate. Caustically, she observed: "We were told to forget; and we forgot quicker than anybody ever could imagine. . . . After four weeks in France or six weeks in America, we pretended to be Frenchmen or Americans. . . . In order to forget more efficiently we rather avoid any allusion to concentration or intern-ment camps . . . [because] it might be interpreted as pessimism."[79] Helplessness, dependence, obsequiousness, shame: These were the lot of the refugee.

Arendt's most incisive exploration of the political cost of stateless-ness, and its connection to the doctrines of human rights, would be artic-ulated in *The Origins of Totalitarianism*. Rights, she argued, are not innately natural or innately human; in essence, she would defend, indeed laud, the artificiality of rights as she had previously lauded the artificiality of the Yishuv. Rights are political *inventions*—human inventions—that attain meaning only in the context of membership within a political community. Without that, unaccommodated man is unprotected man—is, in fact, "the scum of the earth."[80]

Arendt's critique of human rights must still be engaged because it still rings true. She pointed out that, from the start, "the declaration of inalienable human rights . . . reckoned with an 'abstract' human being who seemed to exist nowhere, for even savages lived in some kind of social order." The Rights of Man had proved anything but inalienable: "It turned out that the moment human beings lacked their own government and had to fall back upon their minimum rights, no authority was left to protect them and no institution was willing to guarantee them." Thus the feebleness, indeed fraudulence, of human rights doctrines when divorced from a specific polity: "The world found nothing sacred in the abstract nakedness of being human. . . . It seems that a man who is nothing but a man has lost the very qualities which make it possible for other people to treat him as a fellow-man."[81] Rights must be grounded—rights must be *made* real—within a nation's political institutions. Here again, Arendt stressed the dangers of rootlessness and the necessity of its opposite. A place in the world—the political world of citizenship—and the protection it entails are the prerequisite for a fully human life. For Arendt, the loss of such a polity is equivalent to expulsion from humanity itself.

But what kind of polity could ensure such rights? In Arendt's view, the failure of the interwar European states to protect all citizens—and their substitution of ethnic nationalism for democratic inclusiveness—meant that the sovereign nation-state was dead, or at least should be. In *The Origins of Totalitarianism,* she observed, "Human rights were protected and enforced only as national rights, and . . . the very institution of a state, whose supreme task was to protect and guarantee man his rights as man, . . . lost its legal, rational appearance."[82] National sovereignty became a means by which some citizens were "denationalized," deprived of rights, expelled, and finally murdered. As a result, Arendt came to see the nation-state as the enemy rather than protector of rights, and nationalism as the precursor to what we now call ethnic cleansing. (In Arendt's parlance, "sovereignty" sometimes referred to the establishment of an independent state and sometimes to the ways an extant state shielded its policies from others.) Much earlier, in 1940—even before the Final Solution—she wrote, "The twentieth century has shown us the ultimate consequences of nationalism, as evidenced by horrible relocations of peoples and various massacres, beginning with the Armenians and the Ukranian pogroms."[83] She added that since the nation-state had failed, the "sole salvation" of world Jewry, by which she meant European Jewry, would be a European commonwealth and a European parliament in which the Jewish people would participate. She would cling to this construct even as events outstripped the ideology it represented.

In a sense, Arendt argued that every nation-state not only could but *would* become the Third Reich. The downward trajectory from sovereignty into nationalism and, then, into ethnic fascism was inevitable. What *had* been *must* be. This is akin to arguing that every democracy is doomed because the Weimar Republic failed. And indeed, some German intellectuals argued just that (though Arendt was not among them); in 1939, Max Horkheimer contended that, with the rise of fascism, liberal-democratic states could never be reestablished. It is no coincidence that a large number of the binationalists in Mandatory Palestine were refugees from Germany. They had earned their suspicions of nationalism, and their fears that it led to fascism, in the hardest of ways. As Judith Shklar observed, "One does not forget Weimar easily."[84]

But to see Hitler's Storm Troopers lurking in the shadows of every democracy—or in every movement for national independence—is a kind of paranoid repetition compulsion, which is hardly the basis for sound political judgment. There is no doubt that the Yishuv and, then, the State of Israel have been the object of this compulsion, and not only by Arendt. Zionists and anti-Zionists, leftists and rightists: All have had the greatest difficulty in seeing Israel, and the Israeli-Palestinian conflict, in their particularity rather than as stand-ins for other struggles and other histories. "The reality of Israel is, in large measure, a projection of fantasies, both by those who want to love the place and those who are consumed by hatred for it," observed Israeli-American writer Joel Schalit. "While Israel is as real as any other place on the map, the fact that it was conjured during a time when it literally had no place emboldens both its friends and enemies to treat it as a trope."[85]

Arendt imposed her tropes—her fixations—on Zionism. She believed that "Palestine contained potential solutions to the problems that had led to totalitarianism in Germany," her biographer Elisabeth Young-Bruehl wrote. "In the homeland of the Jews, Hannah Arendt wished to see [enacted] all of the elements which formed the foundations of her political theory."[86] It was this propensity to see Palestine, and then Israel, as a laboratory in which her ideas could be tested that, I believe, led to so many of Arendt's radical misjudgments. The glaring differences between Germany and Palestine, and between the histories of Germans and Jews, were blurred.

Unlike Horkheimer, who would revise his views on anti-Semitism and liberal democracy, Arendt would continue to argue against the sovereign nation-state in favor of federations and grass-roots councils. And despite her dogmatism, I find Arendt's critique of sovereignty to be, in many ways, valuable and far-sighted. Today we see many of the most tyrannical governments, and their policies of torture, massacre, and ethnic cleansing, protected from international pressure under the rubric of sovereignty.

Yet here, too, as in her warnings against partition, a slice of reality was substituted for the whole. It is true that the partition of Palestine led to violence and injustice. The attempted imposition of a binational state or federation would, however, have led to far greater bloodshed and injustice, since neither Jews nor Arabs supported such entities; Arendt's refusal to even consider this is baffling. Similarly, it is true that nation-states have often been guilty of heinous crimes against their citizens and their neighbors. But the fact that sovereignty can be misused as a protective shield for barbarism does not mean that all states will inevitably pervert it in this way, much less that endangered peoples should forgo independent state-hood. The demise of the state, in those places where it has occurred, has led not to peaceful transnational federations, happy multiethnic repub-lics, or self-governing councils. Instead we find the cruel anarchy of *failed* states (Libya, Yemen, Somalia . . . the grim list is long).

When it came to Palestine, Arendt's antipathy to the nation-state prevented her from seeing that an imposed contrivance like federation or binationalism, admired by outsiders but at war with actuality, had consider-ably dimmer prospects than a flawed but reality-based compromise like partition. She refused to acknowledge that what philosopher Seyla Benhabib calls the conflict "between *ethnos* and *demos*" cannot always be solved—or, rather, that it can be, indeed must be, solved in more than one way, that all these ways will be imperfect, and that each solution must respect the unique history of the nation in question.[87] The irony is that Arendt's attempts to untangle the Gordian knot of statehood versus statelessness led her, in the context of Palestine, to solutions that were profoundly anti-political and, as such, contradicted her deepest convictions.

It is interesting to compare Arendt's views on nationalism and the nation-state with those of two people she admired, Rosa Luxemburg and Bernard Lazare. In a 1966 article for the *New York Review of Books* entitled "A Heroine of Revolution," Arendt lauded Luxemburg—who adamantly denied *any* national or Jewish identity—for her insights, character, and revolutionary commitments. But Arendt was highly critical of Luxemburg's "doctrinaire internationalism." Abstract internationalism, epitomized by the socialist motto "the fatherland of the working class is the Socialist movement," was "disastrously wrong," Arendt charged. "It is indeed more than a little disturbing that Rosa Luxemburg herself, with her acute sense of reality and strict avoidance of clichés, should not have *heard* what was wrong with the slogan. . . . A fatherland, after all, is first of all a 'land.' "[88] I cannot read this without thinking of the strong parallels to Arendt herself—parallels of which she was obviously unaware.

Arendt repeated this critique of extreme anti-nationalism in *The Origins of Totalitarianism,* where she addressed the interwar European Left. "The socialists kept implicitly intact the original concept of a 'nation among nations,' all of which belong to the family of mankind, but they never found a device by which to transform this idea into a working concept in the world of sovereign states," she wrote. "Their healthy disinterest in national sovereignty turned into a quite unhealthy and unrealistic indifference to foreign politics."[89] Arendt was not a Marxist or a socialist, and she did not consider herself part of the Left, though she deeply admired Left intellectuals such as Lazare, Luxemburg, Benjamin, and Brecht.[90] Yet her staunch antipathy to sovereignty, and in particular to Israeli sovereignty, reveals the peculiar truth that one can be an *ultra-leftist* without committing oneself to the actual Left.

And despite Arendt's close identification with Lazare, I think she missed some of his key beliefs. Though he loathed chauvinism of every kind, Lazare insisted that national aspirations are not incompatible with internationalism. "At certain moments in history, nationalism is for human groups the manifestation of the spirit of freedom," he wrote. "Internationalism obviously presupposes the existence of nations." He continued, "[I] do not hesitate for an instant in accepting nationalism alongside internationalism. On the contrary, I believe that for internationalism to take root, it is necessary that human groups should previously have won their autonomy."[91] For historically weak and disenfranchised peoples—a category that includes Jews and Palestinians—national sovereignty, and even nationalism, are necessary steps toward the achievement of political maturity.

Nineteen forty-eight was one of those "certain moments in history." It is clear that, *pace* Arendt, the "sole salvation" of world Jewry, and certainly Palestinian Jewry, did not rest on a commonwealth of European nations; if it had, there would be few Jews (or at least Israelis) alive today. Arendt's increasingly desperate suggestions at this time—all the commonwealths and federations and protectorates that would, presumably, link warring peoples in a forced embrace—were, as Scholem immediately understood, recipes for extinction. She could not confront the contradiction between the risks of statelessness and the risks of nationalism (though she was right to see each as perilous). Nor could she confront the irresolvability of Arab and Israeli maximalist claims to the land (though she was right to see each as partially valid). In this, she was actually much *less* realistic than the Zionist leaders she so fiercely assailed. She wished away, rather than grappled with, an existential clash of claims and needs.

Wars, more than any other political event, force the question: Which side are you on? In the 1948 war Arendt did not choose the Arabs and she did not choose the Jews. She chose her fantasies of what *should* be. She chose to insist that a bitterly opposed marriage between two hostile, wounded peoples would result in justice, peace, and national development. Somehow, Hannah Arendt forgot her own warnings about the ruinous perils of worldlessness.

There is another aspect of Arendt's thought that, in my view, led to her flawed analysis of the Arab-Israeli conflict. It is Arendt's idealization of the undesired, the social leper, the excluded: in her words, the pariah.

Arendt loved outsiders and believed there was nobility in being one. This was, I think, as much an emotional predilection as an intellectual one. In her early twenties, while still in Germany, she began an eponymously titled biography of Rahel Varnhagen, a nineteenth-century bourgeois German Jew. It was Arendt's first major work after her dissertation, and many writers have noted her close identification with her subject. Young-Bruehl called it "a very autobiographical biography," while historian Steven Aschheim termed it "her most revealingly personal work."[92] It is not a stretch to say that Varnhagen was both a warning and an alter ego for Arendt. (Of course, by the time the book was published in 1958, much had changed; as one writer noted, "Arendt's great historical subject was no longer the question of whether Jews were fit to enter the salons, but the question of whether Jews were fit to inhabit the earth.")[93]

Arendt used Lazare's paradigm of "parvenus" and "pariahs" as the scaffolding for the book. The former were vilified; the latter, extolled. Rahel "had always stood outside, had been a pariah, and discovered at last . . . that entrance into society was possible only at the price of lying," Arendt approvingly noted. More generally, the pariah is blessed with "an emotionally exaggerated understanding of the dignity of every human being, a passionate comprehension unknown to the privileged. . . . The pariah, precisely because he is an outcast, can see life as a whole." The pariah is authentic, honest, free. The parvenu, in contrast, is a fraud: "Not for a single minute did he dare to be himself. . . . It was necessary for the parvenu . . . to sacrifice every natural impulse, to conceal all truth, to misuse all love."[94]

Rahel was the first in Arendt's long line of courageous outliers; Luxemburg was another. Here again, pariahdom was key. Arendt argued that Luxemburg's Jewish comrades among the Polish socialists developed their universalist, humane outlook because they existed "outside all social ranks" in "truly splendid isolation."[95] She wrote that Heinrich Heine, another hero, regarded the "aloofness of the pariah . . . as the essence of freedom"; as such, he "takes his place among the most uncompromising of Europe's fighters for freedom."[96] Arendt's glorification of the outcast became a sociological principle: "All vaunted Jewish qualities—the 'Jewish heart,' humanity, humor, disinterested intelligence—are pariah qualities."[97] The figures she most admired were mavericks, and the more they were shunned, the better. "Often an era most clearly brands with its seal those who have been least influenced by it, who have been most remote from it, and who therefore have suffered most. So it was with Proust, with Kafka, with Karl Kraus, and with Benjamin."[98]

Arendt's admirers frequently stress her presumed marginality. Young-Bruehl wrote that "self-conscious pariahdom was her personal kingdom." Benhabib noted that Varnhagen's "eventual recognition of her status as a pariah and a Jew . . . provide[s] a parallel narrative, almost a parable, for the experiences and transformations of Arendt's own lifetime."[99] This insistence on Arendt as an outsider has occasionally led to silly analogies, as when Young-Bruehl wrote, "In Berkeley, as earlier in Princeton, Arendt felt as much a pariah . . . as Rosa Luxemburg had . . . in the German SPD."[100] (The SPD acquiesced in Luxemburg's assassination; things like that don't happen in Berkeley.)

Still, it is true that Arendt was an incontrovertibly independent thinker—and person. Hans Jonas, who clashed with her bitterly over *Eichmann in Jerusalem*, noted this in a loving tribute upon her death: "One sensed an absolute determination to be herself."[101] Yet there is a difference between independence, however admirable, and pariahdom. In the U.S., Arendt wrote for influential journals including *Partisan Review*, the *Nation, Commentary*, the *New York Review of Books*, and the *New Yorker*. Her books were widely reviewed; she lectured to acclaim throughout the country and the world; she received numerous prizes and honorary degrees; she taught at prestigious universities; she hobnobbed with New York's intellectual elite.

Arendt's friends saw her as a brave truth-teller who bucked a sheep-like herd of conformists and was in turn ostracized by them: another iteration of the pariah. This became especially noticeable during the controversy over *Eichmann in Jerusalem*, as evidenced in the letters she received and sent. Karl Jaspers, for instance, assured her that animus to the book arose because she had "touched an extremely sore spot for many people, shown their lives to be informed by a lie." However, it is not clear how he made this judgment, since his letters reveal that he did not begin reading *Eichmann in Jerusalem* until three months after he wrote this. Nevertheless, he was sure that Hannah would be vindicated: "A time will come . . . when the Jews will erect a monument to you in Israel."[102] (That time has not come.) This view of Arendt as a solitary warrior speaking truth to power has been reiterated by more recent accounts of her life and work and by Margarethe von Trotta's 2012 film *Hannah Arendt,* which depicts its heroine as an intellectual Joan of Arc whose loneliness of vision is a sign of virtue. An odd tautology is at work here: The pariah is good, wise, and truthful *because* she is a pariah.

Arendt shared this view. Her extensive correspondence during the Eichmann controversy reveals her obdurate refusal to engage the substantive issues that her book raised, even with longtime friends whose views she respected. Instead she insisted, again and again, that the controversy was simply a clash between brave truths (hers) and cowardly lies (everyone else's). In fact she claimed, somewhat astonishingly, that "there *are* no 'ideas' " in her book and that, therefore, "the hostility against me is a hostility against someone who tells the truth on a factual level." This truth was so plain that it lacked any "theoretical and scholarly embroidery."[103] In short, everything she wrote was objectively correct; there was nothing more to discuss. In Arendt's view, the attacks on her book were proof of her accuracy, honesty, and courage.

Arendt was so committed to seeing herself as an outlier and to taking contrarian stands that she imagined opposition when it scarcely existed. "I am glad they hanged Eichmann," she wrote to her friend Mary McCarthy in June 1962. "I know I am in a minority with this feeling."[104] Actually, Arendt was in the *majority* of Jews who, in Israel and the United States, supported the death sentence (though a very small minority of Israeli intellectuals, many of whom were Brit Shalom veterans, did not). Responding to Scholem's criticisms of the Eichmann book, which he loathed, Arendt insisted, "What confuses you is that my arguments and my approach are different from what you are used to; in other words, the trouble is that I am independent."[105] But Scholem was pretty independent too, and he thought that her book *did* contain ideas: "The problem you pose is genuine." He believed that the difficulties lay in Arendt's broad brush, lack of historic knowledge, and malicious sarcasm, not her independence.

"I do not belong to any organization and always speak only for myself," Arendt proclaimed to Scholem.[106] There is no doubt that when it came to Zionism, and then to Eichmann, Arendt stood apart from many of her presumed comrades and proudly bore the self-proclaimed mantle of outcast. The question is what inherent value this had. For there is a difference between departing from the crowd and being wise; loneliness and insight can be synonymous, but only adolescents assume that they always are. Furthermore, it is entirely possible to take an independent stance on divisive issues—as Scholem frequently did—without becoming a metaphorical exile from one's community or people. And so the important question is: What intellectual achievements did Arendt's idealization of the pariah produce, especially in the context of Zionism?

There are several aspects to what we might call "the pariah question" as it relates to Arendt. In her essay "The Jew as Pariah," written in 1944, she mounted an uncompromising defense of the rebellious pariah as the quintessential political and moral actor; her argument has always struck me as simultaneously noble, inspiring, puerile, and ahistoric. Again, Arendt drew heavily, if somewhat reductively, on Lazare's paradigm of pariahs versus parvenus. The dichotomy is not useless, though it is simplistic, since many Jews fit neither category, even in the emancipated West. (The millions of Ostjuden were virtually ignored.) But for Arendt, these were the only choices. The parvenu is again derided as the assimilationist willing to abandon her people and cravenly deny her Jewish identity; parvenus are "the rich, privileged Jews, the nabobs and philanthropists" who falsely claim leadership of the Jewish community.[107] In contrast, the "conscious pariah" cares nothing for society's judgments. She is the proud Jew who fights for political liberation *as a Jew* in conjunction with exploited others, regardless of the cost.

Lazare, who became a Zionist as a result of the Dreyfus Affair, was Arendt's model for the latter: "He knew . . . [that] the emancipated Jew must awake to an awareness of his position and, conscious of it, become a rebel against it—the champion of an oppressed people."[108] The pariah's fight was twofold: against gentile oppression and the Jewish establishment. In Arendt's telling, Lazare was unable to stir the Jewish masses due to Jewish self-denial and Jewish spinelessness. "The pariah simply refused to become a rebel. True to type, he preferred to 'play the revolutionary in the society of others, but not in his own,' or else to assume the role of *schnorrer* [beggar], feeding on the crumbs from the rich man's table."[109] Though Arendt set this part of her essay in the previous century, it is clear that she was describing the present-day failures of the Jewish people as she saw them.

The most controversial part of "The Jew as Pariah" is its section on obligation. Like Lazare, Arendt posited that the pariah must take political responsibility for his oppression and "feel that he was himself responsible for what society had done to him." This obligation was political, moral, even existential. Its refusal made one less than human: "Politically speaking, every pariah who refused to be a rebel was partly responsible for his own position and therewith for the blot on mankind which it represented. *From such shame there was no escape.*" Every human being, even the most despised or exploited, will "be called to account for the things which men do to men."[110] Oppression was no alibi for the absence of agency.

Arendt wrote this in 1944, when Sobibor and Treblinka were churning out Jewish corpses and grievously altering our concept of "the things which men do to men." This passage has therefore been interpreted as a form of blaming the victim, though I think that is a misreading of it. Arendt was calling, I believe, for the oppressed to respond politically *to* their persecution, which is not the same as assuming blame for it. At the end of the essay, she makes clear that all previous Jewish strategies for survival in the European Diaspora were catastrophically bankrupt. (In this, she was the diametric opposite of Maxime Rodinson, a firm believer in assimilation.) "Today the bottom has dropped out of the old ideology. The pariah Jew and the *parvenu* Jew are in the same boat, rowing desperately in the same angry sea. . . . Both alike are outlaws. Today the truth has come home: there is no protection in heaven or earth against bare murder."[111] This was certainly a fitting response to the devastations of 1944; it was also the Zionist position.

To assume pariahdom in Arendtian terms meant, then, to be politically aware, fearless, and active. But a somewhat different meaning of pariah, to which Arendt was equally loyal, is loner: the person who remains aloof from the mass—even, or especially, from his own people. This figure has a long lineage, as in the romantic image of the prophet who stands on the mountaintop. He is solitary and misunderstood; his warnings and his wisdom are unappreciated. He sees clearly *because* he sees from afar; his clarity is based on distance, indeed on height. This height is not only physical but ideological and emotional as well: He looks down on his people and even sometimes views them with contempt. This, too, describes Arendt.

Arendt sought that kind of distance and was proud of it. She was genuinely, and understandably, disheartened by the harsh attacks aimed at her during the Eichmann controversy. But she also took a pugnacious pride in what she called "the war between me and the Jews" and in her isolation from the Jewish community.[112] To Arendt, detachment meant strength—and sometimes, no doubt, it does. And yet I think that Arendt's pride was misplaced. Far from being the source of intellectual discernment and moral virtue, distance was a source of her greatest errors. Her remoteness—her status, often self-induced, of a pariah—accounted for some of the enormous miscalculations in her political judgments.

Arendt's remoteness took several related forms. She distanced herself from the complexities of Jewish history, reducing it to its "antihistory," that is, to anti-Semitism, catastrophe, failed assimilation, and worldlessness. She distanced herself from the tangled political realities and limited political choices in Palestine. And she distanced herself from serious critics, impugning their motives and surrounding herself with flatterers. ("You are conquering the Jews and are the best Jew yourself," Jaspers assured her during the Eichmann controversy.)[113] These disconnections led to the unfortunate mix of abstractness and ignorance that weakened her analyses of Zionism, Palestine, and Israel.

When it came to Zionism, even those who loved Arendt were struck by how uninformed she was. It wasn't only committed Zionists like Scholem who held this view. Jonas, who left Israel after fighting in the War of Independence, recalled, "In Palestine, during the years between the end of the [world] war and the United Nations' decision, . . . we were shocked at the turn in her thinking"; he was shocked, too, by the "odd" and "appalling" reasons Arendt offered for her convoluted positions.[114] Arendt's niece Edna Brocke, an Israeli Sabra who later moved to West Germany and was close to her aunt, remembered: "She often repeated the criticisms of Israel current among many leftists in Europe and the United States, which were usually based on scant knowledge of the real situation."[115] In place of familiarity with political facts—and with the texture of human experience—Arendt substituted political theory, accompanied by a tone of imperious certainty. Scholem mocked this trait as her "sovereign height" and added, "I don't have such sovereignty—and to tell you the truth, I don't think Arendt does either."[116]

This haughtiness was not confined to Arendt's approach to Zionism, though it was most pointedly obvious there. She criticized revolutionaries who fought for workers' control of the factories because they did not adhere to the strict division between the political and the economic: a division that was solely hers. She criticized civil rights activists seeking to desegregate schools in the American South because they did not adhere to the strict division between the political and the social: a division that was solely hers. Zionists, socialists, black activists: In each case, they refused to conform to the theories she superimposed upon them. (Arendt was often disappointed.) And in each case, her ignorance of political realities was at fault. Of course, anyone can misconstrue a complex political situation; anyone can be wrong. But Arendt kept being wrong in the same way. It was this *kind* of wrongness that, Young-Bruehl observed, "left her totally cut off from any possibility of action and without influence" in the Zionist movement—a movement that, contrary to Arendt's charges of stifling uniformity, is one of the most disputatious and least homogeneous in history.[117]

An alternative view of the social critic's role—an anti-pariah position—has been developed by the political theorist Michael Walzer. "The ideal critic is part of his or her society, engaged rather than detached," he argued. "Closeness is the crucial quality of the good social critic." This is not a question of holding a particular political position; Walzer wrote admiringly of George Orwell and Antonio Gramsci, who disagreed about a lot. Closeness is, instead, a matter of ethics: It implies "a way of living with others." And because close critics regard proximity "not only as a moral tie but as a personal engagement, their critique has the sensitivity, intimacy, and grasp of detail that are features of confessional literature."[118] This is precisely what Arendt's writings on Zionism lack. Arendt wrote in praise of "splendid isolation," but that is a poor place from which to understand the world.

Arendt's writings on Zionism and Israel show how easily distance can nurture distortion. Few observers of twentieth-century politics (or, for that matter, twenty-first) would agree with her claim that the pariah—the despised, the exploited, the oppressed—possesses a "passionate comprehension" of every human being's "innate dignity." We have learned too often and too well that today's pariah can become tomorrow's occupier (as in Israel), that former slaves can create new ones (as in Sudan), that those who have been whipped and beaten can build torture chambers for their enemies once they ascend to power (as in Iran and Iraq, Zimbabwe and Congo). Arendt's exaltation of the pariah as a kind of ethical savant was a form of romance—and self-romance.

After 1950—after Israel was founded, won its war of independence, did not make peace, and did not collapse—Arendt largely stopped writing about Zionism, though she often visited her relatives in Israel. (In a letter to Blücher during a 1955 visit, she praises Israel's "incredible" social and economic achievements, observes the anxiety that permeates the country, criticizes its treatment of Arab citizens, decides that the kibbutzim are finished, and notes that "everyone, with very few exceptions, is idiotic.")[119] As a political problem, though, she bid adieu to Zionism, which had proved so troubling for her. "Peace or Armistice" was her last essay that dealt extensively with the subject. "I do not want to have anything to do with Jewish politics any longer," she privately wrote to the editor of the *Jewish Newsletter* in 1953.[120]

But she was not quite finished; bonds, especially deeply ambivalent ones, are harder to break than they sometimes seem. In 1961, Arendt went to Jerusalem to cover the Eichmann trial, which would become her last confrontation—not with Nazism but with Zionism and "Jewish politics."

A vast literature on *Eichmann in Jerusalem* exists. Much of it centers on Arendt's concept of evil, her writings on the Jewish councils (*Judenräte*), and her portrait of Adolf Eichmann. Since the book's publication in 1963 a great deal of historical research has been conducted, archives have been opened, and primary materials unavailable to Arendt have been discovered. Many of her facts, and the broader claims she made based on them, have been disputed, complicated, or flatly overturned. There are few historians today who would agree with Arendt's assessment that

Eichmann was "certainly . . . not" a major war criminal and that, other than professional ambition, he "had no motives at all." Nor would many agree with her startlingly hubristic claim that she knew "the whole truth" about the thorny, indeed harrowing relationship between the Jewish leadership and Jewish deaths.[121]

Yet *Eichmann in Jerusalem* still demands to be read, though for exactly the reasons that Arendt abjured. Far from being devoid of ideas or of "theoretical embroidery," the conceptual questions that the book raises draw us to it. The ways in which terror and dehumanization dissolve solidarity among victims; particularity versus universalism in prosecuting crimes against humanity; the qualities that distinguish genocide from other atrocities; the function of war crimes trials and the value of justice; the distinction between collective responsibility and collective guilt: All remain unhappily pertinent.

Arendt's treatment of these issues in *Eichmann in Jerusalem* was sometimes brilliantly original and sometimes gravely erroneous. Few books remain, for me, so radically inconsistent, which is to say so astute, forceful, and moving at times—and, at others, so infuriating, wrongheaded, and odious. Even after many readings, I find her section on Anton Schmid, the Nazi soldier who helped Jewish partisans, almost unbearably moving, and the lessons she drew from his story continue to challenge me; even after many readings, the language that Arendt employs throughout the book grows no less shocking and no less ugly. I will focus here not on the usual controversies, such as the banality of evil concept. I am interested, rather, in the depictions of Zionism and of Israel that Arendt puts forth, and in how *Eichmann in Jerusalem* connects to more general issues such as sovereignty, which was so central to her critique of the Marxist movement, and to solidarity, which was a key concept in her worldview.

Israel's kidnapping of Adolf Eichmann on the streets of Buenos Aires on May 11, 1960, sparked a worldwide debate—and a flurry of letters between Arendt and Jaspers. Much of their discussion centered on Israel's right to kidnap and try Eichmann and on the purpose of Israel as a state. (Israel may be the only country on earth for which a purpose is required, though neither Jaspers nor Arendt questioned this.) For Jaspers, "This trial is wrongly conceived at its very root." In his view, this was not because the kidnapping's legality was in question but because "what was done to the Jews was done not only to the Jews but essentially to human-kind"; therefore, "a sentence [should be] pronounced by humankind, not by a single state." Here, Jaspers embodies exactly the kind of amorphous universalism that Arendt so forcefully criticized in *The Origins of Totalitarianism*. In any case, practical problems with Jaspers's proposal immediately arose. As he admitted, there was no international body—no "humankind"—that "want[s] to have anything to do with the case."[122]

But Jaspers's critique was based, too, on his view of Jewish "chosen-ness," which posits the Jewish people as both less and more than others. He viewed Israeli sovereignty as a kind of diminution. An Israeli sentencing or execution would "trivialize Eichmann's actions"; the case "should not be reduced to an Israeli issue." National sovereignty itself, Jaspers averred, is "profoundly alien to the Jew"; the State of Israel was simply "a necessary stopgap," which was justified only to the extent that it "has possibilities different from other states." To prove its superiority—or, perhaps, inferiority—Israel should refuse to pass sentence: "It would be good for Israel, I think, to display this *high-mindedness,* to prove true to the Jewish tradition."[123] (Eichmann's defense attorney would also appeal to what he called the Solomonic wisdom of the Jews, though this didn't help his client much.) Jaspers and Arendt also wondered whether the trial would induce an anti-Semitic reaction outside Israel. Though their views differed, neither one raised the obvious, uncomfortable question: Why should the trial of a German mass murderer lead to anti-Jewish, rather than anti-German, sentiment?

For the most part, though, Arendt rejected Jaspers's views, which is somewhat surprising in light of her previous opposition to Israeli sover-eignty. In the Eichmann book itself, she discusses the Israeli court's juris-diction in highly contradictory and sometimes negative ways. In these earlier letters, however, she vigorously defended Israel's fitness to prose-cute. If Eichmann was to be tried, she wrote, "We'll go ahead"—the "we" refers to Israel—since no one else will. (Germany had zero interest in extraditing Eichmann.) But more than practical concerns were at issue. "Israel has the right to speak for the victims, because the large majority of them (300,000) are living in Israel now as citizens," Arendt wrote. "The trial will take place in the country in which the injured parties and those who happened to survive are. You say that Israel didn't even exist then. But one could say that it was for the sake of these victims that Palestine became Israel. . . . In addition, Eichmann was responsible for Jews and Jews only, regardless of their nationality. In other words, other issues and jurisdictions don't come into play here at all."[124]

The only realistic alternative to an Israeli trial, Arendt pointed out, would have been an Israeli assassination of Eichmann in Buenos Aires. She mused, "That, too, would have produced a trial," though obviously of a different sort. In a subsequent letter, Arendt disputed Jaspers's "stopgap" view of Zionism. Israel, she reminded him, speaks for the Shoah's victims but is not confined to them: The state "was finally born of necessity but . . . in no way arose exclusively from that necessity."[125] Zionism—as aspiration, as revolution, as refuge, as facts on the ground—predates the Shoah and cannot be limited to it.

These letters reveal something else: the disconcerting fact that Arendt formed her two most controversial judgments—on Eichmann's character and Jewish collaboration—*before* the trial started. In December 1960, she wrote that the trial will "demonstrate . . . to what a huge degree the Jews helped organize their own destruction. That is, of course, the naked truth." At the start of the trial four months later, she worried that the "very crucial . . . fact of Jewish collaboration" would *not* be dealt with. And it barely was. In other words, the collaboration issue was a preoccupation of Arendt's, not a focus of the trial itself. In another letter, written in December, she explained her wish to face Eichmann "in all his bizarre vacuousness."[126] All this strongly suggests that Arendt's key conclusions, whether right or wrong, did not arise primarily from the trial's evidence but, rather, preceded it. As had been the case with Palestine, Arendt approached the trial as a kind of laboratory that would either realize her ideas or fail dismally. Despite avowing that she was going to Jerusalem "as a simple reporter" who has "the right to criticize" the court "but not to make suggestions to them," she arrived in Jerusalem with precise judgments firmly in mind.[127] Two things are sure: She was not a simple reporter, and she did not mind making suggestions.

The first words of *Eichmann in Jerusalem* are in Hebrew: " '*Beth Hamishpath*'—the House of Justice." This is fitting, because the meta-subject of the book is Israel. In its first ten pages, Arendt discusses Israel's "old prejudice against German Jews," Israeli marriage and divorce laws, anti-Semitism as "the most potent ideological factor in the Zionist movement," Israel's lack of a constitution, "inexplicable" negotiations between Zionists and Nazis before the genocide, the "collaboration of the *Judenräte*," and postwar reparations payments from Germany to Israel.[128]

What emerges without ambiguity in these first pages is Arendt's vehement disdain of Zionism as a movement and of Israel as a society. These become frequent refrains of the book. Thus she tells us of the "radical Zionist" who failed to object to the Nuremberg Laws (an indication of the movement's self-deception, obsequiousness, and poor political judgment); of how Herzl's *The Jewish State* "converted" Eichmann to Zionism; of how Zionists "spoke a language not totally different from that of Eichmann"; of the Nazi regime's "pro-Zionist attitude"—and on it goes.[129] (The role of Zionist groups in the anti-Nazi resistance movements is not mentioned.) It is entirely possible that, after reading Arendt, a young person who knows little of twentieth-century history would regard Zionism and Nazism as ideological and practical allies. Long gone are the days of the 1930s and forties when Arendt viewed Zionism as the clear-eyed enemy of Nazi persecution and participated in the movement as such. Now, in an about-face, the Zionist movement is depicted as the Nazis' helpmate. Arendt was not the first to voice this accusation, but it had previously emanated mainly from the Israeli right wing as an attack on Labor Zionism. As had been the case with her advocacy of a Jewish army, Arendt again found herself in the company of the Revisionists.

Arendt's distaste for actually-existing Israel and actually-existing Israelis pours forth from her letters of this time; the Israeli historian Amnon Raz-Krakotzkin, who is generally sympathetic to her, terms her views "the banality of racism."[130] It is certainly jarring to read Arendt, the great proponent of binational coexistence and Arab rights, disparage the "oriental mob"—otherwise known as Sephardic Israelis—who stand outside the courthouse, "as if one were in Istanbul or some other half-Asiatic country."[131] (All pariahs are not, apparently, created equal.) In her view, it was unfortunate that "the European element [has been] very much pushed into the background."[132] Yet even the European element, at least if it came from the East, can disappoint: Chief Prosecutor Gideon Hausner is "a typical Galician Jew, very unsympathetic. . . . Probably one of those people who don't know any language." As the trial progresses, Arendt will find Hausner "increasingly revolting."[133]

It is not only ethnic prejudice that we see here. Arendt was a true bourgeois—who else would be so obsessed with parvenus?—and it is hard not to notice the class antagonism in her comments on the trial, Eichmann, and Israel. In a 1964 interview, she complained about the "shabbiness" and "shoddiness" of the Nazis, which, she presumptuously claimed, "all of us" have found harder to cope with than the enormous number of victims.[134] All of us? One gets the impression that it was Eichmann's lack of grandeur—his petit bourgeois puniness—rather than his crimes that offended her most. (What if he had been a brilliant intellectual rather than a former vacuum-cleaner salesman?) The same could be said of Arendt's attitude toward Israel, then a poor country, and to the Israeli trial, which she would describe as "so damned banal and indescribably low and repulsive."[135]

As so often, Arendt viewed Israel through the German lens, however distorting that might be. "Everything is organized by a police force that gives me the creeps, speaks only Hebrew, and looks Arabic," she complained. "Some downright brutal types among them. They would obey any order."[136] Though Israel in 1961 bore scant resemblance to Germany in 1933, the echoes of the past drown out the present: "Yesterday I watched the young Jewish generation sitting around a campfire sentimentally singing the kinds of songs we used to know and hate when we were young. The parallels are fatal, particularly in the details."[137] Among the few Israelis who didn't repel Arendt were the trial's three German-Jewish judges—"the best of German Jewry"—especially chief judge Moshe Landau, whom she lauds in a letter to Jaspers as "superb!" ("Let us hope the German Jews gain control," he responds.)[138]

But there is a larger, more important issue than Arendt's scorn for Israel and Israelis: the conceptual focus of *Eichmann in Jerusalem*. Arendt repeatedly reproached the prosecution, sometimes rightly so, for introducing ancillary issues into the courtroom. "Justice demands that the accused be prosecuted, defended, and judged, and that all the other questions of seemingly greater import . . . be left in abeyance," she contended.[139] Surely she is right that the millennia-long history of anti-Semitism cannot be litigated, and that it is the state, not the victims, that must prosecute a crime. This prosecutorial overreach—and the demagogic opportunism that, Arendt believed, it represented—is one of her central themes; as she complained to Blücher, "A lot is presented that doesn't have the slightest thing to do with Eichmann."¹⁴⁰ Indeed, this was the heart of her indictment of Hausner and "his master" Ben-Gurion, both of whom she despised.

Yet from the book's opening pages to its very end, Arendt is guilty of the precise offense for which she lambasted the prosecution. It is impossible to see how the many issues she introduces—the Zionist analysis of anti-Semitism, Israel's marriage laws, the "transfer agreement" of 1933, German reparations, Israel's lack of a constitution—had "the slightest thing to do with Eichmann" or his offenses. And here we find the central paradox—indeed, the central dishonesty—of this book. Arendt uses the trial, perhaps *more* than the prosecution did, to explore a large number of extraneous themes that she deemed important but that were utterly irrelevant to Eichmann's guilt. This is especially true of the most toxic question she raises: the behavior of the Jewish councils. This is a topic that, as her letters show, preoccupied Arendt even before the trial but that, she admitted, was hardly raised in the trial itself.¹⁴¹ Arendt never poses the obvious question: Even if every Jewish leader in every occupied country had collaborated with the Nazis—which they did not—how could that mitigate Eichmann's guilt even one iota?

This is not to say that questions of collaboration were or are unworthy of consideration. On the contrary, they are important and necessary, and the answers to them usually devastating—though more complicated, and therefore more agonizing, than Arendt's simplistic denunciations suggest. But by raising these questions in the context of a book that, Arendt repeatedly insisted, was "a sadly limited" factual report concerned solely with Eichmann's culpability, she leaves the indelible impression that such issues were directly connected to Eichmann's guilt—and, therefore, possibly exculpatory. In fact, the very structure of Arendt's book, and her descriptions and defenses of it, not only suggest but demand this interpretation. Her refusal to address, or even acknowledge, this central contradiction stands as one of the book's greatest failures.

Eichmann in Jerusalem is many valuable things: a reflection on conscience, an indictment of moral and political evasion, a consideration of the link between a criminal individual and a criminal state. But it is not a report and Arendt was not a reporter. She attended less than half the trial; "I want to get away as quickly as possible," she wrote to Blücher after less than ten days in Jerusalem.¹⁴² She was not in the courtroom for Eichmann's cross-examination, which surely yielded insights into his character. She approached the trial with preconceived notions, which became the book's focal points even though the trial took an entirely different direction. Most important, she ignored the gist of the trial itself: witness testimony. Approximately half the trial's 121 sessions were devoted to this—Hausner presented 111 witnesses—though Arendt recounted the words of only three in any detail. This does not mean that Arendt's book is invalid, much less irrelevant. But these factors change the meaning of the book and the ways we should approach it. As the historian Deborah E. Lipstadt observed, Arendt's "agency derived, in great measure, from her status as a witness. Her failure to reveal that she was not there for significant portions of the proceedings constituted a breach of faith with readers."[143]

Arendt arrived in Jerusalem with a dismissive attitude toward the witnesses. On the trial's third day, she complains to Jaspers of "the comedy of speaking Hebrew when everyone involved knows German and thinks in German."[144] Actually, most of those involved—that is, the Israeli survivors and spectators—did not speak or think in German and, in all probability, had no desire to do so. Arendt was clearly implying that, in her view, the trial was essentially an intra-German confrontation between a German defendant and three German judges. The Hebrew-speaking survivors (some of whom testified in their native languages) were, at best, a self-indulgent, time-consuming sideshow. Though Arendt admits, toward the end of her "report," that "everyone should have his day in court," she prevents us from hearing virtually everything the witnesses recounted.[145] It is hard to miss the contempt and irritation in her complaint to Blücher: "The Jews want to pour out their sorrow to the world, and forget that they are there to relate facts. Of course, they have suffered more than Eichmann has. . . . And furthermore: as repulsive as the horrors are, they are not exactly unprecedented."[146] *Of course, they have suffered more than Eichmann has*: This grudging admittance is surely one of the most morally obtuse sentences ever written.

From the book's opening section, Arendt argues for a strict separation between Eichmann's crimes and the victims' pain; the latter, in her view, should be barred from the courtroom. Of Eichmann, she writes, "On trial are his deeds, not the sufferings of the Jews. . . . If he suffers, he must suffer for what he has done, not what he has caused others to suffer."[147] This rigid distinction might be legally possible; humanly speaking, it is not. I know of no recent trial for crimes against humanity or genocide—think, for instance, of Rwanda and Srebrenica—where such an absolute division has been policed, or where survivors have been prohibited from discussing what they saw, experienced, and felt. Though there is vigorous debate in the legal and human rights communities about how wide-ranging victim testimony should be, the public acknowledgement of torment is a recognized aspect of such tribunals. Arendt was not wrong to demand that the trial's focus remain on Eichmann, and the judges often tried to restrict testimony that they deemed irrelevant. But her insistence that the survivors testify as mere conveyers of facts—and her attendant belief that even the most factual testimony could, or should, be cleansed of the anguish embedded within it—makes little sense. The victims' "flayed skin and tortured flesh" *were* facts.[148] Arendt wanted a genocide trial without trauma.

There were, I believe, several interrelated reasons why Arendt suppressed the voices of the victims. Some were intellectual, some psychological, some connected to her attitudes toward Israel.

Intellectually, Arendt was highly suspicious of compassion. This does not mean she was unkind; all evidence suggests that she could be a wonderful friend. But in the public realm—the political realm, the one she valued most—she viewed compassion as a danger. In Arendt's view, compassion—the co-suffering for others—drives revolutions from the political realm of freedom into the social realm of justice and equality. That is where they go wrong.

Compassion "remains, politically speaking, irrelevant and without consequence," Arendt wrote in *On Revolution*. In the French Revolution, she argued, it was the injection of compassion—the desire to alleviate the suffering of the masses—that "suffocated its original spirit" of freedom. Arendt is undoubtedly right that compassion for others can lead to bad political judgments. But so can its absence. (The twentieth century is littered with examples of each.) In the Arendtian hierarchy, compassion gives birth to pity, a sentiment she despised. Superior to both compassion and pity is solidarity because, Arendt posited, "it partakes of reason." Compared to compassion or pity, solidarity "may appear cold and abstract, for it remains committed to 'ideas'—to greatness, or honour, or dignity—rather than to any 'love' of men." Solidarity is based not on feelings of empathy—indeed, not on feelings at all—but, rather, on a respectful but dispassionate "community of interest with the oppressed and exploited."[149]

Greatness, honor, dignity: This is what Arendt valued. All were in short supply in the ghettoes and the camps, whose aim was to demolish those very qualities. Victims who had been crushed by history, and there were many in the Jerusalem courtroom, did not interest Arendt, except to the extent that they elucidated her ideas, sometimes "cold and abstract," about modernity and totalitarianism. This does not mean that she ignored the *fact* of victimhood. Quite the contrary. Arendt was gripped by the twentieth century's violence; *The Origins of Totalitarianism* in particular was inspired and haunted by the Shoah. But the *experiential* suffering of the victims, as explored by writers like Primo Levi, Tadeusz Borowski, and Jean Améry—all of whom limned the excruciating process by which a human being becomes less human—was alien and tiresome to her. Perhaps unsurprisingly, Levi and Améry loathed Arendt's "banality of evil" concept.

Arendt was deeply suspicious of any political viewpoint or program that drew from the well of victimization. And yet, as we have seen, she admired, indeed idealized, pariahs. But the boundary between the two groups is not as sharp as she wished; surely many victims are pariahs, and vice versa. *Eichmann in Jerusalem* reveals Arendt's striking inability to resolve, or even acknowledge, this contradiction in her thought. Faced with the remarkably inventive cruelties, moral and physical, of the Nazi project, she could only querulously complain that the survivors had nothing "exactly unprecedented"—nothing interesting or important—to say. This was an especially startling claim to make in the early 1960s, when the details of the genocide were largely unknown and the very concept of the Shoah had yet to attain the central importance in twentieth-century history, politics, and moral inquiry that it now holds.

If the survivors were testifying about experiences that failed to interest Arendt, they were testifying, also, from a vantage point to which she objected. In *Eichmann,* Arendt describes the Shoah as a crime "perpetrated upon the body of the Jewish people. . . . Only the choice of victims, not the nature of the crime, could be derived from the long history of Jew-hatred." The genocide was an assault not against the Jews per se but on "the very nature of mankind."[150] By this, Arendt undoubtedly meant to connect the larger world to the Shoah: a vital task. She refused the Shoah's isolation as a strictly Jewish matter with which other nations and peoples need not concern themselves, and she stressed the crucial distinctions between genocide and conventional war. Arendt was not the only observer of the trial to make these points, but she emphasized them with powerful clarity.

Yet there is a conceptual flaw here. The genocide, which the Third Reich directed solely against Jews, was, in Arendt's words, a "new crime." But this newness does nothing to lessen the fact that the Jews were its target. Killing Jews as a modern genocidal project makes the crime no less anti-Jewish than killing Jews in an old-fashioned pogrom. To the victims, Arendt's distinction would have connoted exactly the kind of abstract universalism she had criticized so cogently elsewhere. To the victims—who were killed by the Nazis and their helpmates *as* Jews and solely *because* they were Jews—the phrase "only the choice of victims" would have sounded strange if not outrageous, and the emphasis on "mankind" a murky evasion. Jews were killed because they were members of the Jewish people, not because they were members of mankind. Arendt's distinctions become almost absurd when she argues that "these modern, state-employed mass murderers must be prosecuted because they violated the order of mankind, and not because they killed millions."[151] Surely the killing of millions would warrant prosecution too? The Poles and Russians thought so.

The witnesses in Jerusalem did not testify as abstract universals—as "world-citizens," a concept Arendt mocked—on whose bodies the tortures happened to be inscribed. They testified as individuals and as Jews, which is how they experienced the horrors, and in most cases they testified as Israelis, which is who they now were. This particularism—or, one might say, this particular *kind* of particularism—was anathema to Arendt. As Israeli philosopher Elhanan Yakira argues, Arendt's "refusal to recognize the legitimacy and importance of the survivors' testimony, and her rejection of the juridical relevance of the category 'crimes against the Jewish people' amount to a rejection of the Israeli *différend*. . . . It is a negation of the right to an Israeli point of view."[152] The words of the witnesses challenged Arendt to develop a dialectical rather than antagonistic relationship between universality and particularity, that is, between a crime against humanity and the Jewish nation that was its not-incidental object. It also challenged her to recognize Israel as a distinct nation comprising, but different from, European Jewry (and different, certainly, from German Jewry). Her response to these challenges was to largely excise the witnesses.

In doing so, she missed the historic meaning of the trial, which became a transfixing public event—the writer Haim Gouri called it "an open university"—for all sectors of Israeli society and spurred the kind of democratic debate that Arendt usually extolled. Far from being obsessed with the Shoah, Israel had, at the time of the trial, often repressed it. A wall—of shame on the part of the survivors, contempt on the part of the Sabras, guilt on the part of everyone—had isolated the survivors and their experiences from the national narrative. This wall had cracks: There were impassioned debates over German reparations, and the Shoah was taught in Israeli schools. In addition, the Nazi and Nazi Collaborators (Punishment) Law was passed in 1950, only two years after Israeli independence; Yad Vashem, the Shoah memorial and archive, was established three years later. But the survivors who had not actively resisted were often suspected of cowardice or even collaboration; blue numbers tattooed onto forearms were a mark of disgrace. And in an important sense, the Shoah had remained an intra-Jewish affair. The country's major Holocaust trial to date had involved Rudolf Kastner, a Hungarian Jewish leader accused of collaboration. Few Israelis imagined that a Nazi criminal would be tried in their country under their laws.

Yet nothing could hide the intimate, wrenching ties between Israel and the Shoah. Israel was a country where almost every citizen from Europe (or with European ancestors) had lost relatives, where an entire generation never knew its grandparents, where large numbers of displaced orphans' extended families had been killed, where hundreds of thousands of forever haunted survivors had found refuge, and where national legitimacy was partially based on the genocide. The aim of the trial was, in large part, to bring this repressed past into the open through the revelations of the witnesses, who would emerge as distinct individuals from the generic six million. As Tom Segev, one of Israel's New Historians, has written, "In encouraging them to unlock what had been sealed within their memories and to relate their personal stories, he [Hausner] redeemed them and an entire generation of survivors."[153] This was especially important since the Nazis intended the genocide to be a crime without witnesses or survivors—or, at least, without witnesses or survivors who would be believed.

And the trial aimed at something even larger: to reverse the terms of the public conversation within Israel by transforming the survivors, formerly on the defense, into plaintiffs. "The whole conceptual framework under which survivors were seen as suspects had to be changed in order to begin to listen to what they had to tell," Israeli law professor Leora Bilsky observes. "For the first time, the survivors were linked with the accusing party and not with the accused."[154] In short, the trial was a confrontation between modern Israelis, with their ethos of militant self-defense, and what Segev calls "the last Jews." As such, it challenged all segments of Israel's contentious populace to forge new understandings.

This was a complicated and painful undertaking; waves of empathy did not automatically pour forth. Gouri, a native-born Israeli poet and journalist who covered the trial for the left-labor daily *Lamerhav*, wrote of his initial aversion to the witnesses: "I did not want to listen to this broken little man go on and on about his sufferings, his ills and indignities. . . . I did not want to see him, and I did not want to hear him." For Gouri, this disgust was the beginning of a process filled with ambivalence, bewilderment, and unresolved moral doubt. "These, too, are your own flesh and blood," he argued with himself. "They are in a position to demand that you sit through this, that you not run away. . . . There will be no escape and no reprieve."[155] For Arendt, in contrast, witness testimony—the words of the broken little men—was an endpoint, marked by annoyance and moral certitude.

Among the other reporters in the Jerusalem courtroom was the American war correspondent Martha Gellhorn, who covered the trial for the *Atlantic Monthly*. Like Arendt, Gellhorn insisted on Eichmann's troubling sanity, noted his inane use of language, and emphasized the universal import of the genocide. "Since he was not unleashed on the rest of us," she wrote, "we tend to forget that Eichmann despoiled us all. He robbed humanity. . . . Does it by any chance bore us to hear the agony of a people? . . . Do we possibly think that this Trial does not concern us . . . ? . . . We are desperately involved, all of us, everywhere." But unlike Arendt, Gellhorn did not view such universalism as antithetical to Israeli juridical sovereignty or to the specificity of witness testimony; large chunks of her article are devoted to their statements. And unlike Arendt, Gellhorn heard Eichmann testify in full. She records the audience's reactions to him, which included "disbelief, revelation, disgust."[156]

The Eichmann who emerges in Gellhorn's account is not the rather stupid "clown" that Arendt posited but, rather, a cool organization man with a "dazzling" grasp of the Nazi bureaucracy who soon takes over his own defense. (Gouri, too, noticed how, during cross-examination, Eichmann's "amazingly quick mind comes up with a new lie.")[157] The witnesses, and the audience, are depicted as sober and restrained: qualities attained, Gellhorn makes clear, by a Herculean effort to conquer pain. Arendt had written testily of the "witnesses who, country after country, told their tales of horrors," and she complained about their inability to distinguish real horrors from "imagined" ones.[158] Gellhorn, in contrast, describes the witnesses as evincing quiet grief and humility—a direct contrast to the showy histrionics that, Arendt claimed, degraded the proceedings. This disparity in perspectives is attributable, I believe, in part to Gellhorn's admiration for Israel, which she would maintain throughout her long life (and which, much later, would sometimes put her at odds with her young, left-wing friends in London). It was also due to her deep interest in the affliction of ordinary civilians, which she had been witnessing as a journalist, and mourning as a person, since the Spanish Civil War.

Arendt indicted the Eichmann prosecution for its failure to highlight what she regarded as the true nature and meaning of the genocide. In her view, the Shoah was a modern negation of mankind's diversity and not, as Hausner insisted, a continuation of ancient anti-Semitism. Neither of them understood that the genocide assumed such gigantic proportions precisely because it synthesized these two deadly ingredients, and that to choose between them was futile. Arendt pinned the court's failure on the Jewish worldlessness that she so dreaded and that emerged once more as the villain of her tale. "How little Israel, like the Jewish people in general, was prepared to recognize . . . an unprecedented crime," she charged. "This misunderstanding, almost inevitable if we consider not only the facts of Jewish history but also . . . the current Jewish historical self-understanding, is actually at the root of all the failures and shortcomings of the Jerusalem trial."[159]

But if the trial failed in some important ways, so did she; Arendt's "historical self-understanding" was not as complete as she thought. At the courthouse in Jerusalem, she squandered an opportunity to begin to comprehend the subjective damage that profound suffering, utter helplessness, and extreme violence imprint on their victims. The trial presented her with what were, in effect, the wrong *kind* of pariahs. Arendt admired cosmopolitan, politicized intellectuals like Lazare, Luxemburg, and Benjamin, who constituted a kind of pariah elite. But in Jerusalem she encountered, perhaps for the first time, the Polish tailors and Romanian housewives who had been unfathomably debased in the ghettoes and the camps. They were not smart enough to understand why their children had been turned into ashes. Arendt's response was to turn away in pique.

It has sometimes been said that Arendt's language, rather than her arguments, prompted the visceral reactions to *Eichmann in Jerusalem*. During the controversy, Jaspers wrote to Arendt of "the style that some people reproach you for," which he accurately summed up as "ironic, cold, heartless, know-it-all, misanthropic."[160] More recently, in an otherwise perceptive study, Seyla Benhabib refers to Arendt's "terminological infelicities."[161] This euphemism avoids *Eichmann in Jerusalem*'s problems instead of explaining them. For a writer, especially a writer as precise as Arendt, language *is* content: Who can separate the dancer from the dance? As George Orwell argued in his 1946 essay "Politics and the English Language," a writer's choice of words raises not just stylistic or aesthetic questions but inescapably political ones too.

I referred earlier to Arendt's language as shocking and ugly. The shock, and the ugliness, derive from a rhetorical device that she employs at key points in the book. Cleverly, slyly, she takes ordinary words and phrases that are loaded with historic meanings and twists them in perverse ways. It is hard to believe that Arendt did not mean to scald her readers, especially her Jewish readers, by this technique. It functions by innuendo rather than forthright statement, which makes it more powerful or, at least, more insidious. These words and phrases, scattered throughout the book, are like little knife wounds to the gut.

The first example comes at the book's beginning. Arendt opens *Eichmann in Jerusalem* by castigating the "show trial" orchestrated by Ben-Gurion, a charge she will repeat. Of course, like all public trials—and Eichmann's was more public than most—there was a theatrical aspect to the Jerusalem event, in which "the proceedings happen on a stage before an audience."[162] Arendt extends the theatrical metaphor for several pages. She assails Hausner's dramatics. She attacks Ben-Gurion's wish that the trial "show" the enormity of the Shoah to the world. She derides the trial as a sensational "spectacle" that "degenerate[s] into a bloody show."[163]

But to many of Arendt's readers, and certainly to her left-wing ones, the words "show trial" carried poisonous connotations that had nothing to do with theatricality. For them, the phrase could only have evoked the Stalinist purges of the 1930s. Yet here is where confusion sets in. For whereas Eichmann's guilt was certain, the Soviet tribunals were shows precisely because the defendants' *innocence* was a foregone conclusion. Their alleged crimes were the product of Stalin's deranged paranoia; Eichmann's crimes were real. Furthermore, the Soviet confessions were frequently obtained through torture, and the trials, often held in secret, contravened all civilized rules of law. None of this was true of the Israeli trial. Yet the hidden connotations—the Pavlovian associations—of the phrase remain. Is Arendt implying a parallel between what happened in Jerusalem and what happened in Moscow? Is Eichmann the victim of Ben-Gurion as Bukharin was of Stalin? Or is Arendt alluding, instead, to the unknown thousands of show—that is, phony—trials conducted by the Nazis? (She mentions the most famous: that of Georgi Dimitrov, charged with burning the Reichstag.) If not, why use this term, so loaded with hideous meanings?

Arendt continues this technique by her use of the word "selections" and variants thereof. Her book includes a section on Zionist "cooperation with the Nazi authorities" that runs for several pages and delineates the presumably close kinship, in the mid-thirties, between the two movements; thus she negates her own political work and experience. In this section, she writes of the Zionists' desire "to select 'suitable material' " for the kibbutzim and " 'to pick young Jewish pioneers' from . . . the concentration camps." The Zionists, she avers, "somehow believed that if it was a question of selecting Jews for survival, the Jews should do the selecting themselves."[164]

"Selections" is one of the foulest words in Jewish history. It conjures, of course, the Nazi selections, most notoriously at Auschwitz, of those who would be sent to the gas chambers: a fate reserved solely for Jews. This deadly decision was sometimes made immediately upon arrival at the camp and sometimes rendered later, after naked, emaciated prisoners were paraded before camp guards who would assess each prisoner's fitness for continued slave labor. (Jewish prisoners never made these decisions.) This is the crucial, grotesque judgment of which Primo Levi writes at the very beginning of *If This Is a Man:* "Consider if this is a man . . . Who dies because of a yes or a no."[165] It was the primal experience of Auschwitz.

"Selections" are indelibly connected to the camp experience of help-lessness, fear, degradation, and death. As with "show trials," the word immediately evokes feelings of almost overwhelming repulsion. Arendt's implication that Zionist "selections" and those in Auschwitz were parallel—despite the fact that the former meant life and the latter, death—makes this one of the most morally obscene parts of her book.

In short, Arendt developed a rhetorical device in which she would take the worst aspects of terror regimes (Stalin's show trials, Nazi death camps) and link them, either explicitly or by implication, with the Zionist movement or the State of Israel. Another example, so radioactive that it was eliminated after *Eichmann in Jerusalem*'s first edition, is Arendt's description of Leo Baeck, Berlin's chief rabbi and head of its Jewish Council, as the "Jewish Führer." This phrase did exist—but, contra Arendt, it was Eichmann's assistant, not Berlin's Jews, who used it.[166] Baeck's case was complex, for he was a powerful man and a powerless one. His actions in Berlin, and later in Theresienstadt, were criticized by Raul Hilberg and Paul Tillich, among others, just as his refusal to abandon his fellow Jews by accepting sanctuary in America was praised. Arendt, however, was uninterested in the woeful dilemmas that Baeck and others faced (just as she was uninterested in the specific dilemmas that Jews in Palestine faced in 1948); instead, she breezily condemns him with a toxic, and falsely attributed, turn of phrase. This kind of linguistic promiscuity was catching: Mary McCarthy, in defending the Eichmann book, would refer to Zionism as "the Jewish Final Solution." (McCarthy also argued that the *Judenräte* leaders could not be hurt by Arendt's criti-cisms because they were already dead.)[167]

Many critics of the Eichmann book have focused on Arendt's inflam-matory judgment that the behavior of the Jewish leaders "is undoubtedly the darkest chapter" of the Shoah.[168] But it is through her more subtle uses, or misuses, of language that she most severely condemned Zionism, the trial, the Jewish leadership, and Israel. And it is through this manipu-lative misuse of language that she sought to pair, and by implication equalize, Nazi actions and the Jewish reactions to them. (One wonders: If there was a Jewish Führer, were there also Jewish *Einsatzgruppen* and a

Jewish Treblinka?) This verbal fudging of perpetrator and victim tarnishes, indeed degrades, *Eichmann in Jerusalem*. Jaspers inadvertently acknowledged this and thus damned the book—though he thought he was praising it—when he wrote to Arendt, "I am reading on steadily in your Eichmann book. It is wonderful for me. . . . The subject of the Jews' cooperation with the Nazis is only one subject. The subject of the Germans has equivalent weight."[169]

It may be illuminating to briefly compare *Eichmann in Jerusalem* with Primo Levi's *If This Is a Man*; the latter was published in English translation two years before the Eichmann trial, though I do not know if Arendt read it. The differences between the two books, and the two authors, are obvious. Levi's work was a first-person chronicle; Arendt was an outside observer. Levi's subject was a slave labor/extermination camp; Arendt was covering a trial. Levi had the moral authority of a survivor; Arendt did not. Levi was largely unknown when his book appeared in English; Arendt was a famous intellectual by the time she wrote *Eichmann*.

But Levi's book, like Arendt's, addresses the victims' behavior and ethos. In fact, the main focus of his account is the destruction of the prisoners' capacity for resistance against their tormentors and for solidarity amongst themselves. And what he presents is grimmer than anything Arendt wrote. This calls into question her repeated claim that her book had incensed the Jewish community—"the Jews are really quite out of their minds," as she put it—because she told unwelcome truths.[170] For Levi's truths are not just unwelcome but unbearable, at least to this reader. And this has little to do with recitations of physical violence or of outright collaboration, of which there are few.

To the question "if this is a man" Levi replies, essentially: No. And this lost humanity applies not just to the Nazis who control the camp— this we expect—but to their victims too. After a selection for death, Levi registers his disgust at a religious Jew, Kuhn, who thanks God that he has been (temporarily) spared: "Kuhn is out of his senses. Does he not see Beppo the Greek . . . who is twenty years old and is going to the gas chamber the day after tomorrow. . . . Does Kuhn not understand that what has happened today is an abomination, which no propitiatory prayer, no pardon, no expiation by the guilty, which nothing at all in the power of man can ever clean again? If I was God, I would spit at Kuhn's prayer."[171]

What Levi documents is not survival, as the book's cheery American title (*Survival in Auschwitz*) suggests, but its polar opposite: "the demolition of a man." Levi knows that the aim of the Nazis is "to annihilate us first as men," and the book charts their triumph. "Our comrades . . . are marching like automatons; their souls are dead. . . . There is no longer any will. . . . The Germans have succeeded in this." He considers "what they have made us become. . . . We, transformed into slaves, . . . killed in our spirit long before our anonymous death." He condemns the Jewish kapos, who in return for a few privileges betray others; they are "monsters of asociality and insensitivity," yet "rivalry and hatred" dominate *all* the imprisoned. And he damns his own spiritual destruction. "This time last year I was a free man: an outlaw but free." Now, "I am not even alive enough to know how to kill myself."[172]

In the book's horrifying nadir, Levi watches the hanging of a Birkenau prisoner who, along with others, had blown up a crematorium. Hoping to inspire the fellow prisoners who are watching him, the defiant man cries out before death, "Comrades, I am the last one!" In unmitigated shame, Levi recalls, "I wish I could say that from the midst of us, an abject flock, a voice rose, a murmur, a sign of assent. But nothing happened. We remained standing, bent and grey, our heads dropped. . . . The Russians can come now: they will only find us, the slaves, the worn-out, worthy of the unarmed death which awaits us."[173] *Worthy of the unarmed death?* Levi's book is sometimes thought of as a relatively gentle or at least uplifting one, but this is the most lacerating self-judgment I can envision.

All this is excruciating to read. It contradicts the fantasy that although physical resistance was impossible, the prisoners remained spiritually whole or, at least, spiritually recognizable. In fact, Levi's memoir illustrates the "moral collapse" of which Arendt so controversially wrote.[174] Why did Levi's account not elicit a furor? Part of the answer lies in the factors I listed above, which distinguished his book from Arendt's. But another answer, I believe, is to be found in his language, which is the almost perfect inverse of hers.

Though he documents the erasure of dignity, empathy, and "the habits of freedom," Levi's language consistently encompasses his fellow prisoners. Even in destruction, they are "we": He is not apart from, different from, better than they, which is why he earns the right to call them comrades. He judges some severely—Kuhn, Henri, and others; just as he judges himself. As the critic Michael André Bernstein observed, "By its very syntax, . . . Levi's individual response is endowed with a communal point of origin. . . . His insistence upon the communicative and communal function of language . . . is proof, at the level of the word and the sentence, that the Nazis failed to dehumanize him."[175] This is the grammar of humanism. Levi shows, rather than tells, what solidarity is— and the price of its failure.

And this is the grammar that *Eichmann in Jerusalem* sorely lacks. Though Arendt considered solidarity to be the highest virtue, there is little in her book that embodies it. *Eichmann in Jerusalem* oozes with contempt: for Zionism, Israel, Ben-Gurion, Hausner, the Jewish leadership, the Israeli audience, the relatives of the dead, the survivors of hell. There is nary a moment when we recognize a "community of interest with the oppressed and exploited" between Arendt and the people she writes about. This absence of connection cannot be hidden, for it is embedded in her sentences. That is why her theorizing about "mankind" and the crimes against it, though conceptually smart and politically important, sounds so hollow. Arendt notes at the beginning of her book that the court's judges ("all three born and educated in Germany," she reminds us) are "visibly stiffening under the impact of grief."[176] I wonder why that is never true of her.

Arendt's attitude toward the victims and the flippant contempt that suffuses *Eichmann in Jerusalem* are often debated in the context of "love" for the Jewish people, in large part because of Scholem's famous letter in which he accused her of its lack.[177] But it is solidarity, not love, that is the issue here; as Arendt argued so convincingly, they are not the same. Just as she could not admire the pariahs in Israel, despite her frequent extolling of the *idea* of pariahdom, she could not realize a sense of solidarity, despite her ideological admiration of it. Her stance stands in sharp contrast to that of Horkheimer, who came to understand the relationship of the saved to the drowned. In "After Auschwitz," he wrote:

> We Jewish intellectuals who escaped death by torture under
> Hitler have only one task: to help see to it that such horrors
> never recur and are never forgotten, in solidarity with those who
> died under unspeakable torments. Our thought, our work
> belongs to them; that we escaped by accident should make our

solidarity with them not doubtful, but more certain. Whatever
we experience must stand under the sign of the horrors
intended for us as for them.

He concluded, "Their death is the truth of our life; to express their despair
and their longing, we are there."[178]

After writing, and defending, *Eichmann in Jerusalem,* Arendt was finished
with Zionism. She called the book her *"cura posterior,"* which has often
been taken to mean her healing from the Shoah. But I suspect she also
meant that she was cured of Zionism and the wrenching questions it had
posed for her. After all, she had previously referred to attending the trial
as "an obligation I owe my past," and her past was heavily entwined with
struggles for and against Zionism. In any event, the Eichmann book freed
her; after completing it, she told McCarthy that she felt "light-hearted
about the whole matter."[179] (McCarthy did, too. She described the book as
"morally exhilarating," a gift of "joy," and "a paean of transcendence,
heavenly music.")[180] Arendt had apparently mastered the past, or at least
her own past.

But cures are not always complete, and Zionism was like a lingering
illness that plagued Arendt. She became, we might say, an anti-anti-
Zionist, just as she was an anti-anti-Communist. In the midst of the
Eichmann controversy, she firmly dissociated herself from the stance of
the American Council for Judaism, which opposed all forms of Zionism:
"My reason for breaking with the Zionist organization was very different
from the anti-Zionist stand of the Council: I am not against Israel on principle, I am against certain important Israeli policies. . . . Should catastrophe overtake this Jewish state, . . . (even [for] reasons of their own
foolishness) this would be the perhaps final catastrophe for the whole
Jewish people."[181] Despite her dislike of Israel, she rallied to it in times of
risk, such as the 1956 Suez war. Her relationship to Israel was like that of
an alienated, rebellious child to her family: Though full of anger, resentment, and feelings of superiority, she could never separate completely,
and in times of crisis she always came to its defense.

Danger spurred her enthusiasm. She exulted in Israel's victory in the
1967 war: "The Israelis did a wonderful job," she wrote in June. After
visiting the country later that summer, she reported that the situation was

"very encouraging. . . . Nasser should be hung instantly. Feudal rule in the worst sense of the term but under the guise of socialism. . . . And as far as the country itself [Israel] is concerned, one can see clearly from what great fear it has suddenly been freed."[182] She allied herself with Israel in the 1973 war, too: "The Jewish people are united in [support for] Israel," she told a French television interviewer—a unity in which she clearly included herself; and she was stunned, perhaps naively, by the hostility to Israel in the UN that year.[183] She contributed frequently to the United Jewish Appeal and the Israel Emergency Fund. And she continued to visit family members in Israel, including her beloved niece, though Blücher never accompanied her there.

What are we to make of the tortuous saga of Arendt and Zionism? In a 1969 letter to McCarthy, she expressed her ambivalence about Israel, Jewish survival, and the Jewish people in ways that suggest she had not quite worked through her relationship to Zionism—and never would. "If one honestly believes in equality, Israel is very impressive," she wrote, but in the next breath she described the country as a "nearly hopeless business." For her, the central issue was Jewish calamity—which, in Arendt's view, was both danger and salvation for the Jewish people. "The memory [of destruction] will keep the people together; the people will survive. That is *au fond* all that matters, Jews think: Empires, governments, nations come and go; the Jewish people remains. There is something grand and something ignoble in this passion; I think I don't share it." But she repeated her previous belief that "any real catastrophe in Israel would affect me more deeply than almost anything else."[184] Perhaps she did share it.

Arendt's real contribution to "the Israel question" is this ambivalent loyalty and sense of unending contradiction. Yet despite the claims of present-day admirers, she has little guidance to offer in solving the contemporary Israeli-Palestinian conflict. This is not only because the political situation today—in Israel, the West Bank, Gaza, the Middle East, the world—is so different from that of 1948 (let alone 1938). It is also because Arendt's assessments and prescriptions, even at the time of their writing, were deeply flawed.

Arendt's struggles with Zionism were a strenuous, ethically motivated effort to solve the most piercing and exigent problems of her time.

She needed to figure out how the seemingly marginal Jewish Question turned the twentieth century upside down. Despite the mean-spiritedness of *Eichmann in Jerusalem*, the charges against her of anti-Semitism, self-hatred, Jewish betrayal, and anti-Zionism are false and offer little insight into her ideas. But so does an idealization of them—or of her. Arendt's Zionist writings are a model of the pitfalls into which so many commentators on Israel fall: arrogance, ignorance, remoteness, abstractness, and the tendency to see the country, and its conflicts, as a replication of previous histories rather than as uniquely themselves.

Arendt never acknowledged these shortcomings; she was not one to admit she was wrong. But, unknowingly, she summed them up in a 1965 letter she wrote to Jaspers. Predictably, she was criticizing other intellectuals, but her words could have served as a fitting self-assessment: "People ignore reality in favor of their bright ideas."[185]

CHAPTER TWO

Arthur Koestler

THE ZIONIST AS ANTI-SEMITE

LIKE MANY ZIONISTS, ARTHUR KOESTLER despised the Jews of the Diaspora: pungently, if somewhat startlingly, he decried "that eery odour of otherliness, of vagrancy and jugglery which surrounds Mr. Abramowitz who comes from nowhere and belongs nowhere."[1] But unlike most Zionists, Koestler wasn't fond of the Israeli Sabra either: "Dull" and "dumb" were among his kinder assessments. Like many Zionists, he loathed Yiddish, which he regarded as a vulgar jargon "saturated with the smell of narrow streets, of unventilated bedding, mental inbreeding and tortuous ways." But unlike his Zionist confrères, he loathed Hebrew too: Here was a stuffy old language that was "totally unfit to serve as a vehicle for modern thought."[2] Like most Zionists, Koestler was adamantly secular; he railed against the "holiness and squalor" of the Orthodox ghettoes, "teeming with toddlers and vermin." Yet he mocked the Zionists of the secular Left as a feckless "nation of conscientious objectors."[3] When it came to Zionism—and to Jews—Arthur Koestler was a man of deep contradictions and sizable dislikes.

Koestler's incongruities were almost without limit. Though never a fighter himself, he demanded that Jews defend themselves militarily, whether in Europe under the Nazis or in Palestine under the British. But he scorned the pre-state Palmach and was critical of the Haganah. He found the presumed cowardice of Diaspora men emotionally repulsive, though not as sexually repulsive as the presumed strength of Israeli women. He detested Jerusalem for its religiosity—"I have never lived at such close quarters with divinity, and never felt farther removed from it"—but Tel Aviv was no better: "colourless, shapeless . . . the architect's Sodom and Gomorrah."[4] He exulted in Israel's establishment as a state—then immediately turned his back on it as a "totalitarian Lilliput" and demanded that every Diaspora Jew do likewise. In fact, with the founding of Israel, Koestler insisted that every Diaspora Jew should, indeed must, assimilate into Christianity. To do otherwise would doom one's children to, at best, a life of stigma and, at worst, to the ovens.

During several periods in his exceedingly turbulent life, Arthur Koestler was a fiercely committed Zionist. But he was a peculiar sort of Zionist, for he viewed Israel not as the site for the Jewish people's regeneration but, rather, as a means to that people's disappearance. This merciful vanishing act, he argued, would instantly make the world a far more harmonious place.

As he aged, Koestler's views on the Jewish Question became increasingly extreme and peculiar. Yet those views—along with his strenuous attempts to divorce himself from the Jewish people and his belief that Jews themselves were the cause of anti-Semitism—raise important issues about the role of Jewish self-criticism within the Zionist movement. And outside it, too, for many of Koestler's views endure within the Diaspora today, especially among Jews on the left who are most critical of Zionism.

Arthur Koestler is often regarded as a weathervane of the twentieth century's political movements, conflicts, and traumas. In 1945, the critic Granville Hicks called him "a terrifyingly representative figure"; six decades later, the historian Timothy Snyder wrote that Koestler "exposed his mind and body to the fearful spectrum of twentieth-century ideology like a healthy man volunteering for a life of radiation therapy."[5] Koestler was a European Jew, a refugee, and for many years a stateless person; a fiery Communist and equally fiery anti-Communist; an enemy of Stalinist state terror and ardent supporter of the Zionist terrorist underground. You could find him in the Weimar Republic and, then, in France, as they crumbled before the Nazis; in Spain as a Communist spy during that country's civil war; in Palestine and Israel at key moments in their history. He was imprisoned in a fascist jail in Spain and in various internment camps in France and England. He traveled widely, including throughout the post–World War I Middle East and the famine-wracked Soviet Union of the early 1930s. He lived in Budapest, Vienna, Berlin, Paris, Cairo, Jerusalem, and London.

He was a wonderful journalist: vibrant, observant, alert to paradox and the telling detail. (The weary, battered Old Bolsheviks in Moscow were "still glowing in cold devotion, like phosphorescent corpses.")[6] And a terrible novelist: wooden, didactic, mechanical. V. S. Pritchett observed that Koestler's novels "are not novels: they are animated cartoons of a pilgrim's regress from revolution." Harold Rosenberg decried Koestler's "pervading glibness."[7] Irving Howe disparaged *Darkness at Noon*'s schematic, puerile version of Marxism as "a sign of intellectual panic."[8] All true. Yet the novel, Koestler's cri de coeur against the Stalinist purges, is regarded as one of the most important works of twentieth-century literature. And one of the bravest: Koestler's voice was one of the first from within the heart of the militant Left to publicly decry the deformation of the revolution.

Koestler met, and knew, a lot of interesting people. He offered unsolicited (and unaccepted) advice to Nikolai Bukharin and Karl Radek in Moscow and to Chaim Weizmann and David Ben-Gurion in Tel Aviv. He was friends with Walter Benjamin, who gave Koestler half his morphine tablets as they tried to escape occupied France. He interviewed Einstein; he argued with Jean-Paul Sartre (at whom he threw a glass) and Albert Camus (to whom he gave a black eye). He wrote revolutionary leaflets with Wilhelm Reich and was friends with Hanns Eisler. He joined, and quit, political movements with astonishing alacrity: bridge-burning, he called it. With equal alacrity he turned comrades into enemies and vice versa. Thus the former Communist praised Joseph McCarthy and Whittaker Chambers; perhaps more astoundingly, the erstwhile prisoner of Franco urged the Western democracies to align with the Spanish dictator in the fight against Communism, which Koestler likened to the bubonic plague. Every cause he joined, and every place he went, proved crushingly disappointing to him; as he wrote, "The pursuit of Utopia . . . turned me into a Casanova of Causes."[9] The metaphor is well chosen. Koestler had affairs with hundreds of women—"My harem is beginning to wear me out," he once complained—to whom he was often emotionally, physically, and sexually cruel.[10] His politics and his sexuality were intertwined: "The political libido is basically as irrational as the sexual drive," he wrote.[11] In his case that was true—and never more so than when it came to Zionism.

Koestler witnessed the decimation of his generation through state-lessness, purge, execution, torture, and murder. Most of his family died in Auschwitz. Unsurprisingly, he was prone to severe depressions, break-downs (sometimes at opportune times), and occasional suicide attempts. He recalled his devastating losses: "At a conservative estimate, three out of every four people whom I knew before I was thirty, were subsequently killed in Spain, or hounded to death at Dachau, or gassed at Belsen, or deported to Russia, or liquidated in Russia; some jumped from windows in Vienna or Budapest, others were wrecked by the misery and aimless-ness of permanent exile."[12]

Koestler's politics never exactly developed; instead, they were subject to Damascene-like reversals. Rupture rather than synthesis was his style. In the 1920s, for instance, he was an energetic propagandist for the right-wing Zionist movement; in the 1930s, traveling through the Soviet Union as a Communist, he was totally uninterested in the condition of the Jews. He explained, "Each year brought its own revelation, and each time I could only think with shame and rage of the opinions I had held and vented before the last initiation."[13] Much of his life was spent in self-refutation and self-justification. He returned, obsessively, to certain themes and experiences, trying time and again to get them right—or make them right. As one critic observed, Koestler "never quite recovered from finding a monster in the cradle of the revolutionary paradise."[14]

Yet despite Koestler's ideological zigzags, his mode of thinking remained remarkably consistent. Throughout his life, he insisted on either/or dichotomies and deceptively simplified choices. (He would have been at home with George Bush's post–September 11 challenge to the world that "you're either with us or against us." In fact, this was Koestler's unwelcome message to the liberals and leftists of postwar Europe in his fight against Communism.) One could call this worldview Manichean, sectarian, reductive, fundamentalist, undialectical, or even Stalinist; Koestler called it "absolutitis." In his analysis of Zionism, this mode of thinking became grossly exacerbated and led to a series of costly political and moral miscalculations. Certainly, Koestler is the echt twentieth-century man not only because of his tormented relationship to Communism and anti-Communism but because of his equally tormented relation to Zionism and Judaism. As one scholar of Jewish history wrote, Koestler "provides an important illustration and test-case of the failure of . . . [a] generation of European Jewish intellectuals to find an answer to the question of Jewish cultural survival in the modern era."[15]

Arthur Koestler was born to a secular, prosperous family in Budapest in 1905. His later claims that he was "half-Jewish" and "of uncertain and mixed racial origin" are false; all the Koestlers were Jewish, and his mother was descended from a long line of esteemed rabbis.[16] Koestler painted his childhood as devoid of Jewish influences, but this too was untrue. His parents went to synagogue on the Jewish holidays and cele-brated Sabbath dinners; he lived in a predominantly Jewish neighbor-hood near an imposing synagogue and went to a predominantly Jewish school. Arthur was, in all likelihood, circumcised—an odd detail, one might think, but one that will assume importance later. (He was also very short—his nickname in college was "the Dwarf"; this, too, will become relevant.) His paternal grandfather, to whom he was very close, was an Orthodox Jew from Russia who almost certainly spoke Yiddish. Arthur read the Bible in Hebrew, and Biblical references would be liberally scat-tered throughout his writing; he likened his journey through the Communist movement to the search for "a Promised Land—and the plagues were descending on Pharoah according to plan."[17] Budapest's Jewish community was highly educated, cultured, and successful; this was the comfortable, seemingly stable world that enveloped a young Arthur Koestler. It was not traditionally religious, but to call it assimilated is not quite right either.

Koestler's anxieties and self-loathing were among his favorite topics, exhaustively detailed in his diaries and memoirs. He was, he recalled, "an only child and a lonely child; precious, neurotic, admired for my brains and detested for my character."[18] As a schoolboy, he viewed himself as a "pathetic figure" of "boundless timidity and insecurity . . . a small, disgusting tragedy."[19] Adulthood wasn't much happier. His self-described "list of miseries" included "lack of self-confidence," "guilt," "jealousy," "devaluation of friends," "vanity," "lack of personality," "greed," and, coming in at number one, "incest barrier."[20] Shame and humiliation haunt his autobiographical and fictional works. Koestler feared that he was a coward, had a tendency toward betrayal, and harbored homosexual tendencies. He liked to quote Otto Katz, a Communist organizer and onetime comrade, who told him, "We all have inferiority complexes of various sizes, but yours isn't a complex—it's a cathedral."[21] Yet there is a disingenuous quality to this self-flagellation; as Stephen Spender observed of Koestler, "If one keeps on referring to one's 'inferiority complex' it becomes a kind of asset and therefore must cease to be so inferior."[22]

The end of World War I changed the political map of Europe and upended young Arthur's life. As the Austro-Hungarian Empire died, Budapest spun into a whirlwind of political activity. "The most interesting campaigns were on the left," Bernard Avishai has written. "That is where you found the Jews."[23] A Soviet Republic, led by Béla Kun, was established in March 1919. Arthur was an enthusiastic supporter of the Reds, if only because their parades and banners were so exciting and because, despite shortages, there was an abundance of ice cream. But the socialist experiment was short-lived; after a few months, the quasi-fascist forces of Admiral Miklós Horthy, supported by foreign troops, crushed the revolution. Kun was Jewish, as were many of his government officials and supporters, and Horthy's White Terror focused with particular fury on Budapest's Jews: an ominous precursor of the Europe to come. The Koestlers quickly fled to war-decimated Vienna. Arthur was still a young adolescent, but he had already experienced revolution, counterrevolution, and anti-Semitic terror. Nevertheless, he would write of his early years, "I had never been personally victimized or bothered by anti-Semitism"— though being hounded out of your country as it spirals into anti-Jewish violence does seem, at the very least, like a kind of bother.[24]

In 1922, Koestler entered the Vienna Polytechnic. He would later claim that he found the Jewish Question "boring" and had never heard of Zionism. (This is doubtful, in part because Zionist leaders Theodor Herzl and Max Nordau were among Budapest's most prominent figures.) Despite his self-proclaimed ignorance, Arthur promptly joined Unitas, a Zionist fraternity that followed the right-wing Revisionist line of Vladimir Jabotinsky, and he quickly became an enthusiastic, indeed pugnacious, leader of the Zionist student movement. Koestler had no interest in the liberal or socialist-Zionist organizations at his school, or in the socialist pioneers making their way to Palestine. Unitas was dedicated to military uniforms, marches, and duels with the anti-Semitic, Austrian-nationalist students—to "out-Heroding

Herod," as he put it. Its major purpose was "to disprove the legend of Jewish cowardice."[25] Under its tutelage, the Dwarf blossomed.

One of Koestler's major influences at this time was Otto Weininger, an Austrian philosopher who viewed the Jews as a fatally feminized people. (Weininger, who was Jewish, proved his masculinity by committing suicide at the age of twenty-three.) Then, in 1924, Koestler met Jabotinsky and immediately became a dedicated acolyte. For young Arthur, Jabotinsky was everything he feared he, and the Jews, were not. The Revisionist leader was a confident, charismatic speaker. He was, in Koestler's loving remembrance, "a stranger to Jewish tradition" who "detested the turbid mysticism and confused sentimentality . . . of the [Zionist] movement" and "hated the Talmudic dialectics."[26] He had military experience. He exuded fearlessness. He was unapologetic. He was at home in the world, not a tentative guest in it. Best of all, he was, in Koestler's words, "utterly un-Jewish," which meant he was a man's man. Throughout Koestler's life, Revisionism was the Zionist tendency to which he adhered. It was vehemently anti-socialist and anti-Communist, dismissive of the kibbutzim and the Arabs, urban, secular, militaristic, and, eventually, terrorist. (Ben-Gurion referred to Jabotinsky as "Vladimir Hitler.") This was the kind of negative Zionism that viewed Israel, as a young Amos Oz would write in a different context, "as one giant act of revenge for the historical 'humiliation' of the Diaspora."[27]

Koestler didn't consider the secular Jews of Western Europe—Jews like himself—to be really Jewish. Despite the post–World War I experience in Hungary, he viewed assimilation as a resounding success, with Jewish citizenship, civic rights, and social acceptance firmly established. Real Jews—by which he meant poor, stateless, religious, backward, despised Jews—were to be found in Eastern Europe's cramped ghettoes, whose inhabitants he compared to furtive convicts. Koestler didn't actually know any such Jews and had never visited a shtetl, but never mind. "Koestler identified the hum, humor, and humility of Eastern European Orthodox Jews with an impulse to submissiveness," Avishai observed. "He loved to hate Yiddish Jews. . . . He cringed at what he took to be their cringing before the angry God and the angry goy. He knew virtually nothing about them, but seemed to fear that they'd bring out the worst in him."[28] For Koestler, Zionism did not mean the painstaking construction of a new, positive world but the cathartic razing of an old, negative one.

Zionism, he wrote, was "the only cure for a sickness": the sickness of being a frightened, powerless pariah, the sickness of being a Jew.[29]

Every revolution is a synthesis of self-affirmation and self-critique. On one hand, the oppressed assert their dignity and worth—"Black is beautiful"—and, sometimes, their superiority to their oppressors. On the other, they acknowledge that subjugation and powerlessness have damaged them on the deepest psychic levels. The revolution must therefore construct not only a new economic and political order but, also, a new kind of human being, for the old kind has been grievously damaged. W. E. B. Du Bois wrote of the American slave's "submission," "laziness," "resignation," and "infinite capacity for dumb suffering"—qualities that, he observed, persisted after Emancipation.[30] The Bolsheviks spoke of creating a "new man"; their scorn for the illiterate, servile Russian peasantry knew no bounds. The Indian independence movement under Gandhi and the Algerian Revolution under the National Liberation Front stringently criticized the actually-existing cultures of their actually-existing peoples. As Michael Walzer has shown, both movements sought to rouse the masses from "the passivity, the quietude, the deep lethargy" that enfeebled them; the fate of the revolution depended upon this. Gandhi believed that Indians must be *made* into free people who would be "fit" for independence; Frantz Fanon wrote of the need for the "radical mutation" of the Algerian.[31]

The Zionist movement undoubtedly fits within this tradition of self-critique, which it sometimes raised to an extreme pitch. There are several reasons for this, including the Jews' culture of analytic thought and skeptical argument; in addition, many Zionists were strongly influenced by Bolshevik vanguardism. Zionism aimed not only for political independence but for a profound psychic and cultural transformation. "Jewish is beautiful" was not its mantra.

Transformation necessitated destruction. One of Zionism's key aims was *shilat ha'golah*—the negation of the Diaspora, which Zionists viewed as parasitic and debased. Perhaps it is unsurprising, then, that Zionist depictions of the Diaspora Jew often bore a creepy resemblance to anti-Semitic depictions of the Diaspora Jew. Both viewed the Jewish people as deeply flawed. The difference is that the Zionists believed that Jewish inferiority was historically determined and therefore capable of change,

while the anti-Semites believed that the sorry state of the Jews was irreme-
diably rooted in blood, in genes, in the essential.

The term "self-hatred" is overused, and is usually employed as an
insult hurled by one Jew against another. Like "Orientalism," it is meant
to foreclose debate and so should be used with the greatest caution. Yet
there is a line where rational self-criticism *does* curdle into vicious
contempt. Koestler repeatedly crossed it.

Here he is, in his 1949 book about the birth of Israel, describing the
Jew: "Each time you burn him alive, stick a knife into his stomach or
pump gas into his lungs, he pops up again like a jack-in-the-box, with a
more horribly ingratiating smile, and offers you a second-hand suit or a
share of real estate."[32]

And here is Jabotinsky: "Because the Yid is ugly, sickly, and lacks
decorum, we shall endow the ideal image of the Hebrew with masculine
beauty. The Yid is trodden upon and easily frightened and, therefore, the
Hebrew ought to be proud and independent. . . . The Yid has accepted
submission and, therefore, the Hebrew ought to learn to command." In
short, the Israeli must be the "diametrical opposite" of the Jew.[33]

Such views were by no means the monopoly of the Right, which was
a small minority within Zionism. Key Zionist thinkers and Hebrew
writers who were far more influential than Jabotinsky (or Koestler)
propounded similar themes. It is hard to overstate the extent to which
humiliation and shame—emotions with which Koestler was on intimate
terms—recur throughout Zionist literature. Recall that Bernard Lazare
described the Jewish people as "a tribe of slaves." H. N. Bialik's searing
Hebrew poem "In the City of Slaughter," a response to the Kishinev
pogrom of 1903, reserved some of its greatest fury for the "cowering"
Jewish men who, "crushed in their shame," failed to defend themselves,
their wives, their children: The "sons of the Maccabees . . . died like dogs."
As such, they were unworthy of compassion:

> They are too wretched to evoke thy scorn.
> They are too lost thy pity to evoke,
> So let them go, then, men to sorrow born,
> Mournful and slinking, crushed beneath their yoke.[34]

Ahad Ha'am viewed the Jews of the Diaspora, and not only in the East, as
spiritual cripples. A. D. Gordon spoke of the leechlike, "fundamentally

useless" nature of Diaspora Jewry. Yosef Brenner described Diaspora Jews as "gypsies, filthy dogs, inhuman."[35] And in an 1897 essay published in the Zionist newspaper *The World,* Theodor Herzl sounded an awful lot like Jabotinsky and Koestler—and like the Jew-haters who would soon overtake Europe. The Jew, Herzl wrote, "is spineless, repressed, shabby. [His] face shows only miserable fright or a mocking grin—he carries on his dirty deals behind the mask of progress and reaction; with Rabbis, writers, lawyers, and doctors, who are only crafty profit seekers."[36]

In light of the enormous influence of religious Zionists in Israel today, it may be hard to remember that Zionism was originally not just a secular movement but a blatantly anti-religious one. Exilic Judaism yearned for a return to Israel but believed that only the Messiah could make things right, sometime in the distant future. Zionists believed that only men and women could make things right, and that the time to do so was now. (Two thousand years of waiting were, they figured, enough.) For the political Zionists, especially the majority on the left, "religion" and "passivity" were synonymous; therefore, as Walzer has written, "Zionism was, and could only be, the creation of people who were hostile to Judaism."[37]

Koestler was thoroughly secular and firmly adhered to this world-view. But he took it one step further. He rejected not only the Jewish religion but all of Jewish history and culture. Or, rather, he insisted that there *was* no Jewish history or culture. In his view, the Jewish religion, including the Bible and the Talmud, had no unique ethical or intellectual value; Judaism was simply "an inert tradition voided of all spiritual content." Take away the idea of a chosen people—which Koestler would pervert into a racial doctrine—and the return to Israel, "and all that remained would be a set of archaic dietary prescriptions and tribal laws." Hebrew, he claimed, had been dead for two millennia (so much for medieval philosophy and science, the Haskalah, etc.); Yiddish was an ugly mish-mash that could boast no literature of consequence. Jews in the Diaspora, as Jews, had accomplished nothing. In short: "Since the first century A.D. the Jews have had no national history, no language, literature and culture of their own."[38] The Jewish people had survived for five thousand years, but so what? There was no there there.

Koestler's smug confidence in dismissing the religion, history, and culture of the Jews was matched only by his ignorance of them. And though Ben-Gurion, for instance, viewed the Diaspora as a wasteland, not all Zionists did. In fact, there was a lively debate within the movement about how to *incorporate* the Diaspora into Zionism. Ahad Ha'am, Bialik, and Gordon stressed the importance of the Jewish people's cultural continuity; many Zionists, including those as secular as Koestler, believed that invaluable ethical concepts were embedded within Judaism. In any case, Israel can never really sever itself from the Jewish past; as the Biblical scholar Robert Alter observed, "It is *because* of a shared past, onerous yet precious, that these men and women have come together from many lands to live a renewed destiny on this soil."39

In 1936, Yehezkel Kaufmann, a scholar of Jewish history, wrote a remarkable essay, published in Hebrew in Tel Aviv, which took his fellow Zionists to task for their adoption of anti-Semitic arguments. Though there is no reason to think that Kaufmann had ever met Koestler, the essay could have been addressed to him.

Kaufmann himself was a strong critic of the Diaspora. But he vehemently objected to the view that the religion, economy, or cultural habits of the Jews were the causes of anti-Semitism. This was a belief that, since the Enlightenment, had been adopted by Jews themselves—most enthusiastically, perhaps, by Zionists. Thus, Kaufmann charged, anti-Semitism "puts on the disguise of Jewish nationalism. . . . The poison that flows from Jewish nationalist sources is perhaps the most dangerous of all."

In a sometimes mocking tone, Kaufmann pointed out that anti-Semitism had a distressing ability to reinvent itself entirely independent of Jewish behavior. "During the period of the Enlightenment the [Orthodox] Jews were blamed for being hostile to culture, for detesting 'knowledge.' . . . In the following period, the Jews were seized with a great passion for knowledge. . . . Then the anti-Semites reversed themselves and discovered new Jewish faults." The Diaspora's political economy—its dearth of factory workers and peasants—was often blamed for Christian antipathy. Not only was this false ("Is it really true that the Jew isn't a working man?"), it was ahistoric: "The hatred is far older than this social structure, and clearly does not flow from it. . . . What reason can there be to believe that, if the Jews had a larger proportion of farmers and workers, *those* classes would not dislike them?" Contempt for the Jews could not be attributed to the Jewish "jargon"; resentment of the Jews was not due to their talent for business. (Aren't there stores in Paris and Tokyo, Kaufmann wondered?) In fact, Jews could be teachers or tailors, millionaires or ragmen: No matter. Nor did anti-Semitism stem from some innate, evil propensity of Christians. No, anti-Semitism had one cause: statelessness. Jews were "the *eternal alien*" and would continue to be despised until they constituted a sovereign nation. Zionism must aim to change political circumstance, not metaphysical essence: "It is not redemption from *moral sin*, but from *tragic accident*."

What worried Kaufmann most were the psychological and ethical implications of the Zionist self-critique. Zionism, he wrote, assumes that "we must first hate ourselves" in order to forge a movement. But what kind of society could be built on self-hatred? What kind of strength could be founded on renunciation? How to reject, how to repress, so many centuries of life—of sorrow and defeat, yes, but of vitality and accomplishment too? "Faith will not issue from contempt, and hope will not spring from insult," Kaufmann warned. "Pride is the only true nourishment for redemption."[40]

In 1925, a twenty-year-old Koestler suddenly quit college and sank into depression. The next year, just as suddenly, he moved "out into the wilderness among the mosquitos and Arabs"—moved, that is, to Palestine.[41] Though a fervent Revisionist and thoroughly urban in his outlook, he chose to join a left-wing rural commune. He would spend the next four years in Palestine and fail at all his endeavors, yet this is where his journalism career began.

It is no surprise that Koestler was appalled by the commune; the real question is why, given his ideology and personality, he sought it out at all. Located in the Valley of Jezreel, which would become one of Israel's most fertile regions, the collective was at that time bare and impoverished. Koestler unfondly recalled it as "a rather dismal and slumlike oasis in the wilderness, consisting of wooden huts, surrounded by dreary vegetable plots" and "ramshackle dwellings in which only the poorest in Europe would live." The Zionist pioneers were ill, exhausted, overworked, and prematurely aged. Koestler proved useless at physical labor: "After an hour or two of this work, my hands were blistered, my head . . . swam, and my bones felt as if stretched on the rack. . . . Work in the field remained torture." Even the farm implements betrayed him; Koestler bemoaned "that rusty, clotted spade, so different from the gleaming symbol of my dreams of freedom."[42] Before long, the collective kicked him out.

His other ventures were equal fiascos. He started a Revisionist news agency, which acquired exactly two subscribers (one in Latvia, one in Czechoslovakia). He was hired as an assistant to an Arab architect, who fired him, as did the director of a tourist agency. He even failed as a lemonade seller, which seems hard to do in such a hot country. Perhaps most doomed was his work as editor on the *Nile and Palestine Gazette,* a German-Arabic paper that propagandized for Zionism among Arab readers; it lasted for three issues. But he did publish freelance articles on Palestinian life and politics in several European papers. Through a combination of luck, connections, and what he called "shameless bluffing," he was hired as Middle East correspondent by Ullstein, a large, influential, Jewish-owned publisher based in Berlin. Ullstein was liberal, cosmopolitan, modern—the essence of all that would soon be destroyed. Koestler was only twenty-two when hired. He had found his true calling.

The Middle East of that time was a relatively open place, and as Koestler roamed through it he had remarkable access to leaders in Transjordan, Iraq, and Egypt. Some of what he wrote is still prescient. "The British influence doesn't go deep and doesn't touch the national roots of the countries within its sphere of influence—it is a thin enamel crust," he observed.[43] He considered the Wahhabis to be ascetic fanatics. He reported that Iraq's King Faisal told him, "The rebirth of the once so mighty Empire was every Arab's wish. . . . It is a slow process but sooner or later the rebirth of Arabia will become a fact."[44]

Koestler's Zionism did not set him against the emerging Arab nationalist movements that he observed. On the contrary, he "wrote with considerable sympathy of Arab efforts to wrest independence from their colonial masters," biographer Michael Scammell observes. "Oddly, it was his Zionism that prompted him to identify with the Arabs as underdogs and to express a healthy contempt for British policies."[45] In Koestler's analysis it was the British, not the Arabs, who were the main and certainly most powerful antagonists of Zionism.

As a project, actually-existing Zionism underwhelmed Koestler. Unlike Arendt, he either failed to notice or was hostile to much that was being built in Palestine. He disliked the influence of the Russians and Poles—sons of the ghetto!—in Tel Aviv. He had no political affinity for the kibbutzim or the Histadrut, the powerful socialist labor union that dominated the Yishuv. His inability to master Hebrew sent him into angry tirades against it; he insisted that the language would separate Palestinian Jews from European culture (an ironic charge in light of later accusations that Israel is "too Western"). Yet Koestler was discerning about some aspects of Zionism and of Palestine. Describing what he called the Jerusalem Sadness—a syndrome that persists to this day—he wrote of the city's

> tragedy without catharsis. . . . Its inhabitants are poisoned by holiness. . . . Perhaps the most disagreeable are the Clergy, Moslem, Christian and Jewish alike. The Moslem clergy . . . call on the average twice a year for a holy bloodbath. . . . The Jewish clergy was engaged in feuds with the Moslems about the rights of way to the Wailing Wall, and among themselves about the correct method of ritual slaughter; they also encouraged their orthodox disciples to protect the sanctity of the Sabbath by beating up the godless who smoked cigarettes in the streets and by throwing bricks at passing motor cars.

The political atmosphere was equally toxic: "The Husseini clan murdered members of the Nashashibi clan; during the riot season they both murdered Jews; the Jewish parties hated each other, the British, and the Arabs, in that order."[46]

Koestler didn't renounce Zionism at this time. But the romance was gone, at least for a while. He rued, not for the last time, that "instead of Utopia, I had found reality; an extremely complex reality."[47] He returned to Europe in 1929, just before the outbreak of the Hebron riots—an event that would forever alter Palestine, Jewish-Arab relations, and the Zionist movement. In 1930, he moved to Berlin, arriving on the day of unprecedented Nazi electoral gains—an event that would forever alter Germany, Europe, and the world. The next year, he joined the German Communist Party. For most of the 1930s, Zionism and the Jews vanished from his radar.

In 1937—eleven years after Koestler had first embarked for Palestine— Britain's Peel Commission returned from its tour of the Mandate and issued its controversial report. In response to worsening violence between Jews and Arabs, their sharply antithetical political aims, and the cultural chasm between them, the commission urged partition as the only possible guarantor of peace and mutual self-determination. Shortly after this, Koestler traveled to Palestine as a correspondent for Britain's

News Chronicle. "I took the boat from Athens to Alexandria," he remembered. "Half the passengers were Jews, and the other half hated them."[48]

Koestler reported on several aspects of the political situation that would become more prominent in his subsequent writings and that are sometimes overlooked in analyses of the conflict today. In Palestine, he observed, "Among the lower strata of British civil servants . . . there is an atmosphere of anti-Semitism unparalleled anywhere else under the British flag." The Brits regarded Tel Aviv as "some kind of leper city." As for the Arabs, British policy was a "vacillation between extreme tolerance and brutality." Though a campaign of Arab terrorism had been launched, it was no mass movement: Most of the violence was perpetrated by paid gunmen. (There were apparently different prices for killing a Jew, an Englishman, and an enemy Arab.) Moderate Arabs were "too afraid of being bumped off by terrorists if they expressed their views," yet many favored "peaceful compromise."[49]

Koestler's main point was that the partition of Palestine had already occurred. "While you are discussing partition theoretically, in the sphere of economic and cultural life it is an accomplished fact, and the split is complete," an anonymous source explained to him. "If it does not soon get its territorial expression we shall all go to the devil, Arabs and Jews together." In fact, Koestler wrote, "The two communities seem to live on different planets." (Jews and Arabs were already boycotting each other's economies.) As for political programs, the Arabs understandably wanted a state with, to be blunt, as few Jews as possible; they consequently sought to end Jewish immigration. That, too, was understandable, if not exactly an example of international solidarity. But for the Jews in Europe— already under assault from the Nazis and their friends—restricted immigration meant death. Palestine was one of the few places to which hunted Jews could still immigrate, though it wouldn't be for long. "It seemed a hopeless situation," Koestler posited, "for, from their own point of view, both parties seemed to be right."[50] But, he stressed, a self-governing Jewish entity—with its own rural and urban economies, schools, labor unions, cultural institutions, taxes, medical system, and political parties— had already been built.

Partition would be difficult. But it was by no means an artificial imposition on an organic unity, for there was no organic unity. On the contrary, partition *recognized* extant, deeply rooted divisions. "An irrepressible conflict has arisen . . . within the narrow bounds of one small country," the Peel Report stated. "There is no common ground between them. Their national aspirations are incompatible. . . . Neither of the two national ideals permits of combination in the service of a single State."[51]

Marxists—including, most vociferously, Jewish Marxists like Rosa Luxemburg and Leon Trotsky—had long insisted that the proletariat had no country. The advocates of partition thought otherwise, as did overwhelming numbers of Palestinian Arabs and Palestinian Jews. Partition was predicated not on the wished-for unity of all peoples but on the actual differences between two particular peoples, and it implied that coexistence depended upon acknowledging rather than moralistically denying those differences. It was a sober, un-glorious plan that failed to fully satisfy either side. But it was not "racist," "imperialist," or "genocidal," as has since been charged. In fact, it envisioned a reasonable, perhaps even normal, future of development and independence for each community. And the other options were far worse. "The prospects for the future of the Holy Land are one colossal nightmare," Koestler warned in a dispatch published in 1939. "Fear and hatred are growing daily. . . . Britain must act, and act quickly."[52]

The mainstream Zionist movement (but not the Revisionists) accepted the Peel Commission's principle of partition, although the Zionists objected to the proposed borders. Virtually all Arab leaders, within and outside of Palestine, immediately rejected the Peel Report and the prospect of any other partition plan, under any circumstances, at any time. Historian Benny Morris has argued that Arab rejection of partition was overdetermined. Probably so. But in light of the subsequent decades of anguish, blood, and wasted lives, it is hard not to regard this refusal as a world-historic mistake of unforgivable proportions.

Three events pushed Koestler back into Zionism. In 1938, he left the Communist Party. In 1939, Hitler invaded Poland and began annihilating Europe's Jews. That same year, Britain closed off Palestine to virtually all Jewish immigrants through the infamous White Paper.

And so as the 1940s progressed, Koestler devoted himself with furious energy to Jewish and Zionist causes. He no longer viewed a Jewish state as an idealistic project; this time, it was a question of survival. Just as he had defied his former Communist comrades by writing

Darkness at Noon, now he bucked British policies and public opinion, along with the Revisionist line, arguing time and again for partition. He strenuously denounced the White Paper as "a Palestine Munich." He began working with Chaim Weizmann in London. Perhaps most important, he publicized, in print and on the BBC, the horrifying disclosures of Jan Karski, the Polish Resistance leader who brought news of the Jewish extermination to the outside world. (To those who rejected such reports as alarmist, Koestler wrote an extraordinary essay titled "On Disbelieving Atrocities" in which he charged that "the neurotics who totter about in a screened phantasy world because you lack the faculty to face the facts" were accomplices to mass murder.)[53] Koestler was enraged by the British press's refusal to report on the genocide: "Not one paper-headline for 5 million Jews. But for 50 British Officers [killed]—what a ballyhoo."[54] He devised a plan for bombing the death camps, which was submitted to the British government. Distraught over his family's peril—they were trapped in Eichmann's Budapest—he had a nervous breakdown.

In December of 1944, when many journalists were making their way to a recently liberated Paris, Koestler traveled once more to Palestine as a correspondent. He met old friends, including from the Communist Party and the French Resistance. He had a secret meeting with Menachem Begin, then a leader of the terrorist Irgun; Koestler tried, unsuccessfully, to persuade him to cease terror attacks on the British. (Weizmann arranged the meeting, pleading with Koestler to "talk to those *meshuganeh* friends of yours.")[55] He met, too, with Nathan Friedman-Yellin, a leader of the Stern Gang, which had recently assassinated Britain's Lord Moyne on a Cairo street; though this was a moral and strategic disaster, Koestler viewed the Sternist as a noble if tragic figure. (Years later, Friedman-Yellin would become a leading Israeli dove.) Koestler visited a far-Left kibbutz, which he blessed, sort of: "May you prosper and flourish in the Hebrew socialist tradition—and shed . . . your infantile allegiances to Uncle Joe."[56] He met with Arabs in the countryside and noted that, when it came to the Arab-Zionist conflict, "My sympathies are so split that in the end I shall develop schizophrenia." He wrote, "I love this country more than I ever thought," but he concluded that he could never live there.[57]

In the late 1940s, Koestler wrote two major books about Palestine: *Promise and Fulfilment* (1949), a journalistic account of Zionism under the

Mandate, preceded by *Thieves in the Night* (1946), a fascinating and bizarre novel.

Thieves in the Night begins in 1937. It is Koestler's most personal engagement with Zionism—the work in which his political "absolutitis," his sexual obsessions, and his neuroses about being Jewish most clearly merge. The author's stand-in and main character is Joseph, a vaguely left-wing, half-Jewish Englishman who, upon suddenly awakening to his Judaic heritage, hot-tails it to Palestine to join a struggling kibbutz. There were many good reasons, circa 1937, to become a Zionist, starting with Hitler's ascension and the spread of virulent anti-Semitism throughout Europe. Joseph, however, is inspired by a different sort of event. He is disgustedly rejected by his gentile British lover when, in an intimate coital moment, she realizes that he is circumcised. This is what we might call the Phallic Theory of Zionism, and it was, so far as I know, unique to Koestler. (When it was pointed out to Koestler that this episode made no sense even on its own biological terms, he "revised the scene to imply that the penis was no longer erect.")[58]

Joseph has a lousy time on the kibbutz. But he does fall madly in love with Dina, a German refugee who is a "knock-out," perhaps because she too is only half-Jewish. In Berlin, Dina had been sexually tortured by the Gestapo; she is therefore terrified of being touched and incapable of returning Joseph's ardor. One day, while wandering in the hills, she is gang-raped and murdered by neighboring Arabs. Disgusted by his fellow kibbutzniks' passive response to this and other atrocities, Joseph makes a Koestleresque U-turn and joins the right-wing terrorist underground of the Irgun. Again, credulity is strained. "The emergence of a terrorist leader out of a Kibbutz . . . is, of course, humanly possible, but, indeed, very improbable," historian Joseph Nedava observed with admirable understatement. "It would be almost as unimaginable to visualize an Eskimo from the Arctic regions becoming a banana-millionaire in equatorial Africa."[59]

Joseph does not just become a terrorist. *Thieves in the Night* is a veritable *celebration* of terror. The main thrust of the book—and its great deceit—is Koestler's insistence that terror and submission were the sole Zionist choices. Koestler would later defend the Haganah's prewar policy of restrained defense and extol its prowess as a fighting force, but in *Thieves,* the Zionist militia is ridiculed and scorned. And Koestler's terror-versus-submission paradigm is presented not just as a political choice but as a sexual one. Terror is the gateway to being "un-Jewish": to being, that is, a virile man. (Arthur Koestler, meet Frantz Fanon.) Metaphorically, terror restores Joseph's sorely missed foreskin.

Thieves in the Night was a startling reversal of *Darkness at Noon*'s repudiation of terror and utilitarian ethics. This was no small matter, for Koestler had built his subsequent career, his moral critique of Communism, and an entire ethical edifice on that repudiation. Now he insisted, and would continue to insist, that terror was the sine qua non of political power: "Without terror the British would never have cleared out of Palestine."[60] (Arthur Koestler, meet Ismail Haniyeh.) In 1948, when Ben-Gurion's forces fought and defeated the Irgun in the *Altalena* battle—thereby establishing the principle of the state's monopoly on violence—Koestler was appalled, though this was a key moment in the building of Israeli democracy. He admired the terrorists.

In *Thieves*, Zionist terror is depicted not only as necessary but as the epitome of brilliance, strength, and glamour. "Political imaginativeness was nowadays only to be found among extremist movements of the tyrannical type," Koestler wrote. "Nazis, Fascists and Communists seemed to hold the international monopoly of it. . . . Apparently submission to discipline and boldness of vision were not as incompatible as was generally assumed. Those who denied the freedom of ideas were full of ideas and ingenuity; while the defenders of free expression were dull and pedestrian with hardly an idea worth expressing."[61] Not surprisingly, these notions were roundly ridiculed by Koestler's contemporaries. Reviewing the novel in the *New Yorker*, Edmund Wilson wrote that Koestler's terrorists descended to "hate-mongering and mumbo-jumbo." Diana Trilling was aghast at Koestler's concept of the "gunman-messiah." Isaac Rosenfeld simply observed, "All sense and principle desert him."[62]

Koestler's attraction to terrorism was due in part to his enduring loyalty to Jabotinsky, one of the Irgun's leaders and main inspirations. It was due in part to Koestler's thin understanding of Zionism, which he boiled down to a punch-in-the-face of the Jews' enemies. It was due in part to his juvenile insistence on seeing complexity and weakness as synonymous. But it was also due, I believe, to his peculiar personal history.

Koestler is often described as a man of action. And he was. But it is equally true—though often unnoticed—that unlike many men of his generation, and certainly many left-wing men of his generation, he never fought militarily for his beliefs. He did not join the International Brigades in Spain; in fact, unlike his comrades, he notoriously fled from Madrid when the city was under aerial attack in 1937. ("No pasarán" was, apparently, not his motto.) He did not join the French Resistance, the Free French, the British army, the Haganah, or the Irgun. He was, it is true, briefly a member of Britain's Pioneer Corps during World War II, but most of his time was spent seeking release from manual labor—"I am working now eight hours a day in the bloody open air and it is really no fun," he kvetched.[63] After a year with the Corps, he had a breakdown and was released as unfit; thus ended what one biographer called his "brief and inglorious military career."[64] In short, Arthur Koestler was a militarist, not a fighter. It is no great stretch to imagine that his idealization of *other* men fighting—sometimes, as with the Irgun, in the most amoral ways—was a reaction to this. Albert Camus once praised the man who fights by necessity yet continues to despise violence. Koestler turned this on its head: He did not fight, but he found violence rather appealing.

The Koestler who idealized the "imaginativeness," "boldness," and "ingenuity" of terrorist violence cannot be separated from Koestler's feelings of Jewish shame. In *Thieves*, those feelings express themselves in aesthetic disgust. Here is Joseph as he looks at his fellow immigrant kibbutzniks: "Joseph was struck by the ugliness of the faces. . . . His revulsion against this assembly of thick, curved noses, fleshy lips and liquid eyes was particularly strong. . . . He was surrounded by masks of archaic reptiles." (Arthur Koestler, meet Julius Streicher.) In fact, Koestler considered the main accomplishment of early Zionism to be a kind of biological miracle in which the gnarled, stooped denizens of the ghetto had birthed a nation of tall Aryan sons: "mostly blond, freckled, broad-featured, heavy-boned and clumsy; farmers' sons, peasant lads, unjewish-looking."[65] One wonders what Darwin would have thought.

But if Koestler held native Israeli men in some, limited admiration—at least they were "unjewish"—he was revolted by Israeli women, whether immigrant or native-born. Psychologically, this made sense. Zionism's raison d'être, in Koestler's view, was to make the Jews strong; but strong women, especially strong Jewish women, were a far-from-appealing prospect. Consider Joseph's description of the female European immigrants, who present such a stark contrast to half-Jewish Dina's cultured beauty: "The other girls made him shudder in incestuous revulsion. . . . Some acrid spice of their intellect permeated the very pores of their bodies. . . . They were saturated with the long experience of the race which lingered in their eyes and on their skin like the heat of the former occupant in a chair." And again: "The female comrades . . . [were] looking even less attractive than usual. I suppose they sing the Anthem during the act of procreation." But the Sabra women are no better: "these stumpy, dumpy girls with their rather coarse features, big buttocks and heavy breasts, physically precocious, mentally retarded."[66] Later, Koestler would excoriate Israeli women as "insupportable hystericals; their table manners and conversations are on the level of the Cracow ghetto; they don't drink, they don't relax, they aren't human."[67] Arthur Koestler, meet Alexander Portnoy!

Thieves in the Night is the perfect exposition of Koestler's politics of disdain. His reasoning went like this: The original sin of the Jews was their purported lack of guts. Israeli Sabras, however, did not lack guts. Ergo, Israelis had "ceased to be Jews."[68] Since Israel was thus, by definition, "unjewish," it could not create a new kind of Jewish life; it could only put an end to the old. This was a good thing. But it was not a great thing, for the sequel wouldn't be of much use. That was because the Jews had lost their brainy, sophisticated civilization (yes, it did exist) along with their cowardice; the two were umbilically connected. The "Hebrew Tarzans," Koestler complained, were "without traditions, manners, form, style. . . . The humanistic hormones of the mind are absent."[69] In other words: Zionism might solve the Jewish Question, but it would do so by getting rid of the Jews.

Thieves in the Night is a vivid manifestation of Koestler's pathologies. But it also offers a fascinating glimpse into the cultural variety and intracommunal divisions of Mandatory Palestine. We are introduced to the Mukhtar of Kfar Tabiyeh, Koestler's fictional Arab village, who keeps a portrait of Neville Chamberlain, the White Paper's author, on his wall. The Mukhtar's "love for the hills and his country was genuine. . . . He would defend it against the intruders with cunning, courage and ruse. . . . [He] was quite prepared . . . to get himself hanged." There is Moshe, a young settler who regards the kibbutz as a socialist model, not a socialist clone: "I see no reason why we should get excited about Russia, and every reason why they should get excited about us." There are the Zionists who denounce the Irgun—"killing women and children. . . . Fanatics and lunatics, the lot of them"—and for whom Jewish-Arab unity "is as sacred to me as the Ten Commandments."[70] There are the Zionist terrorists, with their horrifyingly contemporary blending of the carnal and the chaste: "Oh, for the relief of having one's wrath exploded with a good, home-made bomb! The act of killing already appeared to him divested of its flesh-tearing, physical aspect, free from the angle of death and pain, as an almost platonic act."[71]

There are the British anti-Semites, who see themselves as philo-Semites: "I am a sincere admirer of the Jews. They are the most admirable salesmen in the world, regardless of whether they sell carpets, Marxism, psychoanalysis or their own pogromed infants." There is the American journalist Dick Matthews, who confesses that although he admires the Zionists, he doesn't really like the Jews. There are the Left Zionists who dream of introducing birth control and socialism to the Arab villagers, and those who respond that the Arabs "are illiterate and live in the thirteenth century and haven't read your Marx." There are Jews who mock the idea of a state as "a selfish, old-fashioned prejudice."[72]

And there are the young Arab intellectuals who dream of a state as the entry *into* modernity—the opposite of old-fashioned—even if they haven't read their Marx. Sounding much like Zionists on the subject of Diaspora Jews, they disparage the Arab peasants as "stupid, backward, and filthy" and insist that "the fantastic injustices of the past" be repaired. One such intellectual, Farid, reflects the rising tide of Arab self-determination, Palestinian pride, and intra-Arab divisions. He argues: "All Arab States have their Parliaments—we are denied it because it would give us a majority over the Jews. . . . Iraq is a country of savages compared to us. . . . It is all or nothing—and now."[73] To criticize these characters as stereotypes or mouthpieces misses the point; of course they are. It is precisely *as* representatives, albeit simplified, that they help illuminate the contradictions of life under the Mandate. And help, too, to reveal the ways in which the antagonists—young Jewish nationalists and young Arab nationalists—sometimes echoed each other with uncanny precision.

Much of what Koestler wrote in *Thieves* sounds absurd (circumcision anxieties? "Hebrew Tarzans"? "humanistic hormones"?), especially to a present-day reader. Yet *Thieves* is important precisely as a kind of worst-case scenario. It shows the harrowing self-contempt to which the Zionist self-critique might lead. It is a warning, too—one that obviously has not been heeded—about how humiliation can generate the seductive false pride of terrorism.

Toward the end of the novel, Joseph sums up his political credo, which doesn't sound too different from Koestler's. It is the key, I think, to why Koestler's political commitments were so erratic and, ultimately, unsustainable: "I became a socialist because I hated the poor; and I became a Hebrew [Zionist] because I hated the Yid."[74] This is the exemplary statement of a fatally conflicted Jew in flight from himself and his people. It is the essence of negative Zionism—the Zionism that, as Yehezkel Kaufmann had warned, assumes that "we must first hate ourselves" before achieving independence, autonomy, and self-respect.

Koestler visited Israel again in 1948. It did not go well. *Thieves in the Night,* which mocked the Left and praised the Irgun, had made him famous, though not necessarily beloved, among Israelis: "Every taxi driver in Tel Aviv had read *Thieves in the Night*—and was eager to argue with him."[75] Koestler had an apocalyptic view of postwar European politics—he expected the Soviets to march into Paris, where they would be joyously greeted by Sartre and Simone de Beauvoir—and he brought this mind-set to Israel. In fact, he almost completely misunderstood the politics of the new nation, and his emotional estrangement from it was patent. In both these ways, he resembled Arendt.

Koestler superimposed the history of the European Left onto Israel. He believed that the antagonism between Left Zionists and Revisionists, especially as played out in the *Altalena* affair, was a replay of Communist-Trotskyist hostilities in Spain. He charged that "under the guise of socialism" Ben-Gurion's Labor Party was creating "a totalitarian party-regime."[76] He likened what he called "Haganahism" to Nazism and Stalinism. He tried once more to convince Ben-Gurion and other Labor leaders to accept the Revisionists into the government and to take an anti-Soviet line, though nobody listened to him. Other parts of the visit weren't much better. He visited a left-wing kibbutz, where "he sneered at almost everything he saw."[77] He hated Tel Aviv.

Most of all, Koestler just didn't like the Jews, especially the "dismal fat middle-aged Jewesses." (In his diary, he wrote, "Already after a few days in this country it is a relief to have dinner with a non-Jew.") He complained that "all my old friends without exception have turned into cranks, monomaniacs or fanatics," though it's possible that some of his old friends thought the same of him. On Yom Kippur, 1948, he warned that "the Jews are a much sicker race than we all thought" and that the Jewish people's "accumulated psychic pus is threatening to flood the new state."[78] The next day he left Israel, never to return.

Promise and Fulfilment, Koestler's second book on Palestine, is a pro-Zionist work, though not because it disparages the Palestinians' fight for independence or slights their fear of Zionism. Like Arendt, Koestler took these seriously. He argued that, though Jewish settlement brought economic development to the Palestinian Arabs, this could be "no possible consolation for the fact that they [Zionists] were gradually taking the country over. The pressure of [Jewish] persecution in Europe, and their superior civilization, made their victory inevitable and in this sense 'historically just,' while according to other standards of value the fate of the Arabs remains a pathetic injustice."[79]

"Superior civilization" are the key words here. Though this concept may grate on our postcolonial sensibilities, it is one with which Marx was quite comfortable (and with which Arendt agreed). Indeed, despite the fact that Koestler was now aggressively anti-Communist, he articulates an essentially Marxist telos, albeit in an overly mechanistic version.

In Koestler's view, Zionism was morally justified due to the centuries of Jewish persecution, the Nazi onslaught, and the Yishuv's social and economic accomplishments. But the *reason* the Jews defeated the Arabs had little to do with morals and everything to do with modernity. For Koestler, the conflict of Arab versus Jew was really the conflict of rural versus industrial, illiteracy versus education, tribe versus nation, despotism versus democracy, religion versus secularism, fatalism versus activism. In short, though couched in ethnic terms, the Arab-Israeli collision essentially pitted the torpid past against the vigorous future, be it socialist or capitalist. The Zionists, Koestler wrote, "did not dispossess or victimize or exploit its [Palestine's] native owners, but substituted themselves for the former by virtue of a historic fatality. They did not come . . . with shotguns, glass beads and fire water; nor with missionaries either. . . . They were the relatively decent and humane executors of the amoral workings of history."[80]

Similarly, he argued, the Haganah won the partition war not because it was braver than the Arab fighters but "because modern European Jews had a greater capacity for initiative, improvisation and coordinated action than their primitive adversaries." And because, too, the sophisticated national unity of the Yishuv contrasted so sharply with the political disorganization of the Palestinians, who were abandoned by their leadership before the fighting started. Of the Mufti and rich landowners, Koestler observed, "Their social programme [was] mediaeval feudalism. They had preached death to Zionism and sold their land to the Jews; . . . and when the showdown came [they] were the first to sneak away to Beirut and Cairo, leaving the helpless masses in the lurch."[81]

But the real focus, and the real culprits, of *Promise and Fulfilment* are the British. Like I. F. Stone, Koestler viewed British imperialism as Zionism's chief antagonist and the major cause of Palestine's agonies, especially after 1947. (Both men would have been astounded by the contemporary British Left's view that, as Tariq Ali put it, "Israel was created in 1948 by the British Empire.")[82] Koestler indicts Britain's Middle East policies as criminal and cruel.

The Balfour Declaration, Koestler argued, was "unorthodox, unpolitic, freakish"; the idea of a Jewish National Home was a strange, indeterminate concoction that resembled "a white negro." But the persecution of the Jews, who endured "in between *autos-da-fé* and gas chambers," along with the building of the Yishuv, made that national home a necessity and a fact.[83]

Jewish and Arab Palestinians shared a resentment of British domination. Koestler argued, however, that the British strongly favored the Arabs, whom they could treat, and control, as traditional "natives." The Zionists, on the other hand, fit into no traditional colonial structure. "British rulers and Zionist pioneers lived in different worlds, spoke a different language, obeyed a different psychology. The Jews thought in terms of the prophecies of Isaiah; of Tolstoi, Marx and Herzl." To the Mandate's administrators, "Isaiah, Tolstoi and the Jewish renaissance were cloud-cuckoo-land."[84]

Koestler summed up the war years of 1939–45 as "essentially the story of Jews trying to save their skins, and of the . . . Mandatory Power to prevent this." The refusal to allow Jews into Palestine—a ban that included Jewish children from Germany and Poland—was "moral perfidy and legally absurd." After the war, hundreds of thousands of stateless survivors languished in displaced persons camps. Yet Britain, though now under a presumably pro-Zionist Labour government, continued its previous policy, thus condemning the survivors to imprisonment in new camps, return to Germany, and, sometimes, death on the seas: " 'The abstract arguments about Zionism and the Jewish State seemed curiously remote after this experience in human degradation.' "[85]

Perhaps most astonishing, the British defied the UN's 1947 partition plan and, in stark contrast to its policy in India, withdrew from Palestine without establishing any self-governing institutions among the Arabs or supporting those that existed among the Jews. Left behind was "a country without legal government, administration, police or public services, cut off from the outside world and ravaged by war." In short, the British *engineered* a catastrophe in Palestine—Koestler termed it "Operation Deluge"—drowning the country in "blood and squalor" and creating "a second Ireland in the Levant."[86]

Koestler's major point is one that would sound strange to much of the contemporary Left—and especially to much of the British Left, for whom anti-Zionism has become the almost nonnegotiable ticket of entry into Left discourse (and which has conveniently repressed Britain's nefarious role in the Arab-Israeli conflict). He argued that Zionism, far from being an extension of British imperialism, was the main *impediment* to British plans in the Middle East. The Zionists' demand, and capacity, for self-rule made British control of Palestine unworkable and redundant. Even worse, the Zionists were interlopers in Britain's desired alliance with (and desired subordination of) the Arab nations. Zionism was, in short, "the nigger in the Levantine woodpile."[87]

Koestler considered Britain's Middle East policies to be a "fanatic appeasement" of the Arab nations, inspired in part by "the bogey of 'setting the Middle East aflame.' " To gain Arab support against the Nazis, Britain had halted Jewish immigration into Palestine. To gain Arab support against the Soviets, it then fought the Yishuv and opposed partition. Britain's substitute proposal was a one-state entity, which in practice meant an Arab-dominated Palestine, though Jews were promised a "guaranteed minority status." The only problem with this plan, Koestler noted, was "the experiences of the Armenian, Greek, Syriac, Kurdish, Maronite, Hindu, Moslem, Sikh and other national or religious minorities in the East. . . . 'Guaranteed minority status' is equivalent to that of a 'licensed persecutee.' "[88] Britain's soothing assurances of multicultural tolerance could not hide the splintered, antagonistic realities of Palestine.

In Koestler's view, the main aim of the British, and especially of its traditionally pro-Arab Foreign Office, was to prevent the formation of a Jewish state; to this end it essentially used the Arab countries. Thus, Koestler charged, the British *"wanted* to be bullied and blackmailed [by the Arab states] out of their commitments to the Jews." They adopted a Machiavellian policy that exploited the Arabs—hid behind them, in effect—in order to achieve their own goals. But those goals were so inconsistent, unworkable, and obviously doomed that they defied logical explanation. "It is futile to search for rational causes," Koestler concluded. "British policy in Palestine . . . is a case-history for the psychologist."[89]

Koestler's analysis is a useful corrective to the facile view of "British-Zionist imperialism." Yet in stressing the British role in fomenting Arab-Jewish strife, he underestimated the force of genuine Palestinian and Arab nationalism, and he ignored the ways in which the Mandate had protected the Yishuv. And unlike Arendt, Koestler did not foresee the persistence of Arab-Israeli hostilities; on the contrary, he expected that Israel would become a peaceful, normal state within ten or fifteen years, "safely established in the Middle East."[90] Most of his other forecasts proved wrong too, in large part because, like Arendt, he viewed Israel through the cloudy lens of previous historic experiences. He predicted that, within a decade, Israel's raucous, multi-party electoral system would be replaced by three parties. (Today, the country's electoral system is one of the most notoriously fragmented among the advanced democracies.) He thought that the use of Hebrew would condemn Israelis to "intellectual sterility." He believed that partition would become an accepted fact and that "in fifty years' time, . . . few will take an interest" in the birth of Israel. And he predicted, not for the first time, that Israel would "become an entirely *'un-Jewish'* country."[91]

Most of all, Koestler believed that with the establishment of Israel, the unhappy Jewish story was at an end: especially for him. In his customarily Manichean fashion, he proclaimed that every Jew must now make "the vital choice": *aliyah* to Israel or Jewish nullification. In other words, it was time for every Jew who remained outside Israel to dissolve his Jewish identification, abandon "the stigma of separateness," and "cease to be an accomplice in his own destruction." The Diaspora should, indeed must, abolish itself. As for Israel, Diaspora Jews (who would no longer *be* Jews) should "wish it good luck and go their own way."[92] In this new project of de-Judaization, Arthur Koestler would lead the way.

Disentanglement proved more difficult than he had imagined. Like the man returning to the wife who, he insists, bores him, Koestler addressed the Jewish Question once again in a 1955 article called "Judah at the Crossroads: An Exhortation." It is one of his strangest essays. He reiterates his previous diktats about child-rearing: "I regard it as an outright crime for parents . . . to impose the stigma of [Jewish] 'otherliness' on a defenceless child." (Koestler is often described as childless, though he fathered an out-of-wedlock daughter, whom he refused to meet, with a married lover.) He repeats his call for assimilation, though he allows that Jews are, understandably, "touchy" on this subject. He asserts that the gentile world will welcome (former) Jews with open arms. He restates his theory that the Jews possess "no cultural tradition." He concludes, "The sooner all this is discarded, . . . the better for all concerned."[93]

What Koestler added here, far more overtly than ever before, was his analysis of the reasons for anti-Semitism. These could be encapsulated in two words: the Jews. Radically misunderstanding the Biblical covenant, Koestler argued that the Jews had appointed themselves members of a "Chosen Race"—a term traditionally used by anti-Semites—to whom God had promised "preferential treatment." Judaism was, therefore, a form of racism; why shouldn't it engender vicious resistance? "The Jewish religion, unlike any other, is racially discriminatory, nationally segregative, socially tension-creating," Koestler charged. It follows that anti-Semitism could never be ended by law, education, enlightenment, democracy, socialism, citizenship, or sovereignty. "It can only be brought to an end by Jewry itself."[94]

For Koestler, even the good things in Judaism led to bad things. The universalist message of Judaism—the "ideals of righteousness and brotherhood"—is in reality a kind of boastful presumption. In fact, it is this "turgid bombast" that "gave rise to the legend of the Elders of Zion and keeps suspicions of a Jewish world-conspiracy alive." Similarly, he charged that the observance of a Jewish Sabbath had led to the "holocausts of Jewish victims burnt, raped, robbed, chased and gassed." (Saturday instead of Sunday had, apparently, driven the world nuts—even begetting Treblinka.) Yet the stiff-necked Jews had insisted on their own course, another example of their "Lilliputian fanaticism."[95] One can picture Yehezkel Kaufmann tearing out his hair.

In his Zionist days, Koestler had expected a Jewish state to automatically solve the problem of anti-Semitism; in his Communist days, he had expected a workers' state to do so. "Judah at the Crossroads" was written only seven years after Israel's declaration of independence, yet Koestler was already impatiently lashing out at anti-Semitism's stamina. He seems to have concluded that if anti-Jewish enmity persisted even after the establishment of Israel, the fault could only lie with the Jews themselves.

As Koestler aged, he increasingly downplayed any Jewish identity and, as an old friend observed, commenced "turning into a regular British snob."[96] But he entered the Jewish—or was it the anti-Jewish?—fray one last time, in 1976, with the publication of *The Thirteenth Tribe*. This was Koestler's attempt to formulate a final—a really, truly final—answer to the Jewish Question that had tormented him throughout his life. (Torment, or at least drama, was his métier; seven years after writing *The Thirteenth Tribe*, Koestler, then aged seventy-seven, committed double suicide with his much younger wife.)

The Thirteenth Tribe takes Koestler's idea of a Jewish "race"—or, as he liked to say, "the dogma of the Chosen Race"—to a new level. The Jewish people are, of course, a mixture of races and ethnicities, including African, Arab, Persian, Berber, and European, as a walk down any street in Israel will quickly show. It has usually been anti-Semites, including Hitler, who have regarded the Jews as a race—a concept that, as the historian Hyam Maccoby wrote, "has no place in Jewish tradition."[97] None of this mattered to Koestler, who continued to deny that the Jews were a *people* with any shared history, traditions, ethics, or culture. Instead, they were simply a genetically linked group. And most members of this group, he claims in *The Thirteenth Tribe*, had descended not from the Semites of the Middle East several thousand years ago but from the Khazars, a now-defunct Turkish tribe who converted to Judaism in the eighth century.

The oddity of this book makes a cogent description difficult. Here, for example, is Koestler on the all-important Nasal Question: "The 'Jewish nose' need not be really convex in profile, and may yet give the impression of being 'hooked,' due to a peculiar 'tucking up of the wings,' an infolding [sic] of the nostrils." The kindest thing that can be (and was) said about *The Thirteenth Tribe* is that it rests on extremely slight evidence.

In Koestler's view, the "fact" that Jews were not Semites meant that *anti*-Semitism was simply a big mistake—or, as he put it in a rather astonishing phrase, "a misapprehension shared by both the killers and their victims." The centuries of exclusion, expulsion, persecution, massacre, and extermination had all been a gigantic misunderstanding based on the "cruel hoax" of the Jews' Semitic origins.[98] (If only Hitler had known the truth!) The Christian hatred of Jews as killers of Christ, the fascist hatred of Jews as Communists, the peasant hatred of Jews as capitalists, the nationalist hatred of Jews as stateless, the reactionary hatred of Jews as modernists, the Arab hatred of Jews as foreigners: All this, Koestler implied, was the result of a terrible confusion. With his new revelations, however, all that history and all that hatred would become wonderfully irrelevant. But so, too, would the Jews, for they were simply the remnant of a long-forgotten Asiatic tribe with no cultural tissue connecting them and no reason to maintain their irksome existence. Presto! The Jewish Problem had been solved.

For decades, Koestler had wrestled with his Jewish identity, alternately fixating on and repressing it. With *The Thirteenth Tribe*, he had finally found a way, as one biographer put it, to "emancipate himself from the 'seed of Abraham' . . . by tracing his lineage to the loins of the Khazar tribesmen."[99] In other words, Koestler had entered what he had once derided as cloud-cuckoo-land.

Arthur Koestler's life and politics were full of sharp dissonances. He was a militant who did not fight. He was a Zionist who was disgusted by Jews. He was a Communist who detested physical labor. He was heir to European Jewry's fertile culture, whose existence he denied. But the greatest irony, perhaps, is that he advocated the auto-dissolution of the Jews, which was a traditionally Marxist position, precisely at the time when he zealously opposed Communism and socialism in all their forms.

A long line of Marxist thinkers regarded the Jewish people as a reactionary, though occasionally heart-warming, anachronism who should and would disappear with the victory of the world revolution. Many though not all of these theorists were Jewish. A young Karl Marx wrote that, because Judaism's essence was "practical need, selfishness, . . . haggling and money," a truly free world entailed "the emancipation of humanity from Judaism."[100] Karl Kautsky believed that "the Jewish nation can only triumph by disappearing." Victor Adler was confident that socialism would lead the Jew "to his tomb."[101] Otto Bauer described the Jews as "a historyless nation" with a "stunted" culture and "decayed" language who had no place in the modern world.[102]

Koestler came to regard Communism as worse than Nazism, yet he echoed these revolutionary Left theorists, sometimes almost verbatim. He thus participated in what the historian Robert S. Wistrich has called an "ethnic death-wish"—a peculiar, and perhaps peculiarly Jewish, phenomenon.[103] As we'll see in the following chapter, Koestler's ideas on the Jewish people closely aligned with those of his contemporary Maxime Rodinson, a lifelong Marxist and anti-Zionist whose politics Koestler would no doubt have detested with the absolutist fervor that defined him throughout a lifetime of tortuous, and tortured, contortions.

PART TWO SOCIALISTS

CHAPTER THREE

Maxime Rodinson

MARXISM, ZIONISM, AND THE ARAB WORLD

"I DO NOT KNOW WHETHER I AM the most famous anti-Zionist in France," Maxime Rodinson wondered in 1981.[1] The answer was probably yes, and it was equally likely that this would have pleased him. A member of the French Communist Party for two decades and then an independent Marxist, Rodinson leveled a critique of Zionism that remains highly influential among leftist intellectuals in the West and some parts of the Arab world. His long article "Israël, fait colonial?," subsequently published in English as a book and translated into Arabic, was the leadoff of *Les Temps Modernes'* landmark 1967 issue on Israel and Palestine. Rodinson answered that question, too, in the affirmative, and his arguments became an authoritative bedrock for many in the New Left. Fred Halliday regarded Rodinson as a moral and intellectual exemplar, while I. F. Stone praised the *Temps Modernes* piece as "by far the most brilliant in the whole volume"—this in an issue that contained forty-seven contributors and ran to almost a thousand pages.[2] But Claude Lanzmann, who edited the issue, later regretted running the piece, and Jean-Paul Sartre suggested that Rodinson be psychoanalyzed to cure his Jewish self-hatred. Rodinson replied that "others, doubtless with somewhat greater justification, have accused me of self-love."[3]

Rodinson's work is important not only for its influence. Equally germane, it bridges the Old Left and the New, and illustrates the continuities and disjunctions between them. Rodinson tried to break with his Stalinist past, yet in crucial ways remained a prisoner of it. In Rodinson's work we can trace the Western Left's trajectory—I would not call it a progression—from defining itself, *as* itself, in the fight for social justice and against fascism to aligning itself as a subsidiary ally in the anti-colonialist struggle. This signaled a fundamental shift in analysis, orientation, and ethics that haunts debates over Israel to this day.

Rodinson was consistently anti-Zionist: so much so that, in my view, he often mounted inexcusably contorted arguments to support his antipathies. Sometimes those arguments contradicted the Marxist universalism that he professed as his greatest value. (Today, those arguments are freely quoted—if not verbatim, then in substance.) Yet he also defied the logic of his anti-Zionism and steadily advocated the two-state solution: even, at times, when addressing an irredentist Arab public. Rodinson's work embraced many contradictions; he was not an easily categorized man.

Maxime Rodinson was born in Paris in 1915 into a working-class family. His parents were Russian Jews who came to France in flight from pogroms. They were secular, anti-Zionist, assimilationist, and Communist—"Russian Stalinists," in Maxime's words, and in each of these identities, ardently so. Maxime's father, Moise, was a garment worker who played chess with Trotsky, organized Jewish trade unions, and helped establish a library for Jewish workers that contained books in Yiddish, Russian, and French; he also "helped preserve the library where Lenin used to look for books," Maxime would proudly recall.[4] His mother spoke Yiddish and had a "horror of rabbis." As a very young child, Rodinson accompanied his mother to left-wing demonstrations, and he taught himself to read by studying the Communist daily *L'Humanité*, which he picked up for the family each morning. Maxime's parents became Soviet citizens in 1924, and although Maxime and his mother wanted to leave France for the USSR, Moise "understood how things were in Russia," as Rodinson later somewhat cryptically explained.[5] In any event, the family stayed. "Everybody around us was anti-Zionist," Rodinson recalled. "My parents, my friends, we were all internationalists, and we had no interest in Jewish nationalism."[6]

The Rodinsons' poverty forced Maxime to quit school when he reached adolescence; he worked as an errand boy and was essentially self-educated. His intellectual drive and aptitude were phenomenal; he studied Greek, Latin, history, and literature on his own. At the age of ten or eleven, he developed a fascination with Islam and began to research it—hardly a typical pursuit for a Jewish boy in France. In 1932, aged seventeen, he passed the rigorous exam for the prestigious École des Langues Orientales despite his lack of formal academic training.

Rodinson became a student, and then a scholar, of Islam and the Arab world—became, in other words, an Orientalist, a term that was unproblematic for him. (He described Edward Said's work on the subject as "a polemic" that was "a bit Stalinist," and was puzzled by the book's popularity in the United States.) He was fluent in multiple languages, including Arabic, Hebrew, Turkish, Spanish, and Amharic. The Hebrew studies displeased his parents: " 'Look how he has stumbled into such foolishness,' " they said.[7]

In 1937—the year of Stalin's purges, the Spanish Civil War, the French Popular Front, and increasing fascist strength throughout Europe—Rodinson joined the French Communist Party; two decades later, he was expelled for publishing unapproved writings. His major books include *Islam and Capitalism, Marxism and the Muslim World, Israel and the Arabs,* and a biography of Muhammad that analyzes the prophet from a materialist and sociological viewpoint rather than a sacred one. Islam's founder had fascinated Rodinson since childhood, and he considered this book "dearest to my heart," though it has been banned in parts of the Arab and Muslim worlds and has not been translated into Arabic. "Probably in an unconscious fashion, I compared him to Stalin," Rodinson once mused. "Both were men of conviction who became men of state. In both cases, true believers were forced by circumstances to face reality, to change, and to resort to the use of power."[8]

In 1940, just before France fell to the Nazis, Rodinson was appointed to the auxiliary military service and sent to Beirut; he soon obtained a teaching post at the French Institute of Arab Studies in Damascus. He remained safely in Syria and Lebanon for seven years—the years of the Shoah—and returned to Paris in 1947. His parents were less lucky: Both were murdered in Auschwitz. Rodinson went on to a prestigious and prolific academic career at the Bibliothèque Nationale and the École Pratique des Hautes Études. He died in 2004 at age eighty-nine.

Though he frequently wrote about Israel and Zionism, Rodinson's main areas of research were the Arab world and Islam. (He often used generalized terms such as "the Arab world," "the Arab people," "the Arab masses," and "the Arab nation.") He consistently asserted a materialist view and wrote, in particular, against the idea of a static, eternal Islamic realm: "The orientalist view that the Muslim world today is simply a continuation of that of yesterday is sheer fantasy." But he argued, too, against Left intellectuals who denied the importance of religion and culture, and he assailed "the infantile . . . 'Third Worldist' revolutionaries who reduce the cause of all international conflicts, past, present, and future, to the dynamic of the capitalist economy and nothing more." He was aware that the East was not simply a less developed version of the West. "The Islamic world has not witnessed the death of God," he warned in 1978, a year before the Iranian Revolution; consequently, the Muslim world had failed to develop an "ideology of moral freedom."[9]

Rodinson was a firm secularist, a stance that caused him trouble in the Arab world, where he was sometimes accused of lacking respect for Islam (and worse). In the early 1960s, when Western leftists were flummoxed by the religious authoritarianism in many newly decolonized countries—"Was it worth fighting to bring to power a moral order that turns out to be a virtual Inquisition?" Rodinson asked—he insisted that the Left continue to assert the values of religious tolerance and separation of religion and state; history had shown that the alternative was persecution, expulsion, and extermination of the Other. He decried the demagogy of leftists who shielded their secularism from the masses as "atheism that is almost ashamed of itself." The intellectual fraudulence, and sheer silliness, of those who claimed to see precursors of Marx, Lenin, and even Mao in the Koran evoked his scorn. Marx "would have been rather surprised," Rodinson noted wryly, to learn that his works prove that "one must believe in a paradise inhabited by houris."[10]

In the 1960s, when the secular political movements of Nasserism and Baathism dominated much of the Arab world, Rodinson foresaw how deadly what we now call political Islam would become (though he could not, of course, have predicted the rise of groups like ISIS). Combining "fanaticism in the service of God" with social goals will wreak "devastating violence," he warned in 1963.[11] He argued that Islam was not inherently incompatible with social progress and intellectual tolerance—he was, of course, well aware of its achievements in former eras. But those eras were long past and could not be romantically recreated. "We are living in the twentieth century. The times are gone when a religious ideology could lead the masses to progressive temporal activity." Rodinson's observations of 1963 are still true, *more* true, today: "Leftist Islam does not exist as a coherent ideology. Rightist Islam, however, is very active." And yet he understood the sturdy, perhaps unshakable role that religion plays in those parts of the world where secularism and anti-clericalism are identified with the repressive state, the ruling class, and foreign conquest. Nor did he belittle spiritual needs. Religion, he wrote, is "responding to the cry of anguish and existential wretchedness that we all feel."[12] In Rodinson's work, religion is neither mere superstition nor part of a secondary superstructure; this understanding is all too rare, even today, among some secularists.

Rodinson often challenged his audiences. In a 1969 speech in Cairo, attended by students from the Islamic university Al-Azhar, he implored his listeners to create a culture of self-criticism, which signaled "that the human conscience is not dead." And he admonished, "There is no holy people." In Algiers in the mid-sixties, he argued for universal rights and an open society: "Societies that turn in upon themselves . . . are societies that are dying."[13] He was not afraid to reassess (some of) his ideas. Thus, in 1978, he caustically observed that socialist-oriented Arab nationalism, especially of the Nasserist tendency, had failed to forge "an escape from economic dependence and underdevelopment. The only achievements of the great Arab nation in the field of power politics and national prestige have been the work of the oil potentates—the most fundamentalist and conservative of Muslims—in selling their oil with the haggling of skilled businessmen and technocrats."[14] The Arab nations, he noted, had been unable even to best puny Israel.

Rodinson knew enough about the Arab and Muslim worlds not to mistake their national liberation movements for social—much less socialist—revolutions. In fact, in 1969 he observed that Marxist movements in the Arab world were almost completely fixated on nationalism at the expense of socialism's traditional universalism. But he was haunted, or at least chastened, by the Communist movement's traditional dismissal of nationalism, which had cost it so much credibility in the Arab world. Time and again he asserted national self-determination as a constituent part of socialism. "Nationalist struggles . . . [are] a necessary stage when the rights of a nation that has been humiliated, oppressed, or even threatened have to be defended." Socialists, he wrote, must link themselves with "the struggle to attain, defend, and consolidate national independence. . . . This struggle is part of the liberating ideal of all socialists."[15] The great exception to this liberating ideal was Jewish nationalism—that is, Zionism—which he regarded as emotionally repellent and politically regressive.

Perhaps because of his extensive travels and contacts in the Arab world, Rodinson reserved his contempt for one particular group: stay-at-home revolutionaries who, from the comfort of the metropolis, urge others into battle. "I marvel at the lack of conscience of Parisian revolutionaries who (like some others) think they have a right to encourage peoples far away to follow a path of agony and bloodshed because they are convinced that it will lead those people—or at least those that survive—to happiness," he wrote in 1978. "If that is Marxism, then I confess openly, I am not a Marxist." He was acutely aware that he should not dictate programs or policies to Left movements in the Third World in the way that the Soviets had imposed their will on local Communist parties. But this abstention would lead him to the opposite mistake: He would fail to adequately confront the moral abyss of terrorism. "True friendship needs honesty," Rodinson told his Algiers audience.[16] He did not always heed this advice.

Though it was not his major focus, Rodinson wrote several books that addressed the Arab-Israeli conflict. In what follows, I will concentrate primarily on those books and related articles (in English translation).

In his controversial contribution to *Les Temps Modernes,* Rodinson laid out not only his indictment of Israel as a colonial state but also, by implication, his analysis of the proper role for the Western Left. The essay is a curious one, because many of Rodinson's key points seem to belie rather than support his conclusions. The piece was a revised version of one he had written in 1953, which he described as "my Stalinist article . . . but I deepened the analysis."[17]

Rodinson begins by quoting an unnamed Lebanese Communist: "The Zionist movement is nothing but . . . exploitation, for the profit of Jewish capitalists. . . . [Israel is] a commercial undertaking and a colonialist platform."[18] Rodinson proceeds to argue *against* this, often sounding like, well, a Zionist. "The motivations of the masses who gave the Zionist movement its strength had little in common with . . . British capitalists," he noted. Zionism grew out of "deep disgust with the oppressive conditions"; the revolt of Zionist Jews was "as justifiable as any other." Moreover, it was "certainly true that the masses" who built the Yishuv were socialist; indeed, the kibbutzim were "perhaps the most advanced example ever seen" of socialism. (A socialism that, he would later note, was free of deportations, purges, and firing squads.) Rodinson points out that the Zionists acquired land legally rather than by theft or military conquest, and that they did not exploit Arab labor. Though the Zionists' disregard for the Arab inhabitants of Palestine was arrogant and led to future conflict, it resulted from "a quite excusable and understandable indifference" rather than a desire to dominate.[19] And after the 1948 war, he argues, the new state's fear of the Arab minority as a potential fifth column was justifiable.

The Jews were desperate people who settled Palestine not to enrich themselves or immiserate others but, Rodinson explains, "because it was the life preserver thrown to them. They most assuredly did not first engage in scholarly research to find out if they had a right to it according to Kantian morality or existentialist ethics." Then came the Shoah, which "lent the call to battle [for a Jewish state] a humane quality without equal."[20]

As for colonialism: Rodinson explains that, in the nineteenth and early twentieth centuries, the word as well as the concept "was essentially taken to mean the spreading of progress, civilization and well-being."[21] The Zionists' oft-condemned search for support from the imperialist states was no different from the Arab nationalist movements' search for support from the imperialist states; moreover, this search was strategically smart, since the imperialist states were the powerful ones. (The massacre of the Armenians was a lesson in the perils of international isolation.) Zionist tactics were, therefore, "perfectly natural given the atmosphere of the period. There is no need for us to moralize." In any case, "belonging to a colonizing group is not the unspeakable and unpardonable crime it is thought to be in cafes along Saint-Germain and Saint-Michel boulevards. Who is innocent of this charge? The only variable lies in the time that has elapsed since the usurping was done. . . . History is full of faits accomplis."[22] For substantial portions of this piece, Rodinson seems to be—and is—constructing a Zionist case.

Then comes the turnabout. After establishing a good argument for the existence of a Jewish state and for the *kind* of Jewish state that the

Zionists created, Rodinson declares that none of this is "at all pertinent." Only one thing matters: "For the Arab masses, acceptance of the UN decisions would have meant unconditional capitulation to a European *diktat*." Furthermore—despite his previous arguments to the contrary—"there is nothing that would lessen the colonial character" of Zionism.[23]

Rodinson does make a rare acknowledgment here—one that, to my knowledge, he never repeated. He admits that had the Arabs accepted the 1947 partition, "the colonial situation could have been left behind at this point and two states, recognized by the UN, could have entered into the realm of international politics." But in his view this refusal, which has had such devastating consequences, cannot be judged or, even, critiqued. He abjures taking any position on "what could or should have been done according to various moral criteria" in 1947 or 1948 (a reticence that would be impossible to imagine on the part of Lenin or other Bolsheviks). Only the insult to Arab pride matters: "The creation of the State of Israel was an outrage committed against the Arabs as a people."[24]

According to this view, nothing can erase Israel's original sin, and every reaction to that sin is rational. "If there is indeed hatred [by Arabs for Israel] that often exceeds all bounds," Rodinson wrote, "it is all based on an objective reality for which the Zionist leaders are responsible: the colonization of a foreign land."[25] And though Rodinson preferred "bloodless solutions"—which distinguished him from the Palestine Liberation Organization and virtually all Arab states at the time—his role, and that of the Left, was to support those who have been so grievously injured. "It is up to the Arabs, who are the ones who have been wronged, to determine what their policy toward Israel will be."[26] Where they lead, he will follow. Nor can any self-defined anti-colonialist make a "moral condemnation" of the Palestinians' use of violence in whatever forms it takes. Rodinson had insisted that the secular Left not pander to what he called the Arab masses on religious grounds; now he was arguing that the anti-imperialist Left *should* pander to the Arab masses on emotional grounds. Easing humiliation was, apparently, the Left's primary task.

Rodinson's 1967 essay is often cited as one of the first to explicate the anti-colonial argument against Israel. But in my view, the subsidiary role for the Left that he envisioned was equally important and, perhaps, had a wider effect. He would reiterate his view of this new position, which sometimes mutated into servility; it would be adopted by a wide array of New

Left activists and intellectuals. Yet it strikes me that this subordinate role was not entirely unprecedented. Rodinson was essentially replicating the servile position of the French Communist Party, perhaps the most Stalinist in Western Europe, vis-à-vis the Soviet Union. Now the Palestinian movement and the "Arab masses" would assume the paramount position, the vanguard position, which the USSR formerly occupied.

This stance posed particular dangers for Rodinson. It would lead him to rationalize the inexcusable: lead him, that is, into a moral quagmire. He was in no way an advocate of terrorism, and he rightly condemned spectators of the Arab-Israeli conflict who incited violence "from a safe and tranquil vantage point."[27] There is no sign of blood lust or vengeance in his work, nor any idealization of the presumably healing properties of violence à la Fanon.

In fact, throughout his writings on Israel and Palestine, Rodinson tried to dissociate himself from Palestinian terrorism. But rather than condemn it openly, as would Fred Halliday, he referred to it with euphemistic vagueness. Thus he wrote, in 1984, that support of the Palestinian resistance "in no way necessarily implies approval of the programs, strategies, tactics, actions, and ideas" of the movement.[28] But what remains of a movement aside from its programs, strategies, tactics, actions, and ideas—especially when, as Rodinson admitted, those tactics "dominate" the movement?

And despite his own nonviolent proclivities, Rodinson was careful to remember his place. The denizen of the First World must not speak too much truth to his Third World brothers, even if he foresaw the ensuing debacles. Thus, in a 1972 dialogue with Daud Talhami of the Democratic Front for the Liberation of Palestine (DFLP), Rodinson expresses some hesitation about the "strategy and tactics" of the Palestinian groups. But, he assures Talhami, "In no way do I desire to enter into discussion and conflict with the representatives of the Palestinian people."[29] This was a time when Palestinian "strategy and tactics" included airplane hijackings and the deliberate murder of Israeli and Jewish civilians in Israel and Europe; 1972 was the year when the Israeli athletes at the Munich Olympics were killed. And in the competition for propaganda-through-terrorism, the DFLP was one of the most notoriously ruthless groups. (Two years after the interview with Rodinson, its guerrillas stormed a school in Ma'alot and murdered more than twenty Israeli students, one of the most loathed events in Israeli history.) Talhami makes clear that in his view "only the language of revolutionary violence can answer the language of Zionist domination"—and, ominously, singles out the revolutionary violence of the Cambodians for particular praise.[30] Given all this, perhaps more "discussion and conflict" were called for on Rodinson's part.

Rodinson's unfortunate delicacy is also on display in his 1968 book *Israel and the Arabs*. He warns the Arab world against the horrific bloodshed that would ensue from an all-out war against Israel and other presumably imperialist states: a war that Mao, the Syrian Baathist government, and other ultra-leftists were urging. Again, though, he immediately demurs, "One is hardly in a position to make moral strictures, however terrible the consequences."[31] Yet Rodinson, who had the ear of many Arab intellectuals, was in an unusually *good* position to forcefully raise such issues. When it came to the Palestinians, his concept of solidarity morphed into the evasion of fundamental ethical questions. Yet Rodinson knew, from his years in the Communist Party, that this supine approach had repeatedly led the Left to moral bankruptcy.

Like Hannah Arendt, Rodinson acknowledged Zionism's accomplishments in agriculture, industry, and the socialist collectives, as well as the suffering and hard work that had produced them. He described Israel in 1968 as "virile, modern and forward-looking."[32] Still, he judged Zionism and the state it created to be a resounding failure. The roots of this judgment can be found, in part, in his unusually rosy analysis of Jewish assimilation. In this respect, he was the antithesis of Arendt, who viewed assimilation as a tragic delusion.

Although the French Revolution had emancipated the Jews, they continued to be seen as separate and not-quite-French. This view was fostered even by some liberals, revolutionaries, and Enlightenment philosophers. In his *Philosophical Dictionary,* Voltaire had described the Jews as "an ignorant and barbarous people, which have long combined the most sordid avarice and the most despicable superstition," while Diderot believed that the Jews "must form a nation apart."[33] The idea of the Jews as an (inferior) nation within a nation ebbed and flowed, though it never disappeared. But it did not achieve fatal meanings until Vichy.

Assimilation remained the goal—"the dominant project of central and Western European Jewry from the French Revolution to the

Holocaust," as historian Martin Kramer wrote.[34] What distinguished Rodinson is his belief that this project had succeeded. In the late nineteenth and early twentieth centuries, he wrote, "Judaism was on the road to complete liquidation." (This last word, which Rodinson frequently used, was an oddly creepy choice given its Nazi and Stalinist connotations.) By the eve of World War II, he argued, the disappearance of Judaism, and of Jewish communities, had been almost achieved. Furthermore, "it is hard to see any reason to consider this trend catastrophic."[35] But it was not only the Jewish religion that was disappearing; so too were the Jewish people, and this too was salutary. In the course of the eighteenth and nineteenth centuries, Jewish communities became "free associations much like political parties or chess clubs," Rodinson claimed. "The notion of a 'Jewish people' had now become outdated. . . . Thus assimilation triumphed, to a greater or lesser degree."[36]

That Rodinson's parents were deported to Auschwitz—by their French compatriots, no less—suggests that this triumph was not quite complete and that Jews were not likened to chess players. In fact, it seems hard to escape Arendt's insight that assimilation was a one-way street on which only the beguiled Jews traveled. Rodinson took the opposite view. "Among the Jews of Eastern and Central European origin," he insisted, "Jewish identity in twentieth century Europe was but a residual phenomenon."[37] Given this virtual erasure, there was no reason to maintain any sort of Jewish community or culture. Marxist theorist Karl Kautsky had believed that the Jews would "triumph by disappearing," but that was decades before the Shoah; Rodinson believed it decades afterwards.

What stopped this gratifying process of liquidation? Nazism, about which Rodinson says little, and Zionism, about which he says a lot. In his view the two were linked, though perhaps not in the usual ways. Rodinson regarded each as a form of coercion; thus he wrote of "people who are Jews only in the Hitlerite and Zionist sense of the word."[38] He repeatedly assailed Zionism for preserving a consciousness of Jewish national identity and collectivity—as if such consciousness should or could have evaporated after the Shoah. The creation of Israel, Rodinson complained, "encouraged sentiments of solidarity among Jews everywhere. . . . I do not believe that this is anything to be happy about." Israel had burdened secular, assimilated Jews with an unwanted identity: "In the countries in which the 'Jewish problem' was on the road to liquidation, Jewish identity has been kept alive for many Jews who did not at all desire it." Rodinson even claimed that "the unconditional solidarity of many Jews throughout the world with Israel . . . confers an apparent plausibility upon" the concept of "the Jewish mobilization for world conquest"—specifically, he wrote, as expressed in the *Protocols of the Elders of Zion.*[39] Like Arthur Koestler, Rodinson believed that Jews were in large part responsible for the hatred of them.

Questions of assimilation and of Jewish solidarity were personal ones for Rodinson. He believed that Israel's actions—and existence—tarnished anti-Zionist Jews such as he. Though he had adhered to the Communist line in 1947, which supported the establishment of a Jewish state, "I did not like it all," he recalled three decades later. "Quite selfishly, I was unhappy about the difficulties this situation held in store for me person-ally."[40] This sense of Israel as a personal affront runs throughout his work. "All the Jews of the earth find themselves caught up, without having been consulted, in the consequences of decisions taken in Jerusalem by a small group of persons whom they did not choose," he protested in 1984. He regarded this as a "shocking and dangerous" situation.[41]

Rodinson's resentment against what he took to be Zionist hegemony over the Jewish world led him to oppose German reparations to Israel. While this had been a furiously contested issue in Israel in the early 1950s, his belated argument was an unusual one. "Among the millions of Jews massacred, many were anti-Zionist or at least non-Zionist," he wrote in 1984. "But that has not prevented the Zionist state from collecting, for its own profit and for the benefit of its projects and decisions, the price of their blood."[42] He seemed unbothered by the fact that, in Israel, the most vociferous opposition to reparations had come from the Revisionist Right, led by Menachem Begin.

This is not to say that Rodinson lacked a Jewish identity. "I feel emotionally concerned with anything that has to do with the Jews in general," he told the DFLP's Talhami.[43] But unlike Bernard Lazare and Albert Memmi, Rodinson maintained that universality and Jewish identity, and certainly Zionist identity, were antonyms. His connection to anything Jewish consisted mainly of *negative* feelings. "The trend I belong to feels a certain repulsion, an irritation, a discomfort vis-à-vis an atmosphere that is specifically and exclusively Jewish," he said, thus joining similarly irritated precursors like Luxemburg and Trotsky.[44] Rodinson's distaste for Jewish culture and tradition sometimes took extreme forms: He wrote that the Sharia practice of amputating hands and stoning adulterers to death is "perhaps a little less spectacular" than Jewish circumcision.[45]

Rodinson felt that his main responsibility as a Jew was to "put one's own house in order" by opposing Zionism.[46] Of course, self-criticism *is* a key part of the Jewish (and Zionist) tradition; dare I suggest there was something quintessentially Jewish—a phrase Rodinson would surely have abhorred—about his approach to Israel? But for him, self-criticism constituted the *entirety* of Jewish identity, or at least the only part worthy of preservation.

And though Rodinson's internationalism was staunchly proclaimed, there were odd aspects to it. He described Israel as a state created "by foreigners for the benefit of other foreigners"; it was an "alien body" imposed on what he consistently called an "Arab country."[47] (This had been the standard Stalinist line until the 1947 partition vote, and it was resumed afterwards.) These descriptions would certainly have confounded Jews who were born in Palestine or Israel. More important: Why is an internationalist using phrases like "alien body" to describe immigrants, especially when many were stateless refugees? Like Arendt's use of "selection" (or Rodinson's of "liquidation"), "foreign" and "alien" have a long and sinister place in Jewish history. Surely Rodinson knew that, for centuries, Jews had been persecuted and expelled from country after country as unwanted aliens. Surely he knew that this was one of Vichy France's rationales for sending his Russian-born parents to their deaths. Surely he knew that the confluence of "Jewish," "foreign," and "alien" was a keystone of fascist and Nazi propaganda; as Isaac Deutscher wrote, "Jews, get out!" was "the old cry" of Europe's anti-Semitic Right.[48] The notion of the alien, disloyal Jew also served as the excuse for anti-Semitic persecutions in the postwar Communist bloc.

There is something disconcerting about Rodinson reviving this language and this idea; suddenly, this cosmopolitan man seems to search for ethnic purity or nativist authenticity. And even on its own dubious terms, Rodinson's charge made little sense. Israel was, certainly, a nation of immigrants, but by the early 1950s a large segment of its population was composed of Jews from the Arab countries—who, not incidentally, had been viewed as "alien" by their Arab neighbors and expelled as such. (This nativism has been revived by the Boycott, Divestment, Sanctions movement. Co-founder Omar Barghouti, who was born in Qatar and raised in Egypt, describes himself as an "indigenous" Palestinian with "*inalienable* rights," while all Jewish Israelis, regardless of birthplace, have only "the *acquired* rights of . . . colonial settlers.")[49]

If Jews were alien to the Middle East—despite having lived there for thousands of years—and had been exterminated in Europe, it is not at all clear where Rodinson thought they should go. This means he had no answer to the Jewish Question. Thus his belief in total assimilation, however fictitious it had proved to be.

According to Rodinson, Israel's baneful effects stretched far beyond its obstruction of Jewish assimilation or, even, its displacement of the Palestinians. Zionism was such a terrible idea, and the State of Israel such a terrible reality, that the situation of the Jews "is more tragic under this glory [Israel] than it often was under humiliation," he wrote in 1968. Far from solving the Jewish Problem, Israel had "played a capital role in regenerating anti-Semitism" in the Arab world where, Rodinson incorrectly claimed, it had been virtually unknown; in Europe; and in the Communist bloc. ("Some Soviet Jews . . . support Zionist ideology. . . . Naturally, this arouses the animosity of the Soviet regime.")[50] The creation of Israel had also led to the expulsion of hundreds of thousands of Jews from the Arab countries, an expulsion that Rodinson regarded as "inevitable" and that did not seem to bother him. (Albert Memmi, born in Tunisia, would have much to say on this.)

And Israel was bad for the Jews. It had yanked them away from their universalist traditions, especially that of the Biblical prophets, whom Rodinson seemed to view as premature anti-Zionists. Whereas Arendt thought that universalism had failed the Jews, Rodinson believed that the Jews had failed universalism. Whereas the Zionist founders envisioned an Israel that would embody the prophetic tradition, Rodinson believed that Jewish sovereignty negated it.

In Rodinson's telling, Israel's effect on Arab culture and politics was even worse. Israel was significantly responsible for the backward state of the Arab countries because the Jewish state "diverts much of the energy and resources of the Arab world from more constructive tasks." Arabs had few options in this matter: "Arab hostility to Israel," Rodinson claimed, "is a necessity arising from the nature of the choices open to the

Arabs in the modern world."[51] In addition, Israel had "partly stemmed" the secularization of the Arab world, a process that, in Rodinson's view, had been proceeding nicely apace.

Emerging from all this is the question of causal relations and culpability, which is at the very heart of every historian's work. It is the historian's job to ask: What led to what? What caused what? Who is responsible? Rodinson addressed these topics in peculiarly confused ways. This confusion is important, for the question of causation is central to the formation of political and moral judgments, and the answers to it have far-reaching consequences.

To say that A led to B—or that B was a reaction to A—is not to say that A is responsible for B. For instance, one could posit (and I suspect Rodinson would have) that fascism was, in part, a reaction to the Russian Revolution. But this does not mean that the Bolsheviks built Auschwitz. Similarly, there is no doubt that the abolition of slavery in the U.S. led to the founding of the Ku Klux Klan and, then, to egregious levels of racist violence, including lynchings, for decades to come. But this does not mean that the abolitionist movement perpetrated those crimes. Nor can feminism be blamed for the backlash against it, including rape and other forms of sexual violence.

This is not to suggest that historic connections and historic causations should not be explored; on the contrary, they must be. This is, for example, the subject of the German historian Götz Aly's 2014 book *Why the Germans? Why the Jews?* Aly argues that a pathological response by Germans to the intellectual and economic achievements of the Jews was a major cause of the Nazis' rise to power and the subsequent genocide. But Aly's moral emphasis is squarely on the pathology, not the achievements; he never suggests that the Jews should have quelled themselves, nor does he indulge in counterfactual fantasies about what would have happened had they done so.

I am not in any way equating opponents of Israel with the Nazis, or the Israeli-Palestinian conflict with the Shoah. I am arguing, however, that when it came to the Arab world's reaction to the founding of Israel, Rodinson's reasoning went askew. The Arabs' eliminationist fury, the anti-modern deformation of Arab societies, the tyrannical nature of their governments, terrorism, the persistence of virulent anti-Semitism . . . Rodinson's unmistakable message was: *Israel caused all this.* The equally unmistakable subtext: If Israel had never existed, what a happy—or at least immeasurably better—place the world would be.

In 1981, Rodinson published an essay titled "Self-Criticism" that looked back on his two decades as a member of the French Communist Party—which, he noted, has "correctly been called Stalinist." "Self-Criticism" is a fascinating piece, and an admirable one in many ways. Unlike many ex-Communists, Rodinson remained a Marxist, and he eschewed the abject self-flagellation in which many former comrades indulged, "as if they had been imbeciles or scoundrels for a certain period of their lives." Nor was Rodinson willing to dismiss Communism as a mistake. "We who paid heed to this demon must blush at our naiveté and at having been unable to gauge accurately the point at which we crossed the threshold into the realm of tyranny. But we have no reason to be ashamed of having been lured by that song, which awakened all that was best in us."[52] Surprisingly, Arthur Koestler held a similar view, at least sometimes. In 1952, he wrote, "In the nineteen-thirties conversion to the Communist faith was not a fashion or craze—it was a sincere and spontaneous expression of an optimism born of despair. . . . We were wrong for the right reasons. . . . There is a world of difference between a disenchanted lover and those incapable of love."[53]

It is easy to understand why Koestler, Rodinson, and millions of others joined the Communist Party in the 1930s, given the worldwide collapse of capitalism and the rise of fascism. Rodinson cited more personal motives too. His parents were proletarian Communists, and he counted himself among "the humiliated and oppressed. . . . The origin of my party membership was a general moral indignation." The question is not why he joined but why he stayed—even through the postwar events of the Slansky trial, the Doctors' Plot, Khrushchev's 1956 speech, and the invasion of Hungary. Rodinson framed the issue well: How, he asked, does a "pure beginning" lead to "complicity in tragic and criminal manoeuvres?"[54] (This is the question many left-wing Zionists, looking at the decades-long Occupation, ask themselves today.) Rodinson offered various answers, including the need to believe that there was at least one place—the Soviet Union—in which a just and egalitarian world was being built.

Today, it is fashionable to ridicule this faith, and easy to forget that it was not confined to Party members. Claude Lanzmann, never a

Communist, recalled, "For a long time the Soviet Union remained like a sky above my head, as it did above those of many men of my generation. . . . And in spite of everything, to our minds it remained the cradle, the future, the assurance of mankind's emancipation."[55] Rodinson recounted how, as the years passed, this sort of yearning merged with "the visceral need not to renounce a commitment that has illuminated one's life." The result, understandable and lamentable, was "the reluctance to recognize the most obvious facts," which led, finally, to "passionate and obstinate blindness." In a rare moment of tenderness, he described leaving the Party, in terms that echoed Koestler's, as "like the moment at which you finally admit that someone you loved does not deserve your love." In the future, he hoped "to avoid falling into a similar mechanism, even if in the interest of another 'good cause.' "[56]

In a slightly earlier essay that addressed the same topic, Rodinson made an astonishing statement: one that sheds light on his worldview while also complicating it. He cites the need for Party obedience—"no army can win without discipline"—though he admits that the Party soldier "might well feel that his orders were sometimes unnecessarily brutal and inhuman." Then he adds: "Yet that radiant world that victory was to bring would free millions of children, *infinitely more innocent than Radek, Rajk, or Slansky*, from . . . eking out a wretched life of poverty."[57] The reference is to three Communist militants (two of them Jewish) who were killed after Stalinist show trials. The claim is an unnerving one, and it leads me to wonder: Why were these three less innocent than the impoverished children of the world? Because of the things they had done in service to the Communist cause? Because of the things they had not done in service to the Communist cause? Is Rodinson implying that the three were somehow *guilty* of the trumped-up charges against them? What is the presumed logic here? More to the point: How could the framing, torture, and murder of innocent Party members somehow help exploited children? How, in short, can one kind of suffering and injustice rationalize the creation of another kind of suffering and injustice?

To his credit, Rodinson never feigned innocence or pretended that he was ignorant of Communism's crimes. "From the very first years, it was possible to know all about the authoritarianism of the Bolshevik Party, the inhuman treatment to which its opponents were subjected, the contempt for the right of peoples to self-determination, the stifling of any critical voice, the atrocities of the repression inflicted on protesting workers and peasants as well as members of the working classes," he bluntly wrote in the 1981 essay.[58] But here, I think, is the abrupt endpoint of his self-perception. He did not acknowledge that these Stalinist crimes in the past—terror, torture, murder—were eerily close to the crimes in the present of the Arab dictatorships (led by Saddam, Assad, Qaddafi, Nimeiry), which he extolled as a *progressive,* or at least necessary, force in their opposition to Israel. In seeking what he believed to be another "good cause"—this time, Palestinian independence—and in his continuing need to find a revolutionary force that would transform the world, Rodinson substituted one blackened sun for another. The obedience he had offered to the Soviets was now bequeathed to the Arab world.

And yet Rodinson's attitudes toward the Arab regimes, and to the question of imperialism, were multifaceted. In a sense, two Rodinsons emerge: the one who wrote about these issues in themselves, and the one who wrote about them in relation to Israel.

As noted, Rodinson did not avoid reproving the Arab regimes; his criticism of Nasser, a veritable god to Arab nationalists, is particularly noticeable. But when writing about the Arab-Israeli conflict, the brutal realities of the Arab states were vastly downplayed. In a chapter of *Israel and the Arabs* entitled "The Rise of Arab Socialism," Rodinson cites specific crimes of the Arab regimes, including Syria's widespread use of torture, Sudan's cruel war against its southern peoples, and Iraq's vicious treatment of the Kurds. But it is particular policies at which he takes aim; he does not argue that these states were systemically deformed. On the other hand, he dismisses Israel in full as "a strange nation . . . chauvinistic and racialist from the Zionist ideology drummed into it . . . encouraged by reading the bellicose texts of the Old Testament."[59]

This stance was due, I think, to the structural fallacy to which Rodinson adhered. In his view, the Arab world in general and the Palestinians in particular were the objects of colonial oppression and imperialist exploitation. Therefore, Arab nationalism—whose sole unifying element was its hostility to Israel—must be upheld at all costs regardless of its lived reality.

Yet here, too, Rodinson's positions were contradictory. He sometimes criticized those who regarded the Middle Eastern states as mere pawns of the imperialist powers, and he ridiculed the New Left's romanticization of the post-colonial nations: "I do not subscribe to the mystique of the Third World, now so widespread in Left circles, and [I] do not beat my breast daily in despair at not having been born in the Congo."[60] And yet in writings spanning more than a decade, Rodinson would recreate the rigid colonial/anti-colonial template—the most Manichean form of Marxist analysis—when he addressed the Israel-Palestine conflict. Thus he would write, "The nationalism of an oppressed nation . . . must be supported in its essential aim." Here he was referring to the Palestinians, and of course he was right. But such a statement also describes Zionism. In Rodinson's view, though, Zionism did not, *could* not, be considered the nationalism of a people that has been "humiliated, oppressed, or even threatened"—though that sounds, to me, like a pretty good description of the Jews.[61]

For Rodinson, the concept of Jews as an oppressed nation—or as a nation at all—was simply an impossibility and Left Zionism therefore an oxymoron. Israel qua Israel was a "colonial amputation" built on "forcibly stolen" Arab lands from the moment of its birth; Zionism, he charged, was thus "almost inevitably . . . reactionary."[62] In his own way, Rodinson believed in Jewish exceptionalism, but his version of the concept was purely negative. Jews do not constitute a persecuted nation; Jewish nationalism is therefore doomed to exploitation and injustice; opposing Israel is ipso facto progressive. In insisting on this paradigm, Rodinson created a perfectly tautological worldview.

The essence of that worldview, which was shared by increasingly large segments of the Left, signaled a significant change. In the older Left, Rodinson noted in 1968, "what interested Westerners was the *internal* structure of the state."[63] Now, where a nation or movement stood, or claimed to stand, on the imperialist/anti-imperialist axis determined the degree of solidarity it deserved, regardless of its practices. (Stalin was an early exponent of this position.) "Internal structure"—an odd term to describe the lived reality of a country or movement—became of perfunctory concern to the anti-imperialist Left. And it was of equally scant interest to Rodinson when it came to what he called "the necessities of the struggle against Israel."[64]

This *tiersmondism*, which surged in the 1960s to 1980s, lives on today; see, for instance, the *New Left Review*'s championing of Hamas,

Hezbollah, and Iran. It presumed to offer protection and support to the formerly colonized world. The great irony is that a kind of Western narcissism is embedded within it. The lives of the people *within* the former colonies—which meant, frequently, their oppression by police states of gross economic, social, and gender inequality—were essentially irrelevant as long as those states or movements opposed the power of the West. Indeed, the less known about those countries, the better; how many Left intellectuals understood anything about daily life in Sudan, Yemen, or Algeria—or, for that matter, Pakistan, Cambodia, or Zimbabwe? And from this perspective, Rodinson's attitude was actually *less* valid than that of many others on the left precisely because, as a Middle East scholar, he knew a great deal about the "internal structure" of the Arab regimes.

In reading Rodinson, I sensed that he knew this and was combating his instincts; at times he sounded like a lawyer who suspects that his client is not the best yet is obliged to defend him anyway. Still, boosting your cause by making demonstrably false statements is not a good strategy. For instance, Rodinson repeatedly stated that the Arab states had recognized Israel "in practice" after the 1948 and 1967 wars, though he must have known this was untrue. He sometimes engaged in flights of fancy, as when he wrote that many Arab states would contribute to a fund for survivors of the Shoah if only the Jews would leave Palestine.[65] (Where such Jews would go was an inconvenient question he sidestepped.) He ignored the Arab states' shameful treatment of the Palestinian refugees—treatment that Sartre had castigated while on a visit to refugee camps in Egyptian-ruled Gaza.[66]

Most of all, Rodinson tried to normalize the Israeli-Arab conflict, which in many ways is sui generis. Israel has certainly developed its own nefarious and unique forms of nationalism, such as its refusal to live within established borders. Rodinson vocally protested these policies, and rightly so. But he often evaded the nefarious and unique aspect of Palestinian and Arab nationalists: their desire not only to build their own states, which is legitimate, but also to eliminate a neighbor, which is not. Rodinson ended *Israel and the Arabs* with a plea that, in the name of peace, the Arabs accept Israel as a (colonial) fait accompli—but added, "No one is so pure as to have the right to *demand* acceptance and condemn the Arabs ... if they continue to refuse."[67] By splitting the difference, he arrived at a thoroughly meaningless position.

What makes this more problematic is that, at the time he wrote this in the late 1960s, the Palestinians' eliminationist aim was loudly and unambiguously articulated; it was the firm center, not the wobbly fringe, of their movement. "The liberation action is not only the wiping out of an Imperialist base but, what is more important, *the extinction of a society*," Fatah proclaimed in 1968. Such liberation would require the "destruction" of Israel's "industrial, agricultural, . . . military, political, economic, financial and intellectual institutions." Lest there be any doubt: "Military defeat is not the sole goal in the Palestinian Liberation War, but it is the blotting out of the Zionist character of the occupied land, *be it human or social.*"[68]

Nevertheless, the following year, Rodinson described the Arabs' nonacceptance of Israel as "perfectly grounded in rationality and ethics, for the basic Arab argumentation seems difficult to refute."[69] In my view, the basic argument seems easy to refute. Yasser Arafat pithily explained in 1972, "Peace for us means Israel's destruction, and nothing else"; this doesn't sound like socialist humanism—or Marxism—to me.[70] Nevertheless, Rodinson continued to insist that even if Arab rejectionism took "brutal and often unrealistic forms, one must . . . seek to understand the profound repugnance" of the Arab people, for they suffered from "a painful amputation that was imposed by force."[71]

The attempt to normalize an admittedly annihilationist program led Rodinson into intellectually disingenuous, or simply false, positions. When he likened the Arab states' non-recognition of Israel to the U.S.'s refusal to recognize Communist China (also a foolish, unprincipled policy), he was forgetting that the U.S. never denied China's right to exist or sought its extinction. When he wrote, "I do not believe that the Arabs of Palestine . . . have ever preached the complete elimination of the Jews from Palestine (except perhaps at moments of excessive excitation by some leaders)," he was forgetting the newspapers, public speeches, interviews, party documents, resolutions, and position papers emanating from the Palestinians, which clearly explained their plans for a massive ethnic cleansing, at best, of Jewish Israelis. (Fluent in Arabic, Rodinson had access to these sources.) And when he wrote, "It is wonderful that this ideological struggle [against Zionism] has so often foresaken [*sic*] the weapons of racial and religious hatred" and then, on the same page, admitted that "critical, mocking, hostile, malevolent, disparaging, or slanderous remarks against Jews" circulate freely in the Arab world, he sounded simply unintelligible.[72]

In 1968, Rodinson devised a particularly strange theory: He argued that the Arab world's venom toward Israel was a gift to the Jews. Recognition of the Jewish state, he wrote, "might have been the salvation of Israel. But it would have been the end of Zionism." Arab hostility was Israel's blessing rather than its curse: "The 'normal' progress of events was fatal for Zionist Israel. . . . If Israel was just a country like any other, why go there, why become attached to it? . . . Zion's salvation lay in permanent danger."[73] The sophistry he had cultivated in his days as a compliantly Stalinist Communist had overtaken him once more.

It is striking that, in his writings on Israel, Rodinson rarely addressed the settlements or the Occupation. This is because he saw all of Israel, not the lands conquered in 1967, as an illegal occupation—or, in the vivid word he preferred, an "amputation."

It is therefore all the more surprising that Rodinson consistently argued against the one-state solution and, by implication, that he opposed the so-called right of return for the Palestinian refugees and their heirs. His reasons were practical, political, and moral.

First, the practical. Rodinson warned Palestinians that their dream of militarily conquering Israel and eliminating it as a Jewish state was a mirage. (Like Noam Chomsky, he regarded the analogy with Vietnam or Algeria as empty, dangerous rhetoric.) "The Palestinian solution is completely unattainable," he warned Daud Talhami. "Israeli tanks are a few kilometres from Damascus and Cairo." Nor would the Palestinians' Arab brothers partake in a "total and very harsh revolutionary war" against Israel, despite their vitriolic grandstanding. Arab unity *against* Israel did not translate into Arab support *for* the Palestinians. "Fraternity with the Palestinians is limited to visits to Palestinian camps by ladies from charity organizations," he caustically noted.[74]

Politically, the "democratic secular binational" state was a nonstarter. In fact, this nice-sounding term was another dangerous delusion. Rodinson understood, as did Halliday and Chomsky, that the Palestinians clearly envisioned a majority-Arab state—not a binational one—with, at most, a Jewish minority with religious rights. He warned that no Israeli, regardless of political persuasion, would even consider this suicidal plan.

Nor would most Europeans. Experience, Rodinson pointed out, "has made us increasingly doubtful about the possibilities of the coexistence of ethnic-national communities [within a united state]. . . . Almost no one believes that this programme is realistic."[75] Support for a unitary Palestinian state, he noted in 1972, was a fringe movement confined, in his view, to right-wingers, anti-Semites, and Maoists: three groups he disdained.

But there was a moral issue to be engaged, too, and Rodinson explicated it clearly and consistently. Though he did not believe in the reality of a Jewish people, he believed in the reality of an Israeli people; though he deplored the founding of the Israeli state, its sovereignty was a fact. And the elimination of that sovereignty—which could only mean the elimination of those *human beings*—was a step too far. Israelis, Rodinson wrote, had formed "a new nationality or ethnic group with a culture of its own"; they were "not a heterogeneous collection of gangs of occupiers who could be sent back where they came from with the greatest of ease."[76] Despite harping on Israel's presumably evil origins, he consistently affirmed Jewish-Israeli nationhood and, by implication, its right to life.

Thus, in 1972, he told Talhami that Israelis and Palestinians "must be represented as distinct communities at the political level, and each must be accorded the right to defend its interests and aspirations"—a stance that hardly accorded with the DFLP's program. A decade later, he reiterated, "Now it is a matter of two peoples, two nations. . . . In our epoch, two peoples cannot coexist within a single state unless each commands its own political structures. Especially when recent history has set them violently against one another." Therefore, "one can speak only in terms of the coexistence of two states."[77] It is dispiriting that the Peel Commission, which advocated partition, made the same assessment in 1937; on the other hand, it is encouraging that Rodinson called this later essay "The Conditions of Coexistence."

Rodinson's stance was an unusual merging of—and departure from—the two paradigms that typically define the Left's approach to Israel. Some leftists view Zionism as a movement for national self-determination and Israel as a historically justified refuge. They argue for the coexistence of a Jewish state next to a Palestinian one. Others see Zionism as inherently racist and colonialist. They argue that the State of Israel should be eliminated in favor of a unified, primarily Arab Palestine.

Rodinson regarded Zionism as a colonial project, one that he resented and disliked. Still, he repeatedly departed from the presumed implications of his colonialist analysis to defend Israel's right to continued existence as a majority-Jewish state. His synthesis of the two positions was and is rare. It was his moment of greatest originality; it is here that he owned the freedom of thought that the Communist Party had forbidden him.

It is tempting, though risky, to accept Sartre's challenge to psychoanalyze Rodinson. Why did a man whose parents were murdered in Auschwitz continue to believe in assimilation's success? Why was he so viscerally repelled by the very idea of Jewish national sovereignty—knowing full well the cost of Jewish powerlessness? Why did he maintain that anti-Semitism could always be explained as a rational, socioeconomic phenomenon, despite abundant evidence to the contrary? These are apparent conundrums, yet there is a logic here. I suspect that Rodinson clung to such beliefs long after history had refuted them as a way to keep faith with his parents. He had been nurtured on steadfast assimilation and anti-Zionism, and he would adhere to them forever. His parents, after all, opposed Zionism before there was a State of Israel, much less an Occupation. "I am anti-Zionist on principle," he explained in 1975. "This was my position long before I understood much about the Palestinian question. It was the position of my family."[78] With a kind of frozen fidelity, he sustained the beliefs his parents had formed in the prewar era, before they, and their world, were obliterated. (In a 1988 interview, Rodinson talked extensively about his parents but never mentioned where, when, or why they were killed.) Unlike Max Horkheimer, he saw no reason to rethink his basic precepts in the aftermath of Auschwitz. In Rodinson's eyes, the Shoah was not a moral, historic, or civilizational rupture.

Another clue to understanding Rodinson must lie in the fact that, while Europe was murdering his parents, the Arab world saved his life by sheltering him throughout the war. (Though at the time even he, the reso-lute anti-Zionist, decided to move to Palestine "if things went badly.") And it was a welcoming world. Damascus and Beirut, and for that matter Baghdad and Cairo, were cosmopolitan cities in the 1940s, brimming with diverse albeit turbulent political, intellectual, and artistic currents. Rodinson thrived during this period; it was then, he has said, that his serious political activity began. He taught Marxism in Beirut and befriended Communist intellectuals in Lebanon and Syria; he would later recall that for them, the 1947 division of Palestine "was like the Hitler-Stalin pact of 1939 had been for us. . . . It was the death of the soul."[79] (Rodinson's first general essay, on Durkheim and Marx, was published in Arabic by the Lebanese-Syrian Communist Party in 1943.) Though he often wrote about "the Arab masses," in all probability it was this sliver of the intelligentsia—secular, educated, French-speaking, modernizing—that he knew well. Their world, too—like that of his parents'—would be largely destroyed, though in their case by internal foes.

Rodinson was acutely aware of, and unsentimental about, the conse-quences of the Arab world's underdevelopment, which is part of the realist Marxist tradition. And though he was not an emotional writer, I suspect that, at times, he was heartbroken by that world, for which he felt such affection. Of oppositional movements in Iran and Egypt, he wrote these chillingly prescient words in 1978: "In both cases a hated brand of authoritarianism was to be overthrown in order to set up a regime in which the people could be mobilized in the cause of another brand of authoritarianism."[80] That same year, on the front page of Le Monde, he denounced the "fascisme archaïque" of the Iranian Revolution.[81] This was his rebuke to an article by Michel Foucault, who idealized the revolu-tion; Rodinson later described Foucault's piece as "completely idiotic." Rodinson added, "Like many philosophers, . . . Foucault was not afraid of giving peremptory opinions on matters of which he was very ignorant. . . . Finally, . . . he abandoned the subject [of Iran], which was better. Then he died."[82]

But Rodinson also had great expectations for the East. In the mid-sixties, he believed that "Islam can travel further along the road to socialism than along the road to nationalism." In 1978, he lauded "the vigor of Marxist thinking" that was "springing up everywhere" in the Arab and Muslim worlds. In his 1979 book, The Arabs, he wrote that extremist political ideologies in the region would probably be "transitory" and were, in any case, "largely the result of conditions imposed on the Arabs against their will."[83] He predicted that the Arab peoples would become disenchanted with Islamic governance and, indeed, with Islam itself: "If the magic potion is ineffective one loses confidence not only in the sorcerer but in sorcery itself."[84] The opposite trajectory, which has come to pass, would surely have grieved him. As I write, the Muslim world reels between the authoritarian repressiveness of Iran and Egypt, the auto-destruction of Syria, the collapse of Yemen and Libya, the fratricidal violence of Iraq, and the sociopaths of ISIS, the al-Nusra Front, the Taliban, al-Shabab, al-Qaeda, and related groups. Liberals, socialists, secularists, democrats, and feminists are in exile, in jail, or worse. The very forces that Rodinson spent his life opposing have ascended with fury, and no "magic potion" to defeat them is in sight.

What are we to make of Maxime Rodinson, whose work embraced so many unresolved contradictions? Fred Halliday praised his rejection of tribal identities, his secularism, and his defense of the two-state solution. In Halliday's view, Rodinson "presented a fresh, independent, and resilient analysis of the middle east's central conflict" and personified "an exemplary 'internationalism' that recognised the rights of the two national groups."[85] Adam Shatz, an anti-Zionist American writer, lauded how "honestly" and "frankly" Rodinson spoke "to his Palestinian friends."[86] Conversely, the Lebanese journalist Michael Young argued that Rodinson's writings "surely nourished many an argument equating Zionism with racism."[87]

Rodinson's work on the Arab-Israeli conflict, like that of almost anyone who writes about it over a long period, can be used in different ways to support decidedly different positions. It is true that he criticized the annihilationist tendencies in the Arab world, the Palestinian movement, and the Western Left; this took courage, especially since he often made those criticisms face to face. He maintained a calm, rational voice in a debate marked by hysteria.

Yet the preponderance of his writings on the conflict was relentlessly hostile to Zionism as theory and practice. It was Israel's presence, not any particular policy, that he blamed for deforming the larger region. His work as a historian was often marked by evasions: about the necessity of Jewish emigration to Palestine, especially during the Nazi years; about the existence of the hundreds of thousands of shattered, stateless Jewish survivors stranded in displaced persons camps after 1945; about the causes of the 1948 war. When analyzing the relation between action and reaction, he misattributed moral culpability. And the delicacy with which he evaded the brutal reality—in terms of strategies *and* goals—of the Palestinian movement and the Arab states vis-à-vis Israel cannot, in my view, be defended. Rodinson was not uncritical of Arab or Palestinian politics. But his well-deserved status as a highly respected and politically committed scholar with deep roots in the region means that he could have spoken out far more clearly. As with Arendt, his writings on the Israeli-Arab conflict are not his best; he became a less intelligent version of himself when he turned to the subject.

Rodinson had a powerful need for a transformative project and a world-historic actor. Losing faith in the Soviet Union, he transferred his bruised hopes to the purportedly revolutionary currents in the Arab world and the Palestinian movement. By doing so, he resisted nihilism and despair. Marxism, he wrote, is "active optimism"; surely we need more of that.[88] But for Rodinson, the cost in intellectual, political, and moral integrity was too high.

This is not to say that Rodinson remained unbowed by history. In a 1988 interview, he looked back on his intellectual trajectory. "In the beginning, I was a communist and optimistic. But now I see that those who have worked out the plans of a better society have in no way succeeded," he confessed. "I have given up 'general' optimism, but one can achieve some things in very limited areas. . . . The outcome of revolutions is not so much in the general improvement of things, but in fresh demands."[89]

CHAPTER FOUR

Isaac Deutscher

A VERY JEWISH JEW

TAMARA DEUTSCHER, ISAAC DEUTSCHER'S WIDOW, titled her biographical sketch of her late husband "The Education of a Jewish Child." Deutscher and Maxime Rodinson were born less than a decade apart, though Deutscher's upbringing was far more typical of Jewish children of their time. (Rodinson's biography might have been called "The Education of a Communist Child.") In an accompanying note, Tamara claimed that Isaac's views on Jews and Israel "remained consistent throughout" his life.[1] It is not clear why this was a good thing, and in any case it was not true. Deutscher's views on Jews, Zionism, and Israel twisted, turned, and changed directions in response to the ironies and shocks of twentieth-century history. Deutscher repeatedly struggled to comprehend, and to master, a Jewish history that he found endlessly perplexing and that stubbornly resisted his Marxist paradigm. Unlike Rodinson, he had an innate feel for the sorrow and tragedy of the Jewish people.

This is not surprising: Tragedy was Deutscher's great subject, and a word he often used. He is known, above all, for his trilogy of biographies of Leon Trotsky, a man for whom the word "tragic," in the classic Greek sense, is if anything mild. Deutscher's work on Trotsky is often lauded, for good reason, as majestic in power and epic sweep, which is also the power and sweep of the Russian Revolution itself. These biographies have served, as one sociologist wrote, as "a kind of Torah for generations of activists."[2]

It is impossible to understand Deutscher's views on Zionism, or any political issue, without grasping Trotsky's influence on his thought. Deutscher was not exactly a "Trotskyist," and, except for a brief period when he was young, he did not belong to any party or sect. But he firmly believed that history would redeem Trotsky's vision: Surely a different, better, truer Communism—"a fully fledged Soviet democracy"—would emerge in Russia to right the wrongs of Stalinism.[3] (This unshakable faith made Deutscher an inept forecaster; he excelled at looking to the past, not the future.) Of course, whether Trotsky would have been any less ruthless or more democratic than Stalin is something that will remain forever unknown, though Trotsky's conduct during the revolution and, especially, as commander of the Red Army offers no reason to think so. As Deutscher wrote with some understatement, Trotsky "would not shun the Red Terror when the time for it came."[4]

Nonetheless, especially in England, where the Communist Party was never strong, many New Leftists would look to Trotsky, and to Deutscher, as exemplars of what they believed was a kinder or at least more flexible version of revolutionary Marxism. But it was not only leftists whom Deutscher influenced. Leopold Labedz, an émigré Polish historian who was fervently anti-Communist, observed: "The scope of the influence of Deutscher's ideas is astonishing. . . . The pillars of the British Establishment listened to him . . . [as did] leaders of the French and Italian Communist Parties. . . . He certainly has not been a prophet without honour."[5]

The iron center of Trotsky's principles, on which he literally staked his life—and lost it—was his confidence in worldwide revolution and his detestation of Stalin's socialism in one country. Because of this influence, Deutscher was in many ways *more* anti-national than Rodinson. Paradoxically, though, Deutscher was also *less* anti-Zionist. He sympathized with and even admired Israel, despite his ideological aversion to it. Much of this is due, I believe, to his deep roots in the world of the Eastern European shtetl: a world that, as Tamara Deutscher wrote, was "so brutally wrecked, tortured, massacred, and obliterated."[6]

Isaac Deutscher was born in 1907 in the small, close-knit, predominantly Jewish town of Chrzanów in the Galician region of Poland. His father, Jacob, was a printer of Hebrew religious literature. Isaac was named for his great-grandfather, an accomplished Talmudist. Isaac began his religious studies, which he would later speak of with disgust, at age four. He was by all accounts a child prodigy, and his father expected him to become a rabbi and a great religious scholar.

Isaac's father (as so often, less is known about his mother) was a pious Hasid. But he was also a progressive intellectual and a Zionist. His idols included Spinoza, Heine, and Lassalle, and he loved German culture. Isaac did not. "I was a Polish patriot," he would recall; he regarded Germany as a political bully rather than a model of enlightenment. Chrzanów was only ten miles from the town of Auschwitz, and Isaac's father admonished him that German was the "world language" he must learn if he wished to venture farther. "You have only to go beyond Auschwitz, and practically nobody will understand you any more, you and your fine Polish language," Jacob warned.[7] Isaac *did* learn; he was a gifted linguist who could speak Yiddish, Polish, and Hebrew and would also master Latin, German, English, and Russian. It was his father, mother, and the rest of the Deutschers who never went beyond Auschwitz, where they were murdered. There is an eerie horror in the fact that Rodinson's parents, who were secular Communists, and Deutscher's, who were observant believers, were all killed in that camp. Auschwitz drew its victims from throughout Europe; the brotherly internationale of which Marxists dreamed was replaced by a depraved internationale of death.

Deutscher witnessed his first pogrom when he was ten years old; as a child, "I lived through three pogroms," he remembered. As a result, the family moved from town to town seeking safety. He was educated at a yeshiva and then a Polish gymnasium, which he fought to attend although Jacob considered it a waste of time. Like many young Jews of his generation, Isaac rebelled against the obscurantism of a religious education—and, in his late teens, the identifying clothing of Hasidic males—though the story of his eating a ham sandwich on Yom Kippur is probably apocryphal. (Similar stories are told by other Jewish atheists of his generation and by secularists of other faiths; Salman Rushdie, whose family was Muslim, recounts a similar story about testing the heavens via pork.) But there is no doubt that it was the secular world of politics that attracted Deutscher as he came of age. While auditing classes in Cracow, where he studied literature, philosophy, and history, he organized a literary circle; one subject of debate—Isaac's choice—was the claim that "Christ was a Jew and a communist." Unsurprisingly, this did not please his Polish classmates; as Deutscher recalled, "All of a sudden I became an intruder, a stranger, I became a 'Yid.' "[8] When he reached eighteen, he moved to Warsaw, where he continued his studies and was quickly drawn to Marxism.

Deutscher did not equate atheism and socialism with a rejection of Jewish culture at this time. He began translating Hebrew poets—including H. N. Bialik, Shaul Tschernichovsky, Avraham Shlonsky, and Uri Zvi Greenberg—into Polish. He wrote his own poems, too, in Polish and Hebrew. Some were published in *Nowy Dziennik*, Cracow's Polish-language Jewish journal, and some praised Zionist achievements ("Mount Scopus brims with fire . . .").[9] This literary background may account for the vivid grace of Deutscher's prose, which is especially striking in the Trotsky trilogy, and especially striking, too, for a writer who learned English as an adult.

In 1925, at the age of nineteen, Deutscher joined the outlawed Polish Communist Party in Warsaw and served on the editorial board of its Yiddish magazine, for which he wrote under a pseudonym. (A friend later noted that Isaac rose through the Party by "sheer brainpower.")[10] In 1931, on the eve of the Great Famine, Deutscher visited the Soviet Union; while there, he turned down offers to stay and teach. The following year, he was expelled from the Party for opposing, as did Trotsky, its disastrously sectarian line, which equated social democracy with fascism and would help pave the way for the Nazi triumph. The official charge against Deutscher was exaggerating the dangers of Nazism, though it is difficult to imagine how one could do that. (Neal Ascherson has noted that this expulsion was a hidden stroke of luck, since "a few years later, Stalin invited the whole Polish leadership to Moscow and shot them.")[11] Deutscher then began writing for *Nasz Przeglad,* a pro-Zionist Polish-Jewish daily; he remained with the paper until, in 1939, it sent him to England, where he would permanently reside. That, too, was fortunate: Like Rodinson, Deutscher avoided death in Auschwitz through exile.

With the outbreak of war, Deutscher joined General Wladyslaw Sikorski's Polish army in Scotland, though he chafed at its anti-Semitism. He learned English and soon began writing for the *Economist* and the *Observer,* for which he became a roving European correspondent. (Covering Germany at the end of the war, he shared a room with George Orwell.) Thus began his decades-long career as a prolific journalist, scholar, lecturer, and public intellectual. In August 1967, at age sixty, he died suddenly while in Rome.

Deutscher's best-known and most quoted work on Jewish topics is his essay "The non-Jewish Jew," which he first presented, in 1958, as a talk to the World Jewish Congress during Jewish Book Week. The essay became the title of Deutscher's one volume on Jewish issues and is reproduced elsewhere and frequently lauded. Though Deutscher's essay is not especially insightful, the phrase "non-Jewish Jew" has seeped into almost promiscuous parlance among Diaspora Jews, especially those who identify as anti-Zionists. (I suspect, however, that many of those admirers would be less enamored of a "non-Negro Negro" or a "non-Arab Arab." While a non-Jewish Jew is praised as a universalist, a non-Negro Negro is scorned as an Uncle Tom and a non-Arab Arab as a self-hating Islamophobe.) Deutscher's essay leads off, and is the self-described inspiration for, Adam Shatz's anthology *Prophets Outcast*, which bills itself as "a century of dissident Jewish writing about Zionism and Israel."[12] Similarly, an appreciation of Christopher Hitchens in the *Jewish Daily Forward* praised the late writer as a non-Jewish Jew and directly connected this to his "steadfast and principled" opposition to a Jewish state.[13] It would be hard to overstate the influence of Deutscher's essay; it is likely that many people who have never read another word of Deutscher on Jewish questions—or, perhaps, on any question—have read it.

And this is not by chance, for "The non-Jewish Jew" shamelessly flatters left-wing, secular, Diaspora Jews. Unlike Koestler, Deutscher did not dissociate himself from the values of Jewish culture so much as narrowly redefine them: In Deutscher's account, those values are the monopoly of people like him. He reopened one of the most tedious debates in Jewish history—"Who is the best Jew?"—by enthusiastically answering in the first person.

Deutscher and Arendt obviously differed on key questions; he would never have subscribed to her theory of totalitarianism, which embraced Nazism and Stalinist Communism. But his concept of the non-Jewish Jew shares much with her notion of the pariah. Many of his heroes— Spinoza, Marx, Heine, Luxemburg, Trotsky, Freud—were also hers. These Jews were heretics and renegades who "transcend[ed] Jewry," Deutscher wrote. "Yet I think that in some ways they were very Jewish indeed."[14]

Because they lived on the margins of society or between cultures, Deutscher argued, they were freethinkers who could imagine the world anew and embrace, indeed conceive, universal values. Jewish universalism thus grew out of Judaism yet negates it; in the universalist vision, "God ceased to be Jewish."[15]

Deutscher also echoed Arendt's conviction that the nation-state, to which Zionism was a purportedly hapless latecomer, was dying. Deutscher knew, of course, of the independence movements surging through the Third World and of the escalating crisis in Algeria. In 1958— the year that he wrote "The non-Jewish Jew"—the All-African People's Congress held its first conference and demanded immediate independence for all of colonized Africa. Nevertheless, Deutscher insisted, "We live in an age when the nation-state is fast becoming an anachronism." He lamented the fact that "the world has compelled the Jew to embrace the nation-state" at this precise moment; though "you cannot blame the Jews for this . . . Jews should at least be aware of the paradox." Deutscher viewed Israel as a negative triumph: It was "the paradoxical consummation of the Jewish tragedy," born from the agony of the death camps.[16]

"The non-Jewish Jew" contains some of Deutscher's most reductive analyses. He suggests that the Shoah resulted from misdirected animus against the capitalist system, which the Jews incarnated: "This is the crux of the Jewish tragedy." (This is the kind of thing that Horkheimer was writing before, though certainly not after, the genocide.) Deutscher concludes by pleading for Jews to "find their way back to the moral and political heritage . . . of universal human emancipation."[17] He clearly implies that the State of Israel is a barrier to, rather than part of, that emancipatory tradition.

Yet the core of this essay, or at least its undeniable subtext, is Deutscher's struggle to maintain his prewar outlook in light of the genocide. His pleas for universalism, and especially his analysis of anti-Semitism, sound almost pro forma, as if he did not quite believe them any more. In the course of the essay, it becomes clear that it is the Shoah, not Israel, that crushed the universalist faith of so many. Deutscher confronts this loss with mournful passion. "We are now looking back on these believers in humanity through the bloody fog of our times. We are looking back at them through the smoke of the gas chambers, the smoke which no wind can disperse from our sight." Revolutionary optimism was betrayed by the twentieth century, in which "the mere words 'solidarity of man' would sound as a perverse mockery to Jewish ears." Nor was there much reason to trust in the future, for the Shoah "has not made any deep impression on the nations of Europe. It has not truly shocked their conscience. It has left them almost cold."[18] Deutscher's internal tug-of-war between ideological belief, the lessons of Jewish history, and the complex realities of the Jewish state would become even more apparent in his reports on his trips to Israel.

If figures such as Trotsky and Luxemburg were, in Deutscher's phrase, "very Jewish indeed"—a description they would have indignantly protested—so too is Deutscher's essay. It is imbued with a view of the Jewish people, or at least some Jewish people, as chosen; and imbued, too, with a deep albeit secular messianism. Deutscher essentially posited: If the Jews can only reclaim, or sustain, their adherence to universalist emancipation, the world might be redeemed. This is a grand, indeed grandiose proposition, and a stirring one, which traces its lineage to the Hebrew prophets. What makes this essay so poignant is the way that Deutscher grapples, as must we, with the knowledge that this universalism—this rootless transnationalism—was in part what made the Jews so vulnerable, so *hated*, and led to the black smoke that we still inhale.

"There is a touch of un-Jewishness about Israel," Deutscher observed, sounding rather Koestleresque, after his 1954 visit there; he noticed in particular the strange sight of Jewish farmers, Jewish soldiers, and Jewish "toughness." Though Deutscher's approach to history was not psychoanalytic, he intuited the dual trauma of many Israelis, in which "a complex and many-sided process of psychological self-uprooting" had combined with "tragic processes of physical displacement. . . . Israel is the State of the displaced person." And he noted, though not without sympathy, that displaced people are often damaged people. "The newcomers are not like the idealists of the previous *Aliyahs;* they are the wrecks of concentration camps, the flotsam and jetsam of European Jewry, and the masses of Oriental Jews, refugees from Arab hatred and revenge." (One wonders if Rodinson ever read this.) Israel's national project consisted not just of building modern industry, agriculture, and cultural institutions but of destroying "all the marks of indignity, all the stigmata of shame, all the yellow patches that Jew-hatred has ever devised."[19] Deutscher understood this process of creative destruction but was hurt that it required the rejection of Yiddish, his beloved native tongue.

In the 1954 article, titled "Israel's Spiritual Climate," Deutscher made clear that there was much in the nascent country that he admired. "There is an egalitarian spirit alive in the working class," he observes. (Ever loyal to Trotsky, he adds that this ethos "flourished in Soviet Russia before it was eradicated by Stalinism.") The kibbutzim, especially those in the Galilee, fill him with delight: "He who has not seen the kibbutz can hardly imagine the boldness and originality of the idea and of its execution." He views the kibbutz as untainted communism in action: far superior, in its political economy and human relations, to the USSR's collective farms. Deutscher attributes this to the differences in human capital that separated the two experiments. The Russian communes "had depended on a backward, sluggish, and intimidated *muzhik* [peasantry], whereas the kibbutzim had been built by the self-sacrifice and courage of idealistic intellectuals and workers."[20] Slyly, Deutscher recounts the story of a Soviet official who visited a kibbutz dominated by the left-wing Mapam Party, which at that time religiously followed a pro-Soviet line. The visiting Russian comrade refused to believe that the Zionist commune had no means of "coercive discipline" and housed no jail. "The Russian did not conceal his incredulity; and he intimated that he thought it a good joke that for once Jews should show their own Potemkin village to a Russian." Unlike Arendt, Deutscher understood the centrality of the kibbutzim to the larger society: "The kibbutz is still Israel's moral power station. . . . It is still the chief bulwark of Israel's defence. . . . The bastions of Israel's Utopian socialism bristle with Sten-guns."[21]

But many things about the new country worried Deutscher, presciently so. The kibbutzim might be unable to sustain themselves, for the country's new immigrants had no interest in either rural living or the abolition of private property. Some kibbutzim had already been forced to hire outside labor, which was previously taboo. The state was too theocratic, the people too nationalistic. The country's borders were bizarre, contorted by "grotesque corridors, bulges, necks, and triangles, carved out by the master carvers of the United Nations." To Deutscher, this illustrated "the stark madness of the nation-state. . . . In Israel you can never escape its mad stare: wherever you go you are always at some frontier or other: 'Look, on the hill over there are the *Syrians!*' "[22] And, he might have added, the Jordanians, Egyptians, and Lebanese.

In addition, Israeli sovereignty had "explosives"—the hundreds of thousands of Palestinian refugees—"built into its very foundations." Yet Deutscher's view was different from that of Rodinson, who regarded Israel as "stolen" and therefore essentially illegitimate. Deutscher was, again, more steeped in tragedy (or, perhaps, in dialectics). Where Rodinson saw one right and one wrong, Deutscher saw the competition of two legitimate claims, which resulted in continuous strife. "One cannot in fairness blame the Jews" for the refugee problem, he wrote, for a people "pursued by a monster and running to save their lives cannot help injuring those who are in the way and cannot help trampling over their property. The Jews feel that the injury they have done to the Arabs is child's play compared with their own tragedy. This is true enough, but it does not prevent the Arabs from smarting under their grievance and craving revenge." As for the future, he predicts, "To the Arabs the Jews are and will for long remain invaders and intruders."[23]

"Israel's Spiritual Climate" is a bipolar piece: Deutscher veers between denouncing Jewish national sovereignty and recognizing its necessity. Once again, there is the view that Israel represents defeat. "To my mind it is just another Jewish tragedy that the world has driven the Jew to seek safety in a nation-state in the middle of this century when the nation-state is falling into decay." Once again, there is the certainty that a non-national future is on the horizon. "The nation-state can prolong its existence only by intensifying all the processes of its own degeneration. In the Third Reich the nation-state found both its zenith and its nadir. . . . Joining now the rank of the nation-states, Israel cannot but share in their decadence."[24]

But Deutscher knew, too, that the Jewish people would not, and should not, return to the powerlessness of the pre-Shoah era. In a remarkable passage he admits to a deeply personal sense of failure and guilt.

Israelis who have known me as an anti-Zionist of long standing are curious to hear what I think about Zionism. I have, of course, long since abandoned my anti-Zionism, which was based on a confidence in the European labour movement, or, more broadly, in European society and civilization, which that society and civilization have not justified. If, instead of arguing against Zionism in the 1920s and 1930s I had urged European

Jews to go to Palestine, I might have helped to save some of the
lives that were later extinguished in Hitler's gas chambers.

Thus, "for the remnants of European Jewry—is it only for them?—the
Jewish State has become an historic necessity. It is also a living reality."
Still, he insists, "I am not a Zionist. . . . The Israelis accept this with unex-
pected tolerance but seem bewildered [by it]."[25]

The bewilderment was Deutscher's, too, as he strained to maintain
his long-standing anti-national principles while recognizing the new and
vexing demands that history had presented. Try though he might, he
could not synthesize the two. In reading this article, I had the distinct
impression that Deutscher wished not only—of course—that the genocide had been prevented but also that history had obediently adhered to
the telos of which Marxists had been so sure. In that framework, the
Jewish people in particular, and national identities in general, would fade
away. Deutscher concludes "Israel's Spiritual Climate" by imagining a
Middle East federation in which Israel might join with the Arab states and
play "a role as modest as are its numbers and as great as are its intellectual and spiritual resources." However, unlike Arendt, Deutscher knew
this was a fantasy. The word he uses to describe it is *Zukunftsmusik,* which
literally means music of the future but roughly translates as "pie in the
sky." "But sometimes," he added, "it is only the music of the future to
which it is worth listening."[26]

Deutscher's transition from anti-Zionism to "abandoned" anti-Zionism in
some ways paralleled Trotsky's. The prophet of Deutscher's books had a
largely secular, Russified upbringing. But Trotsky never claimed any sort
of Christian heritage, and he was puzzled by the term "assimilationist."
Still, he emphatically denied any particular *identification* with the Jews.
When asked, in 1903, whether he considered himself Jewish or Russian,
he replied, "Neither! I am a Social Democrat!" In 1918, when a Jewish-
Russian delegation asked him to ensure that the revolution's commitment
to Jewish equality be maintained, Trotsky "burst into a rage at the reminder
of his national origin and retorted indignantly, 'I am not a Jew, but an
internationalist.' "[27] In one of the rare times that he did speak openly as a
Jew, it was to launch a scathing attack on the Bund, the Jewish socialist
party that was simultaneously anti-assimilationist and anti-Zionist.

Deutscher has some trouble with this: He admits that for Trotsky to self-identify as a Jew "only to refute Jewish demands must have seemed almost caddish to the highly-strung delegates of the Bund."[28] (One can well imagine why they were highly strung.) In any case, Trotsky always maintained that a national identity was antithetical to internationalism.

And yet Trotsky's outlook was inevitably influenced by his Jewish birth: inevitable because of Russia's rabid anti-Semitism. He was raised in an age of pogroms; the years 1881–82, which followed the assassination of Alexander II, were particularly brutal. Trotsky was only a toddler then, but pogroms were a subject of frequent conversation and a source of great fear for his parents. The massacres were "a deeply traumatic experience for Trotsky as a child, and this accounts for the matter always being on his mind," the historian Joseph Nedava wrote.[29] Pogroms appear frequently in Trotsky's writings and speeches; they came to epitomize the degeneracy of the Russians and the debasement of the Jews. This was especially apparent in 1905; Trotsky wrote with blazing fury of the anti-Jewish assaults that swept the country in reaction to the failed revolution earlier that year. His account, titled "The Tsarist Hosts at Work," unsparingly depicts the atrocities, including arson, beatings, rapes, and murders; the brazen cruelty of the perpetrators; and the terror of the crushed victims. "No other Marxist revolutionary . . . matched the passionate quality of Trotsky's evocations of the pogromists in all their hideous savagery," historian Robert Wistrich wrote. "Images of unimaginable suffering, of pain, degradation, and death, were fused in Trotsky's prose into a searing indictment."[30]

Trotsky never specified that the victims were Jews (though his readers would have known this), but he vividly conveys their torment: "Blood-stained, charred, frenzied victims twist and turn in nightmarish panic looking for escape. Some take off the blood-stained clothes from those killed, put them on, and lie down among the piles of corpses. . . . Others kneel down . . . stretch out their hands, crawl in the dust, kiss the soldiers' boots, beg for help. They are met with drunken laughter. 'You wanted freedom—reap the fruits of its labor.' "[31] This sinister, exultant laughter of the executioners would become the terrifying soundtrack of the twentieth century.

Nevertheless, Trotsky insisted that the Jews and their troubles were of no particular concern and held no emotional meaning for him; to one

Jewish-Russian delegation "he declared bluntly 'that Jews do not interest him more than the Bulgars.' "[32] (In his memoir, Chaim Weizmann, Israel's first president, wrote of the "arrogant" Trotsky who "stamped as unworthy, as intellectually backward, as chauvinistic and unmoral, the desire of any Jew to occupy himself with the sufferings and destiny of Jewry.")[33] Trotsky's anti-nationalism was not just a theoretical commitment but was deeply constituent of his being. Unfortunately, he was more of a true believer than some of his comrades, and he was genuinely shocked when Stalin launched anti-Semitic attacks against him in the power struggle after Lenin's death. In exile, though, Trotsky would change. In 1937, he accused supporters of the Soviet Union who denied Soviet anti-Semitism of "not seeing the spots on the sun."[34]

Hannah Arendt once said that, as she came of age, she never imagined that the marginal Jewish people and the marginal Jewish Question would achieve center stage in the world politics of the twentieth century. This was true of Trotsky too. But while remaining anti-nationalist, his views on Jewish oppression, its importance, and its possible solutions changed as the Nazis ascended. By the mid-1930s—earlier than many others—Trotsky understood, as did Arendt, that a lunatic anti-Semitism had taken firm rather than temporary hold of Europe's most developed and aggressive country. And the problem was not only Germany: Trotsky realized that Jews throughout the world were being transformed into hunted prey. "Today decaying capitalist society is striving to squeeze the Jewish people from all its pores; seventeen million individuals of the two billion populating the globe, that is, less than one percent, can no longer find a place on our planet!" he wrote in 1940. "The bourgeoisie has managed to convert our planet into a foul prison."[35] Jews were now ground zero of the international crisis; fascism and anti-Semitism could not be untangled. Battling the former demanded battling the latter, not as a sideshow or out of charitable sympathy but as the very basis of civilizational self-defense.

Of course, unlike Arendt, Trotsky did not become a Zionist. He considered the movement to be a backward, doomed form of romanticism and always regarded it with scorn or, at most, pity. But the events of the 1930s altered him. Unlike Rodinson, he began to doubt the talisman of assimilation. "During my youth I rather leaned toward the prognosis that the Jews of different countries would be assimilated and that the

Jewish question would thus disappear in a quasi-automatic fashion," he told two journalists from Jewish publications in 1937. "The historical development of the last quarter of a century has not confirmed this perspective." He spoke of the Jews as a nation. He dissented from the Communist Party line on the 1929 clashes in Palestine; rather than viewing them as an uprising of Arab anti-imperialists, as the Communists insisted, Trotsky detected the involvement of "reactionary Mohammedans and anti-Semitic pogromists."[36] He lashed out at Britain's White Paper of 1939, which barred most Jewish immigration to Palestine at the precise moment it was most needed. Sounding much like Koestler, he charged that Britain was "interested in winning the sympathies of the Arabs" and "may well transform Palestine into a bloody trap for several hundred thousand Jews."[37] However, all this made him even more certain that Zionism held no solution for endangered world Jewry.

Trotsky sensed that Nazism meant Jewish extermination, and he sensed this before World War II began and the Final Solution was planned and implemented (though Hitler had hardly hidden his intentions). In 1938, after the Munich agreement, he warned a visiting Jewish reporter who suggested a preventive strike against Hitler: " 'Do not speak lightly of a war. You certainly need not pray for war. . . . *Between the* [Polish river] *Warta and the Volga there live seven million Jews—in the coming war they will be annihilated first.*' " And at the end of 1938 he wrote to an American friend, "The number of countries which expel the Jews grows without cease. The number of countries able to accept them decreases. At the same time the exacerbation of the struggle intensifies. . . . But even without war the next development of world reaction signifies with certainty the *physical extermination of the Jews.*"[38] This led him to believe that an immediate territorial refuge, albeit temporary, was necessary to protect the Jews. But, ever the ideologue, he still denounced Zionism.

None of this suggests that Trotsky envisioned the death camps or somehow knew in advance how the annihilation would unfold, as some of his acolytes have suggested. He was not a soothsayer. Nor was his insight into the fate of the Jews an inevitable outgrowth of the Marxist critique of capitalism, imperialism, or even fascism. (At the other end of the political spectrum, Revisionist Zionist Vladimir Jabotinsky had a similar apprehension of the Jewish fate.) In a penetrating essay, the Marxist historian Norman Geras suggested that it was Trotsky's understanding of the *human* (not capitalist) capacity for nihilistic cruelty that was the source of his insight, and that Trotsky may have first gained this understanding from the experience of the pogroms. "There was an element of plain intuition here, spun from Trotsky's broader human sensibility in which something was already known about 'uncontrolled madness,' deadly hatred and the passing of all limits," Geras wrote. "It was out of the kind of understanding which that narrative of his betokens, as much as it was out of his Marxist theorizing about capitalism or fascism, that his anticipation of Nazism's ultimate barbarity may have come."[39]

Indeed, there is something fearsomely prescient in Trotsky's portrait of the pogromist: "The trembling slave . . . feels that he is an absolute despot now. . . . He rules . . . over life and death. If he so wishes—he throws the old woman . . . out of the window, . . . smashes a chair on the head of an infant in arms, rapes a girl in front of the crowd, drives a nail into a living body. . . . There is no torture invented by a brain maddened by wine and rage before which he is obliged to stop short. He is allowed to do everything, and he dares everything."[40] Who can read this today and not think of the ordinary men—doing everything, daring everything, masters of life and death—who made up the Nazi camp guards, police interrogators, prison torturers, and death squads in all their various iterations? These, too, were men who found their freedom in a world of pain and death.

Somewhat surprisingly, with the rise of Hitler and the assault on the Jews, Trotsky acknowledged that a Jewish state would be necessary *after* the worldwide triumph of socialism. According to Deutscher, in early 1937 Trotsky told the *Jewish Daily Forward* that "he had arrived at the view that even under socialism the Jewish question would require a 'territorial solution,' i.e. that the Jews would need to be settled in their own homeland."[41] However, Trotsky refused to call this "Zionism," and he did not think that such a state would be located in Palestine, though he was confident that dispersed Jewry would find "a sufficiently extensive and rich spot under the sun." Similarly, in an essay called "Thermidor and Anti-Semitism," written the same year, Trotsky argued that Jews who desired "their own autonomous republic" would be accommodated under socialism. "The very same methods of solving the Jewish question which under decaying capitalism have a utopian and reactionary character (Zionism), will, under the regime of a socialist federation, take on a real and salutary meaning. . . . How could any Marxist, or even any consistent democrat, object to this?"[42] How indeed? Socialism's magic powers would transform the "reactionary" nature of Jewish nationalism into something else—though this new, improved version still sounds like Zionism to me.

Trotsky was assassinated in 1940, eight years before the State of Israel was born. The annihilation he feared did come to pass, though with a ferocity that even he—who had described Nazism as the "puking up" of "undigested barbarism"—could not have imagined.[43]

Deutscher returned to Israel in 1958 to report on "Israel's Tenth Birthday" for the *Observer*. (A sister of his lived on a kibbutz, and he had an Israeli publisher, Am Oved.) He obviously did not subscribe to Rodinson's theory that Israel had been *given* to the Jews by the imperialist powers as a kind of recompense for the Shoah; on the contrary, he noted that Israelis proudly celebrated what he called "the heroism" of the 1948 war. Deutscher opened his article by lauding Israel's "record of great achievement" in its first decade and expressed, as before, a kind of baffled admiration: "The emergence of Israel is indeed, like all the long and dramatic history of the Jews, a phenomenon unique in its kind, a marvel and a prodigy of history, before which Jew and non-Jew alike stand in awe and amazement, wondering over its significance."[44] "Israel's Tenth Birthday" combines empathy for Israel with warnings to it; Deutscher described himself as Israel's friend despite his many criticisms.

He still worried, and still for good reasons, about the country. The conditions that contributed to its 1948 victory, including Arab disunity and underdevelopment, would not last forever, though Israel seemed dangerously oblivious of this. The Israelis, Deutscher wrote, "might at least take a more sober view of their predicament and chances, and beware being carried away by their new-fangled and already red-hot nationalism. They also ought to get used to the idea that their state is not above criticism: it is an earthly creation not a Biblical sanctity." Israel could not exist indefinitely in a sea of hostility: "In the long run, Israel cannot survive on the borders of Asia and Africa in conflict with Asia and Africa." (Actually, it has survived in just this way, though at woeful cost.) And though "at its very birth it could not help trespassing upon the rights of the Arabs," he argued that Israel had done far too little in pursuit of peace or, at least, sustainable coexistence.[45] This was an indisputably valid point, though Deutscher never discussed Arab intransigence as a factor in this stalemate.

More than Arendt, Deutscher tied Israel's existence to the Shoah. In his view, the genocide provided Israel with whatever justification it had. This was a surprisingly limited view for a knowledgeable historian. Deutscher knew that Zionism predated Hitler, and not just among European Jews; as Albert Memmi would recall of his Tunisian childhood, "From the time my friends and I were twelve years old, long before the sufferings of the European Jews, we conspired, amid an Arab world that had always been hostile, for the construction of a Jewish state."[46] Deutscher knew, too, that some Zionists advocated a Jewish state as a pro-active undertaking to build a Hebrew culture rather than as a defensive response to anti-Semitism.

Yet Deutscher did intuit something important; something that, I believe, is a key to his ambivalence about Israel and that of many others. Deutscher viewed the State of Israel as the bastard child of modern Europe, borne from Western civilization's auto-suicide in the middle of the twentieth century. Israel "came into being not as 'a sublime fulfilment of history's cycle' but as an act of Jewish despair," he wrote. The country was, therefore, "a monument to the grimmest phase of European history, a phase of madness and decay."[47] In this view, Israel is the eternal reminder of bad news, irrespective of either its achievements or crimes. In this view, Israel's patrimony is depraved hatred rather than idealistic hope. In this view, when the world looks at Israel, it sees barbarism rather than civilization—or, rather, it is reminded of how intertwined they are, try though we might to deny this.

Deutscher's ambivalence about Israel was also, I believe, intimately tied to his conflicted feelings about the Jewish world of his childhood. This was a world that had been lost not through natural change or historic progress but through a kind of violence that, he wrote, "defied normal and sane human imagination." He movingly described that world and its people in an appreciation of Marc Chagall that he wrote for the BBC: "Ground down by poverty and persecution, shaken by pogroms, numbed by an archaic Messianic faith, torn between hopes held out by Zionism on the one hand, and revolutionary socialism on the other, Eastern European Jewry was hovering over the precipice. The Jewish *Luftmensch* . . . survived as if by [a] miracle." Deutscher proceeded to praise Chagall's "reconciliation with Jewish history, his surrender to it. He denounces and condemns no one. Over the ashes of Majdanek and Auschwitz he weeps his *Kaddish*, the great prayer for the dead."[48]

Deutscher's own reconciliation was rockier. He veered between sporadic affection for, and increasing aversion to, Jewish culture in general and Israel in particular. The journalist and historian Jon Kimche, a friend, observed that Deutscher spoke of "his Polish Jewish past in an uncritical manner which he never adopted towards anything else. It was a strange contradiction which Deutscher himself never really explained: this demonstratively brutal rejection of a past which he could not resist romanticizing."[49] Actually, Deutscher's approach was not entirely uncritical. In a mid-sixties essay he wrote contemptuously of assimilated Western European Jews and evinced a pride in his religious upbringing while simultaneously condemning Judaism's stranglehold on Jews in the East. "The *Yahudim* of the West, the bourgeoisie and plutocracy, had to carry their Tales and Tefilim [*sic*] as something that would boost their sense of respectability and dignity," he recalled. "We [Easterners] had our dignity and we had no need to boost it. We knew the Talmud. . . . We had grown up in that Jewish past." Yet this tradition, when carried into the present, proved tyrannical: "We had the eleventh, and thirteenth and sixteenth centuries of Jewish history living next door to us and under our very roof; and we wanted to escape it and live in the twentieth century. . . . We could see, and smell, the obscurantism of our archaic religion and a way of life unchanged since the middle ages." He mocked the "fashionable longing" of Western Jews for the shtetl—Martin Buber was singled out—as "Kafkaesque."[50]

Deutscher exhibited a much harsher attitude toward his religious past in an interview he gave just after the Six-Day War. No longer was a religious upbringing or membership in a religious community a source of pride or identity. Now he spoke with disgust of "the medieval figures of the rabbis and *khassidim* jumping with joy at the Wailing Wall; and I felt how the ghosts of Talmudic obscurantism—and I know these only too well—crowded in on the country, and how the reactionary atmosphere had grown dense and stifling."[51] Israel was an overwhelmingly secular country in 1967, which makes one wonder whether Deutscher's furious reaction was inspired more by his unresolved past than by Israel's present. But it is also true that many secular Israelis were equally aghast at the messianic fervor, which would soon find material realization in the settler movement.

It was not only Orthodox Judaism from which Deutscher recoiled. A growing distaste for all aspects of Jewish life manifested itself in his strange repression of Hebrew and Yiddish, the languages in which he had first learned to read and write and understand the world. Deutscher lectured in Yiddish while in Israel, and the journalist S. J. Goldsmith, a British friend, recalled their Yiddish conversations during World War II: "We would sometimes walk . . . through the quiet squares of Bloomsbury—unusually and strangely quiet between air raids—and Deutscher would hold forth in his slow, pontificating voice, and in a very fine Yiddish, about the war and its aftermath."[52] In a 1966 essay Deutscher described Yiddish as "vigorous, pithy, constantly renewing and enriching itself" and bemoaned how the Shoah had reduced it, "almost overnight, [to] a dead language."[53] But at some later point while in England, he apparently forgot virtually all of his Hebrew and most of his Yiddish: an especially odd occurrence for such a fluent linguist. Goldsmith speculated that this so-called forgetfulness was actually "a conscious effort to dissociate himself from everything connected with latter-day Zionism and the Jewish State. How else could a man with an excellent memory and a great gift for languages forget a language [i.e., Hebrew] in which he wrote poetry? . . . It must have been an act of will— Isaac was a very determined man. . . . His Yiddish was halting in his last years—as if he had learned it recently rather than given it up recently."[54]

Whatever his ambivalence toward the shtetl, its vernacular, and Talmudic studies, Deutscher retained a deep love for the Jewish workers' movement of interwar Poland. "Nowhere have I again found this broad, political horizon, this devotion to ideals, this sacrifice, this courage," he wrote in 1958. That movement, though secular, was far from "non-Jewish." But it was Jewish in a particular way: urban, intellectual, socialist. Deutscher tenderly recalled Warsaw's main Jewish quarter, "the Muranów district as it was—among our Nathans and Itzhaks, in our trade unions, in the midst of the Jewish masses pulsing with the warmth of life and revolutionary passion! . . . Unfortunately, that environment no longer exists. . . . [It] bled to death and perished under the ruins of the Warsaw Ghetto."[55] In later life, though, Deutscher seems to have increasingly equated socialism and secularism with a wholesale rejection of Jewish culture.

Enzo Traverso, who works within the Marxist tradition but is critical of it, has written that twentieth-century Marxists generally failed to understand two of their most intensely addressed topics: anti-Semitism and Nazism. Traverso cites a confluence of factors for this failure, including Marxist theorists' anti-nationalism, reductive analysis of religion, unflagging belief in reason, view of history as linear development, resistance to psychoanalytic insights, and overemphasis on class. In the crucial period between the two world wars, Marxists of various tendencies offered different interpretations of the coming crisis. But most were monocausal and each, Traverso wrote, "was incapable of grasping the real dynamic of German anti-Semitism, culminating at Auschwitz. Basically, they perceived anti-Semitism as an epiphenomenon of national socialism, not as a goal in itself."[56] (This weakness continued in the postwar period; it is striking that a leading Marxist historian like Eric Hobsbawm devoted almost no attention to the Shoah in his comprehensive history of the twentieth century.) In Deutscher's writings on Jewish history and Israel, we can observe the struggle between loyalty to classical Marxist analyses and the sometimes reluctant need to reach beyond them—or, at least, to recognize their limits.

This struggle underlies Deutscher's 1966 essay "Who is a Jew?," which was based in part on an interview he gave to the *Jewish Quarterly*. In this article, Deutscher seems to argue most of all with himself. "It goes without saying that classical Marxism made no allowance for anything like the Nazis' 'Final Solution,'" he admitted, and then added, in what must be one of his greatest understatements, "Classical Marxism reckoned with a healthier and more normal development of our civilization in general." Nevertheless, he insisted, he saw no need for theoretical reconsiderations, despite the twentieth century's shattering historic ruptures and moral deformations: "To my mind, the tragic events of the Nazi era neither invalidate the classical Marxist analysis of the Jewish Question *nor call for its revision.*"[57]

This is a curious statement. Classical Marxism predicted that Judaism and the Jewish people would disappear through assimilation; that modernity would vanquish anti-Semitism; and that national borders and national chauvinism would abate as a result of transnational capital, thereby laying the foundation for socialism. Each of these predictions proved breathtakingly wrong. European Jewry did disappear, but through mass murder rather than mass acceptance. Anti-Semitism assumed new, secular, ever more deadly forms. Hysterical nationalist belligerence, aimed at neighboring countries or internal minorities, overtook considerable segments of the European working classes. When Deutscher stuck to strict Marxist theory, his analysis of Nazism was uselessly reductive, as when he claimed that German fascism "was nothing but the self-defence of the old order against communism. . . . European Jewry has paid the price for the survival of capitalism. . . . This fact surely does not call for a revision of the classical Marxist analysis—it rather confirms it." The Jewish annihilation, he insisted, "does not weaken my Marxist conviction, on the contrary, it supports my Marxist *Weltanschauung*."[58]

In criticizing Deutscher's stubbornness, I am not suggesting that Hitler killed Marxist analysis (though he killed many Marxists); on the contrary, philosophers and historians—Theodor Adorno, Horkheimer, Traverso, Norman Geras, Martin Jay, Moishe Postone, and others—adhere(d) to Marxism, often as critical theorists, even after the genocide. But theirs was a broadened, flexible Marxism, one that incorporated approaches and insights from other theories and disciplines. What dismays me here is Deutscher's rigidity. He implies that the Shoah represented no significant detour from the Marxist scheme, and that to rethink, revise, or expand Marxism means to "weaken" it. Here, his Marxism is no longer a fluid tool with which to analyze history; it becomes, instead, a kind of rote fundamentalism—eerily similar to the Talmudic studies against which the young Isaac chafed. Here, his Marxism flattens the complexity of the world instead of illuminating it.

This limited vision reached its nadir in an interview Deutscher gave to the young editors of *New Left Review* less than two weeks after the 1967 Arab-Israeli war. The interview represents Deutscher's last thoughts on Israel and Zionism (he died two months later); it was published in the journal that summer and subsequently turned into an essay for *The Non-Jewish Jew*. This too is reprinted in Shatz's *Prophets Outcast* and is one of Deutscher's frequently cited texts. That is unfortunate, for these are the hastiest thoughts that Deutscher ever expressed on Israel and far from his most insightful. One friend later wondered if Deutscher would have assented to the publication of some of his comments had he lived.

Deutscher warned that Israel's "all-too-easy triumph," and its capture of Jerusalem, Gaza, and the West Bank, might turn into a "disaster."[59] This has proved true, though he never considered that a military defeat for the Jewish state would have made the word "disaster" a grave understatement. In strong language, he rightly admonished Israelis against the belief that lasting security can be built on military victories. But other sections of the interview are clichéd and schematic, based more on abstract ideology and unexamined anger than on a scrupulous analysis of the unexpected, unprecedented situation at hand. The subtleties and complications that marked some of Deutscher's other Jewish writings are harder to find here.

Deutscher assumes a new, sectarian voice in this piece. The man of reason is replaced by the man of vitriol. He rants against U.S. imperialism and neocolonialism—terms he did not ordinarily use—though these were not the causes of the war. At the same time, he downplays the actual events that led to it. He lauds "the Arab peoples struggling for their emancipation," though it is not clear from what or whom they were emancipating themselves by fighting Israel. He assails Israeli "propagandists" who whipped up a "frenzy of belligerence, arrogance, and fanaticism" among their sheep-like fellow citizens—a "striking contrast," he asserts, to their more pacific Arab neighbors.[60] He equates Moshe Dayan with Marshal Nguyen Cao Ky, prime minister of South Vietnam's repressive military junta. (Israeli leftists also despised Dayan as the consummate hawk, but there is no evidence that Israel was becoming a military dictatorship—something that Arendt, too, had prophesied earlier.) Deutscher was always a partisan historian, but he was also a careful, evidence-based one; here he morphs into a polemicist for whom facts are a nuisance.

At the time of this interview, Israelis had made no decisions about the just-captured territories. Many were hoping, indeed expecting, to exchange land for peace. There was no settlement movement. It was Israel's victory, not its policies, that obviously enraged Deutscher; he told one British journalist that the war had "destroyed all 'rapport' between myself and the Jewish feeling" for Israel. "It is sad that this should be so, but I cannot help it."[61] Like Rodinson, Deutscher defended the Arabs' decades-long refusal to recognize Israel; anything else would mean they had "surrendered politically." He put forth the curious theory that Arab threats of destroying Israel were meaningless because the Arabs were quickly defeated. He disparaged Western leftists who had rallied to Israel's defense with the ugly expression " 'Scratch a Jewish left-winger and you find only a Zionist.' " Sartre, who had expressed solidarity with Israel, is the object of particular opprobrium: Deutscher accused of him of lacking "cool judgment" and being "overwhelmed by conflicting emotions."[62] But couldn't the same be said of Deutscher himself?

Deutscher recognized that traditionally injurious themes of Jewish history were being reprised, but he drew the wrong conclusions from this. In previous centuries, he explained, Jews were reviled as representatives of then-burgeoning capitalism; now they were reviled—in his view, with much justification—"as agents of the late, over-ripe, imperialist capitalism of our days." Thus they "are placed once again in the position of potential scapegoats. Is Jewish history to come full circle in such a way?" But the fact that Jews once more "arouse bitter emotions and hatreds in their neighbours" did not lead him to conclude anything about those neighbors or about the durability of anti-Semitism.[63]

Although Deutscher regarded the Arab regimes as Israel's victims, he was simultaneously critical of them. This is not surprising, for he was far from a Third Worldist; indeed, as a classical Marxist, he bemoaned the fact that socialist revolutions had occurred in the impoverished East. In a 1964 essay on Maoism, he wrote, "The impossibility of disentangling progress from backwardness is the price that not only Russia and China but mankind as a whole is paying for the confinement of the revolution to the underdeveloped countries. But this is the way history has turned; and now nothing can force its pace."[64] In the *New Left Review* interview, he lauds, though in a somewhat obligatory manner, the presumably revolutionary nature of Arab nationalism, but he then delineates the faults of the Arab states. These turn out to be serious; they include "a proneness to emotional self-intoxication" and "excessive reliance on nationalist demagogy." More crucial is what we would now call the democratic deficit, which Deutscher describes as "the single party system, the cult of Nasserism, and the absence of free discussion. . . . There is . . . no genuine popular participation in the political processes, no vigilant and active consciousness, no initiative from below." (No mention is made of women's subjugation.) In short, the battlefield defeats of the Arabs were social defeats: "Military inefficiency reflected here a wider and deeper, social-political weakness."[65]

Like Rodinson, Deutscher rejected the Arab states' strategy of militarily conquering Israel, which he viewed as impractical, and their goal of annihilating Israel, which he viewed as immoral. The conflict cannot be "resolved by military means. . . . What they [the Arabs] need far more urgently is a social and political strategy and new methods in their struggle for emancipation. This cannot be a purely negative strategy dominated by the anti-Israel obsession." Arab nationalism must be "disciplined and rationalized by an element of internationalism that will enable the Arabs to approach the problem of Israel more realistically than hitherto. They cannot go on denying Israel's right to exist and indulging in bloodthirsty rhetoric." He calls for the Arab nations to achieve a "real victory, a *civilized* victory": not the destruction of the Jewish state but "an intensive modernization" of their own. Deutscher hoped that this change in orientation would not take much time (he was wrong) and warns, "There is no shorter way to emancipation. The short cuts of demagogy, revenge, and war have proved disastrous enough."[66]

Deutscher urged Israelis and Arabs (he does not speak of Palestinians) to break out of their death spirals and their dreams of ultimate victory; the role of the Western Left was to tell this to each side "as clearly and bluntly as we can."[67] In the ensuing decades, especially the 1970s and eighties, the Left would fail to do so; in fact, many bystanders would goad the Palestinians to increasingly reckless acts of terror (exactly the kind of armchair radicalism that Rodinson despised). One can only wonder, with some wistfulness, what effect Deutscher might have had if he had lived. Yet I doubt that much of the New Left would have been significantly influenced by his urging of mutual Arab-Israeli accommodation. Many Trotskyist groups in Britain would become faithful advocates, or at least supporters, of Israel's destruction. And there is little evidence that Deutscher's critique of the Arab regimes was taken to heart.

Throughout the *New Left Review* interview, Deutscher uses strikingly different tones when he discusses Israel and the Arab states. His analysis of the latter, though critical, is guardedly optimistic. Other than Nasser, the Arab dictators—rather euphemistically referred to as the "more or less autocratic Leader[s]"—remain anonymous. When Deutscher turns to Israel, free-floating hostility erupts: Moshe Dayan looks like "the candidate to the dictator's post"; Israel is "repulsive and reactionary" and acts with "ferocious aggressiveness"; Ben-Gurion is "the evil spirit of Israeli chauvinism."[68] (Actually, Ben-Gurion insisted that the captured territories be quickly relinquished, and warned of dire consequences if they were not.) At the interview's conclusion, Deutscher expresses confidence that the Arab nations "will learn from their defeat and recover to lay the foundations of a truly progressive, a socialist Middle East."[69]

But the 1967 war would have exactly the opposite effect. Stunned by the quick defeat of the Arab forces and increasingly unable to develop diversified modern economies or inclusive democratic institutions, states such as Iraq, Syria, Libya, and Lebanon (and, later, Algeria and Sudan) would descend into the violent convulsions they had promised to Israel. One is reminded of Trotsky's critique of the Comintern under Stalin, which seems to be a fitting description of those Middle East regimes: It was "not only incapable of leading the workers to victory, but cannot even permit them to think through the reasons for defeat."[70] Israelis faced the opposite problem: how to think through the reasons for victory and understand what to do with it. That, too, was a failed endeavor.

If Marxists have a deity, its name would be reason—a direct result of their Enlightenment patrimony. This is one of the ways by which they distinguish themselves from, and attempt to fight, fascism. But the valorization of reason can be a handicap when trying to understand an often irrational world. The frequently unhinged quality of chauvinistic nationalism, including anti-Semitism, is one reason that the Left has so often misunderstood, underestimated, and ignored its power. In both Trotsky and Deutscher, the commitment to reason dueled with the suspicion that some historical forces are, in a final sense, inexplicable.

Trotsky wrote that, even as a youth, "national bias and national prejudices had only bewildered my sense of reason."[71] Yet we have seen that he acknowledged subterranean impulses, like the triumphant glee that accompanies the smashing of a child's head; these, too, determine the course of history. Deutscher, a true child of the Enlightenment, substituted rational causation for the religious faith of his forefathers. Yet he was forced to admit, post-Shoah, that the "goddess of reason was the goddess that failed."[72]

Despite his sometimes simplified explanations of the genocide, Deutscher ultimately expressed a kind of traumatized shock—a negative awe—when he faced the Shoah. To analyze the political, economic, and social causes for the rise of fascism was one thing; to contemplate how millions of utterly defenseless, broken people—humiliated, starved, stripped, tortured—were herded into gas chambers and mass graves was another. It was not just Marxism but the capacity for analytic interpretation itself that stumbled when confronted with this madness. "I doubt whether even in a thousand years people will understand Hitler, Auschwitz, Majdanek, and Treblinka better than we do now," Deutscher predicted in an undated essay called "The Jewish Tragedy and the Historian." "On the contrary, posterity may understand it all even less than we do." Past episodes of extreme persecution and the infliction of excruciating pain, such as the Inquisition, "still [evinced] some human logic." But the Jewish genocide was different: "The fury of Nazism . . . passes the comprehension of a historian."[73]

Deutscher insisted—rightly, I think—that being human, rather than being Jewish, precluded an understanding of Nazism's sheer sadism, which Primo Levi would call "useless violence." "I am sure that it is not my personal involvement in the Jewish catastrophe that would prevent me, even now, as a historian, from writing objectively about it," Deutscher explained. "It is rather the fact that we are confronted here by a huge and ominous mystery of the degeneration of the human character that will forever baffle and terrify mankind."[74] He concluded that a non-historian— a contemporary Aeschylus or Sophocles, perhaps—might shed light on this aporia.

Try though he sometimes might, Deutscher could not sever his connection to the Jewish people. He castigated what he saw as Israel's callous, unnecessary aggression. He forgot Yiddish and Hebrew. He claimed that "the Jewish community is still only negative." He insisted, "I have nothing in common with . . . any kind of Israeli nationalists." And yet the bond remained. "I am, however, a Jew by force of my unconditional solidarity with the persecuted and exterminated," he wrote in the year before his death. "I am a Jew because I feel the Jewish tragedy as my own tragedy; because I feel the pulse of Jewish history."[75] He did not believe that Israel was the answer to the Jewish Question, but he knew that the destruction of Israel would be a staggering Jewish calamity. He did not necessarily believe in the Jewish state, but he definitely believed in the Jews.

Isaac Deutscher was not a non-Jewish Jew. He was a deeply conflicted Jew. Which means that, as he said of his hero Trotsky, Isaac Deutscher was "very Jewish indeed."

CHAPTER FIVE

Albert Memmi

ZIONISM AS NATIONAL LIBERATION

A JEW. AN ARAB. AN AFRICAN. A nationalist. An internationalist. A secularist. A socialist. An anti-colonialist. A Zionist. Few people combine the identities, both inherited and chosen, of Albert Memmi. He not only proudly owned these seemingly disparate affinities but insisted that, though their relationships to each other might sometimes be thorny, they were never inherently antagonistic. His life's aim was to integrate them.

Memmi's writings, which span more than six decades, grapple in bold and original ways with the entangled questions of Jewish identity, social justice, anti-colonialism, and Zionism. Most striking was his ability to reject the either/or polarities of Arab *or* Jew, socialism *or* Zionism, national liberation *or* internationalism. This capacity grew, I believe, out of psychological and moral intuitions as much as political insight. Memmi confronted the catastrophic nature of Jewish history, yet he never retreated into Maxime Rodinson's fantasy of assimilation. He was a militant anti-colonialist, yet he decried the failures of the Third World's post-independence regimes. He was a devoted leftist, yet he sharply reproached the Left's recurring failure to understand the nature of Jewish oppression and the Zionist movement. And far more than Hannah Arendt, Isaac Deutscher, or Rodinson, Memmi understood the urgent necessity and innate dignity of the twentieth century's national-independence movements. Yet he was more astute in recognizing their limitations and dangers.

Throughout all this—throughout a long life of activism, teaching, and engaged writing—Memmi's Zionism remained a proud part of his allegiances, even after Israel became a detested outcast on the left. Memmi turned Rodinson's anti-Zionism on its head. Whereas Rodinson believed that socialist solidarity negated Zionism, Memmi argued that Zionism, as the national liberation movement of an oppressed people, *demanded* the Left's support.

Much of Memmi's work was devoted to exploring the subjective aspects of oppression; in addition to being a political essayist, he was a novelist and poet. He never underestimated the importance of psychology and culture. In a 1996 interview, he said that while Marx was right to stress objective class relations, economic oppression was only the beginning of the human story: "There are always things in the cultural domain that can't be accounted for in strictly economic terms. People don't buy tickets to go to the movies because they have the money but because they need to dream."[1]

Memmi was interested in people, especially oppressed people (the colonized, the proletariat, the poor, immigrants, Jews, blacks, women, himself) as they were: stunted, conflicted, sometimes profoundly misguided—and as they might become. He was an Enlightenment humanist to his core. He wrote in one of his early works, "Either one accepts all the suffering or one rejects it all."[2]

Rather than lean on "scientific" Marxism, Albert Memmi used his life experiences and emotional struggles to lay the foundation of the political ideas he developed. Paradoxically, though, his views on Jewish oppression and the solutions to it were based on material reality more than those of committed Marxists like Rodinson and Deutscher. Memmi's early years were an education in exclusion; one critic described his journey "from the Jewish ghetto of his childhood to the bourgeois Jewish school where he learned he was poor, to the French lycée where he learned he was a 'native,' to the Sorbonne where he learned he was a Jew."[3] And yet, though schooled in "otherness," Memmi became the most inclusive of men.

He was born in 1920 to a Jewish family in Tunisia, which was then under French rule. Memmi's mother was an illiterate Berber Jew; his father, a Jew of Italian-Tunisian stock, was a harness-maker, "somewhat pious," Memmi remembered; "as were all those men of his trade."[4] The

Memmis were poor and lived just outside Tunis's Jewish ghetto. Like Deutscher, Memmi rebelled against religious tradition, became an atheist, and had deeply mixed feelings about the Jewish world of his childhood. That world would come to an abrupt end after two thousand years of existence, due not to the Shoah but to Tunisian independence.

Like Rodinson and Deutscher, young Albert was intellectually gifted. He attended a yeshiva, an Alliance Israélite school, and a French lycée; his languages were Judeo-Arabic, Hebrew, and French. In Memmi's view, there was nothing picturesque about the ghetto: It was a place of "physiological poverty, undernourishment, syphilis, tuberculosis, mental illness . . . an every-day, all-day historical catastrophe."[5] Poverty led a preadolescent Albert to an early, perverse form of class consciousness. "As young Zionists we were so furiously angry at the rich German Jews that we received the announcement of their early tragedies [under the Nazis] rather coldly and, I must confess, almost with satisfaction."[6]

But the ghetto was also a world of solidity and belonging—the very antithesis of rootless cosmopolitanism. Memmi would recall the comfort of its "collective presence," which embodied "a kind of common soul." It was Jewish culture, not the Jewish religion, that he treasured; in fact, he castigated Judaism as "the least comfortable religion there is . . . narrow, mistrustful, fiercely opposed to any innovation." Yet this did not translate into scorn for his religious forebears or for observant Jews; unlike Rodinson, Memmi believed that "one always feels a close kinship with one's own people, even if they repel you."[7]

Though Memmi often described the Jewish condition as one of almost unrelieved estrangement and torment, he was surprised when, arriving in Paris after World War II, he discovered that Jewish-French intellectuals had little sense of a positive Jewish past; this alienation struck him as "utterly ridiculous." In contrast, he considered himself "heir to a powerful tradition and culture"—although, as a free thinker, "that has not prevented me . . . from rebelling frequently against the supremacy of the Tribe, from mocking the words of the ancients." His sense of the relationship between a secular Jewish identity and the Jewish religious past was more dialectical than Deutscher's. For Memmi, secularism incorporated rather than precluded strong ties to Jewish tradition. "In debating against the written and the oral word, I nevertheless am nourished by it," he wrote. "Though I can make fun of details, at heart I do not find it ridiculous to belong to the 'People of the Book.' "[8] Staunch atheism and a grounded Jewish identity were not at war. Unlike Rodinson and Deutscher, Albert Memmi did not aspire to become a non-Jewish Jew.

The social and political position of Tunisian Jews was complex. "We were not even citizens," Memmi recalled. "But, after all, very few people were." Physically and culturally, poor Jews were close to their Muslim neighbors. But Jewish Tunisians were a tiny minority, and in many ways a powerless one. "Even the most underprivileged" Arab, Memmi wrote, "feels in a position to despise and insult the Jew."[9] With shame, Memmi remembered "the extraordinarily fearful timidity of our community in Tunis. We were taught to be nice to everyone—the French who were in power, the Arabs who were in the majority"; with no citizenship or real political power of their own, Jews were "emasculated, castrated."[10] Almost inevitably, the Jewish community looked to the French for protection—though not always successfully, as they would discover at great cost during the Vichy period. Tunisian Jews were colonizers and colonized, advantaged and disadvantaged. Memmi described himself as "a sort of half-breed of colonization, understanding everyone because I belonged completely to no one."[11]

Memmi was a preteen Zionist at a time when the movement seemed at best a utopian adventure and at worst a dangerous fantasy. His education in Zionist youth organizations included "tossing grenades" and learning "the doctrines and precepts of revolutionary action. . . . On Sundays, we would set out for the country, pretending to be Israeli pioneers. We didn't even forget to imitate the internal bickering of the distant, young national movement." His adolescence corresponded to a particularly hopeful time in world politics, and he remembered the year 1936 with special affection: "The entire world seemed to invite me to a marvelous wedding celebration." Though fascism was on the rise, the Popular Front had won the French elections, and in Tunisia there were "joyous open-air meetings" in which "we rubbed elbows with Arab peddlars, Sicilian bricklayers and French railroad workers, one and all dazzled by these new feelings of brotherhood. In Spain, however, the war was beginning, never to end. Yet . . . we cried out joyously: 'No pasarán!' "[12] It was a perilous moment, but a confident one. That "they shall not pass" was a certainty.

In this atmosphere, a distinct Jewish identity seemed self-absorbed, cumbersome, and embarrassing. "I no longer wanted to be that invalid called a Jew, mostly because I wanted to be a man; and because I wanted to join with all men to reconquer the humanity which was denied me."[13] Memmi became an ardent Francophile, in love with French culture and republican principles. "After all, it was they who had invented the remedies after the ills: equality after domination, socialism after exploitation." Zionism ceased to matter: "I thought no more about Palestine. . . . 'The Jewish problem' had been diluted with the honey of that universal embrace." Memmi's anti-nationalism was part of a more general rejection of all presumably bourgeois attitudes and institutions, common to young leftists of his time (and ours). Already, he could detect the death "of religions, families and nations. We had nothing but anger, scorn and irony for the die-hards of history who clung to those residues."[14] Energetic hope and energetic contempt braided together.

In 1939, Memmi graduated from his French lycée in Tunis, winning the country's top philosophy prize. He enrolled at the University of Algiers, but his time there was brief. With the outbreak of war, he was expelled from Algeria and sent back to Tunisia, which was then occupied by the Nazis and the Vichy French. Memmi was sent to a forced labor camp for Jews, from which he escaped; some of his fellow prisoners were deported to the death camps. After the war he finished his degree in Algiers, then moved to Paris for further study in philosophy at the Sorbonne. But here, too, as a Jew and North African, he found that he belonged to "them," not "us."

As with Deutscher, the war and the genocide dented Memmi's faith in Western humanism. "The Europe we admired, respected and loved assumed strange faces: even France, democratic and fraternal, borrowed the face of Vichy." And dented his faith, too, in a universal brotherhood into which Jews would be seamlessly integrated: "I had learned the harsh lesson that *my* destiny [as a Jew] did not necessarily coincide with the destiny of Europe."[15] But his basic convictions remained. Surely a new world, a world of dignity for all, would emerge from the ashes. In 1949, the Tunisian independence movement drew him back home.

Tunisia *was* home, and Memmi viewed the fight for its independence as his own. "How could I, who applauded so wildly the struggle for freedom of other peoples, have refused to help the Tunisians in whose midst I had lived since birth and who, in so many ways, were my own people? . . . Thus, having ceased to be a universalist, I gradually became . . . a Tunisian nationalist.[16] Memmi was a founding editor of the prominent pro-independence magazine *Jeune Afrique*, whose cultural pages he edited for several years. He wrote that he fought for Arab independence "with my pen, and sometimes physically."[17]

Alas, Memmi's love for Tunisia was unrequited. The new state established Islam as the official religion, Arabized the education system, and quickly made it known that, as Memmi put it, "it preferred to do without" its Jews.[18] Despite the Jews' millennia-long presence in the country—"we were there before Christianity and long before Islam," he protested—they were not viewed as genuine Tunisians.[19] Following independence, a series of anti-Jewish decrees made it virtually impossible for poor Jews to make a living. Memmi's hopes for a secular, multicultural republic of equal citizens were dashed. This rejection by his brothers felt deeply personal; it was not just a political wrong turn but an intimate, humiliating wound. An exodus of Tunisian Jews, most to Israel, some to France, ensued; an even larger group would leave after 1967.

The exclusionary measures stunned Memmi. "The ground we had thought to be so solid, was swept from under our feet," he recalled. "We made the cruel discovery that ... socially and historically we were nothing."[20] But the impact on Left intellectuals and the poorer Jewish masses was quite different. In a trenchant 1962 essay called "Am I a Traitor?," Memmi traced the surprising dialectic of Jewish participation in Tunisian independence. It was a *love* of France—of republicanism, secularism, political and civic freedoms—that prompted Jewish-Tunisian intellectuals to fight it. "By pushing their attachment to French ethical values to the limit ... they became the adversaries of French colonization," Memmi explained. "An excess of loyalty to France—to a certain image of France, the finest image," transformed these young intellectuals into anti-colonial revolutionaries.[21] Yet this very fealty to French ideals led them to misperceive the true nature of the independence movement. They assumed that a free Tunisia would model itself on a free France, and they therefore overlooked the liberation movement's Islamic, Arab-nationalist, and culturally conservative aspects.

A chasm opened between the intellectuals and the people of the ghetto. It is not that the ghetto Jews—the poor, the pious, the unschooled—opposed Tunisian independence. On the contrary: "Inside the ghetto, it was not denied that the Moslems were justified in fighting for an end to Moslem misery." But the uneducated shopkeepers and housewives saw what the intellectuals could not: that the end of French rule would not result in an inclusive republic; that their Muslim neighbors regarded them as alien; that Jews would be endangered rather than liberated by the new government. In short, ordinary Tunisian Jews understood the injustice of French rule yet feared its end. "And—why not say it?—the ghetto was right. The intellectuals were self-deceived, blinded by their ethical aspirations."[22] This was a formative experience for Memmi; he would henceforth place himself between vanguardism and populism. Intellectuals might hold positions in advance of the majority, especially on questions like women's rights, but they could not be deaf to the wisdom of the people they presumed to lead.

The Tunisian experience also taught Memmi the necessity of asserting a distinct Jewish position within an internationalist one. The mistakes of the Jewish-Tunisian intellectuals, he argued, stemmed from their insistence that they were *only* Tunisian, and from their confidence that their Muslim countrymen viewed them as such. Neither belief proved true. "The destiny of the Jew too often carries with it a hard nucleus that cannot be minimized," Memmi reflected. "No historic duty toward other men should prevent our paying particular attention to our special difficulties." Internationalism was a primary value, but not at the price of Jewish sacrifice or Jewish suicide. "Beyond the solidarity with all men, there exists a more humble and often less comfortable duty: to come to grips directly with their special destiny as Jews, without worrying too much about being called a traitor by anyone."[23] Tunisia taught Memmi that Jewish identity could not be simply wished away—and that the wish itself was hazardous.

Upon independence, Tunisian Jews were in effect quickly transformed into pariahs. Unlike Arendt, Memmi did not revel in this role. "There may be some pride in that solitude and distance," he wrote. "But I believe that the price for them is too high. Illegitimacy sharpens the mind, to be sure, but it is a very uncomfortable condition." Still, he never regretted his participation in the Tunisian cause; no leftist, he argued, could fail to see the justice of the anti-colonial movements. And he was even somewhat forgiving of the rejection. Emerging states, Memmi observed, tend by their nature to be exclusive as they attempt to create a national identity, though this often bodes ill for the Jews. "It is in the very way in which new nations were born that differences became clear. . . . It is in the way that Tunisia became a nation like other nations that we [Jews] became, as we were everywhere else, a civic and national negativity."[24]

By the time Tunisia became independent in 1956, Memmi had concluded that he could not make a life there despite his championing of its freedom. He moved to Paris, where he remained for the rest of his life as a professor, novelist, and political writer. Soon after arriving in the capital, he visited an older Jewish writer and expressed his confusions about how to be a Jew, a Tunisian, and a French citizen. After listening to Memmi's anxieties, the older writer replied, " 'Well, keep it all; be everything at once.' "[25] Keeping it all became Memmi's project.

In 1953, while working as a high school philosophy teacher in Tunis, Memmi published his first book, *The Pillar of Salt*. Albert Camus wrote the preface, and the novel won the prestigious Fénéon and Carthage prizes. Set in French-ruled Tunis and highly autobiographical, it is the bildungsroman of a poor, eager Jewish philosophy student named Alexandre Mordekhai Benillouche. The novel is a captivating mixture of tenderness and contempt, lyricism and harshness. It is also sensuously evocative. We can almost taste the piece of chocolate (a very small piece, because he is poor) that Alexandre stuffs into his bread; we can almost smell the clean ocean air of Tunis's beach. Alexandre's family is loving, his community protective, and his early years happy and safe. His is "a world of sweetness, all harmony and perfume."[26] Of course it cannot last.

On the basis of his superior intellect, Alexandre is offered an elite French education, all expenses paid by wealthier members of the Jewish community. Here is where his possibilities and his troubles begin. Education opens up his world in wondrous ways: He falls in love with Racine, Rousseau, and Robespierre. Education also separates him from his family and the ghetto. But rejecting his old world does not mean that the new one welcomes him, and Alexandre finds himself in an anguished no-man's-land. Lashing out, he is filled with angry scorn for everyone and (almost) everything: his backward family, pious Jews, medieval Judaic traditions—and, equally, the callousness of the bourgeoisie, the snobbishness of his rich classmates, the hypocrisy of the French, the anti-Semitism of the Arabs. The poor disgust him, but so do the moneymakers; he dislikes his gentile classmates, but his fellow Jewish students are perhaps even worse.

Most of all, Alexandre detests himself. He is not strong enough or brave enough; his manners are awkward, his clothes are shabby, his

French accent is bad, his family is mortifying. What makes this novel so unusual is that Memmi paints his alter ego in the most unpleasant light; one critic wrote that the book's "remarkable depth of self-analysis" is "sometimes so cruel that it has been compared to a surgical operation."[27] In contrast to many autobiographical novels, *The Pillar of Salt* reads as a stinging self-indictment. (At one point Alexandre describes himself as a "mediocre imbecile.")[28] It is Alexandre's primitive, uneducated family, whom he grows to despise with the exacting cruelty of the young, which evokes our empathy. In a particularly wrenching scene, his weary, over-worked father weeps when he realizes that his brazenly secular son will not bury him with Jewish rites when he dies.

And yet Alexandre wins our affections too. We are touched by his yearnings, his woefulness, and his precocious moral seriousness. Alexandre is determined to create a life that will be solely, uniquely his own. But how can he do this, and where does he belong? "I'm African, not European," Alexander broods, "a native in a colonial country, a Jew in an anti-Semitic universe, an African in a world dominated by Europe. . . . How is it possible to harmonize so many discords"?[29] This sense of torment escalates until he reaches a breaking point.

In a crucial chapter, Alexandre is sent to an internment camp for Jews during the Nazi/Vichy occupation. (He volunteers to go there, out of soli-darity with others.) Most of the camp's inmates are poor—the rich and middle classes could buy their freedom—and Alexandre hopes to help them sustain morale in the face of brutality. But he quickly discovers an unbridgeable gap between himself and the others. "I could neither break through the massive suspiciousness caused by their suffering, nor get them to accept me. . . . I came to realize how far my studies and my high-school education had removed me from any possible communion with my own people." I believe that this grim experience—even if somewhat fictionalized—had a profound effect on Memmi's later ideas about the need for progressive intellectuals to school themselves in humility. In one of the novel's most devastating lines, Alexandre admits his feelings for his fellow inmates: "I wanted to love them, and I fear I managed only to be sorry for them."[30]

Four years before Frantz Fanon wrote *The Wretched of the Earth*, Memmi explored the psychic toll that colonialism exacted in his landmark 1957

book, *The Colonizer and the Colonized*. Jean-Paul Sartre wrote the introduction, as he would for Fanon, and Memmi dedicated the American
edition "to the American Negro, also colonized." Memmi's book had a
strong impact on the anti-colonial liberation movements and was praised
by the likes of Léopold Senghor, Senegal's first president, and Négritude
theorist Alioune Diop. But Memmi's work was and remains overshad-
owed by Fanon's, especially in the West, for a number of reasons. These
include Fanon's premature death, his non-white identity, his rejection of
so-called Western values, his exaltation of violence, and the romance of
the Algerian Revolution. In my view, Memmi's is the deeper book, for it
resists Fanon's Manichean outlook and the easy panacea of violence.
Memmi was not a pacifist. But he knew that the creation of freer societies
would depend on the creation of freer people, and that such people could
not be birthed, much less nurtured, by the AK-47.

Whereas Fanon viewed the colonized and the colonizer as "different
species," Memmi viewed them as human beings, albeit of vastly unequal
power; the two were trapped in a suffocating embrace. Memmi seeks to
understand colonization as an objectively racist system and as a subjec-
tively damaging experience; much of the book concentrates on the psychic
impossibilities that colonialism creates. "It is not enough for the colonized to be a slave, he must also accept this role. The bond between colonizer and colonized is thus destructive and creative," he wrote. "One is
disfigured into an oppressor, . . . [a] treacherous being, worrying only
about his privileges. . . . The other, into an oppressed creature, whose
development is broken and who compromises by his defeat."[31] The colonized is not only acted upon, but colludes in his oppression.

It was this psychic mutilation—the colonized's humiliation, self-
hatred, and disavowal of self—that was so brutalizing. (There is an echo
here of Deutscher, writing of the Jews' "stigmata of shame" that Zionism
meant to eradicate.) What made the colonized's situation even more
wrenching was that, in an effort to reject the colonialist's denigration, the
oppressed created counter-myths of their own grandeur, potency, and
unquestionable moral worth. These might provide temporary satisfaction, but they will be deeply destructive to the colonized's future development. "Not only does he accept his wrinkles and his wounds, but he will
consider them praiseworthy," Memmi observed. "Suddenly, exactly to the
reverse of the colonialist accusation, the colonized, his culture, his

country, everything that belongs to him, everything he represents, become
perfectly positive elements." A fatal cultural retrogression is born:
"Everything is good, everything must be retained among his customs and
traditions."[32] Thus an injurious cycle begins; in an attempt to create a
more dignified society, the colonized maims his aptitude for critical self-
assessment precisely at the moment when he needs it most. Zionists
were hardly exempt from this syndrome; Memmi would later charge that
"illusions were born of the accusations of others and through self-
rejection, just as myths were created to counter the accusations."[33]

Memmi's analysis of the historic position of the colonized subject
closely parallels Arendt's description of Jewish worldlessness. "The most
serious blow suffered by the colonized is being removed from history," he
wrote. "He is out of the game. He is in no way a subject of history. . . . He
has forgotten how to participate actively in history and no longer even
asks to do so."[34] Memmi viewed the Third World's independence movements, as Arendt viewed Zionism, as the entering-into-history of the
world's castoffs.

The Colonized and the Colonizer was written only one year after Tunisia
gained its independence. Yet Memmi already intuited, far more incisively
than Rodinson, the crippling position in which the left-wing, Western
anti-colonialist would find himself, or put himself, for the next half
century. For moral and political reasons, the Left would of course support
the independence movements. Yet such movements would frequently
repudiate many of the Left's bedrock principles, which Memmi identified
as "political democracy and freedom, economic democracy and justice,
rejection of racist xenophobia and universality." And so the European
leftist and "leftist colonizer" (people such as himself and Albert Camus)
"discovers that there is no connection between the liberation of the colonized and the application of a left-wing program. And that, in fact, he is
perhaps aiding the birth of a social order in which there is no room for a leftist
as such."[35] Memmi would become a particularly keen observer of the Left's
confused responses to this dilemma.

Memmi was also prescient about the prominent place that terrorism
would occupy in these future struggles, though he could not foresee the
extent of the barbarism to come. It is a very bad sign of the times in which
we live that the terrorism of the postwar anti-colonial movements seems
almost quaint compared to today's beheadings, suicide bombings, mass

rapes, and deliberate targeting of humanitarian workers, doctors, journalists, intellectuals, secularists, teachers, students, and ordinary civilians of every stripe, especially women and girls. Memmi assumed he was writing within a leftist tradition that "condemns terrorism and political assassination"; he termed such actions "incomprehensible, shocking and politically absurd. For example, the death of children and persons outside the struggle."[36] But that tradition was weakening even as he wrote.

The anti-terrorist tradition that Memmi called home has been crippled if not decimated in the past half century; a crucial question for the Left is whether it can be revived. Memmi was particularly revolted by suicide bombings, which came to the fore in the Palestinian movement in the 1990s and have since globally metastasized, and which even now are sometimes falsely rationalized as "primarily a response to foreign occupation," as a 2007 essay in the *London Review of Books* claimed.[37] (Most victims of suicide bombings are unarmed Muslim civilians, often killed in mosques or marketplaces.) Murder-suicide was not just an ugly tactic but something much worse: a "reversal of the gradual humanization of human societies," Memmi wrote.[38] As a civilizational regression, it is a threat not only to its victims but to all people everywhere.

Memmi did not believe that the psychic disfigurements of colonialism could be solved through psychoanalysis on the part of the colonized or goodwill on the part of the colonizer. Colonialist oppression and its handmaid, racism, were structural problems that required structural eradication. "There is no way out other than a complete end to colonization," he wrote toward the end of *The Colonizer and the Colonized*. "The refusal of the colonized cannot be anything but absolute, that is, not only revolt, but a revolution." This was the only road to achieving the goal, the true revolutionary goal, of becoming "a whole and free man."[39] But he always insisted that resistance and terrorism are not the same.

Memmi viewed the Jewish condition as simultaneously sui generis and part of the more general problem of oppressed peoples; he explored this tension in a series of books that followed *The Colonizer and the Colonized*. The betrayal of French and Tunisian Jews under Vichy, quickly followed by the post-independence rejection of Tunisian Jews, had an enormous impact on his ideas about a collective Jewish destiny. "History is made without us," he observed. "Vichy promptly gave up its Jews and in Tunisia we were the first to be handed over. Don't tell me they also gave up the Communists and Freemasons! A man is a Communist of his own choice: it is a free action." No longer could he accept, or not accept, a Jewish identity; no longer could he separate his future from that of the Jewish people. "To be a Jew is . . . not a choice," he wrote in 1962. "It is, first of all, a fate."[40]

Now living in France, Memmi was especially caustic about the assimilationist stance of many French Jews; echoing Arendt, he called assimilation "a solitary comedy" in which only the hapless Jews believed. He addressed, in particular, the tragic delusions of people like Maxime Rodinson's murdered parents. "In the concentration camps, in front of the crematory furnaces, the Franco-Israelites repeated, like Saint Paul: 'I am French. I am a French citizen!' With this firm constancy they would finally win. They would baffle their executioners, and finally gain the esteem of their fellow citizens." When this failed to transpire, Memmi wrote, the victims would reply, "But we were wrongly burned! By a misunderstanding!"[41] Memmi's tone here verges on uncharacteristic derision, as if the victims' self-deceptions angered him almost as much as the perpetrators' crimes.

Portrait of a Jew, Memmi's first Jewish-themed book, was published in 1962. The portrait he paints is not flattering; to be Jewish is to own "a fate of oppression and an alienated culture." What was the nature of that oppressive alienation? Insecurity, anxiety, and anguish, all due to the Jew's precarious status as the perennial outsider. As for Jewish history, it had been "an endless succession of disasters, flights, pogroms, emigrations, humiliations, injustices. . . . Jewish history is but one long contemplation of Jewish misfortune."[42] (He would later write that tragedy had been inscribed on the Jewish people and could not be easily excised.) Pariahdom had not turned Jews into creative, courageous intellectuals, artists, and revolutionaries, à la Arendt; instead it had bred a flock of timorous, maladjusted neurotics. Memmi even quoted Clara Malraux, André's Jewish wife, who compared being Jewish to having syphilis.

The remarkably resourceful nature of anti-Semitism baffled Memmi. Hatred of Jews thrived happily in the First World, the Communist bloc, and the Third World. It was common to vastly different economic systems, religions, and cultures. It was embraced by magnates and proletarians, whites and blacks, believers and secularists, Right and Left;

Memmi described it as "a living thing of multiple heads that speaks with a thousand grimacing faces." Its past was long and its future seemed assured. Perhaps worst of all, it defied rational interpretation. "Today, confronted with that din of explanations, that economic, political, psycho-analytical, historical turmoil, I feel exhausted, depressed," he admitted. "No explanation of this hostility . . . can ever exhaust the subject, can ever reassure me."[43] Memmi never descended into mystical ideas about congenital anti-Semitism, but he refused to reduce such enmity to a mere by-product of capitalism. In any case, whatever the causes, he believed that anti-Semitism deformed the life of every Jew.

In *Portrait of a Jew*, Memmi parts company with a kind of generic universalism and introduces a theme he would subsequently develop: the reality, and necessity, of national identity. "A man is not just a piece of abstract humanity," he argued. People live their lives within particular nations; there is nothing reactionary about this. "True justice, true toler-ance, universal brotherhood do not demand negation of differences between men, but a recognition and perhaps an appreciation of them." Jews in particular had paid a high price for abstract universalism, which suppressed their particular history and particular needs. Now it was time to acknowledge a truth that was existential and political at once: "I am convinced that difference is the condition requisite to all dignity and to all liberation. . . . To be is to be different."[44] By denying these realities, socialist intellectuals separated themselves from the very people in whose name they struggled. After all, most people—revolutionaries like Trotsky and Luxemburg notwithstanding—want to live within a national commu-nity. They do not regard this as an illness in need of cure or a sin in need of expiation.

Memmi was not, however, an exponent of what we now call identity politics. On the contrary, he would criticize the politics of differentiation as they morphed into a kind of narcissistic self-preoccupation. He hoped that the assertion of cultural and national differences would serve as the basis for a sturdy internationalism rather than as an end in itself.

In subsequent books, Memmi's depictions of the ways in which oppression had disfigured Jewish culture grew more harsh; anti-Semites could have a field day with some of his writings. He believed that a posi-tive Jewish identity existed; in this, he parted ways with the Sartre of *Anti-Semite and Jew*, though the two men were philosophically close. (*The Pillar of Salt's* Alexandre is the echt existentialist antihero.) But Memmi echoed the self-critique of those Zionists—Koestler was a prime example—who saw the Diaspora as the breeding ground for a collective personality disorder. And he voiced the same sense of humiliation about Jewish history as Arendt. In his 1966 book *The Liberation of the Jew,* Memmi excoriated "the ghetto culture of oppressed and broken people" and Diaspora Jewry's "cultural asphyxiation." The Jewish people were "socially and historically sick"; Jews inhabited the earth as "the living dead."[45]

The concept of a chosen people, Memmi argued, was profoundly *anti*-Zionist. Rather than serving as the basis for a Jewish state, chosenness was the reaction of an oppressed people to the triple deformity of no country, no army, and no political power. He assailed the peculiar Jewish pathology that equates suffering with superiority. "A painful need to understand consumes the Jew: why this cruel fate? Why is he thrown into this terrible history . . . ? The Election explains it all. . . . It reassures and flatters him, it demands and attracts. It is at the same time the glory and the duty of the Jew."[46] Each catastrophe became proof of moral worth.

To compensate for their misery, the Jews, like the Third World revolutionaries he had analyzed in *The Colonizer and the Colonized,* basked in the myth of glorious traditions, a noble past, and an unequalled cultural legacy. "Culture was our last trump card. . . . It enabled us to smile condescendingly on our executioners."[47] Here, again, is the self-defeating dialectic of the subordinated: The more degraded he is, the more grandiose his sense of self.

With the end of oppression—which for Memmi meant the achievement of political sovereignty—Jews would be able to dispense with the "fabulous fairy tale" of chosenness.[48] The ancient burden and ancient curse would be vanquished: Free at last! Memmi reversed the terms of religious Zionism. Israel was the endpoint, not the realization, of chosenness.

In *The Liberation of the Jew,* Memmi presents himself as an unwavering Left Zionist. He views Zionism as neither more nor less than the national liberation movement of the Jewish people. Jewish oppression and anti-Semitism can be defeated only by changing the objective predicament—dependence, dispersion, minority status, and statelessness—of the Jews. The task of liberation is not only to reject the abjection and grandiosity of the Jewish psyche but to destroy the Jewish *condition.* Rodinson and Deutscher would have agreed on the necessity of this project though not, obviously, on Memmi's solution. Rodinson looked to radical assimilation, and Deutscher to Communist revolution, to transform the Jew.

Memmi looked to Israel. "It was high time we became adult; in other words, non-dependent, neither in fear nor in hope"; the era of partial solutions and "the remedies of slaves" was past. Political independence was the only way to address the composite oppression—psychic and economic, social and political—of the Jews: "Only this collective autonomy will give us at last the daring and the taste for liberty which alone are foundations of dignity." Like Arendt, Memmi believed that individual solutions had come to naught. So too had the collective solutions of "money, science, honors, universality." None of these mattered, for "without liberty all these things will give forth the tenacious odor of death."⁴⁹ As with the colonized, so with the Jews: Nothing short of revolution would do.

Memmi envisoned Israel as the center of Jewish identity around which the Diaspora would reorient itself—a proposition that was anathema to many French Jews. (One can imagine Rodinson's alarm.) "The national solution . . . is the only definitive solution," Memmi insisted. "Israel is not a supplementary contribution, a possible insurance in case of difficulties in the Diaspora; it must be the frame of reference for the Diaspora which must in [the] future *redefine* itself in relation to it." Crucially, though, he distinguished unequivocal support from uncritical support. Israel's treatment of its Arab citizens, its prejudice against Sephardic Jewish immigrants, the influence of the rabbis, and, after 1967, the Occupation: All were subject to his critique. "The actions taken by its [Israel's] governments have often shocked me," he asserted. "I have never denied myself the right to question them or denounce them." None of this, however, prompted him to doubt the need for a Jewish state. Here, too, Memmi's experience as an anti-colonial North African was key. "I only criticize what exists and ought to function better; I never question the existence [of Israel] itself; just as no scandal, no error can make us doubt the necessity of decolonization."⁵⁰

It was statehood, not the mystique of a "promised land," that interested Memmi. (As a secularist he would have asked: "Promised by whom?") He argued that the destruction of Israel would be a greater tragedy than the Shoah precisely because Israel represented the will to survive and a conscious act of regeneration. He concludes *The Liberation of the Jew* on a note of high expectation and deep anxiety: "Israel is hence-forth your concern. It is . . . our only real card, and our last historical chance. All the rest is diversion."[51] Koestler believed that Diaspora Jews could, indeed must, sever themselves from Israel; Memmi found that inconceivable.

Albert Memmi was passionately committed to the Left and one of its frankest critics.

Memmi's adherence to socialism was entwined with his identity as a Jew. In fact, he believed that every Jew, whether in the Diaspora or Israel, *had* to be of the Left; as a persecuted people, Jews required a radically transformed world. "I continued, I continue, to think that socialism is the only honorable, probably the only effective, road open to humanity," he wrote in 1966. "We [Jews] were, in a way, condemned to the Left."[52] Even after the Left's rancor toward Israel became widespread, Memmi affirmed this attachment. Socialists, he wrote in 1975, "are my people, their ethics are mine, and I hope to build with them a world for all; it is among them that you will find the greatest number of Jewish intellectuals, and that is fine."[53]

But there was a problem, and it was large: The Left had betrayed the Jewish people time and again. These betrayals were so extensive and recurrent that, Memmi concluded, they were intrinsic to Left politics rather than random aberrations. In a grotesque version of the repetition compulsion, the Jewish plight of marginality, exclusion, and rejection had been reproduced within the very movement in which so many Jews had placed their hopes and for which they had sacrificed, fought, and died.

For Communists like Rodinson, Jewish identity was a selfish side-show and Jewish nationalism inherently retrograde. Jewish leftists were expected to fight for others; they were the movement's designated altru-ists. Memmi had seen how selflessness was the Jewish revolutionary's ticket of admittance to the socialist fraternity, and this angered him. Caustically, he wrote, "On no condition can anyone suspect him for a moment of thinking of himself or his people. He fights unconditionally for all humanity: a trait which everyone uses and abuses; perfectly abstract, in reality laughable and touching." Jews on the left had often gratefully assented to these conditions, despite their evident folly: "Was there a more foolish or artificial policy (more non-Marxist in the final analysis) than to ask someone to fight only against an injustice of which he is not a victim?"[54]

Memmi argued that this (self-)mutilation was inherent in the Marxist analysis of the Jewish question: *"The failure of the European Left, with regard to the Jewish problem, was no accident."* There is a long line of Jewish Marxists (including Marx) who believed that the Jewish people's existence would and should cease; in traditional Marxism, "a Jew's only duty was to disappear. From what other people could one ask such saintliness?" Memmi asked. "Why such historical masochism?"[55] The Left's general antipathy to national aspirations took a singular, extreme form in the case of the Jews. A socialist might, for instance, oppose Polish nationalism, or at least Polish chauvinism. But he would not deny the existence of the Polish people or look forward to its erasure. That would be a fascist position. Yet in the case of the Jews, self-negation and brotherhood were considered synonymous.

Jewish leftists were thus transformed into what Memmi derided as the movement's "cuckolds . . . accomplices in our own destruction"; fatally naive, the Jewish socialist persisted in "seeing as friends people who would watch him being tortured with indifference." Yet there was no place outside the Left that Memmi could go. "I will not abandon socialism," he insisted.[56] But he also insisted that the socialist movement no longer deny the reality of Jewish oppression or the need for Jewish self-determination.

The Left's hostility toward the "bourgeois deviation" of nationalist aspirations became a crisis as the postwar anti-colonial movements gathered steam. In analyzing this phenomenon, Memmi focused first on France, where the predicament had multiple, intersecting causes. To begin, there was the failure of North African revolutionaries to fight for socialism and democratic freedoms and their acquiescence in religious orthodoxy and oppressive social traditions. Then, across the sea, there was the French working class's conspicuous lack of solidarity with, or actual hostility to, the anti-colonial movements. None of this comported with Marxist doctrine. And though consciously anti-colonial, French intellectuals betrayed a kind of colonialist arrogance. They expected that their politics, worldview, and modern social vision would be shared by their Third World brothers. Surely, they thought, only the shackles of imperialism had sustained practices such as religious obscurantism and the debasement of women.

One reaction to this crisis was the Communist Party's somewhat belated insistence that anti-colonialism *was* socialism (or at least soon would be). It followed that leftists should support the independence movements, no questions asked. Memmi decried this strategy, which was dictated by the Soviet Union and adopted by the French Communists, as a "mania . . . for dubbing any political mutation that they find useful 'socialist and revolutionary.' " Sooner or later, reality would assert itself: "One cannot live forever in a dream world of scholasticism or tactics, and often the real world takes its revenge—when the new leaders send the Communists to prison."[57]

He condemned the opposite reaction too: resentment of the colonized and their movements. "So these colonized people turn out to be greedy, aggressive, blood-thirsty fanatics," he wrote in an essay called "The Colonial Problem and the Left." "Well then, we will be as nationalistic as they are; and since they are making war on us, we will reply in kind." Memmi criticized this stance even as he understood it. "It is a reactionary attitude, to be sure, but . . . the claims it makes are ethical; they are those of a secular humanist bewildered by events, of a universalist who feels himself cheated and who, in a certain sense, has been."[58]

The French Left was truly in a pickle. If it championed the national liberation movements, it lost support among the French working class and sacrificed some of its basic principles. If, conversely, it pandered to French nativism, it renounced a different set of principles and, moreover, *"commits a fruitless suicide,"* for *"the right can always outbid the left on this score."*[59] And so a split, or perhaps a dual if contradictory strategy, emerged: indulging the independence movements and simultaneously ignoring what was actually happening within them.

It quickly became clear that this solution didn't solve much. In choosing to overlook developments in the Third World that it found unsavory, the European Left abandoned "both the universal and the international front," Memmi charged. "For, in the long run, no true internationalist can say: this does not concern me." The other extreme—the populist stance—was predicated on the view that the colonized are always deserving of unwavering support. This too proved destructive, for it "leads to the toleration of every kind of excess—terrorism, xenophobia, social reaction." And far from aiding the colonized, uncritical encouragement "fostered in him every kind of mental and spiritual disorder, and . . . added to the perplexity of those few victims of colonization who had retained a relatively sharp and morally sound political sense."[60] Seeking a kind of solidarity on the cheap, the Left had essentially abandoned the Third World's true progressives and true democrats, who were not necessarily dominant within their liberation movements or at the helm of their new governments.

Memmi wrote "The Colonial Problem and the Left" in 1958. He was charting, perhaps more than he knew, the future trajectory of a large and influential portion of the Left in Western Europe and the U.S. In subsequent decades, many leftists would adopt a bipolar attitude—with all the unhealthiness that implies—to the formerly colonized world and the question of nationalism. They would often take a demotic stance: Think, for instance, of Rodinson and Deutscher praising the presumably revolutionary nature of the Arab dictatorships. But in doing so, a problem instantly emerged. Those regimes were rabidly nationalist, and yet the Left had staked itself, for the past one hundred years, on *anti*-nationalism as a rudimentary principle. Here, I believe, is where Israel became so calamitously useful. The Jewish state enabled the Left to sustain a blistering critique of nationalism, albeit only in the case of one small country, while simultaneously kowtowing to the anti-imperialist and stridently nationalist rhetoric of the Third World.

This explains a glaring if often unnoticed contradiction of Left politics in the postwar period, but especially from the 1960s on. Leftists, and especially New Leftists, were enthralled by Cuban, Vietnamese, Mozambican, Chinese, Algerian, and Palestinian nationalism. But they loathed Zionism as a thing apart. This approach would come to fruition in the 1967 Arab-Israeli war, when much of the Western Left hailed some of the world's most horrifically repressive—and racist—regimes as harbingers of justice and freedom. As Simcha Flapan, a member of Israel's far-Left Mapam Party, would charge: "The socialist world approved the 'Holy War' of the Arabs against Israel in the disguise of a struggle against imperialism. . . . Having agreed to the devaluation of its own ideals, [it] was ready to enter into an alliance with reactionary and chauvinist appeals to genocide."[61]

A decade before this debacle, Memmi saw that such convoluted strategies would spell disaster by harming colonialism's victims and weakening the Left. Memmi called for a radical reorientation of the socialist move-ment. On one hand, it must recognize the validity of national liberation movements, including Zionism. Rather than regarding nationalism as something "stuck in their throats like a bone they are always longing to cough up," leftists should support national independence as "genuine and constructive. To reject it is mere abstract intellectualization: the negation of what is real." On the other, support of the unsupportable—of those who repudiated humane, democratic, and egalitarian principles—must cease. "If we accept nationalism without argument and without reflection, we are again disqualifying ourselves. We must judge it and make up our minds about its errors."[62] Critical acumen was required in all instances; no blank checks would be written.

An important test of the Left's capacity for judgment, Memmi wrote, would be its rejection of terrorism against civilians. Another test was the defense of secularism, which he regarded as a nonnegotiable principle, though he knew that many liberation movements—including sectors of the Zionist movement—did not. By secularism he did not mean imposed atheism or the banning of religious practices. Nor did he share Rodinson's and Deutscher's contempt for religion and the religious (though Alexandre, his young alter ego in *Pillar of Salt,* certainly did). On the contrary, Memmi wrote, it is "destructive, and perhaps unworthy . . . to be ashamed of one's people, to despise their tradition, their culture, and their institutions."[63] But he adamantly believed that a secular public sphere was the only guarantor of free thought and that cultural and reli-gious practices must be subject to the secular rule of law. Once again, he was neither vanguardist nor populist.

More specifically, secularism was indispensable for the psychological and political emancipation of the contemporary Jew: "The tyranny of Moses must be overcome for the modern Jew to be liberated."[64] Memmi expected Zionism to negate Judaism. "The Jew must be liberated from oppression, and Jewish culture must be liberated from religion," he wrote in 1966. "This double liberation can be found in the same course of action—the fight for Israel."[65] Many Zionists shared this view. Some still do. A half century later, however, there is a bitter cast to Memmi's hopes and expectations, given the immense growth and political power of the Orthodox in Israel today.

If Memmi's belief in a secular Israel failed to materialize (or, rather, to last), so did many of his hopes for the anti-colonial movements.

Revolutionary rhetoric notwithstanding, the underdeveloped world failed to sign on to the Left's project, or at least to the one that Memmi valued. "For the moment," he wrote in 2004, "the third world has chosen nationalism rather than socialism, religion rather than Enlightenment philosophy."[66]

"To my Jewish brothers / To my Arab brothers / so that we can all / be free men at last." So reads Memmi's dedication to his 1975 essay collection, *Jews and Arabs*. But the book's stance is not one of cozy fraternity. Writing in the aftermath of the Yom Kippur War, Memmi began by reasserting his identity as "an Arab Jew and a left-wing Zionist." And though he affirms the brotherhood of Arabs and Jews, he announces that Jews have "the most serious of accounts to settle" with their brothers.[67] These included the treatment of Jews when they lived in the Arab countries, Arab refusal to accept Israel, and, most controversially, acceptance of the joint Arab-Jewish population transfer that had transpired since 1948. This transfer was, Memmi asserted, an accomplished fact and the only practical basis for peace. He would build a sustained argument against the Palestinian demand for the right of return.

Memmi's depiction of intercommunal relations in the Arab world is bluntly negative. "No member of any minority lived in peace and dignity in a predominantly Arab country!" Muslims were undoubtedly colonized, but so were Jews: "dominated, humiliated, threatened, and periodically massacred." Memmi poses an uncomfortable question: "And by whom? Isn't it time our answer was heeded: by the Moslem Arabs?" He lambastes the treatment of Jews in Arab countries after 1948. "Must we accept the hangings [of Jews] in Baghdad, the prisons and the fires in Cairo, the looting and economic strangling in the Maghreb, and, at the very least, exodus?" Perhaps addressing Rodinson—the two knew of each other's work—Memmi angrily explains that Zionism was the result, not the cause, of such depredations. To argue otherwise is "historically absurd: it is not Zionism that has caused Arab anti-Semitism, but the other way around. . . . Israel is a rejoinder to the oppression."[68] He reminds the reader that he and his young Tunisian friends became Zionists in the early 1930s in reaction to what they perceived as an implacably hostile Arab world, not in response to Hitler.

"*Jewish Arabs*": This, Memmi says, is what he and his fellows wanted to be. "And if we have given up the idea, it is because for centuries the

Moslem Arabs have scornfully, cruelly, and systematically prevented us from carrying it out." He scoffs at Muammar Qaddafi's suggestion that Sephardic Israelis "go back home." Home to what? Memmi points out the glaringly obvious: "No more Jewish communities are to be found in any Arab country, nor can you find a single Arab Jew who is willing to return to his native country."[69] The State of Israel is the retort to homelessness. Home for Israelis is Israel.

It was in Paris that Memmi first encountered what he called the "fable" of Arab-Jewish harmony, which was cherished by French leftists. (Rodinson was particularly wedded to this concept.) At first Memmi considered it harmlessly silly. But the myth became dangerous after the 1967 war, "when it became a *political* argument" to delegitimize the necessity for a Jewish state and to suggest that the creation of Israel had destroyed an Edenic Middle East. Memmi admits that some Maghrebi Jews, nostalgically homesick as immigrants tend to be, upheld the myth of happy coexistence: "Uprooted people . . . embellish the past." Some native-born Israelis, too, adhered to the fiction in the hope that, if an era of Arab-Jewish amity had recently existed, it could reappear in the future too. "Otherwise the whole undertaking [of Israel] would seem hopeless!"[70] But sentimentality is a precarious basis for politics, and rose-tinted glasses had never served the Jewish people well.

Memmi upholds four principles throughout *Jews and Arabs:* First, the Arab peoples' right to independence and national development. Second, the Jewish people's right to the same. Third, that the crux of the Israeli-Arab conflict is Arab irredentism. (He was writing before Israeli irredentism, in the form of the settler movement, became so powerful.) Fourth, that that the only solution to the conflict is a national one: sovereignty for both Israelis and Palestinians.

Despite the treatment of Jews in Arab countries, pre- and post-1948, Memmi never faltered in his allegiance to the independence movements of the formerly colonized world. He praises Tunisia's Habib Bourguiba, Ghana's Kwame Nkrumah, and Senegal's Léopold Senghor. He insists on treating Arabs as political equals rather than damaged victims. "I am not a 'friend' of the Arabs," he explains. "I have a fairly accurate knowledge of the humiliations they want to erase, the fears they want to exorcise, the hopes that may be stirring in them. . . . I refuse to take an attitude toward them which, at bottom, is paternalistic . . . a mixture of old colonialist scorn and newfound benevolence." Memmi's Zionism affirms rather than negates Arab aspirations. "A Zionist who is aware of the nature of his own cause cannot fail to understand and approve of the Arab peoples' social and national ambitions, even though he may regret coming into conflict with them," he insists. But a relationship between equals entails parallel responsibilities: "Conversely, he is entitled to demand of the Arab peoples, clearly and openly, that they recognize his own demands for liberty and the reconstruction of his nation."[71] Internationalism means nothing without mutuality.

The Arab refusal to recognize Israel had been defended by Rodinson and Deutscher. In Memmi's view, it rested on bad history, bad politics, and bad faith. He forcefully addresses Rodinson's claim that the Middle East in general, and Palestine in particular, are intrinsically Arab-Muslim lands to which the Jews are illegitimate interlopers. "We constantly hear of 'Arab lands' and 'Zionist enclave.' But by what mystical geography are we not at home there too, we who descend from the same indigenous populations since the first human settlements were made? Why should only the converts to Islam be the sole proprietors of our common soil?" Israel, Memmi notes, rests on "a scrap of the immense common territory which belongs to us too, though it is called Arab."[72]

Yet the question of legitimacy was, ultimately, not one of statistics or "ridiculous arithmetic." For Memmi, a Jewish state in part of Palestine was a fact. And it was a fact that was not only justified but *required*. Israel was self-defense; Israel was cultural rejuvenation; Israel was political maturity; Israel was survival. Yet here, too, Memmi charted an independent course. Unlike Jabotinsky and his followers on the Zionist right, Memmi refused to celebrate nationalism; unlike Fanon and his acolytes on the left, he refused to celebrate violence. "I am not an enthusiast of the nation-as-response. I hate violence, and not just other people's violence, my own people's too! . . . Only you cannot, unless you are a hypocrite, ask any being, whether singular or collective, to refuse to defend itself if it is threatened."[73] National chauvinism must be rejected, but passivity was no longer an option.

Memmi also forthrightly addresses the key indictment of Israel's legitimacy: the Palestinian refugees. He found a multifaceted situation rather than a simple tale of oppressors and victims. Approximately 700,000 Arabs left Palestine in 1948 because they were forced to do so, or chose to do so, or were terrorized into doing so; in the years 1948 to 1964, an equal number of Jews left their native Arab countries because they were forced to do so, or chose to do so, or were terrorized into doing so. (The 1967 war produced another flood on each side.) Memmi articulates a truth that to this day is generally taboo: "Let's dare to say: a de facto exchange of populations has come about." *Two* civilian populations experienced a *nakba*—a parallel ethnic expulsion. And while the Palestinian situation was "tragic," it was neither unsolvable nor a world-historic catastrophe. "When you come right down to it, the Palestinian Arabs' misfortune is having been moved about thirty miles. . . . We [Oriental Jews] have been moved thousands of miles away, after having also lost everything." In any case, Memmi insists, neither of these exchanges could or would be reversed, despite the Arab refusal to accept the finality of the first or to acknowledge the reality of the second. Israel would not welcome back the Palestinians any more than the Arab nations would welcome back the Jews. History does not flow backwards; woe to those who deny this. To destroy Israel in order to compensate Palestinians "would amount to resolving a tragedy by means of a crime."[74]

The Israeli-Palestinian conflict, Memmi averred, set two nationalisms against each other. Each was relatively recent and therefore fragile; both peoples "have been and still are victims of human history." The conflict did not, however, set Palestinian revolution against Israeli reaction, Palestinian anti-imperialism against Israeli colonialism, or Palestinian poverty against Israeli riches, despite attempts to impose such interpretations on it. *"There is violence between the Arabs and the Jews because there is an historical conflict between two powerful and partially competing national ambitions, not at all between a social and revolutionary (Arab) movement and a nationalist and imperialist (Jewish) movement."* Framing the conflict in false terms enabled the Left to assail Israel's right to exist and fling it "into the ignominious hell of the imperialist nations."[75] Only by abandoning Manichean oppositions and the flawed history on which they rest could a workable solution be found.

The good news, Memmi reminds us, is that strife between nations can be solved. In Marxist terms, such clashes are conflicts rather than contradictions; they do not call for the negation of either side. The important thing, the urgent thing, was to find a good-enough accord for the future rather than recurrently shedding blood in an impossible attempt to avenge the past. "A mediocre agreement is better than continual war," he pleaded.[76] Reason paired with realism was a practical demand as well as an ethical one.

Ironically, it is Memmi who therefore emerges as the true materialist against the Marxist idealism of Rodinson and Deutscher. "It is not, but definitely not, enough to be an ardent socialist, in order to build a socialist world," Memmi contends. "You have to know how to distinguish between what is possible and what is impossible." The alternative is "revolutionary romanticism, which sometimes gives rise to catastrophes." In what can only conjure Arendt's positions of the late 1940s along with those of contemporary one-staters on the left, he deplores "our friends . . . who, impatient with history, simply . . . reconstruct peoples and regions on the basis of the model they want them to follow."[77] This impatience, too, is a kind of vanguardism, though it often drapes itself in the language of justice and human rights.

In short, Memmi besought Israelis and Arabs to step out of myth and into reality, for only there can politics be made. For Israelis, this meant acceptance of a sovereign Palestinian state; Palestinians, like all other peoples, had every "right to perfect their existence as a nation." Furthermore, Israelis must never forget Palestinian suffering until such national ambitions were met; to ignore Palestinian statelessness, he warned, is "impossible, and dangerous." For Palestinians and the Arab states, reality meant replacing their view of Israel as a temporary, illegitimate trespasser with acknowledgment of the Jewish state as a sovereign nation. "The Palestinians have *never* stopped claiming the *entire* region," Memmi pointed out. "It is our life that is at stake. A day must come when the Moslem Arabs will admit that we too . . . have a right to existence and dignity."[78] Unlike Rodinson, Memmi saw the Israeli-Palestinian conflict as a symptom, not the cause, of the region's political dysfunction and incessant violence.

Memmi wrote these essays in the late 1960s to mid-1970s. The settlements had not yet expanded, nor had Israel veered rightward to the Likud; the Palestinians had not yet spawned the suicide bombers or the fundamentalist fanatics of Hamas and Islamic Jihad. It is grievously painful to acknowledge that, five decades later, some Palestinians and many Israelis have moved further from the ethics of realism for which Memmi pleaded.

National independence is necessary, but it is not an end in itself. The nation's purpose is to abolish oppression, to advance justice, to nurture cultural and intellectual development in an atmosphere of freedom. In a

1972 speech in Jerusalem, Memmi warned Israelis that "there must be respect for social justice; otherwise the nation breaks apart. . . . The prophets must not remain mere myths to which you doff your hat." Zionism, he reminded his audience, had roots in the socialist movement; it becomes a shriveled version of itself if it forsakes that heritage. Nationalism can easily be perverted into chauvinism, aggression, racism. "It is up to the dominated classes, the socialists, ourselves, to fight so that that doesn't happen, *so that the social struggle is not dissociated from the national struggle.*"[79] Sovereignty could—but mustn't—lead to a fetishization of the state.

Memmi regarded the Left's anti-Zionism as indicative of a more general moral and political confusion. He insisted, as would Fred Halliday, that the sine qua non of any humane resolution of the Arab-Israeli conflict was mutuality: No more talk of extermination! "The only truly socialist solution, the most serious criterion for judging whether or not a political attitude is an attitude of the left: does it seriously desire an *agreement* that takes into account the *existence,* the *freedom,* and the *interests* of *both* partners?" Binationalism, Memmi averred, might be a future dream, even a worthy one. But dreams should not hinder the attempt to alleviate suffering, injustice, and violence in the present. (In that case, they become nightmares.) The Occupation was politically and morally wrong. But it was not an existential wrong; it did not lead Memmi to doubt Israel's right to exist. He concludes *Jews and Arabs* with a short article on Israel, written in 1974. "The Jew had no state, no nation, no flag, no land, no language, no culture," he reminds his readers. "Do you know what that's called? It is described as, experienced as, and called oppression."[80]

The establishment of a Jewish state has not, of course, vanquished anti-Semitism. How to interpret this failure? For Rodinson, it proved the foolishness of Zionism's basic goal. For Memmi, the opposite was true. The hatred directed at Israel—from its Arab neighbors, from the Western Left, from anti-Semites on the right—proved the Jewish state's necessity.

"Rarely have I had so little desire to write a book."[81] So Memmi announces in the first line of *Decolonization and the Decolonized,* which has sometimes been interpreted as a refutation of his previous works. (One American critic's review was titled "Albert Memmi's About-Face.")[82] That is a serious misreading. Memmi revisits ideas he began forging in the

1950s. But the criticisms he makes and the values he asserts are a continuation of his previous convictions.

Published in 2004, *Decolonization and the Decolonized* analyzes what has gone wrong in many countries of the previously colonized world. It is a discomfiting book; "I fear I have managed to annoy just about everyone," Memmi admits.[83] This is not a book of nostalgia, regret, or self-flagellation. But it is a book of sadness, disappointment, and anger.

Memmi had not become a colonial apologist; on the contrary, he assails colonialism as "collective slavery."[84] And he never exhibits the contempt for ordinary people that permeates the work of a Third World critic like V. S. Naipaul. Memmi's indignation is directed mainly at political and military leaders ("criminal idiots"), timid intellectuals, and religious fundamentalists. He critiques the widespread fixation on "an archaic golden age and glorious future," a phenomenon especially prevalent in the Muslim world. But he sees this as a way to keep the powerless opiated: "Isn't this what the aristocrats want?"[85]

The book focuses on the Arab world, including North Africa, for that is what Memmi knew best and where he had sustained long friendships. (Its original title was *Portrait du décolonisé arabo-musulman et de quelques autres*.) Nevertheless, his analysis fits many countries in other regions. The post-colonial problems he addresses are sobering: hunger, gross extremes of poverty and wealth, incessant warfare, subjugation of women, persecution of minorities, religious fanaticism, backward educational systems and social customs, conflation of religion and politics, stifled intellectual life, terrorism, state brutality, and an absence of democratic freedoms. "There seems to be no end to the pustulent sores weakening these young nations. Why such failures?" He acknowledges the "understandable postcolonial guilt" of European leftists—which, as a North African, he did not share—but warns that "guilt becomes noxious when it leads to blindness." Mostly, though, he is interested in the internal development, or lack thereof, of the states in question. The book's aim, he explains in a cutting phrase, is to describe people who "are no longer colonized" yet "sometimes continue to believe they are." Describing their situation as "neocolonial" will not take us far; the term is essentially tautological, and serves mainly "as a screen and rationale."[86]

The emphasis on interior reality rather than external subjugation is at the heart of this book's ethos—and of the controversies over it. Memmi did not imagine that foreign exploitation ended on the day a nation won independence; he was acutely aware of the continuing, enormous inequities between the world's rich and poor countries. But he insists, as would Halliday, that the post-emancipation trajectory of a nation or region cannot be understood simply as a reaction to, or product of, Western colonialism. Memmi wants to examine how the formerly colonized nations have *used* the independence for which they suffered and bled. Even the victims of a bad past—of which there are many—can create a livable present and build a viable future. Isn't that the belief that motivates every revolution? For Memmi, the formerly colonized are answerable for their praxis of freedom, just as the former colonizers are responsible for the damage they had wrought.

Much of Memmi's wrath is directed at Arab intellectuals, especially those who now live in the safety of the West. Imprisoned within a self-made fortress—the word he chooses is "autistic"—they are unable to hear, see, or speak the truth to their people. This was no small matter, for Memmi viewed honesty as the intellectual's primary vocation. Arab and Muslim intellectuals, he charges, had virtually ignored "the stupefying phenomenon of suicide attacks. . . . Hardly a word about the condition of women. . . . Not a single statement about the fate of minorities. . . . Almost no one openly opposed the Taliban regime. . . . No one dared to condemn, unless in private, Saddam Hussein." (Luckily, there is one issue that inspires courageous stands: "Nearly everyone had an opinion about Israel's right to exist.")[87] In *The Colonizer and the Colonized,* Memmi had warned that the colonized's shame prevents him from realistically assessing himself, his culture, and his political situation; five decades later, he looked at the rancid fruits of that incapacity.

One of the tragedies Memmi discusses is the ways in which violence has filled the chasm created by the absence of civic institutions. Without the rule of law, power is mediated through the gun and the bomb. He is acutely, indeed tenderly, aware of how deeply the formerly colonized yearn for an end to violence and terror in their lives; surely this is the sine qua non of a normal existence. He castigates the betrayal of that desire: "After decades of independence they are still cutting throats in Algeria, imprisoning people in Tunisia, torturing in Cuba, and condemning the uncovered faces of women in Iran and Algeria. Mass graves have been discovered in Iraq; populations fleeing before imminent massacre have been counted in the hundreds of thousands. . . . In Black Africa . . . entire ethnic groups are massacred. . . . In Algeria the army has maintained a reign of terror."[88]

With almost uncanny accuracy, Memmi foresaw that the democratic uprisings now known as the Arab Spring would fail in the absence of civic institutions and a pluralist mind-set; such rebellions would actually strengthen authoritarian governments *and* the power of fundamentalist groups. "The immobility of the regime allows no room to hope for any immediate change. What is needed is its total collapse. Yet every disturbance results in increased repression," he argued. "The country of the decolonized is a country without law, where there is rampant institutional violence that can only be countered by even greater violence. The fundamentalists know this and await their moment. The 'law of God' . . . will suppress even the few scraps of freedom that have been conceded by the ruler."[89] Thus the wild swings between the brutality of the nominally secular dictatorships and of the religious fundamentalists dedicated to overthrowing them.

And a decade before the *Charlie Hebdo* and Bataclan terror attacks in Paris, Memmi perceptively analyzed the dilemma of Muslim-French citizens, especially those born in France to North African parents. He viewed the French *banlieues* much the way he viewed his childhood ghetto. "Those who extol the romanticism of the ghetto have no idea what they're talking about," he wrote with a touch of annoyance. "Living in a poor suburb [of Paris] is like living in another city." While the parental generation often strove to assimilate, the younger generation rebelled against this, though without formulating a sustainable alternative identity. The problem was not that the young were caught between cultures (so was a young Albert Memmi), but that they had no tools with which to navigate them. "The son of the immigrant is a kind of zombie," Memmi observed. "He is a French citizen but does not feel in the least bit French. . . . He is not completely Arab. He barely speaks the [Arabic] language. . . . He would be hard pressed to read the Koran he waves around during demonstrations like a flag, similar to the head scarf worn by young women."[90] The youths' resistance to assimilation was matched by the refusal of France's white communities to welcome them. Assimilation might be an official ideal, but few on either side seemed to really want it.

Memmi's positions in this last book might be called "neoconserva-
tive," except that there is nothing conservative about them. His critiques
grew out of his commitment to internationalism, reason, and social
justice. He specifically rejects the clash of civilizations thesis: "There is
now a single, global, civilization that affects everyone, including fundamentalists." The dream of separate development and self-sufficiency—
shared by rich and poor nations, albeit for different reasons—is dead.
"We now live within a state of previously unknown dependence," Memmi
insists.[91] The challenge is what to make of that shared destiny.

Both Marxism and neoliberal capitalism had failed the Third World,
which prompts Memmi to raise the challenging question: "So, what
should we do?" By "we" Memmi meant, well, you and me—"All the
inhabitants of the planet, . . . former oppressors, formerly oppressed, and
even those who believe they remain outside history." This is the grammar
of inclusion. And of responsibility: In the family of man, we are all adults.
In a world that appears increasingly fragmented but is in fact permanently interconnected, international solidarity "is not only a philosophical
and moral concept, it is a practical necessity."[92] As he had with Jews and
Arabs, Memmi demanded that we acknowledge interdependence as an
undeniable fact. He believed, as did Arendt, that we are condemned to
share the world with others; that is the human condition.

Maxime Rodinson, Isaac Deutscher, and Albert Memmi belonged to
roughly the same generation and shared many traits. Each emerged from
poverty on the basis of outstanding intellectual abilities; each was a self-
made man. Each came of age during the rise of fascism and, then, the
Shoah; each subsequently observed, and cheered, the emergence of millions
of people from colonial oppression into independence. Each adhered to
principles that were anti-fascist, anti-colonialist, secular, and socialist, and
defined himself as such. Each was a bridge between the Old Left and the
New, and responded to the challenges the latter posed. Each was a brilliant
intellectual. Yet each was wrong about a lot of things: for Rodinson, belief in
a progressive Arab revolution; for Deutscher, faith in a democratized Soviet
Union; for Memmi, expectation that Israel would become a secular and
socialist beacon. Each was, I suspect, a disappointed man.

It was their attitudes toward Israel that separated them most
radically—or, put another way, that starkly illuminated the ways in which

their worldviews diverged. Rodinson, the traditional Communist and confirmed anti-Zionist, viewed Israel as at best a colonial fact and blamed it for the Middle East's relentless political strife. Deutscher, the dissident Marxist, came to accept Israel as a result of the Shoah but turned sharply against it after its 1967 victory. Memmi, the anti-colonialist, believed that Jews and Arabs could and must achieve national independence in tandem. In the following chapter we will see how Fred Halliday, a New Leftist from a younger generation, navigated the tension between anti-colonialism and democratic values with which Rodinson, Deutscher, and Memmi had wrestled. For Halliday, too, Israel would become decisive, divide him from longtime friends and allies in Europe and the Middle East, and force him to reevaluate the bedrock principles of the New Left.

CHAPTER SIX

Fred Halliday

FRED HALLIDAY WAS BORN IN 1946, which means that the Left he encountered as a young man was different from the Left in which Maxime Rodinson, Isaac Deutscher, and Albert Memmi came of age. Antiimperialism had replaced anti-fascism; Third World peasants had replaced European proletarians; the celebration of terrorism had replaced abhorrence of it. What the Egyptian Marxist Mohamed Sid-Ahmed called the "Sixth International"—the Left of Baader-Meinhof, the Irish Republican Army, the Japanese Red Army, the Red Brigades, the Popular Front for the Liberation of Palestine—had come to the fore. These groups were never mass organizations and never defined the whole of the Left, or even the socialist Left. But they challenged other groups to contend with them and to either accept or reject them as self-proclaimed vanguards.

And within this Left, the Palestinian struggle reigned supreme. "For this Sixth International, the Palestinian resistance is a banner," Sid-Ahmed observed in 1976; the Palestinian Rejectionist Front was "an inspiration for the revolt of the dispossessed against the affluent, both in its ends and in its means."[1] This inspiration would result not simply in a glorification of violence but in a *reliance* on violence in place of the slow, hard work of organizing ordinary people to effect political change. Terrorist acts, preferably against unarmed civilians and covered by the world press—shock and awe indeed—were regarded as a major sign of revolutionary commitment, even by individuals and groups who would never have participated in such actions themselves. In other words, the Sixth International pulled much of the New Left toward (or behind) it.

Palestinian terrorism elicited the most enthusiasm and the fewest moral doubts. Albert Memmi had assumed that the Left would naturally disown heinous terrorist acts as "incomprehensible, shocking and politically absurd." He was wrong.

Halliday's journey through the New Left was both unique and emblematic. His ideas, especially about revolution, imperialism, democracy, and human rights, changed dramatically in reaction to tumultuous world events over the course of four decades. This sensitivity to history—that is, to the world—led to charges of treachery. A typical example is Middle East scholar Joseph Massad's 2012 screed on the Al Jazeera website, in which he assaulted a then-deceased Halliday—along with his "Arab turncoat comrades"—as a "pro-imperialist apologist."[2] Yet it was precisely Halliday's intellectual flexibility—his ability to derive theory from experience—that was one of his greatest strengths. Contra Massad, Halliday didn't move from Marxism into neo-imperialism or turncoatism, whatever that is; rather, he developed a sturdier, more humane *kind* of radicalism. Like Memmi, he sought to restore socialism to its heritage—derived from the Enlightenment, from 1789, from 1848—of reason, secularism, freedom, and universal human rights.

This reconnection was not a form of nostalgia. Halliday did not want to recreate the Second International of pre–World War I Europe or the Popular Front of 1936. He wanted to create a new, more authentic progressive movement for the contemporary world. And he knew that this might not be possible—or, at least, that how to do so was up for grabs. He did not discard the sacred category of revolution, but by the turn of the twenty-first century he no longer regarded it as sacred.

Halliday's views on Israel and Palestine were a key part of his political odyssey. Especially after 1967, anti-Zionism would become a foundational—perhaps *the* foundational—principle for the New Left. (Edward Said claimed, "The question of Palestine is the touchstone of contemporary political judgement.")[3] In 1968, Memmi wrote that nationalism was the bone that stuck in the throat of the Left; soon it was Israel that caused the choking. Halliday reevaluated and eventually rejected this antipathy. His views are the clearest example of how Israel became the demarcation line of the New Left.

Halliday's evolution can be seen in a series of articles on Israel-Palestine that, though written separately and at different times, constitute a kind of political bildungsroman. In 1971, a young Halliday—still in his twenties and an editor at the Marxist *New Left Review*—disparaged criticism of the Palestine Liberation Organization's airplane hijackings as a "bourgeois" hang-up; a decade later, he was insisting on a two-state solution at a time when this was anathema for much of the Western Left and virtually the entire Arab world. And though Halliday continued to condemn the Israeli Occupation and rightist Israeli politicians, he became sharply critical of the Left for ignoring, excusing, or supporting the terrorist crimes, religious fanaticism, and exultant militarism of groups like the PLO, Hamas, and Hezbollah. He considered the Second Intifada and its suicide bombings to be a political and moral disaster for the Palestinian people rather than an inspiring example of armed resistance.

Like Rodinson, a formative influence, Halliday was a learned scholar of the Arab and Muslim worlds. But Halliday's intimate understanding of these states' post-revolution trajectories prompted a far more outspoken reconsideration of anti-imperialism as the basic test of leftist commitment. This is not because Halliday became a flunky for imperial power; the crimes of the U.S. in Vietnam and Nicaragua, or of the Portuguese in Mozambique and Angola, had not diminished by a whit. But like Memmi, Halliday did not blame all the Third World's problems—especially repressive dictatorship—on colonialism. In fact, he subscribed to the classic Marxist position that imperial capitalism had the contradictory effect of suffocating *and* developing the Third World. This meant that opposing imperialism, colonialism, or capitalism should be only the start, not the culmination, of Left politics. The job for socialists, Halliday wrote, is "not just to defeat capitalism, but to better it, to transcend it in economic achievement, in culture, in human emancipation and in democracy."4

As the 1960s turned into the seventies and eighties, transcendence and human emancipation became increasingly difficult to discover in the post-colonial world. In response, Halliday came to question the methods and accomplishments of the self-described anti-imperialist movements. "A critique of imperialism needs at the very least to be matched by some reserve about most of the strategies proclaimed for overcoming it, as well as by a certain caution about the utterances of . . . 'the subaltern,' " he argued.[5] The violence and repression of the anti-imperialist regimes were central to his break with the *New Left Review* in 1983 and to his subsequent arguments with much of the Left and the anti-globalization movement. The gaps in their outlooks became even wider as Halliday continued to stress the importance of human dignity and freedom rather than the glories of armed struggle. And when armed struggle morphed into jihadism, those gaps became an abyss.

Like Memmi, Halliday was not a pacifist. Like Memmi, he was equally distant from Fanonism. He did not subscribe to the idea that violence "is a healing medicine for all our people's diseases," as Fatah proclaimed, or that "revolutionary terrorism" is the "essential pre-condition" for freedom, as the German New Left leader Rudi Dutschke insisted to Herbert Marcuse in a 1967 debate.[6] Halliday supported revolutions in the hope that the world's most oppressed peoples would find a path to freedom from tyranny and immiseration. He was horrified to see revolution after revolution turn to blood-soaked vengeance and fearsome repression, especially in countries like Iran and Ethiopia, which he knew and loved.

Halliday's analyses of the Zionist and Palestinian movements, and of the profound mistakes each had made and the crimes each had committed, were entwined with his views on the region's larger crises. (As he pointed out, "The Palestinian question does not exist on the moon, but in a very specific and constraining Middle East.")[7] This does not mean, however, that he thought a regional solution was likely. In fact, what we see in Halliday's writings on Israel-Palestine over the course of more than twenty-five years is a sad and steady *narrowing* of possibilities. Looking back on the 1967 war two decades later, he observed "a triumphalist intransigent nationalism in Israel [pitted] against an often chauvinistic nationalism and blind rejectionism dominant among Arabs."[8] In 2004, he wondered, "If there was a realistic chance for peace in 1967, 1973 and 1993, where is the chance of it now?"; the answer was not good. Two years later, in the immediate aftermath of the war between Israel and Hezbollah, he analyzed the labyrinthine complexity and intensified deadliness of the area's conflicts. The Arab-Israeli conflict had become a hydra-headed monster that "can be said to resemble the European war that began in 1914: another regional conflict . . . [which] suddenly, almost casually, detonated . . . with dire consequences for all and catastrophic for many."[9] In 2009, he cautioned against the hope that a U.S.-Iranian nuclear deal might lead to one between Israelis and Palestinians. The Iranians could not "deliver" Hamas any more than the U.S. could "deliver" Israel.

A healthy respect for history's insistence on outsmarting theory defined Halliday's writings. Though he revered, and was deeply influenced by, Rodinson and Deutscher, I do not think he would have agreed with the latter's claim that the Shoah need not prompt a Marxist to rethink the Jewish Question. Halliday devoted a lot of energy to rethinking. He was especially wary of what he called "Rip van Winkle socialism," in which failed theories are lazily recycled and the sobering lessons of history ignored. (The anti-globalization movement, he charged, had "leapt from the coffin in 1999 like Joyce's Finnegan at his Wake, having learned nothing at all.")[10] In other words, he feared ossification more than so-called deviation; turncoatism didn't worry him at all. And so he instructed his friends: "At my funeral the one thing no one must ever say is that 'Comrade Halliday never wavered, never changed his mind.' "[11] Those who write about radical change are often incapable of it; that wasn't true of Halliday.

Fred Halliday was born in Dublin and raised in Dundalk, Ireland, a town that the *Rough Guide to Ireland* advised tourists to avoid because it was too rough. Dundalk virtually abuts the border with Northern Ireland, and it served as a center for the Irish Republican Army. Unsurprisingly, the Irish Question remained a bedrock for Halliday, though more as a warning than an inspiration. Parallels between the Irish and Israeli-Palestinian conflicts are not hard to find; the unhappy lessons of Ireland, Halliday wrote, include "the illusions and delusions of nationalism" and "the corrosive myths of deliverance through purely military struggle."[12]

Growing up so close to "the Troubles," and to the IRA's border campaign of guerrilla warfare, endowed Halliday with a healthy aversion to the concept of "progressive atrocities," which posits that terrorism against the presumably right targets—Westerners, Americans, the English, Israelis, whomever—is OK. (This term made an unfortunate reappearance on 9/11.) But perhaps it was Dundalk's sheer intractability—also reminiscent of the Israel-Palestine conflict—that made the town such a perfect negative model. In 2005, Halliday recalled a recent visit home: "Talking to a wise long-term observer of the town's affairs, I asked him if, over the past thirty years, anyone around there had changed their mind about anything. He looked at me a bit askance and replied curtly, 'Of course not.' That was all that needed to be said." Halliday's critique of the Provisional IRA, which "battled its enemies to a dead end over the bodies of hundreds of innocents, its struggle finessed or cheered by 'socialist' fellow travelers," was one he would apply to the rejectionist wing of the Palestinian movement.[13] In later years, Halliday explained that the Irish Question clarified the Israeli-Palestinian conflict for him. In each case, he came to support a compromise solution that would recognize the legitimate national aspirations of each group.

Halliday was the result of a "mixed" marriage: His father, a successful shoe manufacturer, was Methodist and Quaker, his mother was Catholic. Even as a child, he was obsessed with world events. A friend from Ampleforth College, a Benedictine boarding school Halliday attended, remembered, "When we met at 11 Fred was already a close follower of the news. . . . He was up on Dien Bien Phu and Suez. [Patrice] Lumumba was a hero. . . . On the whole he was for Chinese imperialism because he was against the American kind."[14]

After graduating from Oxford in 1967, Halliday studied at the School of Oriental and African Studies in London. In addition to hundreds of articles—essays, analyses, interviews, on-the-scene reports—as a journalist and scholar, he authored approximately twenty books on subjects that included Islam, Soviet foreign policy, Middle East politics, Iran, South Yemen, Ethiopia, and the September 11 attacks. He was widely regarded as one of the West's most learned scholars of international affairs; at the same time, he conversed with a general, nonspecialized audience through his journalism. (Perry Anderson, editor of the *New Left Review*, once criticized Halliday for publishing in the "bourgeois media." Halliday replied that the *New Left Review* was "a self-appointed general staff without any troops at our command.")[15] In 1983, Halliday joined the faculty of the London School of Economics, where for twenty-five years he taught, and challenged, students from around the world—including the Arab nations and Israel—and where he was the first director of the Centre for the Study of Human Rights. The intellectual and governing classes of the Middle East are sprinkled with his graduates.

As a young man, Halliday's political home was the revolutionary corner of Britain's New Left; the turbulence of 1968 in particular "shaped the intellectual and moral framework of my adult years," he recalled four decades later.[16] He was deeply involved in the anti–Vietnam War movement and was an early member of the radical weekly *Black Dwarf*, along with Tariq Ali, a leading New Leftist whom he would later censure. (Typical *Black Dwarf* headline: "ALL POWER TO THE CAMPUS SOVIETS!") From 1969 to 1983 Halliday was a member of the editorial board of *New Left Review*; he continued to write for the journal even after they parted ways, not without some bitterness, on key political issues.

An international perspective was not just theoretical for Halliday. He spoke almost a dozen languages, including Arabic, Farsi, Russian, German, and Portuguese, along with a "working knowledge" of Latin. (The Middle East scholar Danny Postel, a friend, remembered a Chicago restaurant dinner at which Halliday conversed "in his near-perfect Persian with the Iranians, his near-perfect Arabic with the Iraqis, and his gorgeous, lyrical Spanish with the Latin Americans.")[17] Beginning as a student in the 1960s, Halliday traveled widely throughout the "arc of crisis" of the Middle East, Southeast Asia, and Africa. He included well-known stops such as Lebanon, Syria, Israel, and Palestine as well as more obscure countries like Afghanistan, Yemen, and Ethiopia.

As a young activist and scholar, Halliday immersed himself in the revolutionary movements of his time and developed a wide range of contacts along the way: trekking with Maoist Dhofari rebels in Oman; working at a student camp in Cuba; visiting Nasser's Egypt, Ben Bella's Algeria, Palestinian guerrillas in Jordan, the Shah's Iran, Marxist Ethiopia, and revolutionary South Yemen. Halliday wasn't shy. In 1971, he proposed to a leader of the Popular Front for the Liberation of Palestine, one of the hardest of hard-line groups, that Israelis constituted a legitimate nation rather than a religious sect—an idea that the entire PLO regarded as heresy at the time. He argued with Iran's foreign minister about the goals of an Islamic revolution. He informed Hezbollah's Sheikh Naim Qassem that the organization's use of Koranic verses denouncing Jews was racist: "A point," Halliday wryly noted, "he evidently did not accept."[18]

Halliday received, and accepted, invitations to lecture in some of the Middle East's most repressive countries, including Saddam's Iraq, where a government official told him without shame or embarrassment that Amnesty International's reports on the regime's tortures and executions were correct. "I have visited some unsavoury regimes," he recalled of a

1980 visit to Baghdad, "but never have I sensed such fear as in Iraq."[19] The Ayatollah's Iran and Qaddafi's Libya also welcomed Halliday, or at least allowed him to enter and speak. And he did; clearly, he was no boycotter. (In a 2009 speech to the London School of Economics, Halliday told the audience: "I'm critical of Israel, but I go to Israel. . . . I believe we should talk to them and argue with them, like anyone else in the world.") But he was never seduced by his government hosts. In 1990, he described Iraq as a "ferocious dictatorship, marked by terror and coercion unparalleled within the Arab world." In 2009, he reported that the new, reformed Libya was just like the old, outcast Libya: a "grotesque entity" and "protection racket" that terrorized its citizens and was ridiculed throughout the Arab world.[20]

Naturally, Halliday made many mistakes. His 1978 book on Iran, for instance, vastly underestimated the role of religion, and he slighted the staying power of Ayatollah Khomeini's regime in its early months. But he evinced a consistent interest in how ordinary people lived through—or, at times, barely survived—transformative political events. He was genuinely interested, too, in what others, including leaders and activists whose politics he abhorred, might tell him. He believed that an activist intellectual's first duty, as Memmi put it, is to tell the truths he discovers "without worrying too much about being called a traitor by anyone."[21]

In 2008, after twenty-five years at the London School of Economics, Halliday moved to Barcelona to accept a research professorship. He loved the city for its beauty and humanity. (Naturally, he became fluent in Catalan.) He died there, of cancer, in 2010 at the age of sixty-four. Though his death, and his life, were largely ignored in the United States, tributes poured in from throughout the world. The British press filled with obituaries; the *New Statesman* titled its remembrance "The Death of a Great Internationalist."

In the course of his life, Halliday witnessed enormous violence and frequently disappointing political upheavals. He was wounded, too, by personal losses: Many of his friends in the Middle East were murdered by a catholic array of government operatives, hit squads, terrorists, and other actors. Halliday had ample reason for cynicism, yet he seemed to have developed robust antibodies to that disease. Like Hannah Arendt, whom he greatly admired, he believed that the modern world was a collective project. In an essay written six months before his death, he described "this world of ours" as "at once fascinating, tragic and, in the repeated outbursts of human hope and decency that mark it, hopeful."[22]

Though the Left's turn to the Third World is sometimes situated in the 1967–68 period, it began much earlier; as we have seen, writers such as Harry Hanson and Memmi were addressing this phenomenon in the late 1950s. In Britain, too, the debate over the Left's altered outlook predated the late sixties. The *New Left Review*, Halliday's intellectual home for fifteen years, exemplified this turn.

In 1963, the Marxist historian E. P. Thompson wrote a memo to the *New Left Review*'s new editorial board. He was clearly unhappy with the journal's recent orientation toward the underdeveloped world. Thompson did not disparage the anti-colonial movements, through which millions of people were gaining national independence—and, hopefully, education, prosperity, citizenship, and freedom. It was the journal's (and, by implication, the larger New Left's) attitudes to these movements that he reproved. Sometimes angrily, Thompson reprimanded his younger colleagues' deliberate ignoring of human rights abuses, state terror, and dictatorship; their romance with violence and idealization of the oppressed; and their belief that so-called Western values were defunct. (Many of the journal's editors were Oxbridge-educated: the products of those very values.) Are you not, Thompson asked his acolytes, "performing the ultimate *trahison des clercs*, acting as the elegiac prophets of a new mystique" by mindlessly celebrating "the culture of the Third World—the more bitter, tormented, virile or barbaric, the better?" He stressed that internationalism is a relationship to be built, not a fait accompli to be proclaimed, and that, "like any other relationship, it must be based upon self-respect."[23]

Though Halliday's work focused on the Third World, and especially on the Arab and Persian Middle East, it was he who would most productively make use of Thompson's challenge. For Halliday, the Arab and Muslim worlds were not idealized symbols of revolution. He spoke many of their languages, lived there for periods of time, and had many friends (and, no doubt, enemies) there. It was precisely this complicated, decades-long intimacy that enabled him to develop his critique of the region's regimes and movements—and, more important, empowered him to view criticism as an act of friendship rather than of betrayal. Implicit in his

work is the understanding that the last thing the citizens of the underdeveloped world need is protection from critical thought or alternative viewpoints. That is precisely what their colonial masters, post-colonial
governments, and religious authorities have shielded them from. Why
should their Western comrades follow suit?

The experience of Iran was foundational to Halliday's political development. He first visited the country when he was nineteen, carrying a
copy of Che Guevara's *Guerrilla Warfare* in Persian translation. Iran was a
country he particularly loved: He reanalyzed its revolution many times, as
if it were a perpetually bleeding wound he could not heal. Halliday
witnessed the country's revolution in its early months and recalled it as
"one of the most challenging periods of my political and intellectual life:
both in understanding and engaging with these enormous and complex
popular mobilisations, and in coming to terms with the repression,
killing and exile to which many of my friends and comrades were later
subjected."[24] It was in Iran, I believe, that the basis for Halliday's later
views on Israel-Palestine, and his staunch opposition to political Islam—
whether Shia or Sunni, Hezbollah or Hamas, Iran or al-Qaeda—was laid.
In addition, he would come to view the Iranian Revolution as a crucial
factor in transforming the Israeli-Arab conflict into a far more lethal and
multifaceted one.

Halliday's initial study of the country, *Iran: Dictatorship and
Development*, was published just before the anti-Shah revolution of early
1979 exploded. The book's last line reads, "It is quite possible that before
too long the Iranian people will chase the Pahlavi dictator and his associates from power, . . . and build a prosperous and socialist Iran."[25]

The dictator *was* soon forced to pack his bags; the ensuing revolution
shook the world and permanently transformed the Middle East. Halliday
subsequently filed eyewitness accounts of the revolutionary turmoil for the
New Statesman; he began in hope and ended in despair. In a January 1979
article, he assured his readers that the Ayatollah's "main demand is
eminently secular—a restoration of the [1906] constitution."[26] But only one
month later, he reported that Khomeini, now returned from exile, was
attacking the Left; in August, he warned that "the militant right," by which
he meant Islamists, was on a ruthless offensive. He described an atmosphere of hysteria, fear, and xenophobia; the outlawing of newspapers and
political parties (criticism of Khomeini had been criminalized); the brutal

crackdown on women, intellectuals, liberals, leftists, and secularists. The suppression of women, in which anti-feminism was married to nationalist fervor and bogus ideas of authenticity, had already emerged: "It is easy for the demagogues of the right to talk of women's emancipation as part of some 'alien' imposition on Iran."[27] But Halliday did not view women solely as victims. It was startlingly evident that large numbers enthusiastically supported their own subjugation; their chants of "Death to Communism!" reprised the prominence of women in European fascism, especially during the Spanish Civil War. Halliday ended with a warning and a cry: Khomeini and his Islamists "are dragging the country towards a bloodbath."[28]

It would be inaccurate to say that the Iranian Revolution upended Halliday. But it introduced him to new and disturbing complexities, ones he would continue to pursue. Here was a revolution that was genuinely popular and genuinely reactionary. Here were women who wanted to abolish their rights. Here were millions of people who conflated medieval forms of religious fundamentalism and twentieth-century anti-imperialism. And here was the beginning, or *a* beginning, of Halliday's synthesis of left-wing radicalism with liberal-democratic principles. In Iran, liberal freedoms—bourgeois freedoms—began to look pretty good. Halliday would later write, "I have stood on the streets of Tehran and seen tens of thousands of people . . . shouting, '*Marg bar liberalizm*' ('Death to liberalism'). It was not a happy sight; among other things, they meant me."[29]

The Popular Front for the Liberation of Palestine (PFLP) was a prominent group within the PLO that viewed the destruction of Israel as an integral part of a worldwide revolution. (It hoped to turn Amman into what it called "an Arab Hanoi.")[30] The group regarded Israel as an existentially illegitimate, racist, and fascist state and defined itself as secular and Marxist-Leninist. Starting in the late 1960s, it pioneered the tactic of high-profile airplane hijackings and hostage-takings to bring international attention to the Palestinian cause. Most infamous was the 1976 hijacking, in alliance with West German leftists, to Entebbe, Uganda, in which Jewish passengers were "selected" for possible execution; other actions included the 1972 Lod Airport massacre.[31] The hijackings and attacks garnered worldwide responses that ranged from admiration to horror; in either case, they helped place Palestinians on the world's political map.

But they also cemented the linkage between Palestinian independence and the murder of civilians.

In 1971, Halliday interviewed Ghassan Kannafani, a noted writer, novelist, and editor of the PFLP's newspaper, for the *New Left Review*. (Several weeks after the Lod attack, Kannafani was assassinated by the Mossad.) This was one of Halliday's earliest pieces that directly focused on Israel-Palestine, and it illuminates his views at that time. The interview is as revealing for what Halliday does not address as for what he does.

Halliday begins by dismissing what he scorns as "bourgeois criticisms" of the hijackings. Kannafani eagerly agrees: "I appreciate the fact that you reject bourgeois moralism and obedience to international law. These have been the cause of our tragedy." What really worries Halliday are the political repercussions of the hijackings, which he describes as "a substitute for organizing the masses" and "a theatrical event that encouraged fantasy."[32] Halliday also presses Kannafani, more than once, on the legitimacy of Israel as a nation in its own right rather than a colonizer of others. "So you don't think the Israelis are a nation?" Halliday asks, to which Kannafani replies no. The PFLP leader also makes clear that he *opposes* a Palestinian state in the West Bank and Gaza, which he derides as the "Maxime Rodinson solution" and "a fantastic intellectual compromise." But Kannafani admits that "at the moment it is very difficult to get the Israeli working-class to listen to the voice of the Palestinian resistance," surely one of the great understatements of the century.[33]

Halliday does not avoid political debate. It is clear that he views the PFLP's strategy as calamitous, despite Kannafani's triumphal rhetoric. It is equally clear that he respects Kannafani, who was regarded as a leading intellectual of the Palestinian Left and perhaps its most talented writer. But what Halliday never questions, or even hints at, are the *ethical* issues raised by the hijackings and other assaults on civilians, such as the PFLP's murder of Israeli schoolchildren near Avivim the previous year.

It was a very different Halliday who, a decade later, published a major essay called "Revolutionary Realism and the Struggle for Palestine."

It is hard to overestimate how radical—and courageous—this article was; with care, knowledge, and intelligence, Halliday dissected the basic tenets that had guided the radical Left at least since the 1967 war. "Revolutionary Realism" appeared more than a decade before the Oslo

Accords and mutual Israeli-PLO recognition; this was a time when many if not most leftists rejected the very existence of a state for the Jewish people. In fact, as Halliday noted, "The claim that Israelis do not have the right to nationhood . . . is so fundamental [on the left] that it is rarely argued for; it is simply assumed."[34] Significantly, he published his essay not in a liberal or social-democratic periodical that was friendly toward Israel but in *MERIP Reports,* a highly informed, widely respected journal of Middle Eastern politics that was (and is) consistently supportive of the Palestinian cause and hostile to Israel. Metaphorically speaking, Halliday was walking into the lions' den.

Halliday focuses on a 1978 book called *Towards a Socialist Republic of Palestine,* which includes a lengthy discussion between an anti-Zionist Israeli leftist and two Palestinian intellectuals about a future binational state. But Halliday's arguments applied, and apply, to the larger Left. He makes clear that his support for Palestinian statehood had not lessened, nor does he advocate "defeatist acceptance. . . . We all know what is meant in Palestine by 'established facts.' " In fact, he asserts that a Palestinian state should comprise half of historic Palestine. He unequivocally supports the refugees' demand to return (a position he would later alter), though he also makes the taboo suggestion that "some population transfers of both Israelis and Palestinians may be preferable." He stresses that he is not "equating the oppressed with the oppressor." And his essay is hardly a love letter to the Israelis, whom he criticizes for their own forms of irrendentism. Israel's denial of Palestinian statehood, he wrote, was racist and Israeli intransigence toward the Palestinians "stubborn, short-sighted, arrogant, messianic." Israel's stance was politically self-destructive to boot: Halliday warns against the "unrealistic and ultimately suicidal obstinacy of the Zionist movement."[35]

But the bulk of the essay was unquestionably addressed to the Palestinian movement and to Halliday's comrades in the Western and Arab Lefts. With cogency rather than vitriol, he demolished Left positions on partition, Israeli sovereignty, a Palestinian military victory, and binationalism. In a key passage, he pleads for what he calls "a mature internationalism" and observes that realism, as opposed to escapist utopianism, "is manifestly absent" from discussions of Israel.[36] He wonders aloud what Middle East the authors of *Towards a Socialist Republic* lived in, since their depiction of the region bore so little resemblance to the actual one.

(I would argue that the Middle East of the one-staters is more fictitious than that of the Orientalists whom Edward Said castigated.)

Like Rodinson, Halliday bluntly confronted the delusions of the Palestinian movement, speaking truths that many either did not see or would not voice and that a series of defeats had, apparently, failed to teach. A military conquest of Israel "is simply a fantasy," he warned. "[It] is not . . . a remotely feasible alternative. Nor will it ever be."[37]

What were the Left's stated reasons for assailing Israeli nationhood? Halliday engages each of them, including the charge that Israel was a recently formed, alien concoction that represented a religious rather than national group. In response, Halliday points out that virtually all states are artificial because the state itself is a modern, manmade creation. That is a fact, not an argument against it. "All nations are in fact historically formed," he contends. "There did not exist a distinct Palestinian nation one hundred years ago, or a distinct Iraqi or Libyan one."[38] The alternative view—which posits an authentic or eternal nation based on blood—leans on nativist or pseudoscientific mumbo jumbo and is hardly a Left position.

Halliday's arguments were globally situated. He looked at the recent history of India in regard to Pakistan, and to Pakistan vis-à-vis Bangladesh, not to evade the specifics of the Israeli-Palestinian conundrum but to release it from historic and political seclusion. "There exists a standard solution" to irresolvable national conflicts: "namely partition, as the examples from South Asia show." Why, he wonders, is Palestine different? Why is Palestine regarded as a sacred whole, and at such great cost? He critiques the notion, which surfaces only in the context of Israel, that the oppression of a weaker nation by a stronger one invalidates the latter's sovereignty. Thus, the treatment of Pakistanis by India and of Bangladeshis by Pakistan "did not mean that the Indians or later Pakistanis had no national rights. . . . And the same applies in Palestine." (One could also think of Turkey's treatment of Kurds, Greeks, and Armenians, Nigeria's of the Biafrans, Indonesia's of the East Timorese, Japan's of China and Korea, Germany's of all Europe, Russia's of Poland, and quite a few other examples.) This singular attack on Israeli sovereignty was, as he tactfully put it, part of "the peculiar way in which the problem of national self-determination is handled" in the case of the Jewish state.[39]

Halliday revisits the issue he had raised with Kannafani a decade ago, though with more directness. Israelis, he argues, are not "a cluster of colons." Nor are they a cluster of individuals who adhere to the Jewish religion. Echoing Rodinson, he argues that Jews in Israel had created a new nation, one with its own indigenous culture and social structures. "The Jews of the world are not a nation, but Israelis are not just Jews," Halliday wrote. "Israelis . . . have a culture, language and history distinct from that of Jews in gentile countries. . . . While Jews do not form a nation, Israelis do."[40] (This was not, of course, a Zionist position, which posits that Jews do form a nation—or at least that every Jew is *potentially* a member of Israel.)

But the rejection of Israeli nationhood is not really rooted in anthropology or in political theories about the origin of the state. Its (only) function is political: "The case for denying the Israelis self-determination has to be made by denying that they are a nation." The converse was equally true: "The logical conclusion of this acceptance is . . . a two-state solution." The consistent, decades-long refusal of the Palestinians to recognize or accept Israeli sovereignty "is not, despite its apparently militant character, either revolutionary or socialist."[41] In fact, it had gravely wounded the Palestinians' moral standing and retarded their political development.

Most of all, Halliday confronts the Left's cherished fantasy of replacing Israel with a "secular, democratic, socialist Palestine," which it used to justify eliminating Israel. "Where will this socialism come from?" Halliday asks. "Neither Israel nor the Arab world is moving in a socialist direction."[42] Even more to the point: Where would this democracy come from? Virtually all Israelis vehemently opposed a combined state and would take up arms against it; the plan was also opposed by most Palestinians. Here, truly, was a vanguard idea, birthed and nurtured entirely from above. Consequently, such a state could be maintained only by force—hardly the best foundation for democracy. Like Memmi, Halliday understood that history cannot be short-circuited, and that two hostile peoples could not be simply crushed together and transformed— whether through wishful thinking or at the point of a gun—into a functioning, much less egalitarian, society: "A respect between peoples, indeed true internationalist co-operation, can only be achieved once . . . the national rights of each nation have been recognized."[43] Forced fusion would lead not to multiethnic harmony but to civil war. Halliday was acutely aware of the reality that many on the left still deny: Unless it is agreed to by both nations, one state is not a marriage but a rape.

The authors of *Towards a Socialist Republic in Palestine* would not, I think, have denied this. In fact, they were quite honest about their plans. They admitted that their envisioned democracy would "impose upon the majority of the Israeli-Jewish population a political regime not of their choice and probably of their liking." A binational state, they averred, would be Arab dominated and would criminalize Zionism, although "that does not mean . . . that every Zionist will go to jail."[44] They openly advocated a state founded on one-party rule, which they rightly understood to be a necessity due to the coercive nature of their project. It was this aspect that, above all, repelled Halliday. The uniparty state, he insisted, is "an unacceptable solution—in Palestine or anywhere else. . . . [It] is a curse that has to be identified, criticized and denounced for what it is: a travesty of socialism."[45]

In any case, Halliday pointed out, the Israelis had *already* built a functioning multi-party democracy, which they had no intention of trading for a violent tyranny. He posed a simple, obvious, but often neglected question: "Why should anyone be attracted to such a [one-party] system in the first place?" And it was not only Israelis who would mistrust this plan; so would Palestinians, who "know enough about one-party socialism in such places as Iraq and Syria to be forgiven for some skepticism about how democratic it is." Far from advancing democracy, binationalism was "in effect a new dictatorship, clothed in a deceptive socialist garb. To say the least, the Palestinians deserve better than this."[46]

In short, the democratic, binational, socialist Palestine on offer would not be democratic, binational, or socialist. Yet the status quo was untenable and unjust. What, then, would a progressive position be? Halliday spells out the answer clearly: "At the risk of being myself accused of giving ground to Zionist propaganda, I would argue that a socialist position on Palestine must include the acceptance of an Israeli, as well as a Palestinian right to self-determination."[47] Far from being an imperialist plot, the two-state solution might serve Palestinians even more than Israelis: "The goal of partition is the only just *and* the only practical way forward for the Palestinians. They will continue to pay a terrible price, verging on national annihilation, if they prefer to adopt easier but in fact less realizable substitutes, and if their allies and supposed friends continue to urge such a course upon them."[48] Refusal of these facts could only aid the refuseniks in each camp.

"Revolutionary Realism and the Struggle for Palestine" raised vital questions, which extend beyond the Israeli-Palestinian conflict, about the nature of socialism and its relationship to democracy. What *kind* of socialism were the one-staters proposing, Halliday wondered: "Saddam Hussein's or the Israeli Labor Party's?" Or, perhaps, "that of Pol Pot"?[49] He cautioned that it was too late in the twentieth century for any leftist to blithely speak of democratic-socialist states, for no such states existed. The socialist bloc did have accomplishments to its credit, but democracy was not among them. Leftists—whether in Moscow or Baghdad—had lost the right to combine "democracy" and "socialism" in one smooth phrase since they had failed to combine them in practice.

It was in the Middle East that both democracy and socialism had encountered the most daunting problems. "Marxism has had to labor under more hostile conditions in the Middle East than in any other part of the Third World," Halliday and his wife, the sociologist Maxine Molyneux, observed in 1984. "Yet the ghastly legacy of its rivals—in terms of political dictatorship, religious fanaticism, nationalist demagogy and socioeconomic weakness in the face of imperialism—hardly diminish the relevance of Marxism to this pitifully divided and misled area of the post-colonial world." Though imperialism was a real and pernicious force, its enemies had established equally if not more despotic regimes. "If the roles of the US, Britain and Israel are clearly inimical, so too are the Baath's nationalist mystifications, Khomeini's fanaticism, Qaddafi's ranting inconsistencies, the confusions of a Fanon and accommodations of a Nasser." In some parts of the Third World, socialism could point to substantive achievements in fighting the grossest forms of poverty and exploitation (contrast Cuba with Haiti). Yet the self-defined socialist regimes of the Middle East had proved "ferociously sectarian" and were particularly hostile to "liberalism, democracy, feminism and other supposedly bourgeois deviations."[50] The fight against imperialism and the fight for freedom were hardly synonymous. Sometimes they were not even acquainted.

The new political map created by the post-1989 collapse of Communism caused Halliday to rethink the question of international solidarity. (Noam Chomsky, in contrast, would argue that no new thoughts were necessary.) Halliday opened a circa 2007 essay about "the crisis of universalism" with an astute and troubling observation: "In the course of the twentieth century something strange, and distorting, appears to have happened to the concept of 'solidarity.' " International solidarity, he argued, requires the defense of others' rights: This is the concrete expression of a universal, shared humanity. Solidarity *means* rights, which recognize the Other as an equal. Yet the championing of solidarity had led to its diametric opposite. Thus, on the left, one found the "widespread disparagement of rights . . . blind endorsement of guerrilla and armed groups, . . . [and] wholesale opposition to humanitarian intervention."[51] Halliday was revisiting the questions Memmi had posed. What does it mean for the Left to support those who ignore, or even reject, humanist principles? *Who* is owed support: anti-imperialist regimes, leaders, and movements, or the people on the ground whom they claim to champion?

Halliday again focused on the Middle East as the prime example of these dilemmas. In that region, he observed, questions of international solidarity evinced exceptional "confusion and disarray." Perhaps the most egregious misstep, in his view, was the Left's refusal to support the military coalition that opposed Saddam Hussein's 1990 invasion and annexation of Kuwait, which in his view was "as clear a case of state aggression . . . as could be imagined."[52] And though the PLO supported the Iraqi despot, he reminded readers that "Saddam has been as much a friend of the Palestinians as is Yitzhak Shamir."[53]

Halliday's position on this war inspired what he called "a stream of abusive letters, character assassination and vulgar misrepresentation by old comrades."[54] Edward Said shunned him; perhaps more painfully, so did the Lebanese leftist Fawwaz Traboulsi, Halliday's closest friend in the Arab world. But Halliday persisted in wondering how presumed progressives could support a sociopathic dictator who was feared throughout the Middle East for his ingenious methods of torture. He noticed a curious syndrome, one that I encountered while researching this book: Many otherwise intelligent people abandon common sense and their ethical compass when it comes to Middle East politics. "It is as if the Middle East has been the graveyard not only of imperial ambitions, . . . but also of clear-headed moral and legal discussion," Halliday tartly observed. And if this was true in general, it was "above all true, of course, for the Palestine question."

Moreover, Halliday argued, there had been "a regression . . . of ominous import" in the Left's attitudes toward Israel, and this regression exemplified a moral crisis of larger proportions.[55]

At least since the time of the Spanish Civil War, the protection of noncombatants had been a cause of the Left, and the deliberate slaughter of civilians considered a key component of fascism. (The worldwide shock provoked by the bombing of Guernica may be equal to the repulsion that ISIS's beheadings now conjure.) But that principle had been abandoned when it came to the Middle East in general and to the Israel-Palestine conflict in particular. Looking at the 2006 Israel-Hezbollah war, Halliday decried "the crimes of the Israelis in wantonly attacking the infrastructure of Lebanon, and denying Palestinians their national rights." But he also voiced a criticism that was (and is) more difficult to find on the left; thus he condemned "the crimes of Hizbullah and Hamas in killing civilians, placing the lives and security of their peoples recklessly at risk, hurling thousands of missiles at civilian targets in Israel and fomenting religious and ethnic hatred."[56]

Halliday denounced the Left's long neglect of the universal laws of war; no longer did he express disdain for the "bourgeois" morality or international laws that he had voiced to Kannafani. Equally important, Halliday now argued that this morality, and these laws, did not apply only to established states. "Today we see across the world movements of solidarity, with the 'Iraqi resistance,' Hamas, or Hizbullah that, while invoking universal principles of war against the Israelis or the US forces in Iraq, fail completely to apply the same principles [to] the behaviour of the guerrilla and other groups, many of them guilty of terrible acts of barbarism, murder, intimidation of civilians." He chastised those on the British Left (he may have been thinking of his *New Left Review* friends) who, "high on their anti-imperialist rectitude, revel in the slaughter of civilian UN officials in Iraq, [while] others condone the killing of children in Israel, and the wanton sacrificing of the security, stability, indeed sanity of the whole population of Lebanon in the name of a self-proclaimed 'national resistance.' "[57] In short, Halliday insisted, non-state actors must respect international rules of war *before* they become states. The absence of sovereignty is not a license to secede from civilizational norms.

Halliday's gradual reevaluation of terrorism had begun years earlier and was most fully explicated in a 1987 article titled " 'Terrorisms' in Historical Perspective," in which he analyzed terrorism perpetrated from above (by governments) and from below (by oppositional groups). He staked out his position with startling clarity: "There is no middle ground where political violence is concerned any more than there is with racism."[58]

Contrary to popular perceptions, most terrorist activity against civilians is government-sponsored and usually well hidden (though not entirely secret, thanks to organizations like Amnesty International). It includes torture, murder, disappearances, forced labor, cruel modes of imprisonment, and sexual violence. In contrast to non-state groups, who use terror to advertise their existence and strength, governments try to hide their most nefarious acts. "The great majority of the acts of terror . . . have been committed by those in power against those who are out of power," Halliday declared. "This does not provide an answer to the question of moral assessment of hijacking, or bombs in supermarkets, but it does provide a moral corrective to some of the selective judgements that are made."[59] Governments often act in far worse ways than their opponents.

Support for the terrorism perpetrated from below, however, was equally indefensible. Halliday attacked what he called the "relativist fallacy," frequently articulated as "one person's terrorist is another person's freedom fighter." Not so. The underlying assumption of this cliché is that "if you believe that someone's cause is just, then whatever he or she does in pursuit of that cause is itself justified." Yet logically and morally, this makes no sense: A just cause does not legitimate a denial of the Other's humanity. "There are, there must be, violent actions which everybody whatever their cultural background can agree are illegitimate," Halliday insisted.[60] To speak of humanity as a whole—as in, "crimes against"—is meaningless without such shared standards and shared prohibitions. Part of what makes us human is what we hold to be taboo.

All terrorism is a short circuit that substitutes immediate fear and panicky responses for long-term solutions. This is equally true of *anti-terror* measures—especially, Halliday argued, those practiced by Israel against the Palestinians, which are predicated on the recurrently discredited belief that Palestinian terrorism can be militarily eradicated. Terrorism almost always strengthens the Right, which is one reason Marxists have traditionally shunned it as a tactic. (Or, at least, used to.) Terrorism's role in thrusting people away from liberal principles has been proved nowhere more clearly than in Israel, where decades of Palestinian attacks on civilians have helped to steadily push the Israeli electorate rightward—and

where Palestinian *and* Israeli opponents of a two-state solution have strategically used such attacks to prevent or derail any agreement.

Halliday remained a strong advocate of two states and, unlike Edward
Said and Noam Chomsky, of the Oslo Accords. Six years after their
signing, Halliday assessed their prospects. The Accords were, in his view,
"greatly unjust to the Palestinians" in terms of territory allotted. Yet they
were a welcome, indeed watershed event, for they opened the possibility
of a sane future for both peoples. (Here was a novel idea: An agreement
could be imperfect, even unfair, and still a necessary step forward.)
Though Palestinian nonacceptance of Israel since 1947 may have been
impractical and self-destructive, Halliday regarded it as understandable.
"No people in the world could easily accept that, in the space of two or
three generations, the majority of their national territory had been taken
by a settler population." Yet the Left's support of Palestinian irredentism
was illegitimate, indeed perverse. "The zenith of this aberrant solidarity
was the 1970s debate on 'Zionism as racism.' . . . There was another
message mixed up in all this, itself a racist one, namely that the Jews in
Palestine had no right to their own state."[61]

Halliday questioned "the aura of tragedy and doom," the cultivation
of catastrophes and *nakbas,* in which Israelis and Palestinians indulge.
Each people, he suggested, should acknowledge that their national
consciousness and their national movements were modern, contingent
creations that arose for particular, political reasons; each should fore-
swear reliance on eternal, holy, or authentic claims to the land. This "does
not mean they have no right to states of their own or that, in the name of
some higher cosmopolitan or binational ideal, they should live together.
Obviously, given the animosities, . . . they cannot live together in one
state. They are, in this as in other respects, normal nations." The end of
perpetual warfare, Halliday argued, rests precisely on the "acceptance that
Israelis and Palestinians are entitled to what other peoples have, neither
more nor less."[62] Despite what their leaders had promised, only prosaic
compromise, not messianic glory, offered deliverance.

Over the next two decades, Halliday would continue to write, with
deepening sorrow and anger, about the Accords. He regarded them as the
only basis for a rational solution to the conflict—and, crucially, as the only
chance the Palestinians would have for a state. He decried opposition to
the agreement by various groups in Palestine and the larger Middle East,

"who for years sought to destroy the one chance for co-existence and peace . . . and then, egged on by their fellow traveling intellectual acolytes in the west, proceeded to trample on Oslo's grave."[63] In contrast, his role models were men like the Arab-Israeli writers Emile Habibi and Emile Touma, members of the Israeli Communist Party, and PLO representative Sa'id Hammami. All supported two states, opposed terror, and were "principled opponents of nationalist intransigence."[64] (Hammami was assassinated by Palestinian rejectionists in 1978.)

As a Middle East scholar, Halliday had been critical of Edward Said's *Orientalism*. ("The thesis of some enduring, transhistorical hostility to the orient, the Arabs, the Islamic world, is a myth, albeit one . . . which many in the region and in the West find it convenient to sustain," he wrote.)[65] With Oslo, a chasm separated the two. As soon as the Accords were signed, Said denounced them as "an instrument of Palestinian surrender, a Palestinian Versailles," and a manifestation of the Palestinian leadership's "supine abjectness." Said doubted that "there was a single Palestinian who watched the White House ceremony who did not also feel that a century of sacrifice, dispossession and heroic struggle had finally come to nought."[66] However, it is not clear how he could have known this. As he told Salman Rushdie in 1986, "You should remember that I haven't been to Palestine since the mid-sixties"; in a later essay, he admitted that he had not visited between 1947 and 1992.[67] Nor is it likely that all Palestinians, who number in the millions, think alike. (Isn't that an Orientalist fallacy?) Said's claim to speak for every single Palestinian is dubious; some of the PLO's most militant activists who actually *lived* in the West Bank, such as Marwan Barghouti, strongly supported the agreements and hoped they would lead to a viable, democratic Palestinian state and a final end to the conflict.

The Oslo Accords left key issues unresolved; this may well have been a fatal weakness. The door was left open for the murderer of Yitzhak Rabin, for the most fanatical settlers, for the suicide bombers of Fatah and Hamas. (Barghouti is now serving five life sentences for participation in suicide bombings during the Second Intifada.) But many possibilities, good and bad, remained at the time of their signing and for years thereafter. As Barghouti told an interviewer in 1994, Oslo "will not automatically lead to independence. This will only come if we set off an irreversible dynamic through the new national mechanisms we set in place."[68] The future was still open, the *meaning* of the Accords in flux. Oslo was a process, not a thing. Its endpoint was not preordained; to insist otherwise is to read history backwards.

Despite its dismal sense of repetition, new factors do emerge in the Israeli-Arab conflict. Since Oslo, they have rarely been good. Halliday assessed the 2006 conflagration between Israel and Hezbollah as a turning point that signaled a radical change in the region's politics. "The assumptions of that post-1967 epoch no longer hold: of territorial compromise, UN resolutions, the pursuit of mutual recognition, and international guarantees," he wrote. "In Iran, and in its allies Hizbullah and Hamas, Israel now has an enemy more resolute, organised and uncompromising than any it has faced since it was established."[69] The conflict had become internationalized in staggeringly intricate ways. It now involved what Halliday called Greater West Asia, a vast geopolitical area that encompasses India, Pakistan, Afghanistan, Iran, Lebanon, Israel, Palestine, Iraq, Libya, and Turkey. All had combined into a witches' cauldron of rivalry, conflict, violence, terrorism, and political dysfunction.

This new situation, Halliday warned, was "more complex, multilayered and long-lasting than any of the individual crises, revolutions or wars that characterised the Middle East."[70] It would demand new approaches and new solutions, though few were on offer. After the 1967 war, Halliday had likened the Middle East to a prairie fire. Since then, the tempo of disaster has only quickened. The stacks of corpses—in Syria, Yemen, Iraq, Libya, Afghanistan—are as yet uncounted, and might never be. None of this could possibly bode well—or has—for either Palestinians or Israelis.

Aside from the families of those who were murdered and of those who died trying to save them, it would be difficult to imagine anyone who was more devastated by the attacks of September 11, 2001, than Fred Halliday. For years he had vocally opposed the United States' policy of arming the anti-Soviet rebels in Afghanistan, a direct and foolish result of America's anti-Communist obsession. Far from aiding freedom fighters, the U.S. had strengthened what Halliday would later call "the crazed counterrevolutionaries of the Islamic right"; after the Soviets left, Afghan militias had plunged the country into a seemingly endless civil war that terrorized civilians and reduced Kabul to dusty rubble.[71] (James Nachtwey's eerie photographs from that time depict a post-apocalyptic moonscape of ruin.)

For decades, Halliday had yearned for the democratic, tolerant, modern forces in the Arab and Muslim worlds to gain ascendance. In the ruins of the World Trade Center, his warnings and his hopes lay in shreds. A friend and colleague, Adam Roberts, wrote that Halliday suffered a severe depression and breakdown soon thereafter.

Afghanistan was a nation that Halliday had studied in depth. His views on its politics were complicated. There were few if any places less likely to produce a successful socialist revolution or more in need of one. Afghanistan was (and is) a largely illiterate, profoundly religious country of deep ethnic-tribal divisions, immiseration, and antediluvian gender relations; Halliday described it as a place of "appalling backwardness." The 1978 Communist victory there was a coup, not a popular revolution. But the Communist program, including land reform and full equality for women, was a progressive one. "It is undeniable that a social revolution is being attempted in Afghanistan," Halliday wrote in 1978; as such, it "deserve[s] the support of revolutionaries throughout the world."[72] This proved naive; two years later, he denounced the revolutionary government's use of starvation and torture, its "grotesque personality cult," and its "climate of terror." But he denounced as well the rabid brutality of the opposition *mujahadeen*, and he supported the 1979 invasion by Soviet troops, a minority position on the left. Halliday predicted that the likely alternative to the Communist regime was "abandoning Afghanistan to Islamic reaction and probably years of inconclusive civil war," which turned out to be right.[73]

Afghanistan's civil war would become crucial to Halliday's thinking about the jihadist movements and all that followed, including the September 11 attacks and the war on terror. He compared Afghanistan's internal war to the civil war in Spain: not in its politics or ethos, but as the incubator of greater violence to come. Afghanistan, he wrote in 2007, was "the devil's kitchen in which all the brews that later poisoned the globe were first prepared."[74] If Halliday was torn between socialist and democratic convictions while the Afghan Communists were in power, he was unambiguous in his loathing of the Taliban and prescient in his understanding of what its 1996 victory meant. Soon after it captured Kabul, he delineated the grim, bizarre reality of its regime—so grim and bizarre that it was met with disbelief by Western bystanders, just as the Khmer Rouge had been. The treatment of women, which he described as "patriarchy with guns," was especially savage.[75]

Five years after the fall of Kabul, the "crazed counter-revolutionaries" struck New York; they have continued to rampage since, though usually outside the West. (Most of their victims are fellow Muslims, though in places like Egypt and Nigeria they also specifically target Christians.) In the aftermath, Halliday formulated a distinctive set of positions. He maintained that, though the U.S. had originally armed the Islamic militias, the responsibility for the attacks rested on those who perpetrated them; that though a military solution to terrorism was impossible, it was necessary to fight homicidal zealots who had declared war; that though Islamic terrorism arose in part from the gross inequities of capitalism, it was not, and could never be, part of any struggle for justice; and that Islamic fundamentalists were the children not of ancient Islam, as they proclaimed, but of modernity, which they loathed. Halliday did not toggle between opposition to international inequalities and opposition to terrorist violence. His vision encompassed both. Indeed, the two were intertwined.

Halliday saw that September 11 did produce a convergence between West and East, though of exactly the wrong kind. A kind of *negative* internationalism—a shared dehumanization—flourished, epitomized by George W. Bush's eager rejection of the Geneva Accords (see under: Guantánamo, Abu Ghraib, black sites) and the widespread use of terror by al-Qaeda, the "resistance" in Iraq, and other groups (see under: bombing of the UN's Baghdad headquarters, Sunni and Shia torture squads, suicide bombers, and ethnic cleansers). In East and West, chauvinist nationalism, racism, and religious hatred were grossly inflamed. Terror proved to be imperialism's handmaid rather than its foe.

The demise of the Oslo Accords was part of this wider international regression. In 2004, Halliday sadly commented on the agreement's breakdown. "Israeli and Palestinian leaders misjudged their opponents, and the broader communities of both sides combined to override reason," he charged. "The blame should be spread widely, and without equivocation, for the disaster is shared." Like Osama bin Laden and George W. Bush, Yasser Arafat and Ariel Sharon were closer to codependents than enemies. Halliday excoriated the PLO leader for his "callous disregard for the interests of the Palestinians or their commitments to Israel" and the Israeli prime minister as "the recruiting agent for Hamas." (Today, each man remains a hero in his own land.) Without peace, Halliday feared, Israel "will

become a land without a future, except one that is too menacing to contemplate."[76] A decade and a half later, I fear that prognosis may be right.

September 11, Afghanistan, the war on terror, Iraq: All intensified
Halliday's disputes with the European and American Left. If the neocon-
servatives who engineered the Iraq invasion of 2003 failed to understand,
or even care about, the consequences of their disastrous policies, some on
the left failed to understand, or even care about, the aims and ethos of the
new opposition forces in that country. At best, the Left devised a kind of
negative internationalism whose only demands were "Troops Out!" or
"No War!," which Halliday derided as a "narcotic incantation" that avoids
difficult political questions.[77] How to create bonds of *positive* solidarity
with the people of Iraq was, in his view, the crucial criterion on which all
interventions should be judged. (In the 1980s he had worked, alongside
Eric Hobsbawm and others, with the London-based Committee Against
Repression and Dictatorship in Iraq.) And at worst, some leftists
expressed actual affinity with the forces of radical Islam or the Iraqi
rebels, which they viewed as a brave new vanguard striking blows against
the empire. To which Halliday responded tartly, "The anti-imperialism of
racists and murderers is a perverse programme."[78]

In the years that followed, Halliday was increasingly dismayed—and
irritated—by affection for this perversion. "Many groups of the Left . . .
show every indication of appearing to see some combination of al-Qa'ida,
the Muslim Brotherhood, Hizbullah, Hamas and (not least) Iranian president Mahmoud Ahmadinejad as exemplifying a new form of international anti-imperialism that matches—even completes—their own
historic project," he rued. This misbegotten alliance deepened as the war
in Iraq intensified; it became even more pronounced during the Israel-
Hezbollah war of 2006. Why, one might wonder, had leftists jumped into
bed with a so-called Party of God? Halliday reminded his readers that
Islam, and Islamism, had for decades been the enemies of socialism,
which they viewed as a Western import and Jewish conspiracy. "Long
before the Muslim Brotherhood, the jihadis and other Islamic militants
were attacking 'imperialism,' they were attacking and killing the Left—
and acting across Asia and Africa as accomplices to the West."[79] Political
Islam might cross national borders, but it was no more internationalist in
the *positive* sense than colonialism or imperialism. As for the so-called

resistance in Iraq, it had "no interest in democracy or in progress for the people of Iraq whatsoever."[80]

Halliday's rift with his old comrades was never more profound, and perhaps painful, than in this period. As Halliday mourned the "monsters" of political violence—"the Madrid bombings, Gaza assassinations, Kosovo killings, Ugandan massacres, Iraqi depredations, Sudanese persecutions"—the *New Left Review* celebrated many of the actors behind these events.[81] Indeed, reading that magazine's analyses of the post-9/11 period is a puzzling and distressing experience. I read, and revered, the *New Left Review* as a college student and for years afterward; it is still considered the premier political publication of the Left intelligentsia in the English-speaking world. Halliday's disputes with the journal are worth engaging precisely because, far from being a throwaway rag, it is a respected pillar of Left thought.

Safely ensconced within the confines of the bourgeois democracies it reviled, the *New Left Review* celebrated some of the world's most murderous forces. In editorials written by Tariq Ali and Perry Anderson, the journal hailed the elections of Hamas (in Gaza) and Mahmoud Ahmadinejad (in Iran), who would bring such grave harm to their peoples. Praiseworthy, too, was the "steady train of blows [inflicted] on . . . the collaborator regime" by the "resistance" in Iraq, whose struggle was likened to the anti-Nazi Resistance in France—a comparison that would, I suspect, have been an unwelcome surprise to veterans of the latter movement.[82]

"It is in the slums that Hamas, Hizbollah, the [Iraqi] Sadr brigades and the [Iranian] Basij have their roots," Tariq Ali, Halliday's erstwhile friend from the *Black Dwarf* days, exulted, thus condensing some of the world's worst human rights violators into one concise sentence. "A radical wind is blowing from the alleys and shacks of the latter-day wretched of the earth . . ."[83] Anderson, however, was not quite as happy; he complained that the Arab Spring had "not produced a single anti-American or even anti-Israeli demonstration. . . . Can this last?" Surely not; surely activists throughout the Arab world would come to their anti-imperialist senses and demand that "the abject treaty Sadat signed with Israel . . . is legally defunct. The litmus test of the recovery of *a democratic Arab dignity* lies there."[84] (The protestors in Tunis, Tahrir Square, Daraa, and elsewhere defined "Arab dignity" in far different—and far more subversive—terms.)

In 2015, Anderson repeated the old demand for a "revolutionary transformation" of the Arab states in order to confront Israel with a "real threat."[85]
The Rip Van Winkle radicalism that Halliday mocked is nowhere more
evident than here. So, too, is the armchair bloodlust that Rodinson had
denounced.

For Halliday, the fundamental dissonance in worldviews that caused
him to break with the journal—its editors' blindness, if not antipathy, to
human rights and democratic freedoms—remained unbridgeable. He told
an interviewer in 2005, "The kind of position which the *New Left Review*
and Tariq have adopted in terms of the conflict in the Middle East is an
extremely reactionary, right-wing one. . . . I think Tariq is objectively on the
Right. He's colluded with the most reactionary forces in the region, first
in Afghanistan and now in Iraq. . . . The position of the *New Left Review* is
that the future of humanity lies in the back streets of Fallujah." Halliday
added that he felt happier reading the UN's Human Development Reports,
or human rights theorists like Amartya Sen and Martha Nussbaum, or
feminist groups engaged in social policy, than the latest issue of *New Left
Review.* "What would a world without the concept of rights be like?" he
asked.[86]

Of course, he already knew the answer, as do we.

Fred Halliday's writings raise exigent questions about contemporary politics, especially when it comes to the Israeli-Palestinian conflict. What is
Left? What is Right? Why is a compromise solution that exists in the
realm of possibility, as advocated by Halliday, considered less progressive
than the rejectionism of Tariq Ali, Perry Anderson, or Edward Said? Why
is the revanchism of the Israeli Right viewed, correctly, as reactionary, but
the revanchist demand of the "right of return" viewed as progressive?
Why are false solutions that guarantee continued bloodshed so admired?

Halliday's writings also illuminate a strange dilemma, one that has
haunted and harmed Israelis and Palestinians alike and made solidarity
between them extraordinarily difficult. In Israel, to be on the left generally
means to support a two-state solution. In the Palestinian and larger Arab
world, and in parts of the West, to be on the left means to *oppose* a two-
state solution in favor of one "de-Zionized" state. I can think of no other
conflict where there is such a disconnect between the Left of a native
country and the Left of the international community.

In the world of politics, there is a crucial difference between fairness and justice; it is one that, I believe, underlay Halliday's work. It is also foundational to the Israel-Palestine conflict, and a key reason it has remained unsolvable. This is illustrated by an engrossing interview Israeli journalist Ari Shavit conducted with Edward Said in the summer of 2000, which was published in *Haaretz* as "My Right of Return." Said told Shavit that, despite the enormous misery it has caused to Palestinians, he continued to defend their rejection of partition in 1947. "It was an unfair plan based on the minority getting equal rights to those of the majority," Said complained.[87]

Said is right. The partition *was* unfair in many ways, as are most international agreements. So were the Oslo Accords, as he and Halliday agreed. So is almost everything about the conflict, including the fact that Israel has been under armed attack, boycotts, and delegitimation campaigns since the moment of its founding. But to insist on fairness means to wait for Godot. Even worse, it means that your children and their children are doomed to be warriors or widows or orphans. A reasonably just solution to the conflict implies, indeed requires, the acceptance of *unfairness* by each side—and acceptance, too, of the fact that decades of carnage and immeasurable sorrow will never be undone, atoned for, justified, rectified, sufficiently acknowledged, or avenged. Said's demand, expressed more than once, that "until . . . Israel assumes moral responsibility . . . there can be no end to the conflict" was an exercise in moralistic grandstanding, not politics.[88]

What can be hoped for is not fairness or mea culpas—where would *they* end?—but incomplete justice, which is the only kind there is. This would entail acceptance of the fragmentary and the finite—which is to say, of the political and the human. Addressing the demands of right-wing Israeli settlers for "absolute justice," David Grossman wrote, "I answered that the person who seeks absolute justice is evading practical decisions, and that I do not seek pure justice nor the settling of historical accounts, but rather possible life, no more than imperfect and tolerable, causing as little injustice as possible. . . . I fear life among people who have an obligation to an absolute order. Absolute orders require . . . absolute deeds, and I, nebbish, am a partial, relative, imperfect man who prefers to make correctible mistakes rather than attain supernatural achievements."[89]

Halliday expressed a similar idea in 2006 when he distinguished between implausible and improbable goals. (Perhaps he, too, was a nebbish.) He listed various aims that are conceivable, such as providing global primary education for every child. This probably won't happen, but it could. "But it is not possible to have an equal world," he added. "It is not possible to abolish the state."[90] This distinction is nowhere more applicable, nowhere more vital, than in Israel-Palestine, whose inhabitants are fixated on maximalist fantasies and who equate impossibility with integrity.

Implicit in Halliday's writings is, I believe, an even more important insight. It is the understanding that realism is the *assertion,* not the surrender, of humane and even revolutionary values. Realism is what enables those values to move beyond theory into lived actuality; it is the enactment rather than the betrayal of principle. Realism lays the foundation for what Marxists call praxis. The outrage that emanated from leftists like Said and from the Israeli Right when the Oslo Accords were signed— the cries of appeasement and humiliation, the moans of defeat—suggested that this lesson had not been learned.

Halliday liked to tell the story of how, in the early twentieth century, Chinese students mistakenly translated the "Communist Manifesto" to read, "Scholars of the world, unite—you have nothing to lose but your shame!" Halliday's work shows what a progressive movement without shame would look like. It would strive for international solidarity without sycophancy. It would insist on economic justice *and* democratic rights as necessary pillars of a world worth living in. It would oppose terrorism committed by states and their opponents in equal measure. It would assert that, when it comes to the Israeli-Palestinian conflict, the reasonable but never absolute needs of each people must be respected; it would know that fantasies of supremacy lead only to ashes. It would have the humility to learn from, rather than willfully rewrite, history. It would be attuned to reality rather than besotted by theory. And it would, in Halliday's words, "have noticed the sufferings of others."[91]

PART THREE AMERICANS

CHAPTER SEVEN

I. F. Stone

THE LIMITS OF ISAIAH

GROWING UP IN NEW YORK CITY in the 1960s and seventies, I spent summers with my family on Fire Island, which at the time was an inexpensive haven for artists, writers, and left-wing intellectuals seeking a quiet reprieve from the city. I remember two neighbors whom my father always pointed out to me with the greatest respect. One was Irv, his friend, who walked with a limp—a most honorable limp, for he was a veteran of the Spanish Civil War's Abraham Lincoln Brigade, which my father regarded as the noblest endeavor of the century. The other was a short, homely man who wore thick Coke-bottle glasses and looked vaguely distracted. He was I. F. Stone, writer and publisher of *I. F. Stone's Weekly*, which battled the McCarthyite persecutions, the Vietnam War, and all sorts of government crimes and misdemeanors. In 1964, my father told me that the Gulf of Tonkin Resolution, which ratified Lyndon Johnson's escalation in Vietnam, was based on cooked-up evidence. My father could only have gotten that information from reading the *Weekly*, because Stone was the sole reporter in the country who dug through the official government documents, discovered the truth, and printed it.

I. F. Stone's political advocacy and reportage stretched from the Popular Front of the 1930s and forties—he cried when Franco crushed the Republic—to the New Left of the 1960s and beyond. He has been called the foremost radical journalist of twentieth-century America—"There was nothing to the left of me but the *Daily Worker*," he once boasted—and the most deeply democratic one.[1] (Throughout his life, he yearned for a synthesis of Thomas Jefferson and Karl Marx.) Stone was also, as one biographer wrote, "more closely identified with the Jewish state" than any other American journalist.[2] Stone viewed his Zionist commitments as the logical, indeed inevitable, extension of his other Left principles. Nevertheless, his relationship with Israel was stormy: loving, worried, exultant, angry.

Stone, too, has been called one of the "outcast prophets" who dared to criticize Israeli policies and who, early on, foresaw the consequences of the post-1967 Occupation. Although a secularist, his criticisms were embedded in what in he called the "Jewish soul" and the values of the Hebrew prophets. Stone was devoted to a thriving Israel and to the Jewish people's survival; he was also genuinely tormented by the suffering of the Palestinian refugees. His writings on the Arab-Israeli conflict were often astute, but they were also marked by strange occlusions—at best, a determined naiveté—that are a jarring contrast to his perceptive writings on Left history, the New Left, and Black Power. As with Hannah Arendt, his prescriptions for solving the Arab-Israeli conflict were often woozily abstract and therefore unpersuasive, though they are frequently quoted. And his relationship to the American Jewish community took on an unattractive note of peeved self-righteousness, the very quality he resisted when he was persecuted in the bleakest years of McCarthyism.

I. F. Stone—Izzy to his friends and admirers—was born Isidor Feinstein in 1907 in Philadelphia. (He changed his name to the less Jewish-sounding "I. F. Stone" in 1937, fearing that a lethal form of anti-Semitism would sweep the country and hurt his children; it was a decision that he regretted.) His father was a dry goods merchant from Ukraine and secular, though the family kept kosher, recited Sabbath prayers, and celebrated Sabbath dinners. Isidor went to Hebrew school and, at his Bar Mitzvah, received Heinrich Graetz's mammoth *History of the Jews*, which he kept throughout his life. His grandmother and an uncle to whom he was particularly close were Zionists.

Isidor's mother, who was plagued by manic depression and would attempt suicide, was almost illiterate in English. Yiddish was his first language—the one he heard at home—and he always regarded it with tenderness. Throughout his life, Stone's speech and writings were inflected with what Bernard Avishai had called the "hum, humility and humor" of Yiddish culture. In 1968, observing LBJ's attempts to bring as many interlocutors as possible into the Vietnam peace talks, Stone caustically wrote: "The more kibitzers the less the danger of reaching an agreement."[3] In 1974, when he was feted at the Cannes Film Festival, where a documentary about him was screened to accolades, a beaming Stone said that he felt like a "Kosher ham." He loved what he called "the democracy of the Bible"; the prophets were a recurring reference in his writings.[4]

As a boy, Isidor was small, almost dumpy, and plagued by terrible hearing and eyesight. (Toward the end of his life, he was virtually blind.) Reading was his main activity—it was listed as his hobby in his high school yearbook; his early influences included Blake, Whitman, Kropotkin, and Spinoza, whom he discovered at thirteen. Books didn't translate into scholastic achievement, however: Stone graduated forty-ninth out of fifty-two from his high school in the small town of Haddonfield, New Jersey, where his family had moved. As he once explained, "School interfered with my reading."[5]

Isidor grew up within the milieu of a flourishing, intensely political Yiddish-language press. His father read *Der Tag*, a liberal paper, but there were many competitors. Stone once explained their intricate hierarchy: "You could always tell the politics of a Jewish household in those days by which Jewish paper they subscribed to. If they were Communists they got the *Freiheit*; if they were socialists they got the *Forvits*, the *Forward*; if they were religious they got the *Morning Journal.* . . . We took the *Tag*. From a literary point of view, it was the best."[6] Journalism was Isidor's first and abiding love. He started his own newspaper, *The Progress*, which he wrote, edited, and published, when he was fourteen; a year later, he was working as a stringer for the *Camden Courier*. At age twenty, already employed by the *Philadelphia Inquirer*, he dropped out of the University of Pennsylvania. School apparently interfered with his writing.

The other milieu that shaped a coming-of-age Isidor was that of left-wing militancy: not in his family, but in the country at large. In 1927, when his editor at the *Camden Courier* refused to let him cover the Sacco and Vanzetti execution, Stone quit the paper and hitchhiked to Boston to attend a vigil for the two anarchists. What impressed the budding reporter and budding radical more than the doomed men's deaths was the solidarity of the living. In Colorado, miners walked off the job in protest; in Rochester and New York City, there were strikes; in Chicago, there were riots. Young Isidor was learning what political camaraderie meant.

Throughout his life, this proud ethic of solidarity, realized most concretely in the Popular Front, was Stone's lodestar. He always believed that the Left would hang separately if it did not hang together. He was haunted by the failure of the suicidally splintered Left in Austria and Germany to prevent the Nazi victory—though he was more critical of the Social Democrats than of the Communists. Spain was crucial: Unlike George Orwell, Stone fervently believed in the Popular Front and a united Republican army. Five decades later, Stone reiterated, "No, the Popular Front was the right idea. Certainly, the Spanish Republic would have been doomed from the beginning without it." He added, "Some of these *ex*-Communists were so *anti*-Communist that they turned against the Popular Front. . . . Ex's have to prove their apostasy."[7]

Stone remained a Popular Frontist long after the front had crumbled. In 1951, he unsuccessfully argued for the creation of an anti-McCarthyite coalition, and he forthrightly aligned himself with the country's ethnic, political, and racial outcasts. "Some of us are closer to Minsk than to the Mayflower. Some are Reds. Some are folk whose skins bar them from many places," he wrote. "We are not quite the kind of people with whom one associates."[8] In the sixties and seventies, he would beg the antiwar movement to transcend its divisions and unite around a set of common demands. That met with an equal lack of success.

Stone was never a member of the Communist Party, though his siblings and many of his friends were. But he followed much of the Communist line until the Hitler-Stalin Pact catapulted him away. Even then, though, Stone never minimized, or disowned, the U.S. Party's achievements in fighting for civil rights and building the American labor movement. Hitler's attack on the Soviet Union returned Stone, and most of America, to Russia's camp. Still, there are those who, in hindsight, reprimand Stone for his presumably inadequate distance from domestic and Soviet Communism. Paul Berman has accused Stone of fostering a "culture of mendacity" in the American Left and of being "in his own fashion, willy-nilly a totalitarian—at least sometimes."[9] This seems insensitive, at best, to the excruciating and unprecedented nature of political choices in the 1930s and forties. As Dan Diner and Jonathan Frankel have written, Jews *couldn't* be anti-Soviet during World War II because "the Red Army alone stood between the Jews of Europe and annihilation."[10] Looking backwards is cruelly easy.

Stone was not a Stalinist, even a willy-nilly one. After a 1956 trip to the Soviet Union, he wrote, "Stalinism was the natural fruit of the whole spirit of the Communist movement . . . a movement whose members had been taught not only to obey unquestioningly but to *hate*. . . . The liquidation of the opposition was not just a duty but a savage pleasure."[11] He argued that Stalinism could not be blamed on one man's criminality; neither could McCarthyism. But Stone never became a professional—or amateur—"ex." Writing of the Cuban Revolution in 1963, he contended, "Those who try to be objective or friendly are dismissed as dupes, and sometimes—as the Stalin years demonstrate—they were. . . . But events have also shown that in the long run the dupes prove less misleading than the doped."[12] Izzy Stone felt he had nothing to apologize for.

As a journalist, Stone worked as copy editor, rewrite man, sportswriter, political reporter, editorialist, essayist, and columnist for some of the country's most influential publications, including the *New York Post,* the *Nation,* the *New Republic,* and left-wing dailies like *PM* and the *Daily Compass.* In the Washington of Franklin Roosevelt, he became one of the city's most influential reporters, enjoying access to the power brokers of the administration and emerging as "the New Deal's favorite radical." He was well known to the American public through frequent radio and, later, television appearances. But by the late 1940s, with loyalty oaths, HUAC hearings, and paranoid anti-Communism in ascent, Stone precipitously became an untouchable. Cold Warrior Arthur Schlesinger Jr., presumably a liberal, described him, in the ugly language of the time, as one of the "Typhoid Marys of the left, bearing the germs of infection."[13]

With the closing of the *Compass* in 1952, Stone found himself unemployed, outcast, and—truly dangerous for a reporter—without Washington sources. Here was a true pariah. But he was not a quiet or defeated one. Squeezing the proverbial lemonade out of lemons—or, perhaps, borscht out of beets—Stone began his self-published, four-page *Weekly,* which has been called "one of the most astonishing feats in the history of journalism."[14] Since no one in official (or unofficial) Washington would speak to him, the *Weekly* depended almost entirely on deciphering seemingly dry documents and publications. Stone scoured everything from government budget reports to obscure magazines like *Motor Truck Facts,* which enabled him to analyze the transfer of supplies from North to South Vietnam. Compared to his previous publications, the *Weekly* was tiny and marginal, but it offered Stone unprecedented freedom. He wrote about anything he wanted: Nixon and Oppenheimer, Alabama and Algeria, Germany and Poland, Vietnam and the Cultural Revolution, the New Left and Black Power, Greece and Chile, the Smith Act and SNCC—and, of course, Israel and the Arabs. During the fifties, the *Weekly* was a clarion voice against the McCarthyite persecutions, arguing clearly and loudly that it was the inquis-itors, not the Communist Party, who were fundamentally un-American. The choice, Stone wrote, "is whether we are to relinquish the standards of Jefferson for those of Torquemada." Crucially, he viewed McCarthyism as a betrayal, rather than the true face, of American democracy, just as he viewed Stalinism as a betrayal of socialism and the Occupation as a betrayal of Zionism. In fact, he later wrote, he never felt *more* American than during the McCarthy era. As he defiantly explained, "Well, I may be just a Red Jew son-of-a-bitch to them, but I'm keeping Thomas Jefferson alive."[15]

Charter subscribers (annual rate: five dollars per year) to the *Weekly* included Eleanor Roosevelt and Albert Einstein. Marilyn Monroe treated every member of the House of Representatives to a subscription. The *Weekly* became required reading not only for the Left, especially the battered remnants of the Popular Front, but also, as the *Jerusalem Post* wrote, "in the very corridors of power" that Stone "enjoyed lacerating."[16] (FBI director J. Edgar Hoover, who spent years hounding Stone, took out a subscription under the nicely Semitic name "Irving Rubin.") By the time an aging Stone closed the publication in 1971, subscriptions had swelled from the initial five thousand to seventy thousand.

In the early to mid-1960s, with McCarthyism vanquished and the civil rights and antiwar movements on the rise, Stone was welcomed in from the cold. Colleges invited him to speak; high-profile newspapers and magazines published him again. When he died in 1989 at age eighty-one, he was lauded by newspapers around the world—including those, like the *New York Times,* which had fired employees during the Red Scare. Stone was praised as a great journalist, a true American, a fearless truth-teller: in short, a mensch.

It is interesting to compare Stone with Arthur Koestler, since their similarities were many and their differences so profound. Born within two years of each other, both were college dropouts, short, and far from handsome. (Stone was once compared to a chipmunk.) Both were superb journalists, autodidacts, secular Jews, and—albeit in very different ways—Zionists. But whereas Stone was deeply rooted in America and the American vernacular, Koestler was the perpetual émigré. Stone loved Yiddish and considered himself a proud son of Jewish culture; Koestler was embarrassed if not repelled by both. And while Koestler spent much of his life scurrying to disown his Left politics and his Jewish heritage, Stone took the opposite approach. Izzy often spoke of "we," by which he meant leftists, Jews, Americans, and, sometimes, Israelis, none of whom he was inclined to disavow.

Stone's secularism, too, was different from Koestler's. Stone thought a lot about the meaning of Jewish history—something Koestler regarded as an imaginary construct—and was profoundly moved by his visits to Israel. He cried when he first saw the Wailing Wall, and he considered Jerusalem "a place to walk with God even if you don't believe in God. . . . I'm a pious Jewish atheist."[17] Unlike Koestler, Stone believed that Diaspora Jews could not separate themselves from Israel's fate.

But it is character more than politics that most distinguishes the two. On a visceral level, Stone simply despised what he termed, during the McCarthy era, "the Crawl": the abject disavowal of political principles and the betrayal of friends, family, and erstwhile comrades. Naming names was anathema to him, and he was especially disgusted when cowardice was mistaken for patriotism. Professional penitents like Koestler's buddy Whittaker Chambers appalled Stone. "No martyrdom was ever more lavishly buttered," he wrote of Chambers; here was the kind of saint "who threw others to the lions and retired to a villa."[18] Though Stone did not enjoy his years of pariahdom, he seemed to have no desire, or at least no need, for the acceptance and respectability that Koestler craved. It is impossible to imagine Koestler describing himself as a "Red Jew son-of-a-bitch," since this was precisely the identity that he most feared.

Like most American Jews, I. F. Stone was neither a Zionist nor an anti-Zionist until the 1940s. As with most American Jews, Hitler changed that.

During the war years, Stone was one of the journalists—along with Koestler, Freda Kirchwey of the *Nation*, William Shirer, and a few others— who maintained a steady, if sadly ineffective, drumbeat demanding help for what Stone accurately called "the fast-disappearing Jews of Europe." Like Koestler, he lambasted Britain and the U.S. for their refusal to open the doors to Jews trapped in Europe; action, not pity, was called for. Stone argued that Nazi crimes were not tragic but, rather, "a kind of insane horror. It is *our* part in this which is tragic." The democracies, hobbled by "weakness, indecision, sloth, [and] inability to act," had shamed themselves.[19]

Stone made the first of his many trips to Palestine in 1945. "I came to Palestine unhappy," he admitted. "But the longer I have been here the happier I have come to feel." The young Jews building the country were, he wrote, "truly heroic" and an inspiration to "all who prize human courage, devotion, and idealism."[20] Most of all, the Yishuv was "the one place in the world where Jews seem completely unafraid. . . . In Palestine a Jew can be a Jew. Period. Without apologies, and without any lengthy arguments as to whether Jews are a race, a religion, a myth, or an accident."[21] Here was positive Zionism: The Yishuv was not just a refuge from hatred but a place of autonomous development. Sympathetic to the Arab fear of economic and cultural subordination within a Jewish state and to the Jews' fear of minority status within an Arab one, Stone argued for partition. Such a solution, he wrote in November 1945, "is ethically right and politically feasible," and he believed it "would be acceptable to a great majority of Jews and Arabs if it were imposed" by the UN.[22]

The next month, though acknowledging the likelihood that Britain might "attempt to liquidate the Yishuv," Stone wrote that he now opposed partition and a Jewish state. He had one reason: He could find no Arabs who would accept them. (This change in thinking was, perhaps, the result a two-hour off-the-record talk Stone held with Azzam Bey, first secretary-general of the Arab League.) He therefore concluded that a binational state was best "until population parity has been reached between Jews and Arabs." The problem, which Stone failed to acknowledge, is that virtually every Arab leader *opposed* both population parity and binationalism—a position that Azzam Bey would almost certainly have conveyed. Nevertheless, Stone expressed confidence that the Jews could "build a secure homeland for themselves among their Semitic brethren."[23]

With the end of the war, Stone became one of the most outspoken advocates of resettling the Shoah's homeless survivors in Palestine, which directly contravened British policy. Now languishing in displaced persons (DP) camps, the survivors "too often found their liberators as callous and indifferent as their Nazi oppressors had been savage and sadistic." Stone made clear that home for the homeless meant Palestine. "They were persecuted as Jews, and most of them now wish to live as Jews, to hold their heads up as Jews. . . . There is really nowhere else for them to go." Like Koestler, he particularly loathed Britain's Foreign Secretary Ernest Bevin, whom he viewed as an appeaser of the Arab upper classes and whose major aim, he charged, was to build "an anti-Soviet bloc in the Middle East at the expense of Jewish aspirations."[24]

Stone's urgent advocacy of Jewish immigration to Palestine led to his 1946 classic *Underground to Palestine*. At the request of the Haganah, he accompanied a group of "illegals" as they made the treacherous journey from the hostile Europe of the DP camps to the hostile Palestine of the British Mandate. With awe, he described this as "the greatest exodus in the history of the Jewish people . . . greater in magnitude, misery, and drama than those from Egypt and Spain."[25]

As in Koestler's *Promise and Fulfilment*, the villains of Stone's book are the British. The key to *Underground to Palestine* can be found in its relatively undramatic first paragraph, which finds the author sitting in the press gallery of the UN Security Council watching Sir Alexander Cadogan, Britain's representative, make "a professionally astringent argument designed to prevent action against Franco." For Stone, there was an unbroken line between the betrayal of Spain and that of the Jews: "In Sir Alexander's subtle apologetics for a Fascist dictator, I had seen one aspect of the Empire's postwar policy. I was soon to see another."[26] And for Stone, there was an equally direct bond between defense of the Spanish Republic and that of the Yishuv.

Like *Ten Days that Shook the World*, *Underground to Palestine* is an eyewitness report and a work of impassioned advocacy. Of the refugees, Stone explained, "I did not go to join them as a tourist in search of the picturesque, nor even as a newspaperman merely in search of a good story, but as a kinsman, fulfilling a moral obligation to my brothers." And since they could expect no help from others, "I was anxious to . . . see what the Jews could do for themselves."[27]

Gathered in an Italian Communist town for their journey, the refugees were a ragtag lot. The largest group was composed of Poles, then Czechs and Dutch. Others came from Hungary, Germany, France, Turkey, Romania, and Greece. There was also "one rather lonely Egyptian Jew";

Stone described the ship as "a floating Babel." Some of the refugees had fought as partisans during the war. Some were survivors of the concentration or extermination camps. Most were relatively young. Their politics were mixed; seventeen political parties were represented, though over half identified as socialist-Zionists. They were Europe's weary riffraff: former tailors, weavers, woodworkers, carpenters, students—hardly the imposing imperialists of later lore. Other than those who had found refuge in the USSR, all were the sole survivors of their families. Stone recalled "one sick old man I called *zeyde* [grandfather] but who told me he had neither children nor grandchildren."[28]

In their ardor for Palestine, the survivors experienced a push away from murderous Europe and a pull toward reconstructing their lives in a new nation. Some told Stone they had never identified as Zionists, or even as Jews, before the Shoah; the degradations, the losses, the ghettoes, the camps, and most of all the global abandonment had changed that. "We have wandered enough," one passenger explained to Stone. "We have worked and struggled too long on the lands of other peoples. We must build a land of our own. *Mir muzen boyen a yiddish land.* [We must build a Yiddish land.]" A girl named Ruth, a former inmate of Auschwitz, confided, "I didn't expect to live, but I was determined to show them how a Jew could die." Stone rejoiced in this defiance; the revelation, he wrote, was "not that they have suffered. . . . The real news is that so many . . . [emerged] with tremendous vitality, with spirits unbroken."[29] Indeed, he had never seen a "gayer" ship, pulsing with pioneer songs and camaraderie. But he acknowledged, too, the cost of the suffering. There were many who had been morally degraded by what they had done to survive and had developed a "fierce and predatory criminality"; others were physically damaged and spiritually crushed.[30] And perhaps Stone was too seduced by the exuberance of the "unbrokens": Even they had been horrifically violated. Israel was built in large part by people whose primary experience was devastation—people whose trust in the world, in the words of Jean Améry, had been shattered.

In any case, the gayness was not to last. The ship begins running out of food and water and, severely overloaded, is in danger of sinking. Its SOS is refused, more than once, by the British. The human cargo includes pregnant women and the sick; its lower deck becomes inferno-like. The nauseating stink, the noise, the heat, the illness, the desperation to escape are overwhelming; like a recurring nightmare, the Hobbesian conditions of the concentration camps are quickly recreated. "A few of the cleverer, stronger, and more unscrupulous seemed to get back on deck," Stone wrote, but some "seemed too utterly spent to move. A kind of fierce Darwinian struggle went on in that hold and in that struggle the men seemed to become less than human. It was like being in a den of wolves." Back on deck, Stone encounters a German psychologist whom he had previously befriended and who had been trapped down below. "I had never seen a man's face so changed in a few hours. . . . The pleasant young man I knew had the look of a creature cowering under oppression. He must have looked that way . . . in Buchenwald."[31] Here, in concentrated form, is what Primo Levi documented in *If This Is a Man:* how fragile what he called the scaffolding of civilization proves to be under conditions of physical brutality and psychic helplessness.

After additional miserable misadventures, Stone's ship finally sails into Haifa harbor with a Star of David flag waving. The British eventually allow it to land, though it is among the last to do so. (British policies prohibiting Jewish immigration would subsequently harden.) "An Arab guard . . . gave us a friendly *sholom*," Stone concluded. "I was in *Eretz* at last."[32]

Stone's "Epilogue" is a fervent plea for Jewish settlement in Palestine and an equally fervent attack on the British. And it shows how the journey to Palestine changed him. Back in Cairo, he discusses the political situation with friends yet finds himself "curiously uninterested in all their talk. I had begun to feel like a DP myself." For the surviving Jews—and, now, for Stone—"Palestine is not a matter of theory." He no longer quibbles about one state or two but, instead, encapsulates the Zionist case at its pithiest: "These Jews want the right to live as a people, to build as a people, to make their contribution to the world as a people. Are their national aspirations any less worthy of respect than those of any other oppressed people?"[33]

Pithy or not, this question fell on deaf ears in London. Stone had become convinced that the British government would offer the Jews only "disappointment, betrayal, and attack. . . . The British Empire is now waging a war designed to smash what the Jews have accomplished in Palestine." (As a high British military official reasoned, "The world took the killing of six million Jews and if we have to destroy half of Tel Aviv, the world will take that, too.") Like Koestler, Stone viewed the Muslim-Arab bourgeoisie, who were Britain's allies, as a retrograde force: phobic about the Soviet Union, fearful of the immiserated Arab masses, hostile to the modern ideas the Jews had brought to Palestine. The British-Arab coalition, Stone charged, offered backwardness and oppression to both Arabs and Jews. And though a binational Palestine might still be a nice idea, "I think the Jews must look to themselves."[34]

Underground to Palestine ends in anger and hope. Despite the odds, Stone was certain of a British defeat and a Zionist victory. The Jews, he wrote, had nothing to lose and therefore nothing to fear. "They who knew the SS are not terrified by the British. They who saw the gas chambers are not frightened by a naval blockade." He informed Azzam Bey, whom he greatly respected, "*Nothing will stop the people I traveled with from rebuilding a great Jewish community in Palestine.*"[35] He predicted that the British would emerge from their Palestinian sojourn covered in shame.

The material in *Underground to Palestine* first ran as daily dispatches in *PM;* circulation swelled to 250,000, making the paper profitable for the first and only time. Along with Martha Gellhorn, Stone was now the country's best-known Left journalist—and, among American Jews, its most loved.

Underground to Palestine is an immensely moving document. "I came to love these people," Stone wrote; I did too.[36] But a troubling contradiction is embedded within it—one that, in various iterations, would bedevil Stone's later writings. Stone believed that Jewish immigration to Palestine was the indisputable cause of all freedom-loving, justice-seeking peoples. At the same time, he continued to insist, "I am more than ever convinced that Jews and Arabs can live together in peace. There is no such ill feeling in Palestine between Jew and Arab as exists in Czechoslovakia between Czech and Slovak."[37] Whether out of optimism or ignorance, he ignored the fact that virtually all Arab leaders regarded an influx of Jews to Palestine—Stone's imperative—not as an expression of freedom or justice but, rather, as a form of imperialist aggression and religious blasphemy. And the international solidarity that Stone always championed was nowhere to be found. The Arab leaders emphasized that Jewish suffering was not their fault and, therefore, of no concern to them.

In the years leading up to Israel's independence, Stone continued to report from Palestine for *PM,* the *New Republic,* and the *Nation.* In his stress on the Yishuv's resilience, national unity, and quotidian humanity, his dispatches were highly reminiscent of Gellhorn's from Spain (though his were more optimistic). In a May 1948 article called "Tel Aviv Quiet, But You Know There's a War On," Stone reported, "I know the war goes on. A great battle was under way at Bab el Wad to clear the Jerusalem road. . . . But in the sunny streets here swarming with busy folk, there is no feeling of anxiety. There is a great pride in speaking to visitors; a deep confidence in themselves, and the chief danger seems to be the infernal bicyclists."[38]

Two days later, Stone attended the short service at which the Yishuv's leaders declared Israel's independence. (He later noted that it was the only meeting in the Zionist movement's history which started on time and contained no long speeches.) He praised "the Jewish masses for their courage in insisting on proceeding with the establishment of a Jewish state in spite of dark hints of reprisals." He exulted in the Haganah's capture of the western Galilee but stressed that "Israel prefer[s] peace to glamorous military victories." Still, Stone knew that swords, not just plowshares, were sometimes needed; Franco and Hitler had taught him that. "Fear of an armed Jewish state seems the best way to make the Arab nations accept peace. And peace is what the Jews want and . . . what the world needs. But if it is to be war, the Yishuv intends to make its enemies pay long and dearly." The Egyptian air force, as expected, would begin bombing Israel the next day; nevertheless, Stone observed, "I talked to many angry people, but I have yet to see panic in Tel Aviv. . . . Life goes on with vitality, color and zest. . . . The people one encounters in the streets and cafés just naturally and quietly expect the Jewish state to win. In the meantime, they are prepared to take it on the chin."[39]

That same year, Stone teamed up with Robert Capa, the world's most famous left-wing photographer, to produce the book *This Is Israel*. (Photojournalists Tim Gidal, who had immigrated to Palestine in 1936, and Jerry Cooke, an Odessa-born refugee from Hitler, also contributed to the volume.) In iconography, *This Is Israel* echoes Capa's 1938 *Death in the Making*, his plea for Spain—though again, as the titles suggest, the book on Israel radiates far more hope. *This Is Israel* documents the building of a country based on a synthesis of military resilience, agricultural productivity, democratic institutions, and cultural rejuvenation. There are photographs of the ordinary, often smiling men and women who made up the "people's army"; of the building of the kibbutzim; of the children's schools; of the café crowds in Tel Aviv; of the "illegals" trapped behind barbed wire; of family reunions; of the beach, the sea, the promenades; of dance performances, concerts, and theater productions. The subjects of these photographs look simultaneously heroic and prosaic; that is precisely their appeal. Yet something is missing: the Arabs. There are few pictures of them.

Stone organized his text like a fable. Chapter headings include "The Pains of Birth: in which Israel seems doomed by diplomatic duplicity and Arab ambush," "Lusty Baby: in which the Jews implement partition for themselves," and "The Wicked Midwives: in which the Foreign Office and the State Department try to bring about a stillbirth." He emphasized three points. First, that the Arabs had promised, and attempted, what Azzam Bey called "a war of extermination" against Israel.[40] Second, that the U.S. State Department, the British Foreign Office, and the United Nations had tried to undermine, indeed strangle, the nascent Jewish state. Finally, that while the UN squabbled, the Israelis had implemented partition on their own and gained control of the areas allotted to them, just as they had built a state before it was officially recognized as such. If the word "self-determination" means anything, *This Is Israel* is a paean to it.

Stone would later develop a very different take on the events of 1948. But here, as an eyewitness, he was scornful of the Arab armies. "The Arabs showed little fighting heart," he reported. "One people cared enough to die and the other didn't." Like Koestler, he charted the Palestinian flight, which commenced before the official war began. "The Arabs very early began to run away. First the wealthiest families went. . . . While the Arab guerrillas were moving in, the Arab civilian population was moving out."[41] He noted the mélange of unsavory volunteers who joined the Arab forces, including former Nazis, Polish reactionaries, and Yugoslav Chetniks: hardly a progressive alliance.

Stone documented the Haganah's successful evolution (similar to that of the Spanish Republicans) from an assortment of disparate militias into a disciplined, united army. He exulted in the Israelis' "determination, ingenuity, and devotion which filled a Jew with pride headier than the cold mountain air."[42] He hailed the "heroes" of the Jerusalem siege, especially Gershon Agronsky, who maintained the *Palestine Post*'s daily publishing schedule throughout the blockade. (Stone was, first and last, a newshound.) He was unapologetic about Israel's territorial gains during the war, which he saw as ethically justified and militarily required; as he would later note, "The 1947 plan in effect left Israel split into three parts, strategically indefensible, wide open to enemy attack. No stranger boundaries were ever drawn."[43]

In *This Is Israel,* Stone rejects any moral equivalence between aggressors and defenders—between the Arab forces "who had taken up arms against the UN" partition agreement and "their intended victims." He identifies Israel's strength as stemming from a hard-earned self-sufficiency in all realms. "How badly this experiment in turning the other cheek fared," he wrote of the Zionist learning curve since the attacks of 1929. Since then, the Jews had taught themselves to "handle the rifle as well as the plow."[44] Gone is his previous talk of binationalism, confederation, and Semitic brotherhood. Israel can depend only on itself.

In text and subtext—in its celebration of Israel's prowess, its spirit, its ethics, its *necessity*—this is one of the most pro-Zionist books ever written. It is also one that, in subsequent years, Stone would amend, and that is not excerpted in his collected works.

The year 1956 was one of building tensions in the Middle East; Stone visited Israel and wrote frequently about the worsening political situation. In a February dispatch, he reminded readers that the 1948 war was the result of Arab aggression and reiterated that "the Jews had no recourse but to fight for their lives."[45] He devoted an entire issue of the *Weekly* to the Arab-Israeli conflict—which had now expanded into an international conflict—charging that "Britain would like . . . to use Israel to overthrow Nasser and then to make a settlement at the expense of a weakened Israel."[46] He stressed that there could be no turning back to 1947; an Arab-Palestinian state next to Israel was now inconceivable if only because Jordan would not relinquish the land it had seized in the 1948 war. (Nor would Egypt give up Gaza.)

He also made a strong plea for the resettlement of the Palestinian refugees, an issue that was far from a world concern at the time. Stone argued that resettlement was something that the stateless Palestinians *and* the Israelis desperately needed. In the latter case, the reasons were political and moral: "We dare not treat the Arab as human dirt swept out of the land without dirtying ourselves."[47] This warning did not, however, lead Stone to rethink the moral necessities of 1948; he reminded readers that "if the Arabs had won, they would have been merciless and primitive in their revenge. . . . The Yishuv would have been destroyed and its people slaughtered." But he insisted that the Arabs, too, had had a right and a reason to fight, for they regarded a Jewish state as an "alien invasion." Because of this moral ambiguity, "the price of our victory was to find ourselves morally in the wrong. For there in the camps across the borders were new refugees whom this time we had made."[48]

Stone clarified that this resettlement could not be within Israel proper; he did not uphold any "right" of return. Nevertheless, the refugees' future was the responsibility of Israel and the Jewish Diaspora, and he urged a world Jewish campaign to champion the Palestinians' plight. "We must find a way to make new homes for them. . . . We must resettle the refugees or at least demonstrate to the utmost our sincere desire to do so."[49] This was, he wrote, a worthy challenge for Isaiah's descendants.

I read this today with a what-if sense of angst: How different history might be if Israel, and world Jewry, had followed Stone's lead. Again, though, I have a nagging sense that a willful obtuseness, or at least an avoidance of difficulty, underlies the beauty of Stone's simple moral urgency. The Arab countries steadfastly refused to resettle the refugees and corralled them, as Sartre had angrily noted, in impoverished camps designed to inculcate hatred. How could a world Jewish campaign change this? The Arab world insisted on the liberation of Palestine, by which it meant the obliteration of Israel. How, then, would the resettlement of the refugees lead to peace?

To the surprise of some, Stone supported the Israeli-French-British invasion of Egypt in 1956. The Arab states, he argued, had been flooded with powerful weapons from Russia and the U.S., and were increasingly bellicose toward Israel. Syria had moved arms into Jordan. Iraqi troops were on the border, seemingly in preparation for an attack, though "Mr. Dulles saw no reason for alarm." Meanwhile, *fedayeen* guerrillas—"these terrorist squads are Nasser's special pride"—were causing steady casualties in Israel. "All we can hope for now is if the deed were done, 'twere well—as Lady Macbeth said—it were done quickly. If Nasser could be toppled . . . peace might be patched up."[50]

But the next week, Stone abruptly recanted: Preemptive aggression could not be supported. "Because so many bonds attach me to Israel, I am ready to condone preventive war; I rejoiced when my side won," he admitted. "Israel's survival seemed worth the risk to world peace. And this is how it always is and how it starts, and I offer up the mote in my own eye." Still, he asked, "What were all those Migs . . . which Moscow poured into Egypt . . . ? What was Nasser doing when he boasted that he would soon exterminate Israel? . . . And from the Arab side I can hear the recriminations about the homeless refugees it was their sacred duty to revenge. . . . The quarrels of nations are as difficult to unravel as those of children, but the pistols are no longer toy."[51]

These seesaws pointed to an internal three-way conflict that would become steadily more acute for Stone. He was torn between defending Israel's security against unrelenting hostility, upholding the international rule of law, and respecting Arab self-determination This triangular dilemma would be a source of confusion and pain.

Stone's trip to Israel in the summer of 1964 filled him with joy. "To see Israel again after eight years is to be struck at every turn by the triumphant evidence of progress," he wrote in a dispatch titled "An Affluent Society But Living Beyond Its Means." He reveled in the sense of security (the 1956 Sinai invasion, he noted, had done some good); in the vitality; in the flowers blooming everywhere. "It is impossible not to be optimistic" about the "dynamic, confident and expanding Israel of today." But, as with Isaac Deutscher, the joy was clouded with worries: about Israel's economy, burdened by enormous defense expenditures; about the prejudice against Sephardic Jews; and about the "humiliation" of the Arab-Israelis, which "fills one with despair."[52]

Nineteen sixty-seven: In the lead-up to what he feared would be another Arab-Israeli war, Stone linked tensions in the Middle East to those in Southeast Asia. The U.S.'s renewed bombing of North Vietnam, he charged in early June, would defeat any attempts by the superpowers to defuse the Middle East. Moscow, Stone observed, "seems to be taking out on Israel the humiliation Washington has imposed on it in Vietnam." Stone worried about Israel's dependence on the U.S., which had hardly been furthering the cause of world peace. "How can Johnson call for restraint when he has shown so little? How can the U.S. champion freedom of the seas in Aqaba when it has done its best to destroy the principle by blockades around Cuba and North Vietnam?" He assailed the

U.S.'s combativeness toward the socialist bloc: "How can we try to calm down Arab calls for *jihad* against Israel when we have been building up a holy war spirit of our own in years of cold war propaganda?"[53]

But he did not question support for Israel; in fact, under the headline "On The Pro-Israel Left," he approvingly quoted a recent public statement signed by fifty French intellectuals led by Sartre. While identifying themselves as "friends of the Arabic peoples and opponents of American imperialism," they stressed that the precondition for peace was "the security and sovereignty of Israel," and they declared "incomprehensible the identification of Israel with an imperialist and aggressive camp." Stone called on Cairo and Damascus to end "their flamboyant declarations" to destroy the Jewish state.[54]

In the June 12 issue of the *Weekly* and the July issue of *Ramparts*, one of the New Left's premier magazines, Stone laid out his initial reactions to the Six-Day War. Unlike Deutscher, Israel's victory did not immediately lead him to turn in anger against the country. On the contrary, he identified himself as someone who wanted Israel "to live and grow in peace," and he praised "all she honorably won in marsh and desert." Far from identifying Israel as an imperialist agent, he reminded readers of her perilous position: "On the one side are the superpowers for whom she has been a pawn; on the other the Arabs for whom she is an enemy."[55] If Israel *had* been overrun by the Arab forces, "it could expect little more than a few hand-wringing resolutions" from the global community, including the U.S., France, and England. Jewish history, especially twentieth-century Jewish history, had taught the Jews "how little reliance may be placed on the conscience of mankind."[56] Israel was a small and essentially isolated country, not a mighty empire.

Stone was of course relieved that Israel had prevailed ("the troubles of victory are better than those of defeat").[57] But he stressed that triumph made a peace agreement and a solution to the refugee problem all the more urgent; military prowess would otherwise mean little. He still supported "a predominantly Jewish state," but he believed it could be linked in fraternity to a Palestinian one and to Jordan. The key to Israel's survival—the only key, the sine qua non—was amity with the Arab world. "The challenge to Israel is to conquer something more bleak and forbidding than even the Negev or Sinai, and that is the hearts of her Arab neighbors," Stone wrote. "It is to understand and forgive an enemy, and thus convert him into a friend." Israel must reconcile with her neighbors and become part of the ongoing "renaissance of Arabic unity and civilization."[58] He urged a return to "the Grand Design" of the 1947 partition plan and concluded by quoting Isaiah's prediction of a blessed peace between the peoples of Israel, Assyria, and Egypt.

These articles reveal Stone's considerable strengths as an analyst of the conflict. Much of what he wrote proved right—not just morally but politically too. His prediction that, without signed treaties, Israel would become increasingly embattled and militaristic; his prophecy of increased Arab humiliation and rage; his call to heed the suffering of the refugees; his insistence that repeated wars, even if won by Israel, could never substitute for a political solution; his warnings against Israeli hubris and the nation's loss of moral stature—all unerring. Though his language was less virulent than Deutscher's, Stone, too, rued the country's "present mood of military elation and religio-national fervor about Jerusalem. . . . This is the blindness of high tragedy."[59]

One cannot definitively know, of course, what the Arab world's reaction would have been to an Israeli plan to hand back the newly conquered territories in return for recognition, security, and a comprehensive peace. Alas, no such offer was forthcoming, at least publicly. Surely it was worth the risk to try, and there were Israelis, including within academia, the government, and the military, who urged this course. "The Arab states are unable to break out of the vicious circle of hatred, frustration, and suspicion, of injured national pride and the feeling of inferiority in the field of modernization," Yehoshua Arieli, a history professor at Hebrew University, argued in a 1969 issue of the leftist Israeli-Arab magazine *New Outlook*. "The government of Israel will have to break the circle."[60] Devising a two-state solution—recognition for recognition, state for state—was paramount. In the decades since 1967, Zionism has failed this imperative; as historian Jonathan Frankel wrote, a movement that had "developed all the instincts necessary to survive as underdog could not adjust to the much more complex role that comes with the possession of real power." This is Zionism's tragedy: After two thousand years, Jews had achieved true sovereignty yet were "paralyzed" by it.[61]

Still, the chances of a peace offer's success were hardly good—and to many, hardly conceivable—and Stone's articles make equally clear how distant he had become from the political realities of the Middle East. (Two years later, he would praise Lebanon as a stable, multicultural model for "what sooner or later must develop" between Israelis and Palestinians.[62] In fact, tensions between Lebanese Muslims and Christians were already brewing, and in 1975 the country exploded into a ferocious fifteen-year civil war that left it in ruins.) The Israeli victory in June was quickly met by the Arab League's Khartoum Resolution, which promised "no peace with Israel, no recognition of Israel, no negotiations with it." Accolades, funds, and arms poured into the PLO, which stressed armed struggle as the sole road to liberation; terrorist attacks soared. What Stone called the grand design of partition was no more acceptable to the Arab states and the Palestinians in 1967 than it had been two decades earlier; the PLO stated its unequivocal view that Zionism was "fascist" and must be expunged. Stone's assumption that Israelis and Palestinians shared a parallel yearning for peace was simply false; as Yasser Arafat explained to Oriana Fallaci in 1972, "The end of Israel is the goal of our struggle, and it allows for neither compromise nor mediation. . . . We don't want peace. We want war, victory."[63] One could dismiss this as mere bombast, but for many years there was little in the PLO's actions to contradict it. And Stone seemed to have reversed cause and effect. As he had reported in 1948, the refugee problem was the result, not the origin, of the conflict. Indeed, the PLO made plain that it was the 1947 partition, not the conquests of 1967, that it intended to avenge.

Equally important, the Arab renaissance on which Stone pinned such hopes was hard to detect. In fact, the 1967 war would lead to the ascension, or consolidation, of the Arab world's cruelest regimes and dictators: Saddam Hussein in Iraq, Hafez al-Assad in Syria, Muammar Qaddafi in Libya—and to ultra-Left groups within the PLO. (Political Islam also gained new adherents, though this was less noticed at the time.) These were men who regarded peace with Israel as sacrilege, as abasement, and as existential threat: Anti-Israel incitement was their strongest suit with which to appease their disenfranchised citizens. Many Western leftists, including Stone, failed to address, or perhaps understand, the nexus between the 1967 war and intensified repression within the Arab states. This interdependence was clearer to some Israeli leftists. As Shlomo Avineri observed in 1969, "The tragedy of Arab society is that the conflict with Israel reinforces exactly those traditional traits . . . that have already hindered its adaptation [to modernity]. . . . Unless there emerges something like Arab Zionism that will have the courage to disentangle itself from a millennium and half of Arab history in the same way as Zionism attempted to emancipate the Jews from two thousand years of Jewish history . . . the chances for peace in the Middle East are slim indeed."[64] Isaiah's vision didn't mean much to Yasser Arafat, Hafez al-Assad, or George Habash; if anything, they sought to beat plowshares into swords.

Stone's rupture from much of the American Jewish community, and from his previous work, came in an August 1967 essay he wrote for the *New York Review of Books* called "Holy War." In tone and substance, this piece is so different from the article in *Ramparts* that it is hard to believe that they were separated by only one month. The essay was, ostensibly, a review of Claude Lanzmann's issue of *Les Temps Modernes* devoted to the Arab-Israeli conflict. But Stone's piece functioned as an occasion to lay out what the *New York Review of Books* billed as a "new approach" to the conflict. It was an approach that Stone would follow fairly consistently in subsequent years.

Turning first to *Les Temps Modernes,* Stone praised Maxime Rodinson's contribution, which condemned Israel as colonialist, as "by far the most brilliant in the whole volume," though he did not explain why. Stone found it significant that Rodinson "refused, for reasons of principle, to appear in the Arab ensemble. . . . He is too much the humanist (and in the last analysis no doubt the Jew) to welcome an apocalyptic solution at the expense of Israel's existence."[65] (This wasn't quite right; Rodinson later explained, "I was neither Arab nor Jewish, religiously speaking. Sartre and Lanzmann gave me a bad time.")[66] Stone assailed the position of Moroccan journalist Tahar Benziane, who blamed Jews for their history of persecution and who "sees the only solution not just in the liquidation of Israel but in the disappearance of world Jewry through assimilation."[67] This was, Stone charged, "classic anti-Semitism"—and precisely the kind of "disappearance" that Rodinson and Arthur Koestler had vigorously promoted.

Most of "Holy War," however, was devoted to a harsh critique of Israel and to a revision of Stone's previous writings. Throughout the 1940s and fifties, he had identified the Zionist struggle as an anti-imperialist one; now he argued, albeit in a somewhat convoluted fashion, that the Yishuv's

fight against the British failed to prove it was "not . . . a colonial implanta-
tion."[68] Now he assailed the Haganah's "terrorism"—though in a strongly
worded 1946 piece he had denounced that description as a "smear." (At
the time, he described the Haganah as a disciplined, democratic people's
army whose fighters were "no more gangsters than . . . the men of
Concord or Lexington.")[69] Now he denied any symmetry between the
expulsion of Palestinians from Israel and of Jews from the Arab countries. Yet he suggested other symmetries that were highly dubious. Thus
he likened Moshe Dayan's definition of Israel as a majority-Jewish state—
which Stone had supported in the past—to Spain in the time of the
Inquisition. There is something dispiriting about all this: dispiriting not
because Stone was criticizing Israel but because he was descending into
lazy, imprecise arguments to do so.

Of course, there was nothing wrong with Stone changing his mind
on key questions: 1967 was not 1947. What is strange about this essay is
Stone's refusal to acknowledge, much less explain, these dramatic shifts;
he wrote as though he did not have two decades' worth of impassioned
writings on Jews and Arabs behind him. This refusal is particularly
surprising given the strong personal connection to Stone that his readers
treasured. He was writing for people who had followed him for years and
looked to him for guidance; surely he owed them some insight into the
"why" behind his new thoughts.

Stone now assailed the very idea of Jewish sovereignty, which he had
championed in *Underground to Palestine, This Is Israel,* and many other
writings. Israel, he charged, was "racial and exclusionist," a site of "moral
myopia" and "Lilliputian nationalism," and a sad refutation of Jewish
universality. "The greatness of the Prophets lay in their overcoming of
ethnocentricty," he claimed. "Here lie the roots of growing divergence
between Jew and Israeli; the former with a sense of mission as a Witness
in the human wilderness, the latter concerned only with his own tribe's
welfare."[70]

There are several questionable aspects to these claims. It is not clear
why Jewish nationhood is more inherently tribal (or racist, or exclusive)
than the Palestinian, Vietnamese—or American—varieties; indeed, trib-
alism and nationalism are often opposed. Stone's attempt to convert the
prophets into anti-national Jews of the twentieth century—living,
perhaps, on the Upper West Side instead of in Canaan—was at best

misguided; the ancient Hebrews' genius was precisely their ability to *synthesize,* perhaps for the first time in human history, the national and the universal. Stone's implication that the (American) Jew was far more ethically advanced than the Israeli—a claim often made by left-wing Jews of the Diaspora—was arrogant and unsubstantiated, and it sidestepped the radically different circumstances that each group faced. The demand that the Jews function as a "Witness in the human wilderness" was nothing less than Stone's version of the chosen people: a lodestone that, as Albert Memmi had argued, Zionism was designed to eradicate. And perhaps flayed Jewish bodies and crushed Jewish souls had testified enough; as Lanzmann wrote of the Shoah, "Again—and one hopes for the last time—the Jewish people has fulfilled its role as the people who bears witness."[71]

Stone's essay reeks of nostalgia. He seemed to yearn for the halcyon days when the stateless Jewish people could be moral symbols—brimming with ethical power but devoid of the practical kind—rather than citizens of a modern nation confronting the rights and responsibilities of sovereignty under extraordinarily difficult conditions. This does not mean that Israel's policies toward the Arab world or the Palestinians were above reproach; quite the contrary. But Stone's critique was not so much a political analysis as a finger-wagging sermon. As the Biblical scholar Robert Alter wrote soon after the Six-Day War, the Jewish people were no longer "ghostly emissaries of some obscure mission, but men like other men who need to occupy physical space in a real world before they can fulfill whatever loftier aspirations they may have."[72] Stone's essay clarifies what was so fundamentally problematic, so fundamentally *evasive,* about his position. Modern Israelis can't turn themselves into Isaiah any more than modern Americans can turn themselves into Tom Paine. The writings of the prophets are an ethical inspiration, not a how-to manual for solving a modern political conflict.

The foreword to the original edition of *This Is Israel* was written by Bartley Crum, a lawyer who had defended many Communists. He wrote that when it came to Israelis, his friend Izzy Stone "knows what is in their minds and in their hearts."[73] Stone progressively lost this knowledge. In a 1969 article, he once again conflated the Haganah, the Irgun, and the Stern Gang and defended Palestinian terrorism. "Their motives are as honorable as were ours," he wrote; the terrorists, he suggested, represent "the best of Arab youth."[74] But in the 1940s, Stone hadn't thought that the Irgun was honorable or that it represented the best; he had vehemently disowned its members as "quasi-fascist terrorists."[75] In fact, Stone's 1969 comments reveal a surprising obtuseness about Israeli "hearts and minds." This was the time of the PLO's bombings, hijackings, and murder of Israeli civilians, accompanied by the perpetrators' joyous boasts—precisely the "savage pleasure" that Stone had condemned in the Stalinists. It is hard to believe that any Israeli, including those on the left, would have read Stone's words without at best a sense of betrayal and, at worst, a stab of disgust.

Stone never turned against Israel. "Those who cannot forget the holocaust are filled with anguish, as I am, lest we live to see another in Israel," he wrote in 1975. And he insisted on the need for a "double vision" when it came to the Middle East: a recognition of Israel's vulnerability in the midst of a hostile Arab world *and* of its unjust Occupation. Yet he increasingly relied on platitudes. "The lesson of the holocaust is not to be learned in the war colleges but in our prophets," he wrote in 1975. "The lesson of the holocaust is that to treat other human beings as less than human can lead to the furnaces. The way to honor the dead is to see the Palestinian Arab as a displaced brother. . . . Isaiah says Zion shall be redeemed by justice."[76]

Who can argue against brotherhood and justice? As moral imperatives, they are unequalled. But the Shoah was a knotty, continent-wide event involving millions of victims and perpetrators; is there really only one, simple lesson that can be learned from it? And isn't it possible that different peoples—say, Germans and Jews—have *different* lessons to learn? Was it only a dearth of brotherhood that led to the Third Reich? What lessons should the Jews take from the catastrophe? As for the contemporary situation—the Israeli-Palestinian conflict—Stone was once again dodging uncomfortable realities in favor of fuzzy truisms. As one reader, an old friend of Stone's, responded, "What if the 'displaced brother' doesn't recognize Israel as a brother? What if the 'displaced brother' openly calls for the death of his brother?"[77]

Stone did criticize the Arabs' "sterile rejectionism," which had led to so many debacles for them, and he worried, as did Fred Halliday, that the Palestinians would miss the historic moment to attain a state. Yet unlike Halliday, Stone in his universalism became less, well, universal:

He concentrated almost exclusively on Israel's crimes. This was due in part, I think, to a genuine sense of outrage and shame over the ugliness of the Occupation, which began to overshadow all else. But the problem with shadows is that they can obstruct vision. Stone was increasingly unable to view Israel's opponents in a clear light, which means he was increasingly unable to assess the tangled politics of the Middle East. That is why, when the Camp David Accords were signed, he could confidently write that "the Arabs cannot reject the agreements, and the peace process."[78] Yet every Arab state and the PLO promptly did just that, and Egypt became the outcast, not the hero, of the Arab world.

One could view Stone's one-sided criticisms of Israel as evidence of his deep connection to the country. And they were. Unlike Koestler and Rodinson, Stone felt that, as a Jew, he was responsible for Israel. Yet his reluctance to reprove, or clearly see, Israel's foes stands in curious contrast to his writings on the American Left in this period.

As one of the country's earliest supporters of the civil rights movement and opponents of the Vietnam War, Stone was a hero to much of the New Left. The admiration was mutual. He was elated by the brave young organizers of SNCC: "I regard them with reverence," he wrote in 1963.[79] He embraced Students for a Democratic Society at a time when many Old Leftists eyed them with suspicion. Though he viewed the Black Muslims as racists, he admired Malcolm X, especially the later Malcolm, praising him as a "remarkable" and "brilliant" man. "In simple imagery, savagely uncompromising, he drove home the real truth about the Negro's position in America. It may not be pleasant but it must be faced."[80] Even in 1969, when factions of the antiwar and black liberation movements had embraced delusions of instant revolution, Stone defended them. "I feel that the New Left and the black revolutionists, like Luther, are doing God's work . . . challenging society to reform or crush them."[81]

Yet admiration didn't prevent Stone from calling out the extremist New Left's devolution into nuttiness. And unlike many white radicals, he was unafraid to criticize his black counterparts. He charged that the separatist program of Black Power "is not practical politics; it is psychological therapy," and he accused Stokely Carmichael of "New Left *narodnik* mysticism."[82] He refused to romanticize the riots in black ghettoes as political uprisings; indeed, he mocked the looting of liquor stores as "the debut of Marxism-Liquorism in revolutionary annals."[83] The Weathermen, for their part, were drowning in "a mishmash of ill-digested pseudo-Marxist rubbish" that "spurns every normal base of revolutionary support and ends up squarely in the clouds." He decried the group's "tendency to glorify violence for its own sake" and warned, "Political suicide is not revolution."[84] (Stone's niece, Kathy Boudin, was a member of the group.) In other words, in domestic politics Stone maintained the "double vision" that he let slide when it came to the Middle East. He could denounce the revolutionary suicide of Weather Underground leader Bernardine Dohrn, who represented, and threatened, almost no one. But he refrained from calling out the revolutionary suicide of Yasser Arafat, who was leading millions of followers to disaster.

There are, I believe, several reasons for this. First, Stone simply knew much more about American history and politics than he did about the Arab world. But the difficulties had deeper roots. Stone was the victim of a narcissistic fallacy: the belief that everyone shares your essential aims and worldview. It was inconceivable to him that Israelis and Arabs were not working in tandem toward what he called "that haven they have all so long desired."[85] It was inconceivable to him that many Palestinians, and their allies in the Arab world, did *not* want peace—though he accused Israeli leaders of precisely that. It was inconceivable to him that the Israeli Left and the Arab Left were not essentially aligned. It was inconceivable to him that a successful compromise could be viewed as a degrading defeat by extremists on each side, or that rational, realizable political aims were not on everyone's agenda. In short, it was inconceivable to him that the Arab-Israel conflict was not filled with people, or at least leaders, who were more or less like Izzy Stone.

Contrary to Stone's assumptions, the outlooks and aims of the Left in Israel and the Arab world were, and to a large extent still are, in direct opposition. As we noted with Halliday, to be on the Israeli Left largely meant (and means) advocacy of the two-state solution; to be on the Arab Left largely meant (and means) opposition to that project. A clear illustration of this paradox can be found in an absorbing 1974 book called *Arabs & Israelis: A Dialogue,* originally published in French and, then, in English and Hebrew.

The dialogue was conducted over several days between Saul Friedländer, an acclaimed Israeli historian of the Shoah, and the Egyptian Marxist known as Mahmoud Hussein. This was the pseudonym of Bahgat

Elnadi and Adel Rifaat, who wrote as one. (Born in Egypt, they had been imprisoned by Nasser and, at the time of the dialogue with Friedländer, were living as political exiles in Paris.) The interlocutor was the leftist French journalist Jean Lacouture, who considered himself sympathetic to both sides. Mahmoud Hussein was chosen, Lacouture explained, because he was virtually the only Arab intellectual who would agree to speak with an Israeli of any political bent. The dialogue makes for important, albeit disconsolate, reading. For it reveals that the two sides of the Arab-Israeli conflict resided, as Stone himself had written in 1967, "not just in separate rooms, . . . but in separate universes."[86] Indeed, this dialogue encapsulates the larger tragedy of the Israeli-Palestinian conflict. In the years when Israel had a sizable and influential liberal-Left eager to make peace, the Palestinians were dedicated to the destruction of Israel; by the time the PLO was forced to recognize Israel, much of the country had moved to the right.

Friedländer was a member of Israel's liberal-Left. His commitment to Zionism was based on a belief in the need for a Jewish state and, equally, on the promotion of "certain moral values . . . justice for the Jews first of all, yes, but justice for other people too." He explained that a solution to the conflict was necessary to end the plight of the Palestinians and for Israel's moral health. Far from advocating Israeli expansionism, he believed in the "self-limitation of Zionism," by which he meant Israel's need to share the land with others.[87] In practical terms, he advocated a two-state solution, based on a series of gradual withdrawals from the Occupied Territories in order to build mutual Israeli-Palestinian trust. Year later, this would become, in essence, the strategy of the Oslo Accords.

But Friedländer emphasized that the sine qua non of any negotiation—let alone agreement—was the Palestinians' permanent, unequivocal acceptance of Israeli sovereignty. A Palestinian state must be "the end of the road," not "the first stage in a process whose second stage would be the destruction" of Israel.[88] The self-limitation of Zionism did not mean the suicide of Zionism. Friedländer stressed that no Israeli, including those on the left, would accept a non-Zionist Israel and that Palestinian suffering, though real, did not prove that Zionism was bankrupt. (Jacobo Timerman made a parallel argument about Palestinian nationalism when he wrote that Palestinian "crimes and mistakes are not proof that their historic claim [to a state] is not right and just.")[89]

Friedländer viewed the conflict as a confrontation between two rightful claims. Any solution must "preserve both our sense of reality and our sense of justice."[90]

Mahmoud Hussein expressed a series of very different viewpoints. Arab nationalism was "exactly the opposite" of Zionism, he argued. The former is anti-colonialist, freedom-loving, and rejects complicity with foreign powers; the latter is inherently imperialist and domineering. The early pioneers of the Yishuv were racist; this was the basis of their dedication to Zionism. Hussein expressed the Arab world's "pride" and "joy" in the *fedayeens'* terrorist operations—and stated that, in any case, Israel bore the blame for them. Israel was responsible, too, for the political and economic underdevelopment of the Arab nations, for the Jewish state had not "allow[ed] the Arab masses to turn their efforts . . . to the problems of democracy and economic well-being."[91] How Israel, then a country of 3 million, had kept 100 million Arabs in thrall remained unexplained.

Hussein returned repeatedly to the twin concepts of dignity and humiliation. The former, he contended, had been stolen from Arabs by Israel and the West, the latter imposed upon them by the same forces. However, a two-state solution would only exacerbate this problem, for it would end the Arab boycott of Israel and allow the Jewish state to compete with its neighbors. Hussein was certain that Israel would win any such competition; its technological and economic superiority would constitute an "economic occupation of the entire region."[92] Thus another cycle of Arab dishonor—and revenge—would commence. Indeed, Hussein mocked the very idea of peaceful coexistence between Israel and a Palestinian state, which would be unequal in too many ways.

In any case, two states were not in the cards. Though the debate throughout *Arabs & Israelis* was consistently cordial, Hussein was, in a sense, Friedländer's—and Stone's—worst nightmare. (And could be Exhibit A for the Israeli Right.) The "ultimate objective" of the Arab resistance, Hussein explained more than once, was a single state; a Palestinian state next to Israel would constitute only a "transitional" phase to this final goal. For strategic purposes, the Palestinians might temporarily agree to such an entity. But this would do nothing to satisfy their "fundamental aspiration" and, therefore, could not end the conflict.[93] In contrast to Friedländer's Zionism, there was no "self-limitation" to Hussein's nationalism.

It was in describing the road to this one state that Hussein departed from what Friedländer had called the sense of reality. In Hussein's view, Israelis and Arabs were oppressed by the same force: American imperialism. He was confident that Arab and Israeli progressives would therefore build "parallel movements" that would unite them in a *"common fight against the common* enemy." Indeed, the transformation of Israel into a non-Zionist state—that is, its destruction as a home for the Jewish people—would take place "with the voluntary, conscious participation of the Israeli masses." Israelis would throw off the cruel Zionist yoke; Hussein anticipated "more and more deliberate revolutionary disruption contrived by the Arabs and the Israelis themselves." Like Friedländer, he explicated a baseline demand: Arab acceptance of Israel hinged on Israel's "total break . . . with the capitalist West."[94]

Mahmoud Hussein was not a lumpen, stateless refugee living in a camp but an educated cosmopolitan residing in Paris, where he was exposed to a free press, a plethora of political tendencies, and sophisticated political debates. It is difficult to understand how anyone who considered himself a materialist, as he did, could enmesh himself in a series of political prognostications so blatantly untethered to either facts or possibilities. At the end of this dialogue, Friedländer fell silent; Lacouture interpreted this as a hopeful sign.

But in an afterword, Friedländer suggested otherwise. Each man concluded with a statement that illustrated the chasm between their worldviews. Friedländer observed that "the basic Arab aspiration" was "the disappearance of Zionism"—something that, he had clarified, was not remotely acceptable—though he cautioned against "slamming the door" to negotiations if even a glimmer of hope remained. Hussein charged that "the main obstacle" to peace was Israel's "mistrust" of the Arab world and reliance on force, yet the aims he described affirmed the reason for those qualms and the necessity of that force.[95] It is hard to know how I. F. Stone would have answered all this, or how Isaiah would have helped him to do so.

Three decades after its original publication, *Underground to Palestine* was reissued, appended by two essays expressing Stone's updated thoughts on Israel. The second article, called "The Other Zionism," was a tribute, à la Arendt, to Jewish binationalists; Stone wrote in praise, too, of the

Palestinian binationalist Fauzi Darwish el-Husseini. But unlike Arendt, he acknowledged a major problem with the binationalist idea: the paucity of "other" Palestinians, be they binationalists or two-staters. El-Husseini, Stone noted, was assassinated by fellow Palestinians, as were the few who had joined him. "Never before (or since) has a Palestinian Arab leader dared openly to negotiate with the Jews and sign an agreement with them," Stone admitted.[96]

The more interesting essay concerned Stone himself; he titled it "Confessions of a Jewish Dissident." Once more, he pleaded for Palestinian statehood, and he rightly criticized the frosty reaction of Israeli officials to Anwar Sadat's path-breaking visit to Jerusalem the previous year. But most of the "Confessions" concerned Stone's place within the American Jewish community. While political debate within Israel remained vigorous, he lamented that he was "ostracized" in his own country for his contrarian views. And marginalized, too; dissidents, he wrote, were virtually excluded from the American press. Synagogues no longer asked him to speak. Jewish readers accused him of self-hatred, treachery, and worse.

Stone's biographers have documented how genuinely painful this rejection by his fellow Jews was—these were, after all, Izzy's people. It is undeniable that Stone's essays provoked hysterical and nasty reactions— qualities that he always gracefully eschewed. *Midstream* writer Joel Carmichael accused Stone of aligning with "ax-grinders, propagandists, hacks and cranks."[97] In the same journal, Marvin Maurer called him "the comrade of those who call openly for the massacre of all Jews in Israel," a proponent of "an end of the Jewish state," and—just for a bit of Red-baiting—a "long-standing support[er] of 'Marxist-Leninism.'"[98] In the *New Republic*, Marie Syrkin condemned Stone for propagating "PLO apologetics" (though Stone seemed, if anything, oblivious to key parts of the PLO's program).[99] Every American writer who writes about Israel is aware of the rancor that deviation from the Israeli hard line inspires; there is no question that this animosity rained down on Stone and that it hurt.

Yet it would be a mistake to see Stone simply as the victim of unfair attacks, for other reviewers and readers had more thoughtful responses to his work. Was it really true that Israel sought only to avoid negotiations? Was it Israelis who had glorified martyrdom? Was the bloodlust of the Middle East solely an Israeli creation?

A perceptive review of Stone's "Confessions" came from the Israeli politician and diplomat Abba Eban. He stressed his admiration for Stone and his agreement with Stone's two-state position. But he argued that Stone's advocacy of magnanimity as the key to peace had little to do with the realities of the conflict. In 1947 Eban, like Stone, had spoken with Azzam Bey. The Arab leader had explained, "You might get your state if you win the fight for it. But any idea that the Arabs will accept you without fighting to prevent your existence is ridiculous." More recently and more relevantly, Anwar Sadat had confided to Eban that Egypt became reconciled to Israel's existence " 'because of your strength, not because of your or our righteousness.' " Eban wondered why Stone's sense of universal brotherhood did not extend to "the athletes shot through the head in Munich while they were trussed up like animals . . . the schoolchildren on whom the Palestinian 'warriors' turned a machine gun . . . the busload of Israelis murdered in horrifying brutality." All these, he wrote, "cry out of their graves for I. F Stone's tribute of human solidarity, and get nothing from him but stony silence."[100]

Several aspects of Stone's "Confessions" were, in my view, not quite kosher. He asserted that Palestinian nationalism was based on the simple desire for "a state and a passport."[101] This was not exactly the PLO's position; at the time Stone was writing, the organization reiterated its blood-drenched strategy to eradicate Israel. (There was little talk of passports.) And while it is true, as Stone wrote, that the Marxist-Zionists of Hashomer Hatzair originally supported binationalism, it is equally true, as he failed to note, that they abandoned that position by late 1947. Binationalism was always a frail child whose life depended on trust. It died for a reason.

On a personal level, Stone's complaints were unappealingly querulous. Nor were they accurate. Far from being silenced, he was publishing regularly in high-profile journals; the two new essays in *Underground to Palestine* had appeared in the *New York Review of Books* and *Harper's,* two of the country most prestigious outlets for the journalism of ideas. Thick anthologies of Stone's writings, including those critical of Israel, were being regularly issued by a leading American publisher. Criticisms of Israel were not difficult to find. "I doubt whether Stone had a hard time to get his 'Reflections' into print, and I rejoice that this is so," Eban wrote. "He needs no Voltaires."[102] And Israelis were hardly ignorant of the criticisms lodged against them; as Eban noted, his own library contained Arendt, Rodinson, and Chomsky, among others.

"Confessions of a Jewish Dissident" displays a lack of political proportion that was uncharacteristic of Stone. It was written at a time when Eastern bloc and Soviet dissidents (whom Stone mentioned) and dissidents in the Arab world (whom he didn't) were censored, arrested, exiled, disappeared, tortured, and killed. Indeed, the term "dissident" was associated with such persecution. Stone's appropriation of the word for his obviously more benign circumstances manifests an unappealing self-pity. Being shunned by the B'nai B'rith is a far cry from languishing in a Soviet psychiatric ward or an Iraqi prison.

Stone wrote continuously, and always in heartfelt ways, about the Arab-Israeli conflict. But on some fundamental level, he refused to take either Israelis or Palestinians seriously in the post-1967 years. He ignored the role of Palestinian terror and the agonies of Jewish history on the Israeli psyche; my sense is that this, as much as his advocacy of Palestinian statehood, estranged him from many American Jews (and, no doubt, Israelis). This astigmatism was a political handicap. Stone understood, and empathized with, Palestinian humiliation and rage. But he failed to comprehend the Israelis' sense of vulnerability, grief, distrust, and fear, all of which flourish alongside their military power. (Prime Minister Levi Eshkol described this mind-set as "Samson the Nebbish.") As Arie Eliav, a leader of the Israeli Left, once observed, "You take three million Jews from a hundred-odd countries with their . . . ghetto mentality . . . and bring them in. You put a hundred million enemies, Arabs, around them. . . . We've got all the right to be . . . paranoid and schizophrenic . . . because of the 2,000 years [of exile], because of the traumas, and not less because of the horrible attitude of the PLO."[103] The problem was not that Stone refused to submit to this traumatized mentality—which would be, and has been, a terrible basis for policymaking. The problem was that he could not recognize it as a political factor.

Stone was rightly critical of Israeli militarism and ultra-nationalism, but he failed to engage, or even notice, the irredentist strain of the Palestinian movement and the larger Arab world. Those factions of the Palestinian movement—and they were hardly insignificant—whose political aspirations had little in common with a two-state compromise were largely written out of Stone's account. It is as if everything Mahmoud Hussein said, and everything he represented, did not, *could not*, exist. Instead, Stone posited a more manageable world of Israeli aggression and

Palestinian victimhood—not as part of the story (which it is) but as the whole story (which it isn't). Unlike Halliday's views of the conflict, which deepened as time progressed, Stone's outlook began to resemble a stripped-down morality tale. This was not because Stone was anti-Israel, whatever that means. On the contrary, I believe he never stopped loving Israel, just as he claimed. It is far more likely that he closed his eyes to unpalatable realities because he so desperately hoped that a solution could be found and, just as desperately, sought to avoid hopelessness and despair. He was right about the unequivocal need to end the Occupation, but wrong to assume that this would necessarily lead to peace. He was right about the need for two states, but wrong to think that its only opponent was the Israeli Right.

I. F. Stone remains a beacon for me. He has so much to teach: about how to be a journalist, an American, a Jew, a defender of freedom, a person of courage. He never stopped reminding us, especially in his writings on Israel and Palestine, that the Other is human and, therefore, redolent of dignity and deserving of respect. This is dangerously easy to forget. But what Izzy Stone cannot do is guide us to a holistic solution to the Arab-Israeli conflict, for he shielded himself from too many of its toughest and most obstinate quandaries.

CHAPTER EIGHT

Noam Chomsky

THE RESPONSIBILITY OF INTELLECTUALS

IN 2016, AN OFTEN HILARIOUS MOVIE CALLED *Captain Fantastic* portrayed a left-wing, off-the-grid family that eschews the celebration of traditional American holidays; instead, it celebrates Noam Chomsky's birthday each year, during which it sings heartfelt odes to "Uncle Noam." The film, though fictional, accurately captures the strange, indeed unique place that Chomsky occupies in the American political landscape. In one sense, Chomsky is an intellectual outcast. You will not find him writing for journals such as the *New York Review of Books,* and many intellectuals, including on the left, regard him as a one-note dogmatist. At the same time, Chomsky is an extraordinarily prolific writer whose works are widely read—sometimes becoming best sellers—and who is idolized as a sage, especially by young people. The Jewish magazine *Tablet* calls him "the world's most quoted living thinker," which is hard to verify but might be true; publications as disparate as *Foreign Policy* and the *Journal of Palestine Studies* have hailed him as the world's most significant public intellectual. The *New Statesman* named him one of the top fifty "heroes of our time." (He came in at number seven.) The *Nation* magazine dubbed him "America's Socrates." Internationally, Uncle Noam is certainly the best-known, and probably best-loved, representative of the American Left.

The Israeli-Palestinian conflict is one of Chomsky's chief interests. Since the late 1960s he has written hundreds of thousands—perhaps millions—of words on the subject and often spoken on it; he describes this output as "a series of books, huge number of articles, constant talks all the time, thousands of them, interviews."[1] He often contradicts himself, which makes writing about him difficult; you can find a quote from Chomsky to support a variety of positions. But he has put forth a few major, consistently articulated arguments over a period of decades, which I aim to assess in this chapter. Here, I will try to discern not only what he thinks but, equally important, *how* he thinks.

Perhaps because of his work in linguistics, Chomsky is regarded as an expert on virtually any topic he addresses. There is an irony in this, since his best-known political essay, "The Responsibility of Intellectuals," was an attack on the very concept of the expert. Nonetheless, his knowledge of the Arab-Israeli conflict is viewed as deep and wide (except by Israelis, who pay him no heed, and in the Arab world, where he is little known). Edward Said praised Chomsky's profound familiarity with the "history, social reality and political philosophy" of Israel and his "breathtaking" command of facts.[2] The Dutch-Palestinian scholar Mouin Rabbani has lauded his "encyclopedic knowledge."[3] The most surprising—no, shocking—thing one learns when immersing oneself in Chomsky's Middle East writings is how inaccurate these descriptions are. In fact, many leading Left historians and journalists who concentrate on the conflict and are knowledgeable about it give virtually no credence to Chomsky's work. The other surprise is the degree to which Chomsky, who prides hard-headedness, is guided by wishful thinking. This is due, I believe, to concern rather than loathing for Israel—albeit in a highly convoluted way. Edward Said may have been right when he observed, "Chomsky hates Israel . . . in such tones of harsh judgement that only a Jew could have done his hating so effectively."[4]

Chomsky would dispute this; he insists that, when it comes to Israel, "emotional connections" are "kind of irrelevant. . . . When we get down to the moral issue, it's independent of one's personal background."[5] Nonetheless, I believe that a brief biographical sketch may illuminate, and perhaps complicate our understanding of, his views.

Avram Noam Chomsky was born in Philadelphia in 1928, which means that, like many other figures in this book, he was formed by the Depression, the rise of fascism, and World War II. His parents, immigrants from Russia and Lithuania, were cultural Zionists who were deeply immersed in the revival of the Hebrew language. Chomsky's father, William, was a prominent Hebrew grammarian. Noam recalls spending Friday nights reading Ahad Ha'am with him. His mother, Elsie, was a leading figure in Hadassah, the Zionist women's organization.

Like Maxime Rodinson, Isaac Deutscher, and Albert Memmi, Chomsky was a brilliant child. When he was ten, he wrote an essay for the school paper lamenting the fall of Barcelona to Franco's fascists; soon after, he was reading proofs of his father's doctoral thesis. At the age of sixteen, he entered the University of Pennsylvania (I. F. Stone's sort-of alma mater), where he studied linguistics and philosophy. Hebrew remained central to his intellectual development; his master's thesis was titled "The Morphophonemics of Modern Hebrew." He earned a doctorate while still in his late twenties and became a full professor at the Massachusetts Institute of Technology at the almost unheard-of age of thirty-two. He has said that "one of the reasons why MIT became a great university" is that Harvard wouldn't hire Jews.[6]

In the late 1950s, Chomsky attacked the prevalent school of behaviorism and then developed the novel, indeed heretical idea that the learning of language is based on innate biological structures that exist in every human brain. Though initially scorned, Chomsky's theories are now dominant (if not uncontested) in his field. There is no doubt that he revolutionized the worlds of linguistics and the science of mind; scholars of these disciplines live in the post-Chomskyian world as surely as biologists live in Darwin's and physicists in Einstein's.

As a teen, Chomsky identified with Hashomer Hatzair, a socialist-Zionist group, though he never joined because "they were split between Stalinist and Trotskyite, and I was anti-Leninist." He regarded the partition of 1947 and the establishment of the State of Israel the following year as "a tragedy" and claims this was true of "most of the people I was closely connected with."[7] (That is unlikely; by late 1947, Hashomer Hatzair, like virtually all Left Zionist groups, had abandoned binationalism.) In 1953, Chomsky and his wife, Carol Schatz, went to live in Hazore'a, a Hashomer Hatzair kibbutz, which he remembers as "incredible in spirit."[8] The Chomskys planned to return to Israel for good after Noam earned his PhD but decided otherwise, though for professional rather than political reasons. It is interesting to contemplate how Chomsky's life—and the political world—would be different had Chomsky become an Israeli.

Chomsky came of age politically with the Vietnam War. Like I. F. Stone, he began opposing the U.S. intervention in the early sixties; this was a courageous, unpopular stance at the time. His aforementioned 1967 essay, "The Responsibility of Intellectuals," with its clarion call for the demands of the individual's conscience against the state, was widely circulated and is now regarded as a classic of polemical writing. Since then, Chomsky has never strayed from a profoundly internationalist perspective; he has championed often-ignored liberation struggles and forgotten peoples, sometimes long before others even noticed them. He has also never strayed from the view that the United States' power is the world's most villainous force. The world, however, did not remain frozen in 1967 (neither have the Vietnamese), which means that Chomsky's worldview has subsequently resulted in some extremely odd positions, such as downplaying the carnage of the Khmer Rouge and Slobodan Milosevic's ethnic cleansers. In his unwavering focus on imperialism as original sin, Chomsky is, in a sense, the anti-Fred Halliday—or, perhaps, a Fred Halliday who never evolved.

The simplicity of Chomsky's worldview is the source of its power and popularity: America as the epicenter of evil plays well to leftists in both the West and the Third World. Some of this is simply Pavlovian anti-Americanism, but some is grounded in genuine repugnance towards the U.S.'s history of antidemocratic coups, invasions, and support for bloody dictatorships. Our list of crimes is long and shameful: the overthrow of Mossadegh in Iran, Árbenz in Guatemala, and Allende in Chile; the destruction of Vietnam; support for the anti-Communist massacres in Indonesia, the death squads in El Salvador, the Contras in Nicaragua. . . . Still, there is a logical lapse in Chomsky's thinking, which is especially surprising for a logician. That the U.S. has done bad things does not mean that all bad things are done by the U.S.; that the U.S. has committed crimes does not mean that everything the U.S. does is criminal.

Chomsky's greatest split with other segments of the Left occurred over the Bosnian War. He strongly opposed NATO attacks on Milosevic's forces and has praised, and defended, the work of journalist Diana Johnstone, who has spent a lot of energy arguing that because the Srebrenica victims were "men and boys of military age, this cannot be genocide."[9] In a 2015 interview with *Jacobin* magazine, Chomsky described Srebrenica as "a Serb response" to "murderous Bosnian militias." (Chomsky is certain, nonetheless, that Slobo was "horrified" by the slaughter.)[10] And while Said has praised Chomsky as a man of "noble ideals repeatedly stirred on behalf of human suffering and injustice," the Balkan conflicts, like the Cambodian genocide, showed that Chomsky's concern for human suffering and injustice can be decidedly selective. Asked by a *Guardian* reporter about Srebrenica's victims, Chomsky scornfully lashed out: "That's such a western European position. . . . Go to Laos, go to Haiti, go to El Salvador. You'll see people who are really suffering brutally."[11]

Chomsky's critique of neoliberal capitalism and the injuries it causes is potent. But his hatred of the "western position," and especially of the U.S., has generated indiscriminate thrashings. It is one thing to criticize the flaws of the Nuremberg Trials, another to denounce them as "a farce." It is one thing to oppose the U.S.'s post-9/11 invasion of Afghanistan, another to doubt Osama bin Laden's proclamation of responsibility for the attacks "because he may be boasting."[12] It is one thing to critique the U.S. media, another to claim that "the phrase 'U.S. invasion of Iraq' . . . cannot be mentioned" by American journalists, a ludicrous assertion that even the most cursory Google search will disprove.[13] Chomsky has a tendency to glide from important insights to wrong-but-understandable analyses to inexplicable foolishness to outright fabrications.

It is not surprising, then, that Chomsky functions as a litmus test for leftists. Where you stand on Uncle Noam says a lot about your worldview. The Israeli-Palestinian conflict is the quintessential example of this.

As with Marx, there is an early Chomsky and a late Chomsky, particularly when it comes to Israel and Palestine. Chomsky began publicly addressing the conflict in 1969 with a speech to the Arab Club at MIT; it was reprinted in *Liberation,* a leading journal of the New Left. His views remained fairly consistent until 1975. In this period, he expressed his oft-stated, and still-held, position that a majority-Jewish state is by definition undemocratic, despite the fact that many of the left-wing Israeli journalists on whose work he depends hold the opposite view. "The belief that a Jewish state with non-Jewish citizens can be a democracy guaranteeing equal rights to all is not tenable," he wrote. Israel, he has argued, is "a state based *on the principle* of discrimination."[14] But he also contended, in contrast to the Left's laser-like animus toward Zionism, that "Israel is a state like any other; Zionism is a national movement like any other." He endorsed the Zionist belief that "a normal human existence" demands a national home.[15] Like Albert Memmi, he pointed out that " 'internationalism' does not imply opposition in principle to national ties"; like Hannah Arendt, he praised "the extraordinary creativity and courage of those who made the desert bloom."[16]

And he had few illusions—though this would change—about the Palestinian movement. The Palestine Liberation Organization, he noted in 1974–75, "remains opposed to any plan that involves recognition of Israel, [or] conciliation with it" and seeks to " 'liquidate' " every aspect of Israeli society. Chomsky described this program as "suicidal," "hopelessly irrational," indeed "insane."[17] It was also morally heinous, for it would involve, he wrote in 1970, "the destruction by force of a unified society, its people, and its institutions—a consequence intolerable to civilized opinion on the left or elsewhere."[18] He warned the Left against mistaking the Israeli-Palestinian conflict for the anti-colonial struggles in Algeria or Vietnam. And he criticized the PLO's plan for a "secular democratic state" in Mandatory Palestine—the one-state solution—noting, as had Fred Halliday, that such a configuration would be neither secular nor democratic. Nor would it be binational. "What they have in mind," Chomsky bluntly explained, "is an Arab state." In 1974, he advised fellow leftists not to conflate their political vision with that of the PLO: "The Palestinian movement is sometimes described in the West as a movement of revolutionary socialists, but this is far from an accurate characterization."[19]

At the same time, Chomsky criticized the Israeli strategy of excluding the PLO from negotiations as cynical and arrogant. He warned that the Occupation and Palestinian terror might combine to destroy Israeli democracy—which, if it came to pass, would be the most Pyrrhic of victories for the Palestinians. Israeli repression and a continuing Occupation, he predicted, would only strengthen Palestinian irredentism and "might . . . destroy whatever was of lasting human value in the Zionist ideal."[20] Chomsky stressed that Israel's self-appointed friends in the American Jewish community—those who supported settlements and rejected a Palestinian state—were in fact Israel's enemies. All these warnings were, unfortunately, prescient; in my view they have been Chomsky's main contributions to the debate. It is more than too bad that they were not heeded.

Here was the quandary, as Chomsky described it in the late 1960s
and early 1970s: Israel wanted peace and national survival, but it refused
to acknowledge the just national aspirations of the Palestinians; yet the
Occupation of the Palestinian territories would not end until Israel's
national legitimacy was accepted, its security guaranteed, and the irredentism of the PLO abandoned. He thus accurately articulated the major
dilemma of the conflict, which has of course radically worsened in the
succeeding decades.

How to untie the Gordian knot of the Israeli-Palestinian conflict,
which has demoralized so many—including, I believe, Chomsky?
Beginning in the early 1980s, Chomsky devised a new solution—or,
rather, a new analysis. Though he has claimed that his views on Israel and
Palestine have remained largely constant (a dubious virtue, in any case),
in fact he embarked on a radically new direction, or at least a substantially
new argument. From that point, and continuing to this day, Chomsky has
claimed that in the mid-1970s, the PLO—an umbrella of various, often
murderously warring groups representing disparate constituencies—had
in effect performed an abrupt about-face. So too had the entire Arab
world, which Chomsky depicted as a unified bloc despite the viciousness,
then as now, of its inter-state conflicts. Chomsky argued that, starting
precisely in January 1976—the date is important, as we'll see—the PLO
and the Arab nations accepted Israel and sought a peaceful, political, two-
state solution. He specifically included the Iraqi, Syrian, and Libyan dictatorships in this pacific coalition. He has adhered to this analysis ever
since and has more recently extended it to include Hamas and Iran.

Who in the world would rebuff this admirable axis of peace? According
to Chomsky, it has been intransigently opposed by *all* American presi-
dents, *all* Israeli leaders, and *all* Israeli political tendencies, including the
Labor Party, socialist-Zionist groups, and organizations like Peace Now. He
has repeatedly vilified the Israeli Left, including peace activists such as
Amos Oz, whom he particularly detests, as "rejectionists." Indeed, in
Fateful Triangle, his longest and most sustained work on Israel and
Palestine, Chomsky argues that the very "goal" of Zionism, from its earliest
days, has been that of "avoiding any political settlement"—an odd description of the movement that accepted partition as early as 1937.[21] Conversely,
he claims that the Arab states have presented a virtual united front for
peace. For instance, in *Fateful Triangle,* he approvingly cites Saddam

Hussein's peaceful intentions toward Israel and chastises the Jewish state for refusing to respond positively to him. This was the same Saddam who funded the most murderous Palestinian terrorists, such as Abu Nidal, and who would attack Tel Aviv with Scud missiles. And of course there *have* been signed accords—between Egypt and Israel, Jordan and Israel, and the PLO and Israel. But Chomsky dismisses them all as "rejectionist throughout"; he also disparages the idea of land-for-peace as a fraud.[22]

In constructing a world where Arab dictators and PLO militants spent decades seeking peace and Amos Oz opposed it, Chomsky has, unsurprisingly, been forced to ignore the actual history of the conflict. Though a leftist, Chomsky is anything but a materialist. For instance, he makes no mention of the rise, and the power, of the Palestinian Rejectionist Front, whose name was self-explanatory; of the PLO's "nonnegotiable" rejection of the 1981 Saudi proposal because it implied the recognition of Israel; of the so-called phased strategy, through which the establishment of a Palestinian state on the West Bank and Gaza was publicly articulated as the first step toward the elimination of Israel—in essence, a Trojan horse, as Mahmoud Hussein had so forthrightly explained to Saul Friedländer. Chomsky has also virtually ignored the Palestinian movement's many decades of terrorism, which have led even left-wing Israelis to often despair of a compromise. Also unheeded was the PLO's credibility problem—what some left-wing writers called the flagrant gap between its sometimes peaceful pronouncements and its subsequent violent actions.[23]

No, the foundation of Chomsky's analysis is not the actual, on-the-ground, highly complex history of this conflict and this region. Rather, Chomsky rests his argument almost completely—dare I say religiously?—on a little-known, and never passed, United Nations resolution of January 23, 1976.

It would be impossible to overemphasize Chomsky's dependence on this document; for over thirty years, he has cited it dozens of times in his writings. It is central to *Fateful Triangle* and recurs even in recent books, such as 2015's *On Palestine*. For Chomsky, 1976 is the year when Everything Changed—absolutely, definitively, incontrovertibly—and when, in his view, the moral calculus of the conflict was permanently realigned. In *Fateful Triangle* he argues, "With all its evasiveness, unclarities [*sic*], incompetence, and deceit, the PLO has *for years* been a more *unambiguous* advocate of a non-rejectionist peace settlement than *any* organized group in Israel."[24] In October 2014, he opened a speech to a packed audience at the United Nations by lauding the 1976 resolution.

How does Chomsky explain the fact that this history has been so misunderstood, indeed so hidden? Why is this truth "virtually unknown in the United States"?[25] (And, one might add, elsewhere.) After all, in the 1970s and eighties the PLO was not an unknown or little-noticed independence movement; the Palestinians were not the East Timorese or Kurds. On the contrary, the PLO was awash in cash, prestige, and attention. It was recognized by more countries than recognized the State of Israel. Its pronouncements and actions regularly landed on the front pages of all the major Western and Israeli newspapers, as well as in the censored presses of the Soviet bloc and the Arab countries. The PLO had consulates, sometimes embassies, in cities throughout the world; media relations centers; its own news service; and intellectually sophisticated spokesmen who were eagerly quoted. Yasser Arafat freely expounded on his ideas in long interviews to everyone from Oriana Fallaci to *Playboy* magazine. In 1983, Thomas Friedman, then the Middle East correspondent for the *New York Times*, described a PLO press conference in Amman that was so crushed with reporters that they lined four flights of stairs trying to gain entry.

For Chomsky, the disappearance of the supposedly true history of the Israeli-Palestinian conflict is neither a problem nor a mystery. It is an asset. For Chomsky, as for all conspiracy theorists, *the less well known something is, the more likely it is to be true.* Thus he writes darkly of how the manufacturers of consent have "interr[ed] the corpse" of the conflict's history; the 1976 resolution, he told the UN, has been "vetoed from history."[26] But the odd thing is that leftist journalists and historians, including those who are extremely critical of Israel, strong supporters of the Palestinian cause, and noted scholars of the region have apparently participated in this enormous cover-up.

For instance, Rashid Khalidi, the Edward Said Professor of Modern Arab Studies at Columbia University, takes no notice of the 1976 resolution in his book *The Iron Cage*, which is subtitled "The Story of the Palestinian Struggle for Statehood." Indeed, Khalidi writes that not until 1988 did the PLO unambiguously, which is to say, meaningfully, accept Israel and two states—though even then, he notes, the Palestinian movement continued its love affair with violence. (Khalidi, an unwavering advocate of Palestinian rights and opponent of the Occupation, raises a question that Chomsky doesn't: "If the Palestinians wanted to make peace with Israel within its 1967 frontiers, why were militant Palestinian groups killing Israeli civilians within these borders?")[27] Ditto Maxime Rodinson, the self-described "anti-Zionist." In sharp contrast to Chomsky's praise for the PLO's supposedly peaceful intentions, Rodinson sadly wondered why the Palestinian organizations lacked what he called the "political courage" to adopt a realistic, non-annihilationist line.[28] French journalist Alain Gresh, a specialist on the PLO and former editor in chief of the left-wing *Le Monde Diplomatique,* pleaded for this same courage in 1983. In his book *The PLO: The Struggle Within,* Gresh beseeches the organization to abandon its attempts to destroy Israel and, instead, align itself with the Israeli peace forces—the very forces at which Chomsky sneers. Eqbal Ahmad, the leftist Pakistani activist and scholar, made the same plea. He recalled meeting with PLO leaders after they were kicked out of Beirut in 1982; Edward Said attended too. Ahmad begged them to drop their irredentist program, recognize Israel, and "develop a viable, acceptable peace proposal that . . . the world, as well as decent Israeli opinion, could not afford to reject." All for naught: "When we came out of the meeting, Edward looked literally paper white. He was angry and disappointed. He shook his head," Ahmad recalled. "That's the last time I saw Arafat."[29]

Yezid Sayigh, the Middle East scholar who has sometimes represented the Palestinians in negotiations with Israel, never bothers to mention the 1976 resolution, or the supposed sea change it heralded, in his painstakingly detailed, 900-page study of the Palestinian national movement titled *Armed Struggle and the Search for State,* which covers the years 1949 to 1993. On the contrary, Sayigh charts the rise of the Steadfastness and Confrontation Front, a group consisting of four Arab countries and the PLO, which rejected any recognition, ever, of Israel. In fact, in direct contradiction to Chomsky's analysis, in 1977 the Palestine National Council reaffirmed its commitment to liberate all of Mandatory Palestine through armed struggle and, upon victory, to expel all Jews who did not "set aside their racist Zionist affiliation."[30] (This was the precise program that Chomsky had previously labeled "insane"; now he simply ignored it.) Matti Steinberg, Israel's foremost authority on the Palestinian movement, who bases much of his analysis on Arabic documents, concurs with Sayigh, Khalidi, and the others. "The principle of armed escalation within Palestine was reiterated in *all* of the PNC's decisions leading up to the 19th Convention (November 1988), which *for the first time* accepted the partition of Palestine into two states," Steinberg writes.[31]

There is no indication that any of this history has fazed, or even influenced, Chomsky or that he has read the works of these experts. (And experts do, in fact, have their uses.) Indeed, when one looks at Chomsky's voluminous endnotes, a disturbing if not ominous pattern emerges: One of the sources that Noam Chomsky relies upon most is . . . Noam Chomsky. That is why reading large chunks of his work assumes a particularly frustrating, indeed autistic, aspect. The reader scurries from one Chomsky citation to another, trapped in a self-referential world that I began to think of as Chomskyland.

Nonetheless, I became fascinated by the 1976 resolution, upon which Chomsky's analysis hinges, and so I went back to the source. ("It takes a little work to discover the essential facts," Chomsky once wrote.)[32] What I found told me a lot about his methodology.

In book after book, Chomsky characterizes this resolution as "quite clearly" establishing the PLO's acceptance of Israel's sovereignty and claims that, from 1976 on, "The Arab states and the PLO continued to press for a two-state solution."[33] And he habitually describes the resolution as having been "proposed by the PLO and the Arab states" or, sometimes, as "introduced by the Arab 'confrontation states' (Egypt, Jordan, and Syria)."[34] He affirmed these claims in his 2014 United Nations speech.

None of this is true. First, the resolution was proposed by Benin, Guyana, Pakistan, Panama, Romania, and Tanzania. Not one is an Arab country, much less a "confrontation state," and only one of the six had voted against the Zionism-is-racism resolution two months earlier. Second, while the resolution explicitly affirms the "inalienable" national rights of the Palestinian people, it mentions Israel to deplore it. Third and most important, the resolution does not propose a two-state solution. Though it speaks vaguely of peace and secure borders for all, it demands the right of return of the Palestinian refugees. Virtually all Israelis, including those on the left, regard this as the *antithesis* of the two-state solution—something of which Chomsky was, and is, acutely aware. For decades, Chomsky has promiscuously cited this resolution, yet never once has he accurately delineated its sponsors or provisions.

But the most revealing thing to note, though Chomsky has never done so, is the UN debate that surrounded the resolution. The Arab representatives who spoke hardly support Chomsky's argument that they, much less the entire Arab world, endorsed peace. The Libyan representative praised the Zionism-is-racism resolution—which, he claimed, reflected "international public opinion"—and condemned what he called "the Zionist aggressive entity." (The dreaded "I" word—that is, Israel—could not be uttered.) His major point, which was seconded by Syria, was that UN Resolution 242—the so-called land-for-peace resolution—had been "bypassed" by the racism resolution and was now "irrelevant."[35] This means that the position of these two states was the precise *opposite* of what Chomsky has claimed. In addition, the Syrian representative castigated the "Zionist entity" as an "expansionist aggressor" and *mocked* the idea of "secure and recognized boundaries."[36] Neither man hinted at recognizing Israel or supporting two states.

The most important speaker in this debate was Farouk Khaddoumi, the PLO's representative and a member of its Central Committee. He was the last speaker and, for understandable reasons, the most passionate. Khaddoumi used his time (I am not quoting out of context) to assail the "onslaught" of "racist Zionism" and "Zionist colonialism and aggression," which is "responsible for the [region's] continuing wars, bloodshed, misery and turmoil." He described Israel as "a State that is predicated on an immoral basis" and therefore "cannot possibly be susceptible to moral considerations." He ended by assuring his fellow diplomats that, in fighting "the Zionist-imperialist alliance," the Palestinians' "armed struggle victory is inevitable."[37] Needless to say, Khaddoumi, too, made zero references to two states.

Through what powers of alchemy does Chomsky transform this resolution, and these speeches, into an olive branch—one he has repeatedly excoriated the stiff-necked Israelis for rejecting? How did the proudly defiant, anti-Zionist "Axis of Resistance" suddenly renounce its existential purpose and melt into its meek opposite? Chomsky's profound misrepresentations of this resolution and the political positions it articulated—misrepresentations that he repeats time and again, as if that would somehow make them true—are staggering. Even worse, he has constructed an entire edifice, moral and political, on these fallacies.

But the problems with Chomsky's analysis are even deeper. It is not only that what Chomsky says happened in 1976 did not happen. More important, it *could not* happen.

Nineteen seventy-six was the year in which Lebanon's civil war began to spin out of control. Israel was bombing PLO training camps in retaliation for cross-border raids by Palestinian guerrillas. The PLO, which was bitterly split between pro- and anti-Syrian factions, was engaged in daily street battles with various Lebanese militias. Into this volatile brew came Iraq, Egypt, and Syria, which, competing for prominence, backed rival factions in a series of shifting alliances. All this would culminate, later in the year, in Syria's invasion of Lebanon and its military assault *on* the PLO. The idea that in this particular year, in the midst of this particular war, all these hostile factions would suddenly unite and reverse their long-standing animus to Israel, their one common enemy—the idea is, frankly, inconceivable. I repeat: It did not happen and it could not happen—something Chomsky would have known had he widened his blinkered field of vision.

To reject Chomsky's manufactured history does not mean defending the aggressive ultra-nationalism that swept through Israel after 1967. It does not mean defending Israel's hubristic slighting of its Arab neighbors. It does not mean defending Israeli intransigence, the settlement enterprise, or the Occupation. And it does not mean rejecting Palestinian statehood. As Amos Oz explained in 1991: "Unlike Chomsky, I have always believed that the P.L.O. has been one of the most extremist, fanatic and uncompromising movements of our times. Not in terms of what they have done to us, the Israelis, but in terms of what they have done and are still doing to their own people. Nonetheless, self-determination is not granted to people as a reward for good behavior."[38] But it does mean demanding a narrative of the conflict that is truthful and holistic. That is the responsibility of intellectuals.

There is yet a third reason why Chomsky's claims about the PLO were not just wrong but impossible, one which offers further insight into the problems with his overall approach. Despite his voluminous writings on the Israeli-Palestinian conflict, he seems to have little interest in the Palestinians themselves or the movement they built. They are objects, not subjects. Thus he writes of the "helpless Palestinians"; "their story is one of unremitting tragedy."[39] Palestinian (and Hezbollah) terror, infrequently mentioned, is always framed as a response to noxious Israeli provocations, never as a conscious strategy. Not surprisingly, then, Chomsky has little understanding of the role of violence in the Palestinian movement.

Unlike liberation movements such as that of the Vietnamese Communists or the African National Congress—or, for that matter, the Zionists—the PLO's political program was minimal. What kind of society did it want to create? Would it be multi-party or uni-party? Socialist or capitalist? What did it mean by "democratic" and "secular"? In part because the PLO was an amalgam of competing interests, demographic groups, and political philosophies, and in part because Yasser Arafat (and his comrades) were not Ho Chi Minh, Nelson Mandela, or David Ben-Gurion (and their comrades), these questions were never answered. Nor were institutions, or even proto-institutions, created to address them. Violence—the practice of it, the idealization of it, the moralizing of it, the eroticization of it—filled the space left by this political lacuna. Thus Rashid Khalidi writes of "the inability of the PLO leadership to understand the limits of violence. . . . What was necessary was the reeducation of Palestinians away from armed struggle." He continues, "This incapacity was most clearly revealed during the second intifada starting at the end of September 2000, when the militarization of what started as a popular struggle . . . ultimately led to disaster for the Palestinians."[40]

This political void—not some innate bloodlust—is why, even after it officially renounced terrorism in 1988, the PLO continued to practice it; this is why Palestinians have been trapped for decades in the hell of "martyrdom," in both its religious and secular versions, which is surely the greatest barrier to Palestinian modernity. Yezid Sayigh explained, "The guerrilla groups composing the PLO consistently described the armed struggle as the principal, even exclusive, means of liberating Palestine throughout their evolution. . . . The problem for the PLO was that it lacked other instruments of policy, other means of constructing its state-in-the-making. . . . The principal guerrilla groups had not undertaken a serious attempt to transform their society at any point." From the movement's inception, Sayigh observes, violence was "the necessary mobilizing theme" and "defining dynamic" of national consciousness.[41] This would have crucial repercussions for the post-Oslo era. As Oxford academics Hussein Agha and Ahmad Samih Khalidi, who have represented the Palestinians in negotiations, wrote in 2017, "Without 'armed struggle,' the national movement had no clear ideology, no specific discourse, no distinctive experience or character."[42]

It is hard to square this with Chomsky's assertions that Palestinian terrorism is simply a reluctant reaction to Israeli power and that the "Palestinian resistance . . . has remained remarkably disciplined." It is even harder to accept his view that in this sense the PLO was "quite different from the struggle of the Jews of Palestine for a Jewish state," which he identifies with "murder . . . assassination . . . and many atrocities."43 Arafat and some of his associates did, at times, attempt to renounce terrorism (especially when speaking to the West). But not consistently and not for long. Such a move threatened to split the PLO, weaken its popularity in the refugee camps, strengthen Hamas, endanger support from some Arab states—and could easily have led to Arafat's assassination. This doesn't mean that the Palestinians had no options; on the contrary, they had several. But each was risky and none was painless. The idea that a UN proposal, or any other document, could solve these structural contradictions, which have plagued the movement since its birth, is benighted.

Basic knowledge, research, fact-finding, an informed and capacious perspective: These, too, are the responsibility of intellectuals. So is a respect for the constraints of history, which is to say for what is possible at any given moment. Chomsky simply lacks the humility this demands, which has freed him to propound theories that are startlingly unmoored from actuality. He does not understand that political reality, which is to say human beings, cannot be twisted into whatever shape we desire. He does not grasp the fact that history and its "helpless victims" have no obligation to support our ideological precepts.

In this, Chomsky parts company with Marxist historians, or at least the best of them. Eric Hobsbawm once warned that the purpose of history is not "to discover or devise legitimations for our hopes— or fears—for human destiny."44 Eugene Genovese went further. Addressing the demands for so-called relevant history by militants of the New Left and Black Power movements, he warned, "Ideologically motivated history is bad history and ultimately reactionary politics." Genovese insisted that political commitment "does not free us from the responsibility to struggle for maximum objectivity. . . . Only ruling classes . . . have anything to gain from the ideological approach to history."45 These historians understood that, as Hobsbawm wrote, political partisanship influences the questions a scholar asks but can never determine the answers he finds. Chomsky has turned Hobsbawm and Genovese upside down.

Chomsky views the Palestinians as unconstrained in their search for peace. They are free, at virtually any moment—say, 1976—to beat their Kalashnikovs into plowshares. His view of the Zionist movement is the diametric opposite: It is overdetermined at every moment. Contingency, choice, chance, error, courage, folly, tragedy: All are in scant supply. In his telling, Zionism is not a fluid, extraordinarily variegated movement—encompassing fascists and democrats, racists and humanists, capitalists and socialists, mystics and secularists—that, often in crisis and struggling to survive, has undergone a series of tumultuous transformations since its founding. Chomsky's Zionism is something else: a consistent, static *thing*, with aggression and expansion imprinted in its DNA. Its story is stringently preordained.

Take, for instance, the 1982 Lebanon War, in which Israel tried to push the PLO out of Lebanon and into Jordan in the triple hope of crushing the organization, establishing an Israeli-friendly regime in Beirut, and precipitating the fall of the Jordanian Hashemites. (The Israeli historian Zeev Sternhell described these aims as "so delusional that nobody dared state them openly.")[46] As the country's first nondefensive war since the Suez attack of 1956, the war in Lebanon is widely viewed by Israelis as a watershed—and a political and moral debacle. For Chomsky, though, it was simply more of the same. "The thinking behind Israel's terrorist operations in Lebanon is no secret. It was outlined . . . long before, by David Ben-Gurion," he claims in *Fateful Triangle*.[47] (He cites himself as the source for this.) The very concept of change is anathema: "It is of no service now to pretend that [Menachem] Begin and [Ariel] Sharon have introduced something radically new into Israeli social or political culture or military practice in West Beirut"; doing so is a ploy "to cover up the *real* history of Israel." In fact, Chomsky makes the startling claim that the seeds of the 1982 invasion were planted *in 1932;* five decades later, Israel was simply "realizing plans that have early antecedents in Zionist thinking. It had long been hoped that Israel's boundaries would ultimately extend to the Litani River in southern Lebanon, one part of Ben-Gurion's 'vision.' "[48] What had happened between 1932 and 1982? Well, nothing at all. The intervening five decades were, apparently, an uneventful blank slate.

In the worst tradition of Left sectarianism, Chomsky is especially hostile to Israeli leftists who opposed the 1982 war. These men and women viewed the aggression toward Lebanon as a departure, which means they regarded Israel as a moral agent with choices to make. They saw Lebanon as a profoundly disastrous milestone in their nation's history and anguished over it as such. Chomsky mocks this as a form of self-flattery. He attacks Amos Oz as a disseminator of "familiar falsehood" about the war and Jacobo Timerman, whose book *The Longest War* is a stinging indictment of it, as a spinner of "concoctions" with a "remarkable record of falsification."[49]

These critics never suggested that the war was a fluke or could be flippantly excused as a mistake. Yet it also wasn't inevitable, much less the fulfillment of a grand master plan. They recognized that Begin and Sharon represented a deep current in Zionism—but by no means the "real" or only one.

In 1993, Hobsbawm wrote that "the fundamental experience of everyone who has lived through much of this century is error and surprise." The twentieth century humbled Hobsbawm: "The discovery that we were mistaken . . . must be the starting-point of our reflections on the history of our times."[50] But there are no errors, surprises, or mistakes in Chomskyland. Thus, in 2017, Chomsky insisted that the world situation—the world of ISIS beheadings and President Donald Trump—is "very comprehensible and very obvious and very simple."[51] And in a certain sense there are no *people* in Chomsky's world—only wooden actors playing out the fixed roles and inexorable fates he has assigned them.

Some of this may be due to Chomsky's emphasis on structures rather than humans; as Avishai Margalit once observed, Chomsky "seems to lack any kind of anthropological curiosity about the people involved" in the Israeli-Palestinian conflict.[52] That is why Chomsky could write an essay on the Second Intifada that didn't actually discuss the Palestinians— who, one might have thought, were key. Instead, he used the occasion to revisit his well-worn tirades against the U.S.—hardly a major player in the event—and to incorrectly refer, yet again, to the 1976 UN resolution. The Palestinians were almost nowhere to be seen.

Chomsky's use, or misuse, of the 1976 UN resolution is part of an unfortunate pattern that characterizes his work. The array of forces in the

Arab-Israeli conflict is multifaceted, indeed Byzantine. It consists of numerous, ideologically opposed Israeli parties and tendencies; a plethora of sometimes warring Palestinian groups; a baffling panoply of Arab states practicing what Rashid Khalidi called "predatory mores," who often loathed each other as much as if not more than they loathed Israel and who were frequently in violent disputes with the PLO; and the interests and interventions of the two superpowers. The historian, political analyst, or activist of this conflict must, therefore, be able to recognize, juggle, and synthesize many contradictory factors.

Chomsky is peculiarly unsuited to this task. Instead, he devises a strikingly simple account of a strikingly un-simple conflict. In lieu of grappling with multiplicity, he takes one partial, small seed and engorges it so that it stands in for the knotty whole. It is true, for instance, that *some* Palestinian groups began a halting, deeply ambiguous, bloodily internecine, and still-incomplete journey away from revanchism in the late 1970s. But this bears no relation to the stark, absolutist reversal that Chomsky describes; indeed, his claims make the subsequent persistence of the conflict incomprehensible. And when a smidgeon of reality is mistaken for the whole, the spot of verisimilitude does not retain, much less increase, its truth value. On the contrary, a tiny seed of truth is crushed when it is made to support an entire edifice. The Manichean history that Chomsky presents demands that he cleanse away, misrepresent, ignore, and deform an immense amount of evidence. This is nothing less than intellectual fundamentalism.

This sort of intellectual lustration emerges again in Chomsky's treatment of 1971—which, after 1976, is his favorite and most discussed year of the conflict.

In 1971, President Anwar Sadat of Egypt offered Israel peace and recognition in return for the Sinai. This was a brilliant and courageous act. Prime Minister Golda Meir and her cabinet rejected him; this was a stupid and cowardly one. (As Shlomo Ben-Ami wrote, "It was clearly Israel that did not miss an opportunity to miss an opportunity in those years of dramatic change in Egypt's strategic thinking.")[53] The consequences of Israel's arrogant error were immense. It is very possible that the 1973 war instigated by Syria and Egypt, with its attendant deaths on all sides, could have been avoided, along with the profoundly negative domestic repercussions that the war produced within Israel. Though

Golda is idolized by many American Jews as a sort of sort of proto-Zionist grandmother—simultaneously militant and snuggly—she is despised by the Israeli Left.

Chomsky has been criticizing Israel's 1971 decision for decades, and he is right to do so. The trouble emerges when he extrapolates from it. He often states that Israel chose militarism over compromise in 1971 and never looked back: Israel "has adhered to that [1971] policy ever since," he wrote in 2014.[54] This is an odd claim in light of the peace treaty Israel subsequently signed with Egypt, which would indicate that Israel *reversed* its 1971 policy. But the greater problem is that, as with 1976, Chomsky once again spins a fantasy of peace. Israel "could have had peace in 1971," he has frequently asserted; a different response to Sadat "would have ended any significant security threat"; Egypt offered "a full peace treaty."[55]

But Egypt didn't offer this, for the simple reason that it couldn't. Egypt represented no one but itself; the PLO and the other Arab states were in no way beholden to it. Nor did they regard it as a leader—quite the opposite. When Egypt and Israel signed their treaty, the Arab states erupted in fury; Gresh describes this as "a distinct hardening of the whole of the Arab world."[56] Several Arab nations, including Syria, immediately formed the pan-national Steadfastness Front, which rejected any negotiations and any compromise with Israel. This was, likewise, the position of an enraged PLO, which categorically rejected the treaty and did its best, albeit unsuccessfully, to undermine it. Egypt was not hailed as a model, as I. F. Stone and many others had hoped. On the contrary, it was denounced as a traitor, expelled from the Arab League, sanctioned, and boycotted; it became the pariah of the Arab world in the same way that the Boycott, Divestment, Sanctions (BDS) movement hopes to make Israel the pariah of the entire world. After the 1979 treaty, terror attacks against Israel remained a central part of the Palestinian movement, as did the irredentist program. In short, there was no way that Egypt did, or could, offer Israel anything approaching a utopia of "full" peace and security. Israel committed a terrible blunder in rejecting Sadat. But everything we know—which is to say, the subsequent history—suggests that the rest of the Arab world, and certainly the Palestinians, would have continued their war against Israel even had Israel's actions been far wiser.

Why is Chomsky unable to grasp the picture in full? Why does he insist on a shrunken, which is to say falsified, account? There is something almost childlike about his refusal to consider multiple, sometimes discordant factors. And something privileged, too. "When I listen to the brilliant anti-Zionist arguments of George Steiner or Noam Chomsky, to a certain degree I envy these people," Amos Oz told *Partisan Review* in 1982. "Theirs is a simple world."[57]

Frankly, I am not sure if Chomsky's distortions are due to laziness—that is, he just doesn't know what he's talking about; or if they are conscious misrepresentations; or if they are the unconscious result of ideological ossification, which prevents him from absorbing, or even noticing, factors that might complicate his theories.

Perhaps all three ingredients are at work. But I suspect that there is another aspect to his method. Chomsky has always insisted that he cares about Israel's continued existence. I think this is genuine, though it is a kind of care that, buried under a mountain of animus, is difficult to detect. Chomsky's work on the Arab-Israeli conflict is not political analysis or research-based history in any recognized sense of those terms but, rather, an expression of wishful thinking about might-have-beens. I think that Chomsky *wishes* that the PLO and the Arab world had offered recognition and peace in 1976, just as he wishes that Israel could have attained lasting security in 1971. He is always looking for the magic bullet, which means he is unable to grasp the tragic—that is, existential—aspects of this conflict. As a critic once observed of the writer Peter Handke, Chomsky gives voice to "a political emotion" rather than "a political truth."[58]

Of course, there is nothing wrong with emotions or wishes; on the contrary, they should be honored, for they illuminate our vision of a better world. Especially in the Arab-Israeli conflict—so intractable, so anguishing, so exhausting—I do not think we can relinquish hope. (Four years after his son was killed in the 2006 war with Hezbollah, the novelist David Grossman described despair as an unaffordable luxury.) But to mistake one's fantasies for facts, or one's hopes for truths, is a dangerous and narcissistic game. Chomsky plays it often.

This remarkable ability to see only what he wants makes Chomsky the most unreliable of narrators. This (in)capacity surfaced again in the imbroglio over a speech given by Father Daniel Berrigan, a hero of the antiwar movement, in 1973. The incident, notorious at the time, sheds light on how Chomsky filters information, especially when it comes to Israel.

On October 19, 1973—in the midst of the Yom Kippur War, when Egypt and Syria attacked Israel—Berrigan addressed the Association of Arab University Graduates in Washington, D.C. The speech was widely circulated: Within two weeks, it was printed in *American Report,* a publication of the antiwar group Clergy and Laity Concerned, then published in *Liberation* and as a pamphlet called *The Great Berrigan Debate.* The lecture elicited visceral reactions from a variety of people, including Irving Howe, *Village Voice* writers Nat Hentoff and Paul Cowan, and radical pacifist Dave Dellinger; *Liberation* wrote at the time that Berrigan's speech "has precipitated a conflict rivaling that of his burning of draft documents."[59] Critics accused the activist priest of one-sidedness, ignorance, and anti-Semitism; defenders painted him as a brave, taboo-smashing truth-teller. Berrigan's civil disobedience in the antiwar movement was deeply admired by Chomsky, who quickly came to Berrigan's defense and mounted a scathing assault on the critics.

Chomsky addressed the Berrigan speech in his 1974 essay "The Peace Movement and the Middle East." By his account, the speech was an admirably even-handed, nonpartisan critique of Israel and the Arab nations. "He condemned both sides in harsh terms," Chomsky wrote of Berrigan. "He refused to 'take sides' and urged nonviolence." Chomsky highlighted "Berrigan's unmitigated condemnation of the Arab states" and argued, "Berrigan does not give a balanced appraisal of Israeli society, any more than he gave a balanced account of the policies of the Arab states." This last was an odd defense: By concentrating on what Berrigan did *not* say, Chomsky avoided the troublesome issue of what he did. It also implied a strange equivalency. Was Israel, dominated by the Labor Party and the Histadrut, really the equivalent of Baathist Syria and Iraq? Chomsky concluded that charges of anti-Semitism were "simply another fabrication" because "nowhere does Berrigan suggest that the Arabs were right and the Jews wrong. . . . Berrigan nowhere suggests that an end be made of the State of Israel." The real aim of the speech's critics was to "stifle discussion"—though it seems to me that they sought to start one.[60]

I read Chomsky's defense before I read Berrigan's speech, and I experienced the same shock in reading the latter as I had with the 1976 UN resolution and debate. The gap between Berrigan's speech and Chomsky's description is not immense; it is irreconcilable.

Berrigan opens his speech by modestly explaining that he is a "non-expert in . . . the subject you have invited me to explore." This turns out to be his truest statement. Early on, he does launch a critique of the Arab regimes for various faults and crimes, though seeking to eliminate Israel does not appear on his list. The Arab states are condemned for "their capacity for deception," "their contempt for their own poor," "their willingness to oil the war machinery of the superpowers," and "their cupidity masked only by their monumental indifference to the facts of their world."[61] But the Arab world is then quickly dispensed with, and Berrigan devotes the bulk of the speech—more than four thousand words—to an apocalyptic denunciation of Israel.

Berrigan begins this section with a proud though obviously false proclamation: "I am a Jew, in resistance against Israel."[62] (This desire to enter into the Other was perhaps a sign of the times; think of John Updike's 1963 novel *The Centaur,* in which the white antihero tells his black mistress, "I want to be a Negro for you.") But this assumed identity has a purpose: It serves as a moral prophylactic for what follows. After all, isn't any Jew entitled to say anything about Israel? More important, isn't any Jew, even a self-professed "non-expert," actually a maven on the subject?

In Berrigan's view, Israel had presented the world with something new: "a criminal Jewish community." The Jewish state was characterized by "domestic repression, deception, cruelty, militarism." Israel's original sin dated from the Shoah, from which the Jewish people had evidently learned the wrong lessons. Peaceful Isaiah became bloodthirsty Moloch: "The Jews arose from the holocaust . . . like warriors, armed to the teeth. . . . They flexed their muscles; like the goyim . . . Israel entered the imperial adventure."[63]

Berrigan proceeds to offer a sociological and political analysis of Israel—a country he had never visited or, apparently, read much about. (Biblical scholar Robert Alter would write of the speech, "One may be understandably disenchanted with professional experts, but that does not entitle, say, a lecturer on Lapland to be unaware of the fact that Lapland has a very cold climate.")[64] At a time when the kibbutzim and the Histadrut were enormously influential, Berrigan charged that Israel epitomized "the failure to create new forms of political and social life for her own citizens." Ignoring Israel's vibrant, contentious political culture, he derides its "narcoticized public. . . . It is an Orwellian transplant, taken bodily from Big Brother's bloody heart. In Israel, the democratic formula is twisted out of all recognition." He chastises Israel's "huckstering" of lies to the international community. He notes how "logical" it was that "racist ideology," which he explicitly links to the Nazis, was now "employed by the State of Israel." (Berrigan would later claim—falsely—that he had not used the term "Nazi.") And woe to any Israeli who dared criticize its merciless dictators. "Her peacemakers, her men of truth and wisdom, are dispensed with. . . . They have neither power nor voice. . . . Many of them are in prison. . . . Terrorism and violence and murder is [sic] applied to dissidents."[65] (It is possible that some of the Arab students in attendance found this description better suited to Saddam's Iraq, Assad's Syria, or Boumédiène's Algeria.)

The most disturbing aspect of Berrigan's jeremiad is its smarmy combination of philo-Semitism and anti-Semitism; or, more precisely, the way the former was used to justify the latter. Whatever Chomsky's views on Israel, it is surprising that he did not object to (or even notice) this. Albert Memmi had written that, with national sovereignty, the Jewish people could drop the burden of "chosenness." Berrigan would have none of that. His speech drips with sentimental hokum about Jews as the world's great, suffering messengers of morality, or what he called "her historic adventure," apparently forgetting that this adventure has been entwined, especially in Christian theology, with her role as the world's designated villain. For Berrigan, Jews in the past were good: Through noble affliction they taught him his "conception of faith and the transcendent." But Jews in the present—that is, Israelis—are neither afflicted nor noble, and therefore a threat to the world's moral hygiene: "For it is of moment to us all . . . that Jews retain their own soul, . . . so that Jews might be the arbiter and advocate of the downtrodden of the earth."[66]

In Berrigan's view, Israel represented neither the revival of the Jewish people nor the creation of a Hebrew culture but, rather, the triumph of Thanatos: "It is a tragedy beyond calculating, that the State of Israel should become . . . the tomb of the Jewish soul." In sum: "The dream has become a nightmare."[67]

How was it possible for Chomsky to omit not some but all of this from his account of the speech? His views of Israel accorded in some ways with Berrigan's, though at the time they were not so hostile. Why not delineate the speech's major points and explain the ways in which he thought they were and were not correct? Instead, Chomsky deliberately ignored the speech's gist, cherry-picked a few unrepresentative sentences, and presented this sliver as the whole. His anodyne account imparts no sense of the speech's full content or, equally important, its emotional tenor—an aspect of politics to which Chomsky is habitually deaf. (After hearing Chomsky speak to a Berkeley conference in the early 1980s, I. F. Stone commented, "He doesn't hear the poetry of a social movement.")[68] Chomsky's description here is no more accurate—no more *faithful*—than his depiction of the 1976 UN resolution, or of the PLO's subsequent positions and actions, or of the Israeli-Egyptian situation.

Chomsky also addressed the Berrigan speech in the February 1974 issue of *Liberation*. (He called the piece "Daniel in the Lions' Den.") There, he admits, "I did not particularly like Berrigan's address. . . . I disagree with him about a number of questions"—though he never identifies any of them. Instead, he devotes the article to painstakingly delineating Israel's democratic flaws and attacking Berrigan's critics, whom he accuses of "falsehoods," "fabrication," "personal attacks and distortions," and a "mixture of confusion and invective."[69]

This was an indication of things to come: In the following years, vitriol would become Chomsky's trademark. Opponents of his ideas, or even those who differ from them, are toadies for power, propagandists, fabricators, hysterical fanatics, and hypocrites. Fred Halliday is unserious, Amos Oz spreads "carefully cultivated illusion."[70] Journalists are charged with being unable to quote Chomsky accurately, to understand his ideas, or to exhibit either intelligence or honesty. (The *New Yorker's* editor, David Remnick, who has written extensively reported articles on the Israeli-Palestinian conflict, is "too depraved to even discuss" and "reflects astonishing ignorance" on the subject.)[71] One of Chomsky's frequent accusations is adherence to Stalinism, as when he condemns "the Stalinist character of the American Zionist institutions," or the "Stalinist practices" of the Israeli press, or "the old-fashioned Stalinism" of pro-interventionists in Bosnia.[72] He is less interested in debating ideas than in eviscerating those who hold them.

Admirers of Chomsky might cheer this bombast: The lonely prophet, still unbowed, speaks truth to power! But even the powerless are subject to ridicule. Samuel Korb, an MIT student, wrote to the school's paper in "amazed" dismay after a teach-in on divestment from Israel. Chomsky, the event's main speaker, publicly humiliated a student who asked him a question by calling her "an imbecile." "What is this man so afraid of?" Korb asked.[73]

What, indeed? Whatever the answer, it is difficult to square Chomsky's verbal bullying with his oft-proclaimed dedication to the free flow of ideas and information, a culture of dialogue and dissent, and a more egalitarian world in which every human being can participate. In a sober, beautiful 1969 piece for *Liberation* called "Some Tasks for the Left"—the best and most humane thing Chomsky ever wrote—he urged Left activists to "be motivated by compassion and brotherhood" and to reject "dogmatism, fantasies and manipulative tactics."[74] That Chomsky—the "early" Chomsky—has long since disappeared.

Anyone who writes as much as Chomsky must make mistakes; even the most careful scholars do. But when it comes to Israel, Chomsky's inaccuracies are so numerous and ideologically consistent that one wonders whether to consider them errors in the traditional sense of the word. (To my knowledge, he has never acknowledged or corrected any of them.) Certainly they cast grave doubt on those who, like Edward Said, viewed him as a fount of knowledge on Israel. Chomsky's mistakes are not ones of, say, getting a date or place wrong; such faults would be random and singular. His errors, if such they are, recur over decades, sometimes almost word for word. Chomsky views himself as an objective disseminator of facts, but some of his facts are not facts. Here are a few of them.

It is not true, despite Chomsky's claims, that before 1948 the "native Jewish inhabitants of Palestine" were "largely anti-Zionist"—unless by "native," a word freighted with moral gravitas for Chomsky, he means the tiny, politically irrelevant group of Orthodox Jews who came to Palestine in the late nineteenth century.[75] It is not true that "[Chaim] Weizmann's 'liberal Zionism' had breathed its last by 1946"; it remained the country's leading credo for decades.[76] It is not true that the PLO charter—which rejected partition, declared Zionism racist and fascist, and defined Palestine as solely Arab—contained views "comparable to that of the Labor Party."[77] It is not true that "Israeli doves" live in "desperate fear of a political settlement" with the Palestinians; this is their most profound hope.[78] It is not true, as Chomsky frequently claims, that no political differences separate the Israeli Right and Left; on the contrary, Zionism is an ideologically heterogeneous movement and Israel a highly fractious society—ready, perhaps, to split apart.[79] It is not true that Israel's army is "mercenary"; it is as close to a people's army as any other, if not closer.[80] It is not true that the Israeli state imposes "draconian censorship laws"; Chomsky acknowledges that he relies on the Hebrew press for much of his information.[81] It is not true—and never has been—that Israel is "considered barely more healthy economically than Angola, Haiti, El Salvador."[82] It is not true that "no one has ever condemned Israel for aggression"; it has been denounced by assorted UN bodies more than any other country.[83] It is not true that the Soviet Union had "rather limited ambitions in the Middle East" and was a "passive player in the region"; it became a key force in the region after the 1956 Sinai campaign, was as aggressive and influential as the U.S., and was a key actor in the lead-up to the 1967 war and in arming the Arab states.[84] (As *Al-Ahram*, Egypt's official newspaper, reported in October 1968, "United States' political influence in the Middle East has dwindled altogether. . . . The growing Soviet presence in the Mediterranean is outflanking NATO.")[85] It is not true that a "broad political spectrum" of Israelis "advocated support for Saddam's atrocities" against the Kurds. Beginning in the mid-1960s, Israel sent weapons, medical supplies, and military instructors to the Kurds; Israel is the only Middle Eastern state that supports an independent Kurdistan.[86] It is not true that the lack of democracy in the Arab world is due in part to the "long-standing commitments . . . of the Zionist movement from its origins."[87] (Need we say more on that?)

Chomsky's false statements extend beyond Israel itself. It is not true that Iran is part of the "international consensus on a two-state settlement"; this would come as a very big surprise to Ayatollah Khamenei.[88] (Chomsky should check out the Supreme Leader's Twitter account, which rivals Donald Trump's in its hyperactive rancor.) In fact, as *Al-Monitor* reported in February 2017, Iran has *increased* its support for "Palestinian factions fighting Israel," putting this "at the top of its agenda."[89] Nor is it true, *pace* Chomsky, that Hamas and even, perhaps, Hezbollah are included in that international embrace.[90] Hezbollah's leader, Hassan Nasrallah, recently predicted that hundreds of thousands of fighters from across the Muslim world might join its next battle against Israel, whose demise he eagerly anticipates—and promises.

And far from being on essentially the same page, as Chomsky implies, Fatah and Hamas represent "contradictory and competing forces pulling in different strategic directions," Hussein Agha and Ahmad Samih Khalidi point out.[91] In August 2017, Hamas officials visited Tehran; they subsequently described the relationship with Iran as "fantastic" and boasted that Hamas and Iran are working "day and night [on] developing our military strength in order to liberate Palestine."[92] Chomsky insists that Hamas "has long been calling for a two-state settlement," but this is an odd way to prepare for one.[93]

What *is* true, and what Chomsky relentlessly documents, is that Israel is guilty of horrific human rights abuses in the Occupied Territories, as it was in Lebanon during the 1982 war. It is precisely as a left-wing Zionist who hopes that Israel ends the Occupation and rejuvenates its humane principles that I say this. I urge readers to look at the sober but scathing reports of Israeli groups like B'Tselem, MachsomWatch, and Breaking the Silence.

Chomsky depends on Israeli sources for much of his information, but in his emphasis he differs somewhat from these groups. He has little interest in things like house demolitions, land seizures, or checkpoint closures; instead, he tirelessly offers almost prurient descriptions of sadistic violence. He tells us of a gang rape with a dog; a woman beaten with rifle butts; a man genitally tortured.[94] (These are attributed to Israel's Lebanese allies, but Chomsky clearly holds Israel directly responsible.) He recounts Israeli soldiers who force Arab workers to masturbate, attack with leather whips, club a three-year-old child, throw an eleven-month-old baby on the floor, rake an adolescent along barbed wire, and threaten to "fuck" young boys in a West Bank school.[95] I assume that Chomsky's purpose—there are pages upon pages of this in *Fateful Triangle*—is to disgust and enrage the reader. And he does. He also deadens her; reading Chomsky is like being trapped in a room with a jackhammer. Chomsky must, surely, be motivated by deep solicitude for the victims of Israeli violence, and he is right to expose these crimes. Yet one senses no real empathy or grief for the victims—which flood every page of Timerman—but, rather, a cold, grim anger that approaches self-satisfaction.

As for Palestinian terror, Chomsky offers only rare, curiously vague descriptions: PLO behavior has been "often sordid and politically stupid."[96] There are no details to sicken or shock us, which means there is no cruelty, no sadism, no victims who suffer anguish or pain. (To Shylock's question, "Do we not bleed?," Chomsky's answer seems to be no.) And by framing Palestinian terror as a *reaction*, he misunderstands it as a *strategy*—one that, as Steinberg explained, aimed to "solicit the attention of the international community and bring the intervention of the superpowers to bear."[97] In fact, sometimes Chomsky questions the very existence of such terror. Palestinian atrocities, he writes on the first page of *Fateful Triangle*, are "often invented" and exist in a "world of fantasy."[98]

There are three problems with Chomsky's denial of Palestinian terrorism. But the lack of balance is not one of them: Israel has a powerful army, and has unquestionably inflicted more violence and death on the Palestinians than vice versa. The first problem is that Chomsky's obliviousness cripples his ability to understand Israeli politics; as Meron Benvenisti wrote of Hamas's suicide bombings in 1996, the bombings "threatened to make a shambles of Israel's agreements with the Palestinians. . . . The bombings are political, not military, acts. The danger they pose is not to Israel's survival but to a political process."[99] Second, it leads Chomsky to view the Palestinians as mere puppets of Israel rather than as political actors in their own right. Unsurprisingly, the Palestinians beg to differ; as their ambassador to the UN politely admonished Chomsky in 2014, "It is not only the Israelis who are . . . dictating the future of the Palestinian people, nor the Americans. . . . We [Palestinians] are in the forefront. We are not a footnote. We are a key player."[100] The third problem, and the biggest, is the lack of a dialectic. In Chomsky's view, Israel's violence exists in a void. It lashes out, but against no one and nothing.

Chomsky has spent decades insisting that Israel has no security concerns and never did. Even in 1974, when the PLO and the Arab states were, by his own admission, pledged to Israel's destruction, he contended, "In no case was the issue one of security." Two decades later, he reiterated, "The problem . . . has never been security."[101] (He sometimes cites himself as the source for these claims.) He has written that Israel faced no serious dangers in the lead-up to the 1967 war. He scoffs at the idea that Hamas's tunnels, which burrow into Israel, pose any threat; the mere idea is "transparently absurd" and "ludicrous."[102] In his speech to the UN, he praised Hamas's "definite pattern" of restraint; the group's real (and presumably only) "crime," he sardonically claimed, was winning the 2006 Palestinian elections.[103] As for Hezbollah's 130,000 long-range missiles, which are aimed at Israeli cities: They are never mentioned.

All this raises a basic question—a great black hole in the midst of Chomsky's work—that he does not address. That question is: Why is there a conflict at all? He depicts the Israelis as mad dogs on a rampage. They reject peace again and again. They seek militarism, torture, death; they launch savage war after war on their peace-loving neighbors. They waste their wealth on useless armaments and send their children to be maimed and killed in equally useless battles. Their fears are mere paranoia. They destroy rather than create. Chomsky prides himself on being a rationalist and logician. What is the logic here?

Chomsky avoids this question because he has no answer, and he has no answer because he has created a fictitious Palestinian movement. The best he can offer is the feeble suggestion that Israel seeks "control over the territories and their resources."[104] But the Palestinian territories are relatively resource-*poor*, aside from water—this is not the Congo—and in many respects the Occupation is an economic burden, as are the settlements, on the Israeli state and the Israeli taxpayer. His reasoning here is similar to his claim that NATO turned against the Serbs because the latter represented the last, brave resistance to neoliberal capitalism.[105] Chomsky's mono-causal worldview paints him into a corner. He is forced to rely on the kind of vulgar Marxism—on an economic reductionism— that Marx himself disavowed.

Perhaps the most striking, or at least instantly noticeable, aspect of Chomsky's rhetorical method is his dependence on analogies and comparisons, even when they make no sense. As mentioned, Chomsky never departs from an internationalist perspective, and in this he upholds a long-standing commitment of the Left. Unfortunately, he has transformed this principle from an ethic of solidarity into a strategy of evasion. Chomsky suffers from an ailment I think of as Anti-Imperialist Attention Deficit Disorder. Ask him about al-Qaeda and he'll zip over to Nicaragua; ask him about Bosnia and he'll talk about East Timor; ask him about Rwanda and he'll discuss Vietnam. This can be irritating, yet one can't help but be awed by the sheer inventiveness of Chomsky's obfuscations. Questioned by the BBC as to whether the U.S. had a right to invade Afghanistan after 9/11, Chomsky answered that Britain had never attacked West Belfast in response to Irish Republican Army bombs. This led to the following exchange:

QUESTION: Why would any country attack itself? Why would Britain attack part of Britain, part of the United Kingdom?
CHOMSKY: Excuse me, because West Belfast was the place where the bombing was originating.
QUESTION: They were a part of the United Kingdom.
CHOMSKY: Makes no difference.
QUESTION: Doesn't it?[106]

In terms of Israel, the most toxic analogy is the Shoah; it is used by all sides in the conflict. Chomsky has rightly criticized Israel's opportunistic exploitation of the genocide for political gain; this was especially destructive in the run-up to the First Lebanon War, when Begin compared Arafat to Hitler and the PLO guerrillas to the Nazi army. (Timerman wrote that in Lebanon, the Israeli people's *"moral integrity . . . died of a false analogy."*)[107] For Chomsky, this reliance on the Shoah is an essential, perhaps even structural, Israeli neurosis. "How readily the terminology of the Nazis has been adopted in Israeli and American Zionist rhetoric," he charges. In his view, Israelis have an "almost pathological need to imitate the [Nazi] posturing."[108]

But the pathology—the repetition compulsion—may be Chomsky's. In the lead-up to the Six-Day War, he writes, Israel's "propaganda" against Nasser "effectively mimicked Goebbels."[109] He describes Israel's foreign policy as supportive of "those who employ the methods of Himmler's extermination squads."[110] Israel's assault on the PLO in Lebanon is paralleled to the Nazi invasion of Czechoslovakia, while attacks on Hamas-led Gaza are likened to Lidice and Oradour. Justifications of Israeli military actions, such as by the historian Robert Tucker, are equated with Hitler's rationales for Nazi aggression and viewed as equally specious. And here is Chomsky's analysis of Hamas's attacks on Israeli civilians, which takes a particularly circuitous route. After first claiming that the attacks are "a fantasy of [Israel's] apologists," he changes his mind and adds: "The rocketing is criminal, and it is true that a state has the right to defend itself against criminal attacks. But it does not follow that it has a right to defend itself by force. . . . Nazi Germany had no right to use force to defend itself against the terrorism of the partisans. Kristallnacht was not justified by Herschel Grynszpan's assassination of a German Embassy official in Paris."[III]

Such reasoning—it is difficult, at least for me, to even attempt to untangle this—also emerges in the debate over Israel's right to exist as a state for the Jewish people, which really means its *lack* of a right to exist as a state for the Jewish people. Israel's legitimacy has been challenged—by words, boycotts, and guns—since the day it declared independence in 1948, and the country has been the obsessive object of UN condemnation. Chomsky argues, however, that Israel's situation is entirely normal because *no* state recognizes the sovereignty of any other. "States do not have a right to exist," he claims; the "right to exist," he adds, is "accorded to no other state in the international system."[112] These are mysterious, indeed meaningless statements, and especially strange coming from a man with such reverence for UN resolutions. (The UN is, of course, predicated on the fact that states do have the right to exist and consequently do recognize each other.) Again, Chomsky relies on analogy to make his point; this time he finds his example not in the Third Reich but closer to home. "Mexico does not accept the right of the USA to exist sitting on half of Mexico," he asserts. It follows that "there is no more reason to expect Palestinians to accept the 'legitimacy' of Israel . . . than there is . . . for Mexico to accept the 'legitimacy' of the United States, which stole much of its land." Indeed, Chomsky (if no one else) refers to Arizona as "occupied Mexico."[113] He has failed to notice the salient fact that Mexico has no political faction, whether of the Left or Right, that rejects the U.S.'s existence or seeks to wage war against it.

It is easy to mock "occupied Mexico"; it is hard not to. But a serious point is at stake. Hannah Arendt wrote that the process of thinking originates in the premise that "A and B are not the same"; originates, that is, in the ability to make distinctions, to think precisely, and to think anew.[114] Chomsky repeatedly fails to meet this Arendtian challenge. For Chomsky, history and politics are a series of weary repetitions to which we owe nothing but weary Pavlovian responses. A and B *are* the same, as are P and Q, X and Y. They all blur together in an ahistoric and ultimately apolitical muddle.

Ethics begin in the capacity to discriminate. The younger Chomsky realized this. In a 1967 forum in New York City, he debated Arendt, Robert Lowell, and Conor Cruise O'Brien on "the legitimacy of violence as a political act"—a debate that was urgently informed by the Vietnam War and the protests against it. Chomsky's views were nuanced and his tone modest. He mulled over ideas, suggested arguments, and sometimes respectfully disagreed with others.

In this debate, Chomsky disputed Arendt's distinction between politics and morals, and he rejected the dichotomy between tactics and morals. He argued, "If tactics involves [*sic*] a calculation of the human cost of various actions, then tactical considerations are actually the only considerations that have a moral quality to them." He praised the transformative power of nonviolence and the existential cost of its opposite: "Immense harm is done to the individual who participates in violent action. Almost invariably he becomes much the worse for it." Conversely, he noted, there is "the kind of maturity and dignity, and depth of understanding, that was in fact reached by many of the Southern Negro participants in the civil rights movement." He continued, "That kind of moral, human transformation . . . might even save the world from destruction."[115]

Most important, Chomsky intuited the symbiotic relation between the political deeds of a revolutionary movement and the society it will subsequently build; he overtly took issue with Régis Debray and, by implication, with Fanon. Chomsky posited, "It seems to me, from the little we know about such matters, that a new society rises out of the actions that are taken to form it, and the institutions and the ideology it develops are not independent of those actions; in fact, . . . they're shaped by them in many ways. And one can expect that actions that are cynical and vicious, whatever their intent, will inevitably condition and deface the quality of the ends that are achieved." He added, "There is a relationship between absence of terror and . . . success in achieving a just society."[116]

There is an immense and mysterious gulf between this man and the Chomsky of today. Perhaps it was created by too much frustration and too many defeats. For whatever reason, the "later" Chomsky—today's Chomsky—has forgotten the costs of terror; instead he romanticizes Hamas. Today's Chomsky rarely addresses questions of "moral, human transformation." Today's Chomsky cannot distinguish between the Mexico-U.S. relationship and the Arab-Israeli one, or between the Nazi state and the

State of Israel. In Arendtian terms, today's Chomsky has, quite literally, stopped *thinking*, and in the process abandoned his moral compass.

In the present, Chomsky continues to adamantly oppose the Oslo Accords, which he views as the "unilateral rejection of Palestinian rights."[117] He despises the Palestinian Authority as a "quisling regime" and its security forces as the "Vichy police."[118] His understanding of the conflict's history remains puzzling, as when, in 2014, he described the 1967 war thus: "Israel performed a major service to the United States by destroying secular Arab nationalism . . . and supporting radical Islam, which the US supported."[119] Yet unlike many on the left, Chomsky rejects the Israel-South Africa analogy. In fact, he argues that the position of Palestinian-Israeli citizens within the Green Line is utterly different from that of blacks in apartheid South Africa, while the situation of stateless Palestinians outside it is worse. He has often spoken out against the BDS campaign, which takes its inspiration from South Africa—and is the only movement I know of that is premised entirely *on* analogy. (This kind of metaphorical dependence, though dramatic, is dangerously rickety; as Bernard Avishai has pointed out, "Comparable cruelty does not necessarily entail a similar political architecture.")[120]

I find myself in rare agreement with Chomsky here, and am (pleasantly) surprised that the master of analogy rejects this one. Chomsky considers himself a ruthless foe of woolly-headedness and sentimentality; it is this aspect of BDS that seems to most irritate him. "You have to ask what is going to help them [Palestinians], not what is going to make me feel good," he wrote in a much-discussed 2014 piece in the *Nation*.[121] In his writings, BDS emerges as a kind of intellectual fuzz; he told a meeting of United Nations correspondents that the boycotters had failed to ask the most basic questions about the relationship between tactics and aims.

Chomsky's opposition to BDS is based on intellectual, strategic, and what I (though perhaps not he) would call moral grounds. The three often merge.

Israel is not South Africa, Chomsky warns, just as he previously cautioned that it is not Algeria or Vietnam: "The South African analogy . . . is a very dubious one."[122] He has delineated the many differences in the histories, politics, and struggles of the two countries. Unlike in South Africa, the Israeli-Palestinian conflict consists of two national movements. Unlike South Africa, "Palestine" has never functioned as a unified state. Unlike apartheid South Africa, there is no broad-based coalition of groups within Israel who oppose the current regime: "Spokespeople for the BDS movement may believe they have attained their 'South African moment,' but that is far from accurate."[123] Unlike in apartheid South Africa, there is universal suffrage within Israel's Green Line; Chomsky has called BDS's demand for an end to discrimination against Palestinian Israelis "empty and meaningless."[124]

It is extremely doubtful that the international community will endorse an economic boycott of Israel, as it did, relatively easily, with South Africa. In fact, it is likely that even BDS's most enthusiastic supporters use Israeli inventions and products; it is even more likely that developing countries have little desire to deprive themselves of Israeli technological breakthroughs in medicine, irrigation, desalination, and crop production. The Israeli economy exploits—but is not dependent on—Palestinian labor. There is little chance that Israel will be sanctioned by the international community; on the contrary, many countries, including India and the far-Left government in Greece, draw closer to it, as do some Arab and African nations.

In particular, Chomsky opposes BDS's demand, which it sometimes obfuscates, for the right of return. Such a demand, he wrote in 2014, is not supported by international law, has "virtually no meaningful support . . . beyond the BDS movement," and is "a virtual guarantee of failure. . . . There is no reason to expect Israel to accept a Palestinian population it does not want." He strongly opposes the boycotting of Israeli universities, calling it hypocritical ("why not boycott Harvard"?) and antithetical to academic freedom. And useless, too: "What good does it to do to the Palestinians? . . . And of course it does not affect Israel in any way at all."[125]

Chomsky also objects to the one-state solution. Israelis and Palestinians, he points out, have "two separate cultures, different languages, different traditions." (And, one might add, a river of spilled blood between them.) He perceives that a unified state would be an antidemocratic one in which Palestinian *land* is annexed but in which Palestinian *people* will lack rights. Those "who are proposing a one-state settlement . . . are in fact serving . . . the occupation," Chomsky told the *Journal of Palestine Studies* in 2012.[126] In other words, one state would be "a gift to the jingoist right" rather than a victory for the Left.[127] In reality, he says, only two choices exist: an annexationist Israel or two states. In 2014, he told the UN that he believed a two-state solution was still eminently viable, and he urged the delegates to take the long view.

Yet his understanding of the two-state solution remains unique. He continues to insist that all Israelis are united in opposition while their most truculent enemies—Hamas, Iran, perhaps Hezbollah—are on board. (It would be interesting to see him give a speech to this effect in Gaza City, Tehran, or Beirut.) It is depressing to see a Lebanese television clip of Chomsky schlepping around southern Lebanon with a smiling, turbaned Hezbollah commander, who looks like the proverbial cat with his captured canary.[128] Chomsky *does* insist that Israel has as much right to sovereignty as any other nation—though as we have seen, for Chomsky that's a pretty iffy proposition. Ultimately, though, such Talmudic distinctions are probably irrelevant. Chomsky's readers, and certainly his fans, are no doubt most influenced by the fusillades of fury he steadily hurls at the country—a fury he directs at no other state or non-state actor in the Middle East. Israel, he contends, is an "ugly" and "sadistic" society defined by "criminality," "utter hypocrisy" and "moral depravity."[129] His 2014 speech to the United Nations was an adamantine critique of Israel's "long history of . . . crimes," which is fine; he omitted the Palestinians' same long history, which isn't.

And he gravely misunderstands the catastrophes of the Arab world today. He has said that Sunni-Shia conflict in Iraq, and perhaps the whole region, was negligible until the U.S.'s 2003 invasion, which suggests an alarming ignorance of Iraqi, Middle Eastern, and Islamic history. In fact, Chomsky's ironclad anti-imperialism makes him one of the least useful analysts of the Middle East. As the writer and activist Sam Hamad wrote on *Syria Deeply*, an independent website, "Chomsky is a political rock, unchanged by the elements and unaltered by time, no matter how powerful the tidal waves of change crashing against his worldview. . . . The stasis that defines his approach has left him unable to reckon with the Arab Spring's complexities and contradictions."[130]

Chomsky would, I think, agree with this assessment, or at least its first half; as he wrote with disdain several years after the fall of the Berlin Wall, "There are no fundamental changes, and no 'new paradigms' are needed to make sense of what is happening."[131] (Compare this to Hobsbawm: "There can be no serious doubt that in the late 1980s and early 1990s an era in world history ended and a new one began.")[132] Similarly, in response to a question by Israeli journalist Amira Hass, Chomsky described the Arab Spring as "not that different from what's happened before. . . . It is nothing new"—a claim the uprisings' activists would surely contest.[133]

Here is where we find the key to Chomsky's worldview and its weakness. His loyalty to principle has morphed into a crippling ideological rigidity that prevents him, time and again, from apprehending what is happening in the world around him. He views the reassessment of ingrained ideas as a betrayal of principle rather than as the wellspring of intelligence. He remains choleric, yet in a very real sense he has fallen asleep. He is the personification of Halliday's dreaded Rip Van Winkle.

Chomsky is sometimes considered a libertarian socialist or socialist anarchist; as such he is strongly antagonistic to the idea of the state, which he has described as an inhuman institution that traffics in violence and repression. This is an unanswerable indictment because it is true. But it is also true that states, in their good-enough versions, provide their citizens with access to health care and education; establish, and guard, their freedoms; protect their safety (sometimes, yes, through violence); fight corruption; defend the rule of law and the rights of minorities; produce, distribute, and sometimes redistribute goods and wealth.

Chomsky has never recognized any of these virtues. He has long held that the solution to the crises of the Middle East is state collapse or, as he puts it, the "no-state solution." In 2015, he proposed that the fix for a broken Middle East is "if the whole state system erodes in the region."[134] But by that year the whole state system of the region *had* eroded, indeed exploded: Think of Iraq, Yemen, Syria, and Libya. The result of this enormous, world-altering breakdown has not been the emergence of the nonstate, nonsectarian community of internationalists of which Chomsky has always dreamt but, rather, a plunge into anarchy and shocking violence that has created a giant exodus of desperate refugees *to* those nations with strong, functional states. (If you're looking for a non-state utopia, you don't seek asylum in Germany.) This refugee flood has been a major factor in the rise of right-wing, nativist populism in the Western democracies and the overturning of traditional politics within them. New paradigms *are* needed: As Yassin al-Haj Saleh, a Syrian leftist who spent sixteen years as a political prisoner in Syrian jails, commented simply,

"Syria changed the world."[135] The Arab Spring did not prove the irrelevance of the state; it showed, instead, what happens when countries cannot build states that are worthy of their people.

Once again, Chomsky's ideology has blinded him. He cannot comprehend change. He cannot recognize newness. He cannot understand what the refugees are running from and what they are running toward, or what the crowds in the squares and the streets were demanding. He cannot see that the Middle East is not Chomskyland.

In 1970, Chomsky wrote that he hoped to forge an approach to the Arab-Israeli conflict that was "somewhat realistic and more or less humane."[136] He has failed on both counts. Whatever one's politics, it is simply impossible to *understand* the conflict from his work. When you immerse yourself in Chomsky's writings, you learn an awful lot about how Chomsky thinks and about Chomsky's obsessions. But you learn little about the world itself. The shame, and the crime, is that he has misled generations of young people, who know little if anything of Israeli, Arab, or Middle Eastern history; who will not check his sources or see through his deceptive uses of them; and who have little way of knowing how divorced from actuality many of his analyses are. Moreover, he has taken bedrock principles of the Left such as internationalism, twisted them into unrecognizable caricatures, and thereby betrayed them.

Many of the authors discussed in this book have refused the harsh, complicated realities of the Arab-Israeli conflict, preferring to project their a priori theories, hopes, wishes, and antipathies onto it. This has hobbled them as analysts and activists. With Noam Chomsky, the flight from reality reaches its apotheosis. The man who once demanded an end to dogmatism, fantasy, and manipulation on the left now revels in them. He has become his own nightmare. And to the extent that he is considered "the leading intellect of the American left," he is our nightmare, too.[137]

Conclusion

THE GENIUS FOR FAILURE

THE ISRAELI-PALESTINIAN CONFLICT is often called intractable; though it changes, it endures. Various explanations for this strange persistence have been offered, including the claims of religion and history and the interference, or noninterference, of outside powers. In my view, one of the conflict's most distinct, and distinctly ruinous, aspects is the refusal of reality by each side. When it comes to Israeli fantasies, the Western Left has been an acute and invaluable critic—though these very criticisms have sometimes led it to scorched-earth policies and false solutions. Simultaneously, the Left has been the worst enabler of Palestinian delusions—and offered a poisonous array of its own.

In the half century since the end of the Six-Day War, an enormous web of Israeli self-deceptions has become plain for all the world to see. Some observers, and some Israelis, saw the looming dangers at the time. Three months after the war, in response to the nationwide debates over what to do with the recently conquered Jordanian-Palestinian, Egyptian, and Syrian territories, an advertisement ran in the Israeli daily *Haaretz.* "Our right to defend ourselves against annihilation does not grant us the right to oppress others," it said. It continued:

> Conquest brings in its wake foreign rule. Foreign rule brings in its wake resistance. Resistance brings in its wake oppression.

> Oppression brings in its wake terrorism and counterterrorism. . . .
> Holding onto the territories will turn us into a nation of
> murderers and murder victims. . . . Let us leave the occupied
> territories now.[1]

The Israeli lie is, quite simply, the denial of these facts. Israelis—not all, but a seemingly overwhelming number—have told themselves that the Palestinians are not a people, or that this people does not desire or deserve national sovereignty. (There is something cruelly perverse about this; as historian Walid Khalidi has written, statehood for the Palestinians "would end their anonymous ghost-like existence as a non-people. . . . Of all peoples, the Jewish people are historically qualified to understand this.")[2] Israelis have told themselves that the Occupation is relatively humane or only temporary. They have told themselves that they can oppress another nation without wreaking havoc on their own democratic institutions. They have told themselves that ruling over others will not foster racism within Israel itself. They have told themselves that they can be safe while sitting atop a volcano, despite its inevitable periodic eruptions. They have told themselves that the Bible can be used as a real estate manual, and that the events of the ancient past and the demands of a modern state are one. They have told themselves that the setting of borders is not a key constituent of every sovereign state. They have told themselves that missed opportunities will reappear. They have told themselves that they can avoid solving the agonizing dilemmas they face—that God, or the U.S., or some equal substitute will come to the rescue—and that the social fabric of the country won't tear if that avoidance persists. They have told themselves that the rest of the world won't notice any of the above, and that the outside world doesn't matter anyway.

An astonishing level of denial is necessary to sustain these beliefs. Noam Sheizaf, a founding editor of the left-wing Israeli magazine +972, recently compared the Israeli mind-set to that of a person "who falls from the 80th floor and shouts as he passes the 30th floor that he's doing just fine and even enjoying the view and the fresh air."[3]

Liberals, leftists, progressives—call them what you will—both within Israel and in the West have made these arguments for fifty years: though, obviously, without success. So has every person discussed in this book (with the possible exception of Arthur Koestler), despite their wide disagreements about Zionism itself.

But the position of many liberals, leftists, progressives—call them what you will—extends way beyond this critique. In fact, the position of many leftists today, especially in the United States and England, is as fraudulent as the Israeli positions described above. This places them within a long and unhappy tradition.

Socialists, and especially Communists, were in the forefront of the fight against fascism. But when it came to Jews, and the Jewish people, and the Jewish Question, a crippling blindness developed in thinker after thinker and, astonishingly, persevered even as Hitler rose to power. In 1931, Otto Heller, a leading Austrian-Jewish Communist, published an influential book called *Downfall of Judaism* that mocked Zionism as "the last, most desperate and most wretched kind of nationalism."[4] Although he was writing as Nazi Storm Troopers surged through the streets, Heller was sure that the Jewish Question was almost solved and that anti-Semitism, like the state, would soon wither away. Another prominent Jewish theorist of the time, the Belgian Abram Leon, was originally a Marxist-Zionist but converted to Trotskyism and, therefore, to radical anti-nationalism. In 1942, while a member of the Belgian Resistance, he wrote *The Jewish Question: A Marxist Interpretation*, which has enjoyed an afterlife as a foundational text (cited by, among others, Maxime Rodinson). Leon condemned Zionism as "an ideological excrescence" and an unnecessary one; thanks to the magic of the dialectic, the "very exacerbation of anti-Semitism prepares the road for its disappearance."[5] Shortly thereafter he was murdered in a Nazi concentration camp; Heller met the same fate. And when it came to anti-nationalism, no revolutionary leaders could surpass Rosa Luxemburg and Leon Trotsky. Each insisted that any loyalty to national identity was an antiquated residue that held no interest for the working classes, who would warmly welcome their Jewish brothers and sisters as equals-in-arms. Unfortunately, as the historian Walter Laqueur observed, "The Polish, German, or Austrian working class neither needed nor wanted the Jews as allies; they wanted to get rid of them."[6]

This book has contained many examples of such calamitous obliviousness, albeit with less severe personal consequences. Hannah Arendt, in the midst of an existential war, demanded the formation of brotherly binational councils (and mocked those on the front lines who knew more than she). Maxime Rodinson insisted that Jewish assimilation and integration into the wider society had succeeded, despite his parents' deportation to Auschwitz by the French. I. F. Stone predicted that the Arab world would hail peace between Israel and Egypt and cited Lebanon as a model of ethnic-religious coexistence shortly before it exploded into civil war. Noam Chomsky converted the Palestine Liberation Organization and the larger Arab world of the 1970s and eighties into two-state advocates of peaceful coexistence (a position that, he contends, Hamas and Iran support today). Each of these writers struggled for decades to navigate what British socialist Mervyn Jones called the "labyrinth" of Zionism; their failures prove that the Jewish Question is an ongoing argument with no final answer. But these writers also shared, at least in the instances cited above, a treacherous readiness to substitute ideology, wishful thinking, or sheer fantasy for reality.

These same attributes have characterized, and crippled, the combatants in the Arab-Israeli conflict itself. Each side's shared—and greatest—delusion, as Hannah Arendt wrote in 1948, has been a refusal to see the Other as a "permanent reality." Each clung to an almost childlike belief in magical disappearing acts; each has failed to accept that the other should not and can not be driven from the land.

Starting with the Six-Day War, those who denied this fundamental fact became increasingly, indeed enthusiastically, adamant. Israel's hubris soared to delirious heights, leading to the belief that "Greater Israel" would usher in messianic redemption—or, for the secular, that the political goals and moral imperatives of 1947 could be simply cloned onto the political goals and moral imperatives of 1967. The Left indulged in messianic delusions, too, though of a different sort. Much of the Left supported the PLO in its maddest schemes, despite the warnings of supporters like Rodinson and Alain Gresh (and, for a time, Chomsky). There was, first, the organization's goal of abolishing Israel and expelling its Jewish inhabitants and, then, of overthrowing the Jordanian state (another country that, in the early PLO's view, had no right to exist). Other strategies included destabilizing Lebanon, supporting Saddam Hussein, and suicide-bombing Israelis into submission. All ended in defeat and had diametrically opposite results than intended: These included expulsion from several Arab countries, geographic isolation, financial and political collapse, the separation barrier, checkpoints, and, within Israel, the continued rise of the Right and the crippling of the Left. Looking back from the vantage point of 1992, Khalid al-Hasan, a member of Fatah's Central Committee, decried his move-ment's "genius for failure," which he attributed to "arrogance, . . . chaos, confusion, ignorance, . . . and intellectual and mental blockage."[7]

Nonetheless, warm feelings for those days of glory linger—most of all, perhaps, among leftists in the West. Typical is a recent essay on the 1967 war by Sherene Seikaly, a history professor at the University of California and editor of the academic *Arab Studies Journal*. "Those six days marked the transformation of the Palestinian guerrilla from a passive actor . . . into a central icon of a new global age of revolution," she exults. "The parallels between and solidarities across Cuba, Vietnam, Algeria and the Black Power movement . . . were exhilarating and everywhere to be seen." In her view, it is unfortunate that the Palestinians would eventually "begin the ostensibly realistic and ultimately devastating process of allowing the six-day war to set the terms of political action" by accepting a "delineation of Israel and Palestine"—by accepting, that is, the necessity of two states. Though she admits that the armed struggle was "deeply flawed," it remains her source of inspiration; Seikaly urges historians to discover "the history of the fedayeen not in the 1960s, but the 1950s, the 1930s or indeed the nineteenth century" to create what she calls the politics of hope. She seems dangerously unaware of the connection between her idealization of "exhil-arating" armed struggle and the bleeding of the current Middle East, which, she admits, is a "paralyzing landscape of despair" marked by refu-gees, civil war, foreign intervention, and "vigilante Islamism."[8]

Seikaly is not alone in attempting to revive or recirculate the failed ideologies of the past. Witness the current favored strategies of the Western Left: the return of the Palestinian refugees to Israel and, closely connected, the one-state solution. (I concentrate here on the U.S. and England, where these goals arc most popular.) These demands show that not much has been learned; the genius for failure is alive and well. And they ensure one thing only: not the politics of hope but the continuation of bloodshed. Anyone who encourages these "solutions" is guilty of polit-ical malpractice.

The partitions, dictatorships, and wars of the twentieth century (and, now, the twenty-first) created scores of millions of refugees. A partial list includes Indians, Pakistanis, Bengalis, Burundians, Rwandans, Armenians, Germans, Poles, Ukranians, Lithuanians, Iraqis, Syrians, Afghans, Algerians, Bosnians, Croats, Vietnamese, Cambodians, Laotians, Haitians, Kurds, Kashmiris, Darfuris, South Sudanese, Somalis, Eritreans, Ethiopians, and Congolese. And, of course, millions of Jews from Europe and the Arab world. Like the Palestinians, some of these refugees chose to leave; like the Palestinians, many more were forced to leave or terrorized into leaving. Like the Palestinians, almost all lost homes, lands, or businesses; suffered the collapse of their worlds; and witnessed the killings of their families and friends.

Proponents of Palestinian return, such as the Boycott, Divestment, Sanctions (BDS) movement, often frame this demand as an ordinary one that is universally recognized. In practice, the opposite is true. What distinguishes the Palestinians is not that their return has been denied. In fact, this is precisely what they *share* with others. Most of the millions of the world's refugees have not been repatriated; most never will be. Nor, almost certainly, will their children or grandchildren or great-grandchildren. One would be hard-pressed to find a case in which millions of refugees and their descendants have returned to a country from which they were exiled in the midst of a war that they started, especially when many of those returnees reject the legitimacy of the extant nation and their population might overwhelm it.

What *does* distinguish the Palestinians is that, for decades, they have been kept in a cruel political limbo and, often, in impoverished refugee camps: by the Israelis, by their "brothers" in the Arab world, and by their own leadership. What also distinguishes them is that they have often refused political solutions in favor of insisting on an ephemeral "right."

This sort of radical nostalgia has a name: reaction. Its face is set firmly to the restoration of an imagined past rather than the building of a modern future. The Palestinians and their supporters are not, of course, unique in building a movement based upon this genuine yearning for an invented past; Slobodan Milosevic's "Greater Serbia," for instance, was another. In fact, as I write, reaction has made a worldwide comeback. Donald Trump promises to make America great again; Marine Le Pen will do the same for France. So will ISIS—the world's greatest revanchists—for the Muslim world. And, of course, there is the irredentism of the Israeli Right; in its imagination, resettling the West Bank will create a new race of King

Davids, or hasten the Messiah, or redeem Jewish history. "What is Zionism all about?" Tzipi Hotovely, a Likud cabinet member, asked, and then answered: "Zionism is really about going back to Zion, going back to Jerusalem, *going back to all those biblical places.*"9 It is not the self-creation of Tel Aviv—which expresses the cultural and political revolution of the modern Jewish people—but the *re*-creation of the beloved, ancient, ostensibly more perfect past that is at the heart of this vision.

It can be argued that Zionism, from its inception, also represented a return, and in an important sense this is so. That is why, in 1905, Zionist activists rejected a proposal that they settle in Uganda (though it's hard to imagine how doing so would have turned out well). But that argument evades too many crucial factors. First, the goal of the Zionist movement was to generate a thoroughgoing cultural revolution and build a new Hebrew democracy—the opposite of Tzipi Hotovely's return. Second, many, and at a certain point virtually all, of the Jews who flocked to Palestine were fleeing the hells of Russia and, then, of Germany, Poland, Romania, Hungary, and too many other places. Especially after the United States imposed strict quotas in 1924, and as country after country slammed its doors despite the spread of fascism, *most Jews had nowhere else to go.* I have never heard a compelling argument from an anti-Zionist about what else these "scum," to use Hannah Arendt's mordant phrase, should have done (other than, perhaps, die). Third, by the time of the partition—indeed, by the 1930s—the Zionists had built a functioning society with viable political, economic, and civic institutions. The question was not whether to "grant" or "give" the Jews a state; the question was whether to destroy one. That is a question that remains.

The Left has usually opposed any program that seeks to reverse history; indeed, such opposition has been at the heart of the term "progressive." Yet when it comes to the Palestinian struggle, the opposite holds true. Only in the case of the Palestinians is the radical nostalgia of return, and the irredentism that it fuels, considered progressive, or revolutionary, or touted as the ultimate justice.

In this view, Israeli irredentism is right wing and bad while Palestinian irredentism is left wing and good. Its corollary: The Israeli memory of—or obsession with—the Shoah is hysterical, opportunistic, and destructive. The Palestinian memory of—or obsession with—the *nakba* is sober, principled, and productive.

The question is: Why?

To understand, it is helpful to look at the one-state or "binational" proposal, for which the right of return is a stalking horse.

Partition, as Fred Halliday pointed out and as most historians know, has been "a standard solution"—though not necessarily a perfect or happy one—to resolve intractable national conflicts. Post–World War II partitions include India and Pakistan, Pakistan and Bangladesh, Cyprus, Yugoslavia, Czechoslovakia, East Timor and Indonesia, Sudan, and—the mother of all partitions—the breakup of the Soviet Union. (Future possible partitions, whether wise or not, include Spain-Catalonia, Iraq-Kurdistan, and England-Scotland.) Some of these partitions were peaceful, others hideously violent. Some resulted in viable states, others in crippled ones; some led to democracies, others to dictatorships. But there have been no suggestions—other than in the case of Israel and Palestine—that the partition be *un*-done.[10] No matter the circumstances of the birth or the health of the child, it is widely understood that any such plan would result in the crushing of extant institutions, the denial of long-sought independence, political chaos, massive population shifts, and ethnic violence. When it comes to Israel and Palestine, however, the undoing of partition is viewed as the road to peace and a more perfect democracy.

Many people on both the Right and Left argue that the Occupation and the settlements have already erased any meaningful partition between Israel and Palestine. In Israel, the Right celebrates this while the Left despairs (though much of the Western Left rejoices in the belief that this spells the end of Zionism and will lead to one state). This assessment may be correct; the two-state solution is often depicted as a listless patient lying supine on her deathbed. Yet this conventional wisdom about a presumed fait accompli is the subject of far more dispute than is sometimes recognized.[11] Nathan Thrall, the Jerusalem-based Middle East analyst for the International Crisis Group, argued in 2017, "In fact, Israelis and Palestinians are now farther from a single state than they have been at any time since the occupation began in 1967. From [Menachem] Begin's autonomy plan to Oslo and the withdrawal from Gaza, Israel and Palestine have been inching steadily toward partition. . . . And the supposed reason that partition is often claimed to be impossible—the difficulty of a probable relocation of over 150,000 settlers—is grossly overstated."[12]

It is tempting to look at a map of the West Bank, littered with little dots that denote Israeli settlements, and throw up one's hands in despair. But as Thrall indicates, the details behind the dots are more complex than is apparent at first glance. Shaul Arieli is a retired senior officer in the Israeli Defense Forces who is considered the leading authority on the settlements, and his research points to a perplexing paradox: While the settlement movement has amassed tremendous political power, it has failed in its major objective.

Starting with the Likud victory in 1977, the settlement enterprise aimed to create a Jewish majority in the West Bank, which would allow Israel to annex the Occupied Territories while remaining majority-Jewish. Aside from the East Jerusalem area, this project has been a flop. According to Arieli, as of 2016 most of the West Bank remained overwhelmingly Palestinian: In the Mountain Ridge, 92.3 percent of the population was Palestinian; in the Jordan Valley, 93.4 percent; in West Judea and Samaria, 82.3 percent. Only in what is known as the Jerusalem Envelope has the demographic balance been fundamentally altered, with Palestinians now constituting only 46.5 percent. Overall, though, the Palestinian population in the Occupied Territories, including East Jerusalem, stood at 82 percent; for a variety of demographic reasons, these figures are unlikely to substantially change. Palestinians also continued to own the over-whelming amount of land in the territories—though they are not always allowed onto it.[13]

And though the settlements are dispersed, most are small: Of the 126 settlements, 111 have a population of fewer than 5,000 people (with 60 having fewer than 1,000). A plurality of settlers are concentrated in a small number of communities that hug the Green Line, which would almost certainly be incorporated into Israel proper, with land swaps, in any peace deal. Thus, Arieli writes, "With the exception of Western Samaria, which is adjacent to the Green Line, and of the Jerusalem area, the Israeli presence [in the West Bank] is negligible in both demographic and spatial terms." He concludes that the settlement project was "an illusion, rather than a vision . . . a pretentious scheme" that failed—and deserved to.[14]

Sociologist Gershon Shafir concurs. Drawing on Arieli's work, he reports that settlers account for 4.7 percent of Israel's population (though this makes their political potency even more impressive—or despair-inducing, depending on one's viewpoint). Shafir estimates that approximately 27,000 settler households would need to be evacuated for a viable two-state partition. That's a lot of people—but a minuscule proportion of Israel's Jewish population of over six million.[15]

Mouin Rabbani, a senior fellow at the Institute for Palestine Studies, argues that the two-state solution cannot be judged a failure because it was never tried. "There's no evidence that it has been seriously attempted, least of all in the context of the Oslo agreements," he told an interviewer in 2016. "There's no evidence it cannot be done."[16] In fact, as Walid Khalidi points out, it is the one-state framework that was "already tried . . . during the 30 years of the British Mandate, and we know what happened even though the balance of power was at first massively in favour of the Palestinians."[17]

The good news, then, is that the demographic facts can at least "demystify the irreversibility thesis," as Shafir writes.[18] The bad news is that the problem is not one of geography, arithmetic, or population statistics but of political will—which is, admittedly, the toughest thing to change, and which has always been at the crux of this conflict. Can Israelis and Palestinians overcome their irredentist illusions; can they exit from grandiose myth into prosaic reality?

For many proponents of the one-state solution, however, the facts—on the ground or elsewhere—are irrelevant. They are concerned not with the Occupation and 1967 but with what they view as the original sins of 1947 and 1948 (and even, in some cases, of 1917, the year of the Balfour Declaration). Israeli sovereignty—statehood for the Jewish people—is the problem, not the Occupation. "Zionism has never found justification in principles of political equality," writes Judith Butler, a prominent feminist academic, anti-Zionist, and BDS activist. "One cannot find solutions within its terms." Butler, an advocate of Palestinian return, writes that "it is not possible to restrict the problem of Palestinian subjugation to the occupation alone," for to do is to "forget the claims of 1948."[19]

Butler is honest about the fact that when she speaks of binationalism she means a single state where "Jewish Israelis would have to set aside their Jewishness." But she assures her readers that "dismantling the structure of Jewish sovereignty and demographic advantage" will "clearly

. . . be better for the Jews." In fact, such a dismantling will clearly be better for everyone, for it will "eradicate all forms of discrimination on the basis of ethnicity, race, and religion."[20] In this view, the destruction of an extant national community, which is usually considered an act of aggression, is now deemed a democratic project. (Jean Améry, in a 1976 speech to Germans in which he decried the New Left's anti-Zionism, described this as dialectical hocus-pocus.) Ariella Azoulay and Adi Ophir, two far-Left Israeli intellectuals who now live in the U.S., admit that the problems with any one-state entity include "the national question, differences of tradition and custom, aspirations and fears, traumatic memories and residues of hostility and hatred, anger and vengefulness." They are confident, however, that these could be "dealt with by organizations of civil society alongside state mechanisms that bear an equal responsibility to both nations."[21] Alas, I hear echoes of an equally confident Otto Heller and Abram Leon predicting the imminent end of anti-Semitism when I read statements like this.

One-state advocates consistently maintain that any such state must come about peacefully. "Stop using stones, bullets, and explosives," urges Lama Abu-Odeh, a Palestinian-American law professor based in the U.S., in an essay called "The Case for Binationalism."[22] I believe their commitment to nonviolence is genuine. But an air of unconvincing abstraction hovers over their proposals, and the details on offer do not bode well. In the *Middle East Journal,* Leila Farsakh, a Palestinian political economist who teaches in the U.S., suggests that Jews in the new state would constitute a "repentant entity" and be expected "to become *de facto* Palestinians."[23] This sounds a lot like the early PLO's generous offer to allow Jews to remain in Palestine after its so-called liberation if they renounced racist-imperialist Zionism, or of the Egyptian Marxist Mahmoud Hussein's plan to create a non-Zionist state "with the voluntary, conscious participation of the Israeli masses," who would join with Palestinian refugees to throw off the Zionist tyranny. Needless to say, the Israeli masses did not find these plans appealing, nor are they likely to do so now.

Equally useless—and unattractive—is BDS's policy of "non-normalization." This strategy, which bans any contact with Israel or Israelis, has been a long-standing practice in many Arab countries and, especially, among Arab intellectuals. Israelis haven't been hurt by this; its victims are prominent Arab writers, such as Lebanese-born Amin Maalouf, Algeria's

Boualem Sansal, and Egypt's Ali Salem, who have been vilified when they dared to cross the line. Palestinian-Israelis are boycotted too; writer Hisham Nafaa, who lives in Haifa, was refused a contract by a Lebanese publisher because, it explained, "We can't work with someone who holds an Israeli passport"—this from a country that has *denied* passports and citizenship to Palestinians, and segregated them in miserable camps, for over a half century.[24] Non-normalization confines Arab audiences to an airless anti-Zionist prison where, as in all prisons, debate is stifled and ignorance ensured. Ziad Doueiri, an immensely talented Lebanese filmmaker, has been declared "eternally" persona non grata by BDS because he shot part of a film in Israel; BDS prevented him from showing his subsequent movie—an allegory about the Lebanese Civil War that stars Palestinian actor Kamel El Basha—at a film festival in Ramallah. Such is the righteous morality—or, one might say, the idiocy—of non-normalization.

BDS claims to be a successor to the South African anti-apartheid struggle—a claim that, as Noam Chomsky and others have pointed out, rests on a series of counterfeit analogies. What's striking, though, is that non-normalization is the polar opposite of the South African movement's strategy and ethos. The African National Congress's leadership and allies included many whites, and it worked with a broad, multiracial united front of organizations. In contrast, BDS co-founder Omar Barghouti treats Jewish Israelis like carriers of a contagious disease; he refuses to even speak to Jewish Israeli journalists (unlike Palestinian organizations, including Hamas). One might well wonder how a presumably ethnically integrated state can be created through a movement based on ethnic segregation. Barghouti loves to quote Desmond Tutu and Nelson Mandela, but he isn't Desmond Tutu or Nelson Mandela; if he were South African, he wouldn't have even *talked* to Joe Slovo, the white (and Jewish) head of the South African Communist Party, the ANC's closest ally.[25] In this way as in others, BDS's attempt to leech onto the South African movement while obviating its content is an intellectual and moral sham. (I believe, however, that attempts to stifle the movement's right to speak and organize—whether by the Israel government or any other—are profoundly undemocratic and must be unreservedly opposed.)

And so, once again, we are slouching toward what Arthur Koestler called "cloud-cuckoo-land." Magically and mysteriously, the forced merger of two peoples—with a century of killing each other's children between them—will be peacefully accomplished and, moreover, lead to the establishment of a stable democratic polity. There is a frightening naiveté (at best) at work here—and naiveté has never been a friend to either Jews or Palestinians. This may be why Amos Oz regards one-state proposals as "a sad joke. After a hundred years of bloodshed, tears and agony, you cannot expect Israelis and Palestinians to jump into a honeymoon bed."[26] One-state advocates present themselves as hard-headed realists, but Oz likens their vision to a sentimental Hollywood movie and calls it kitsch.

At a conference in New York several years ago, I heard an anti-Zionist Jewish Israeli (yes, there are a few) praise the one-state entity. With curiosity, I approached him after his talk. This man was a learned academic with a firm grasp of history. Through what political process, I asked, will such a state come into being? What kind of army would it have, and how would Hamas's suicide bombers be incorporated into it? What kind of constitution would be written, and by whom? How would conflicts over education, the relation between religion and state, the legal system, and the status of women be adjudicated? What would its foreign policy be, and would it become a member of the Arab League? Somewhat sheepishly, he averred, "Well, it's not really possible—but it's a *good idea.*"

In the West, advocates of this good idea seem blissfully heedless of the fact that, in Israel, it is the province of the ultra-Left and what Oz calls "the loony Right"; the latter, unlike the former, is neither tiny nor powerless. (One problem with boycotts is that they prevent you from knowing what's going on.) The world, and especially the Middle East, offer many examples of states that have not, *pace* Butler, "eradicated all forms of discrimination," much less offered full political rights—and, in quite a few cases, *any* political rights. And in the Israeli Right's version of this plan—the only likely version, if there is one—equality of citizenship would be neither the goal nor the result. Uri Avnery, who was the first Israeli to secretly meet with Yasser Arafat (when doing so was illegal) and was founder of the anti-Occupation group Gush Shalom, explained what Western one-state activists and BDS might not understand:

> Since I witnessed the rise of the Nazis during my childhood in Germany, my nose always tickles when it smells something fascist, even when the odor is still faint.

> When the debate about the "one-state solution" began, my
> nose tickled.
> Have you gone mad, I told my nose, this time you are dead
> wrong. This is a plan of the Left. It is being put forward by
> leftists of undoubted credentials, the greatest idealists in Israel
> and abroad, even certified Marxists.
> But my nose insisted. It continued to tickle.
> Now it appears that the nose was right, after all.
> This is not the first time that a kosher leftist plan leads
> towards extreme rightist consequences.

Ethnic cleansing, Avnery wrote, is the "final stage" of the one-state plan, which is one reason why, like Chomsky, he considered it a gift to the Right. There is nothing in the domestic Israeli balance of political power to suggest that a leftist variant would triumph; there is overwhelming evidence that it would not. To believe otherwise is to be hostage to an unwarranted sense of self-aggrandizement: exactly the mistake that the PLO, egged on by its supporters, made for so many years. Citing the horror movie *Rosemary's Baby*, Avnery concluded, "The attractive leftist vision of the one-state solution may grow up into a rightist monster."[27]

In other words, a one-state *Israel* will mean Israeli sovereignty over all of Mandatory Palestine, with Palestinians in the West Bank as noncitizens. (It will not be binational.) A one-state *Palestine,* as Halliday, Chomsky, and others have pointed out, will mean an Arab state, with Jews as a presumably protected minority. (It will not be binational.) These states would be radically different yet essentially the same. Each means the death of the Zionist project, and neither would be even remotely democratic.

Various kinds of power differentials and inequalities between Israelis and Palestinians are often downplayed or repressed by one-state proponents, as if the acknowledgment of reality—that is, of politics—is an insult. The less powerful will suffer for this. Walid Khalidi warns that given the chasm in power and organization between Israelis and Palestinians, in a one-state entity "the Palestinians would be lucky if they had enough land to plant onions in their back gardens and to bury their dead alongside." He exhorts BDS to give up its one-state illusions and focus on ending the Occupation instead of on "delegitimising Israel itself."[28] Hussein Agha, an Oxford University academic who has represented the Palestinians in negotiations with Israel, cautions that "a utopian binational democratic secular state" would turn out quite differently than its proponents imagine. In light of the Israelis' "vast resources and superior development," Palestinians "would be transformed into an underclass." He explains, "The people on the Palestinian side who talk about the one-state solution do not consider the realities of how that state would function. They do not realize that a binational state would only accentuate their grievances."[29]

But it is detestation of Zionism per se, not defense of the Palestinians, that often inspires the one-staters, especially among leftists in the West. In this view, Jewish political power is unhealthy, unholy, even evil—"an ideological excrescence" indeed. Hannah Arendt expressed this aversion when she castigated Israeli self-defense in the 1948 war, proposing a contorted, unworkable series of imagined entities—anything, anything other than a state. For some, statehood for the Jewish people is *uniquely* tainted, which is why Maxime Rodinson could denounce Zionism as reactionary while affirming that "the nationalism of an oppressed nation"—he was definitely not thinking of the Jews—"must be supported in its essential aim." Isaac Deutscher took a comparable position when he castigated the Israelis for winning the 1967 war while praising "the Arab peoples struggling for their emancipation." Weren't the Israelis struggling for their survival?

Butler expresses this repugnance toward Zionism when she lovingly looks back to a pre-state past: "It is not the Moses who leads the people out of the wilderness who is most important here, but rather the one who *wanders,* a motif that is affirmed time and again by Jewish philosophers."[30] Far be it from me to disparage the Diaspora, of which I am a member; it has indisputably been a brilliant contributor to the making of the modern world. But I do not wander (neither does Butler), though my Lithuanian and Russian grandparents did, and it was not an ennobling motif for them. Exilic nostalgia overlooks too many centuries of ghettoization, grinding poverty, exclusion, expulsion, slaughter, genocide—not to mention despair, fear, and shame. (In 1930, the French journalist Albert Londres reported on the despised, supine "Wandering Jews" of Eastern Europe: "A thick layer of hatred covers them like stone.")[31] It is unclear why Butler and others regard Palestinian statelessness as Bad (it is) and Jewish statelessness as Good (it wasn't). Wistfulness for the Jewish past prefers the ether to the earth; it refuses the basic ethical demand of what Gershom Scholem called "living responsibly, inside history."[32]

It also refuses to honor, or at least recognize, Israel's cultural, political, scientific, and intellectual accomplishments, and the ways it has transformed the existential condition of the Jewish people. (Londres, again, arriving in Tel Aviv: "Heads uncovered, clean-shaven, . . . and chests raised high. . . . It's a miracle! Their backbones have straightened.")[33] And it's hard not to notice that wandering hasn't worked well for the millions of now-stateless refugees from the Middle East, Africa, and elsewhere. Most people want a home where they can grow roots, develop their cultural-national values, and feel safe; when the Left denies this, it simply strengthens the Right. The glories of nomadism are celebrated mainly by people who are not nomads.

There is a long-standing debate as to whether critics of Israel are necessarily anti-Semitic. Of course they are not—just as critics of affirmative action or of looser immigration policies are not always racists or Islamophobes. But sometimes they are. This point seems self-evident, and therefore a diversion from important issues. Neither Noam Chomsky nor Judith Butler is an anti-Semite; on the contrary, each identifies strongly with aspects of Jewish culture and with the Jewish people. The question isn't what lies in their hearts but, rather, whether their analyses of the conflict are correct and whether their proposed solutions will grievously harm that people. I believe the answer to the first question is no and to the second is yes. And, I admit, I am flummoxed by those who see no conceivable connection between contemporary animus toward Israel and centuries of animus to the Jewish people itself.

Ironically, some versions of anti-Zionism—by which I mean opposition to a democratic state for the Jewish people—are, in their own way, an assertion of Jewish superiority. Max Horkheimer (though not an anti-Zionist after the Shoah) expressed this thought when he wrote, in the early 1960s, "Jewry was not a powerful state but the hope for justice at the end of the world. They were a people and its opposite, a rebuke to all peoples. Now, a state claims to be speaking for Jewry. . . . How profound a resignation in the very triumph of its temporal success."[34] There is something beautiful in this thought, and something dangerous; it is a secular version of the "chosen people" idea, which Albert Memmi criticized and which secular Zionism aimed, but failed, to abolish. It suggests that the Jewish people are extraterrestrial messengers of knowledge, or modernity, or ethics, or spiritual values—anything but an actual people living in an actual place. As Robert Alter observed shortly after the Six-Day War, many intellectuals—he cited I. F. Stone in particular—are "intensely uncomfortable with the idea that the Jews should want and have a flesh-and-blood existence as a people in the real geography of this world."[35]

The very idea of Jewish political power makes many people I know, especially fellow Jews, squirm with discomfort. Self-determination is fine, except for us: We are above such selfish, mundane needs. The problem is that a reading of Jewish history—an *experience* of Jewish history—cannot support this view. This does not mean that statehood, much less the state, should be an object of worship. But it is puzzling, especially in the context of the Middle East—the world's most unstable and violent region—that it is the Jews who are being urged, not for the first time, to reject (or is it "transcend"?) unnecessary, anachronistic statehood in favor of a metaphysical universalism that none of their neighbors practice.

For many Western leftists, justifiable fury over the Occupation has led, albeit mistakenly, to anti-Zionism. But for others, opposing Israel's very existence, and boycotting it, are what the journalist Tom Wolfe called "status life" symbols. Liberal or radical American Jews, in particular, seem to find Israelis embarrassing (so intense! so nationalistic! so paranoid!), much in the way that Arthur Koestler was mortified by his Eastern brethren (so poor! so religious! so backward!). Contemporary anti-Zionism is a way to project that you are not a racist or an imperialist—especially important to the British, given their racist, imperialist history—and, heaven forbid, not an Orientalist. It is a way to show that you are allied with the victims, the non-whites, the colonized, that you belong to the club of the good guys; it is a way to show that you are woke. It conveys, that is, a series of feel-good attitudes about yourself, often without having the faintest knowledge of the histories, much less the political realities, that you are addressing.

There is a weird symmetry between the Israeli settlers and the Palestinian revanchists; although they are deadly enemies, they share a worldview. Each is a prisoner of 1948 (and earlier). The settlers believe that a sovereign nation can act like an accordion, expanding at will after statehood has been established. This land fetish is the negation, rather than the fulfillment, of political Zionism; it has turned Israel into a deviant state. The Palestinian irredentists believe they can return to, and perhaps recreate, a pre-1948 Palestine, as if the events of the past seven decades could be erased—and as if they had no role in how those events transpired.

The symmetry is not, however, equal. Israelis have attained a state and Palestinians haven't; and with statehood comes responsibility for one's fate. Despite the external threats (see under: Hezbollah), Israel's internal perils may now be most serious. It is up to Israel to save itself from a future of what David Grossman called "a binational state, or an apartheid state, or a state of all its soldiers, or a state of all its rabbis, all its settlers, all its messiahs."[36] It is up to Israeli democracy (despite its many failures, I do not enclose that term in sarcastic quotes) to rescue itself, reassert itself, revive itself, improve itself, before it is too late. The political task it faces is to convince the Israeli center that ending the Occupation is in its own *self*-interest without downplaying the attendant, undeniable risks and uncertainties.

I do not know if Israel can or will reclaim its democracy. Perhaps it is already too late; if so, the hope that motivates this book is a lament. And if that democratic revival does fail—which, in my view, means the suicide of Zionism—Israelis will have only themselves to blame. Certainly the Nation-State Law—which narrowly passed the Knesset in July 2018 and was opposed not only by the Zionist Left and the Arab Joint List but by many centrists and, even, Israel's president—was a horrible leap backwards. (Contravening Israel's Declaration of Independence, with its clarion assertion of equality for all citizens, the new law stresses exclusion; one centrist lawmaker described it as "a poison pill for democracy.")[37] But, especially in America, it is up to those who consider themselves progressives, liberals, humanists, or leftists to try their hardest to strengthen Israel's democratic organizations—especially since a series of U.S. governments, along with the American Jewish community, have been the indispensable enablers of the settlement movement. In place of boycotting, this means supporting groups on the ground who are fighting for Israeli democracy and Palestinian rights, such as Combatants for Peace, Breaking the Silence, B'Tselem, Peace Now, MachsomWatch, and Blue White Future. (Why should we allow Jared Kushner and Sheldon Adelson to define the term "pro-Israel"?) Of course, condemning Israel in full is a lot easier, and more thrillingly theatrical, than making crucial political distinctions. But, logically speaking, it is hard to see how boycotting Israel will ply voters away from the Likud any more than boycotting the U.S. would convince Americans to abandon Donald Trump.

Ending the Occupation is the necessary condition for Israel's political-moral reclamation. However, it is doubtful that doing so will heal the furious divisions within either the Israeli or the Palestinian community. On the contrary: For each, war unites, peace plans divide. ("In the Israeli-Palestinian conflict the possibility of peace without agony was missed long ago," Shlomo Ben-Ami wrote in 2006.)[38] Nor will an end to the Occupation mean the end of the conflict: There will be no peace now. Yet it is the prerequisite for anything and everything else.

Nissim Calderon, an Israeli writer and longtime anti-Occupation activist, explains, "A situation of no Occupation and no peace will be much better than the present one. We will not be the rulers of people who hate us, we will not deny their right to self-determination, we will care only about security on the border. The advantages of non-Occupation without peace are enormous: at last a fixed, internationally recognized border to the State of Israel; saving the Jewish democratic state; and weakening the fascist and undemocratic tendencies in Israeli society."[39] Hussein Agha agrees that the conflict will continue beyond the establishment of a Palestinian state—to which, he says, many Palestinians are not necessarily oriented. But he too urges, "Let's end the occupation, have two states, and at the same time address those other, deeper issues to try to achieve a genuine resolution of the conflict. What shape that will take, I really do not know. It's not something that can be dealt with in a prearranged plan. We have to find creative ways."[40] Agha's ability to reject false certainties, and his *openness* to the future, are all too rare and desperately needed. Some on the Zionist Left are also trying to devise new ways of configuring the future; Bernard Avishai, for instance, has proposed a confederation of two states—independent political entities that would work closely together on security, water, the environment, and the economy.

In 1981, Fred Halliday broke with many of his friends on the left when he published his essay called "Revolutionary Realism and the Struggle for Palestine." He noted that denial of Israelis' right to statehood was so fundamental to the New Left that the assumption didn't need to even be articulated, much less argued.

By "revolutionary realism," Halliday did not mean a passive acceptance of facts on the ground or a Kissinger-esque policy of realpolitik. For Halliday, realism meant what he called mature internationalism: the rejection of escapist fantasies, rewritten histories, and utopian schemes that lead to catastrophe—not for the stronger party but for the weak. Rather than dividing Israeli and Palestinian nationalisms into evil and noble, Halliday insisted that the only ethically defensible—*and* realistic—position was support for each group's claim to national dignity and self-determination. It was the Palestinians, he warned, who would pay a steep price if the one-state illusion was pursued, even if that illusion was swathed in friendly terms like democratic, secular, binational, socialist, or the right of return.

Everything Halliday wrote then remains true. He, too, believed in living responsibly, inside history.

The opposite of realism isn't principle; it is pathology. To reject realism makes you—and your children—into slaves of the past and strangers to the future.

NOTES

INTRODUCTION

1. The quote is from Judith Butler, who added that it was important to raise "the question of whether there are other options besides violence." While morally admirable, this makes her statement even less comprehensible, since Hamas and Hezbollah proclaim that the violent destruction of Israel is their central mission. The Labour leader is Jeremy Corbyn.

2. Jacqueline Rose, *The Question of Zion* (Princeton: Princeton University Press, 2005), 17; see also 98, 55.

3. This refers to statements by Linda Sarsour.

4. A notable exception was journalist Vincent Sheean.

5. Harry Hanson, "Britain and the Arabs," *New Reasoner* (Autumn 1958): 4.

6. Associated Press, August 16, 1967.

7. Keith P. Feldman, *A Shadow over Palestine: The Imperial Life of Race in America* (Minneapolis: University of Minnesota Press, 2015), 72, 77, 81.

8. Hans Kundnani, *Utopia or Auschwitz: Germany's 1968 Generation and the Holocaust* (London: Hurst, 2009), 49.

9. Simcha Flapan, *The Arab-Israeli War of 1967 (A Reply to Isaac Deutscher)* (Tel Aviv: International Department of the United Workers' Party—MAPAM, 1968), 14. The United States' strong alliance with Israel developed after the 1967 war and, especially, after the 1970 battle between Jordan and the PLO. Israel had no dependable allies in the 1967 war; at the time, it was reasonable to speak of the country as nonaligned.

10. Enzo Traverso, *The End of Jewish Modernity*, trans. David Fernbach (London: Pluto Press, 2016), 83.

11. Fouad Ajami, *The Dream Palace of the Arabs: A Generation's Odyssey* (New York: Pantheon, 1998), xvi.

12. Traverso, *End of Jewish Modernity*, 16, 17, 104, 103.
13. See Stanley Aronowitz, "Setting the Record Straight: Zionism from the Standpoint of Its Jewish Critics," *Logos*, Summer 2004; Perry Anderson, "The House of Zion," *New Left Review* 96 (November–December 2015); also Traverso in *End of Jewish Modernity*.
14. Benny Morris, *Righteous Victims: A History of the Zionist-Arab Conflict, 1881–2001* (New York: Vintage, 2001), 91.
15. Shlomo Ben-Ami, *Scars of War, Wounds of Peace: The Israeli-Arab Tragedy* (New York: Oxford University Press, 2006), 15.
16. Mervyn Jones, "Israel, Palestine and Socialism," *Socialist Register* 7 (1970): 63, 65.

1. ARENDT

1. The first quote is from Amnon Raz-Krakotzkin, "Jewish Peoplehood, 'Jewish Politics,' and Political Responsibility: Arendt on Zionism and Partitions." *College Literature* 38, no. 1 (Winter 2011): 63; the next two from Jeffrey Isaac, *Arendt, Camus, and Modern Rebellion* (New Haven: Yale University Press, 1992), 211–12; the last from Gabriel Piterberg, "Zion's Rebel Daughter: Hannah Arendt on Palestine and Jewish Politics," *New Left Review* 48 (November–December 2007): 55.
2. See, for instance, Sol Stern, "Hannah Arendt and the Origins of Israelophobia," *City Journal* (Winter 2012).
3. Hannah Arendt, *The Jewish Writings*, ed. Jerome Kohn and Ron H. Feldman (New York: Schocken, 2007), 129.
4. Jewish Virtual Library, "Hannah Arendt, 1906–1975," http://www.jewishvirtuallibrary.org/hannah-arendt.
5. Lotte Kohler and Hans Saner, eds., *Hannah Arendt/Karl Jaspers Correspondence, 1926–1969*, trans. Robert and Rita Kimber (New York: Harcourt Brace, 1992), 197.
6. Max Horkheimer, "The Jews and Europe," in *Critical Theory and Society: A Reader*, ed. Stephen Bronner and Douglas Kellner (New York: Routledge, 1989), 90, 91. To his credit, Horkheimer would later develop a far richer analysis of anti-Semitism and disown this essay; it was reprinted, over his objections, in the late 1960s by German New Leftists who adopted its analysis.
7. Elisabeth Young-Bruehl, *Hannah Arendt: For Love of the World* (New Haven: Yale University Press, 1982), 109, italics in original.
8. Hans Jonas, *Hans Jonas: Memoirs*, ed. Christian Wiese, trans. Krishna Winston. (Lebanon, NH: Brandeis University Press, 2008), 178.
9. Bernard Lazare, *Antisemitism: Its History and Causes*, ed. Robert Wistrich (Lincoln: University of Nebraska Press, 1995), 142, 152, 156.
10. Heinrich Graetz, *The Structure of Jewish History and Other Essays*, ed. and trans. Ismar Schorsch (New York: Jewish Theological Seminary of America, 1975), 70, 94.
11. David Biale, *Power and Powerlessness in Jewish History* (New York: Schocken Books, 1986), 6.

12. Hannah Arendt, *The Origins of Totalitarianism* (Cleveland and New York: Meridian Books, 1962) [orig. 1951], 8.

13. Arendt, *Jewish Writings*, 378.

14. Ibid., 315.

15. Yuri Slezkine, *The Jewish Century* (Princeton: Princeton University Press, 2004), 1, 2.

16. Hannah Arendt, *Essays in Understanding* (New York: Harcourt Brace, 1994), 12.

17. Arendt, *Origins of Totalitarianism*, 120, emphasis added.

18. Arendt, *Jewish Writings*, 146, 143.

19. Lotte Kohler, ed., *Within Four Walls: The Correspondence between Hannah Arendt and Heinrich Blücher, 1936–1968*, trans. Peter Constantine (New York: Harcourt, 2000), 20.

20. Arendt, *Jewish Writings*, 182, 184, 164.

21. Ibid., 394.

22. Ibid., 434.

23. Ibid., 434–35, 437, 434.

24. Ibid., 435.

25. Zeev Sternhell, *The Founding Myths of Israel: Nationalism, Socialism, and the Making of the Jewish State*, trans. David Maisel (Princeton: Princeton University Press, 1998), 47.

26. Bernard Lazare, *Job's Dungheap* (New York: Schocken, 1948), 42–43, 99, 43.

27. Sternhell, *Founding Myths of Israel*, 47.

28. Arendt, *Jewish Writings*, 218, 262.

29. Ibid., 163, 137.

30. Kohler and Saner, eds., *Hannah Arendt/Karl Jaspers Correspondence*, 410. At a party in 1945, Arendt told Mary McCarthy that she had been sent to a concentration camp, though she later admitted this wasn't true.

31. Arendt, *Jewish Writings*, 137; 255–56, italics in original; 263.

32. Elhanan Yakira, *Post-Zionism, Post-Holocaust: Three Essays on Denial, Forgetting, and the Delegitimation of Israel*, trans. Michael Swirsky (Cambridge: Cambridge University Press, 2010), 254–55.

33. Arendt, *Jewish Writings*, 227–28. Toward the end of the war, the British army did form a Jewish Brigade, which liberated a few of the camps.

34. Arendt, *Jewish Writings*, 145.

35. Ibid., 138–39.

36. Ibid., 166.

37. Kohler and Saner, eds., *Hannah Arendt/Karl Jaspers Correspondence*, 98.

38. Arendt, *Jewish Writings*, 376, 377.

39. Ibid., 384, 339.

40. Ibid., 55, 353.

41. The Peel Commission of 1937, for instance, noted that "the zeal shown by the fellaheen in the late disturbances was religious and fundamentally in the nature of a Holy War." See Benny Morris, *One State, Two States: Resolving the Israel/Palestine Conflict* (New Haven: Yale University Press, 2009), 52.

42. Jacqueline Rose, *The Question of Zion* (Princeton: Princeton University Press, 2005), 86.

43. Arendt, *Jewish Writings*, 431, 432, 434, 184, 170.

44. Ibid., 424–25.

45. Ibid., 343, 347.

46. George Lichtheim, *The Concept of Ideology and Other Essays* (New York: Vintage, 1967), 117. Lichtheim was referring specifically to Arendt's *On Revolution*.

47. George Prochnik, *Stranger in a Strange Land: Searching for Gershom Scholem and Jerusalem* (New York: Other Press, 2016), 305.

48. John B. Judis, *Genesis: Truman, American Jews, and the Origins of the Arab/Israeli Conflict* (New York: Farrar, Straus and Giroux, 2014), 215. For other historians, see Walter Laqueur, *A History of Zionism;* Benny Morris, *One State, Two States;* Neil Caplan, *Failed Diplomacy;* Tom Segev, *One Palestine, Complete: Jews and Arabs Under the British Mandate;* Yoav Peled, "Zionist Realities," *New Left Review* 38 (March–April 2006), http://newleftreview.org/II/38/yoav-peled-zionist-realities-debating-israel-palestine.

49. Arendt, *Jewish Writings,* 197.

50. J. Bowyer Bell, *The Long War: Israel and the Arabs since 1946* (Englewood Cliffs, NJ: Prentice-Hall, 1969), 35.

51. Seyla Benhabib, *The Reluctant Modernism of Hannah Arendt* (Thousand Oaks, CA: Sage Publications, 1996), 39.

52. Arendt, *Jewish Writings,* 352, 366, 371.

53. Ibid., 360, 436. Arendt's criticisms here are particularly puzzling in light of her celebratory writings on the American Revolution, in which she posited state-founding as the sine qua non of political freedom.

54. Ibid., 350, 351.

55. Ibid., 349.

56. See, for instance, Chapter 3 of Dagmar Barnouw's *Visible Spaces: Hannah Arendt and the German-Jewish Experience* (Baltimore: Johns Hopkins University Press, 1990).

57. Arendt, *Jewish Writings,* 395, 401, 389.

58. Nir Hasson, "A Fight to the Death, and Betrayal by the Arab World: The Most Disastrous 24 Hours in Palestinian History," *Haaretz,* January 25, 2018, https://www.haaretz.com/middle-east-news/palestinians/.premium-1.833130.

59. I. F. Stone, *This Is Israel* (New York: Boni and Gaer, 1948), 21. Azzam Bey's threat has been widely quoted, including in the Egyptian daily *Akhbar al-Yom* on October 11, 1947. See also Benny Morris, *Righteous Victims: A History of the Arab-Israeli Conflict, 1881–2001* (New York: Vintage Books, 2001), 219.

60. Arendt, *Jewish Writings,* 385–86; Hannah Arendt, *Eichmann in Jerusalem: A Report on the Banality of Evil* (New York: Penguin, 1977) [orig. 1963], 226.

61. Arendt, *Jewish Writings,* 398.

62. See, for instance, Jacqueline Rose's praise of Arendt's "uncanny prescience" in *The Question of Zion,* 84.

63. Arendt, *Jewish Writings*, 397.

64. Ibid., 399.

65. Ibid., 425.

66. Ibid., 423, italics in original; 429, 450.

67. Ibid., 428.

68. Hannah Arendt, *On Revolution* (New York: Penguin Books, 1990) [orig. 1963], 257. This was a somewhat strange accusation in light of the Bolshevik victory in 1917, which suggests that Lenin's party had, indeed, learned a few things in the intervening years.

69. Arendt, *Jewish Writings*, 447.

70. Ibid., 450.

71. Judith N. Shklar, *Political Thought and Political Thinkers* (Chicago: University of Chicago Press, 1998), 367.

72. Gershom Scholem, *A Life in Letters, 1914–1982*, trans. Anthony David Skinner (Cambridge: Harvard University Press, 2002), 331.

73. Ibid., 330, 332.

74. Ibid., 332.

75. Arendt, *Jewish Writings*, 254.

76. Hannah Arendt, *Between Past and Future: Eight Exercises in Political Thought* (New York: Penguin, 1993), 221.

77. Hannah Arendt, "Introduction: Walter Benjamin, 1892–1940," in Walter Benjamin, *Illuminations*, trans. Harry Zohn (London: Fontana, 1973), 33; Richard J. Bernstein, *Hannah Arendt and the Jewish Question* (Cambridge: MIT Press, 1996), opening page.

78. Arendt, "Introduction," in Benjamin, *Illuminations*, 15.

79. Arendt, *Jewish Writings*, 265.

80. Arendt, *Origins of Totalitarianism*, 267.

81. Ibid., 291–92, 299–300.

82. Ibid., 230–31.

83. Arendt, *Jewish Writings*, 130.

84. Shklar, *Political Thought and Political Thinkers*, 371.

85. Joel Schalit, *Israel vs. Utopia* (New York: Akashic Books, 2009), 29, 33–34.

86. Young-Bruehl, *For Love of the World*, 229.

87. Benhabib, *Reluctant Modernism of Hannah Arendt*, 43.

88. Hannah Arendt, "A Heroine of Revolution," *New York Review of Books*, October 6, 1966, http://www.nybooks.com/articles/1966/10/06/a-heroine-of-revolution/; italics in original.

89. Arendt, *Origins of Totalitarianism*, 40–41.

90. As she wrote to Scholem in 1946: "I have never been a Marxist (nor have I ever been 'dialectical'). People here generally regard me as an anti-Marxist, which is far closer to the truth." She would reiterate this during the Eichmann controversy: "I do not belong to 'the intellectuals coming from the German left.' " See Scholem, *Life in Letters*, 333 and 398.

91. Lazare, *Job's Dungheap*, 73, 75.

92. Young-Bruehl, *For Love of the World*, 38; Steven Aschheim, "Introduction," in Steven Aschheim, ed., *Hannah Arendt in Jerusalem* (Berkeley: University of California Press, 2001), 4.

93. Jewish Virtual Library, "Hannah Arendt, 1906–1975."

94. Hannah Arendt, *Rahel Varnhagen: The Life of a Jewess*, ed. Liliane Weissberg, trans. Richard and Clara Winston (Baltimore: Johns Hopkins University Press, 1997) [orig. 1958], 244, 248–49, 241, 244.

95. Arendt, "Heroine of Revolution."

96. Arendt, *Jew as Pariah*, 72, 75.

97. Arendt, *Jewish Writings*, 274.

98. Arendt, "Introduction," in Benjamin, *Illuminations*, 19.

99. Young-Bruehl, *For Love of the World*, 39; Benhabib, *Reluctant Modernism of Hannah Arendt*, 10–11.

100. Young-Bruehl, *For Love of the World*, 295.

101. Hans Jonas, "Hannah Arendt, 1906–1975," *Social Research* 43, no. 1 (Spring 1976): 3.

102. Kohler and Saner, eds., *Hannah Arendt/Karl Jaspers Correspondence*, 511, 527.

103. Carol Brightman, ed., *Between Friends: The Correspondence of Hannah Arendt and Mary McCarthy, 1949–1975* (New York: Harcourt Brace, 1995), 148, emphasis added; 146.

104. Ibid., 136.

105. Arendt, *Jewish Writings*, 470.

106. Ibid., 470.

107. Arendt, *Jew as Pariah*, 78.

108. Ibid., 76.

109. Ibid., 78.

110. Ibid., 77, emphasis added; 78.

111. Ibid., 90.

112. Kohler and Saner, eds., *Hannah Arendt/Karl Jaspers Correspondence*, 632.

113. Ibid., 518.

114. Jonas, *Memoirs*, 180.

115. Edna Brocke, " 'Big Hannah'—My Aunt," in Arendt, *Jewish Writings*, 515.

116. Scholem, *Life in Letters*, 434.

117. Young-Bruehl, *For Love of the World*, 184.

118. Michael Walzer, *The Company of Critics: Social Criticism and Political Commitment in the Twentieth Century* (New York: Basic Books, 2002), xii–xiii, xv.

119. Kohler, ed., *Within Four Walls*, 283, 282.

120. Young-Bruehl, *For Love of the World*, 291.

121. Arendt, *Eichmann in Jerusalem*, 258, 287, 125.

122. Kohler and Saner, eds., *Hannah Arendt/Karl Jaspers Correspondence*, 413, 420, 413.

123. Ibid., 420, 424, 419; 425, italics in original.

124. Ibid., 415.

125. Ibid., 415, 423.
126. Ibid., 417, 435, 410.
127. Ibid., 417, 435, 410, 417.
128. Arendt, *Eichmann in Jerusalem*, 3, 10, 11.
129. Ibid., 40, 61, 63.
130. Raz-Krakotzkin, "Jewish Peoplehood, 'Jewish Politics,' " 72.
131. Kohler and Saner, eds., *Hannah Arendt/Karl Jaspers Correspondence*, 435.
132. Kohler, ed., *Within Four Walls*, 354–55.
133. Kohler and Saner, eds., *Hannah Arendt/Karl Jaspers Correspondence*, 434; Kohler, ed., *Within Four Walls*, 358.
134. Arendt, *Jewish Writings*, 488. Arendt's contempt for Israel was typical of many German Jews, including those who had settled in Palestine during the Hitler years. The Israeli journalist Azriel Karlebach (himself of German origin) observed in 1943, "They flock around the shallow water of the yishuv, lapping at it with the tips of their tongues, then turn away with expressions of disgust, muttering daintily about the stench." Tom Segev, *The Seventh Million: The Israelis and the Holocaust*, trans. Haim Watzman (New York: Hill and Wang, 1993), 51.
135. Kohler, ed., *Within Four Walls*, 357.
136. Kohler and Saner, eds., *Hannah Arendt/Karl Jaspers Correspondence, 1926–1969*, 435.
137. Kohler, ed., *Within Four Walls*, 357.
138. Kohler and Saner, eds., *Hannah Arendt/Karl Jaspers Correspondence, 1926–1969*, 435, 434, 436.
139. Arendt, *Eichmann in Jerusalem*, 5.
140. Kohler, ed., *Within Four Walls*, 363.
141. Arendt complained that "the Jerusalem trial failed to put before the eyes of the world" the question of the Jewish Councils "in its true dimensions," but admitted that she nevertheless "dwelt" on it. Arendt, *Eichmann in Jerusalem*, 125.
142. Kohler, ed., *Within Four Walls*, 358.
143. Deborah E. Lipstadt, *The Eichmann Trial* (New York: Schocken Books, 2011), 180.
144. Kohler and Saner, eds., *Hannah Arendt/Karl Jaspers Correspondence*, 434.
145. Arendt, *Eichmann in Jerusalem*, 229.
146. Kohler, ed., *Within Four Walls*, 364.
147. Arendt, *Eichmann in Jerusalem*, 5, 9.
148. Ibid., 249. Arendt was quoting from the judges' ruling.
149. Arendt, *On Revolution*, 86, 222, 88, 89, 88.
150. Arendt, *Eichmann in Jerusalem*, 269, 268.
151. Ibid., 272.
152. Yakira, *Post-Zionism, Post-Holocaust*, 300.
153. Segev, *Seventh Million*, 351.
154. Leora Bilsky, "Between Justice and Politics," in Aschheim, ed., *Hannah Arendt in Jerusalem* (Berkeley: University of California Press, 2001), 250.

155. Haim Gouri, *Facing the Glass Booth: The Jerusalem Trial of Adolf Eichmann,* trans. Michael Swirsky (Detroit: Wayne State University Press, 2004) [orig. 1962], 31, 33. Gouri focuses less than Arendt on the role of the Jewish Councils and more on the refusal of the Allies to try to halt the genocide. But he also repeatedly raises the painful question of whether the Yishuv could have done more to save its brethren: "We shall not at this point call ourselves, too, to account, although some day, heaven help us, we shall have to do so." See Gouri, 103.

156. Martha Gellhorn, "Eichmann and the Private Conscience," *Atlantic Monthly* (February 1962), http://www.theatlantic.com/past/docs/issues/62feb/eichmann.htm.

157. Gouri, *Facing the Glass Booth,* 200.

158. Arendt, *Eichmann in Jerusalem,* 223, 224.

159. Ibid., 267.

160. Kohler and Saner, eds., *Hannah Arendt/Karl Jaspers Correspondence, 1926–1969,* 541.

161. Benhabib, *Reluctant Modernism of Hannah Arendt,* 176.

162. Arendt, *Eichmann in Jerusalem,* 4, and see also 5–9.

163. Ibid., 6, 9.

164. Ibid., 59, 61.

165. Primo Levi, *Survival in Auschwitz,* trans. Stuart Woolf (New York: Simon and Schuster, 1996) [orig. 1947], poem unpaged.

166. See Young-Bruehl, *For Love of the World,* 363.

167. Mary McCarthy, "The Hue and Cry," *Partisan Review* 31, no. 1 (1964): 86, 83.

168. Arendt, *Eichmann in Jerusalem,* 117.

169. Kohler and Saner, eds., *Hannah Arendt/Karl Jaspers Correspondence,* 530.

170. Ibid., 626.

171. Levi, *Survival in Auschwitz,* 129–30.

172. Ibid., 26, 51, 55, 91, 143–44.

173. Ibid., 149–50.

174. Arendt, *Eichmann in Jerusalem,* 131. Arendt was not referring specifically to the camps, but to Jewish society more generally.

175. Michael André Bernstein, "A Yes or a No," *New Republic,* September 27, 1999, 35–41.

176. Arendt, *Eichmann in Jerusalem,* 4.

177. Arendt's equally famous riposte to Scholem—"I don't love the Jews . . . I *belong to* this people"—is often cited by her admirers as a wonderful example of cosmopolitan, non-tribal identity. But these admirers almost always ignore the rest of Arendt's reply, which is nothing less than a rejection of secular political action. Arendt recounts a conversation with Golda Meir in which the latter explained, "as a socialist I do not believe in God. I believe in the Jewish people." Arendt calls this "a horrible comment" and continues, "The magnificence of this people once lay in its belief in God. . . . And now this people believes only in itself?" This is somewhat astonishing in light of Arendt's vilification of Jewish passivity and "worldlessness," and her

demand for Jewish political agency. See Arendt to Scholem, July 20, 1963, in Scholem, *Life in Letters*, 399, italics in original.

178. Dan Diner, *Beyond the Conceivable: Studies on Germany, Nazism, and the Holocaust* (Berkeley: University of California Press, 2000), 116.

179. Young-Bruehl, *For Love of the World*, 329; Brightman, ed., *Between Friends*, 168.

180. McCarthy, "Hue and Cry," 91.

181. Young-Bruehl, *For Love of the World*, 361.

182. Kohler and Saner, eds, *Hannah Arendt/Karl Jaspers Correspondence*, 672, 674–75.

183. Young-Bruehl, *For Love of the World*, 456.

184. Brightman, ed., *Between Friends*, 249.

185. Kohler and Saner, ed., *Hannah Arendt/Karl Jaspers Correspondence*, 593.

2. KOESTLER

1. Arthur Koestler, *Promise and Fulfilment: Palestine, 1917–1949* (London: Macmillan, 1949), 194.

2. Arthur Koestler, *Arrow in the Blue: An Autobiography* (New York: Macmillan, 1961) [orig. 1952], 110–11, 205.

3. Arthur Koestler, *Thieves in the Night: Chronicle of an Experiment* (London: Macmillan, 1961), 279, 295.

4. Koestler, *Arrow in the Blue*, 199; Koestler, *Promise and Fulfilment*, 325.

5. Granville Hicks, "Arthur Koestler and the Future of the Left," *Antioch Review* 5, no. 2 (Summer 1945). Snyder's quote can be found on the back cover of Michael Scammell's biography, *Koestler: The Literary and Political Odyssey of a Twentieth-Century Skeptic* (New York: Random House, 2009).

6. Arthur Koestler, *The Invisible Writing: An Autobiography* (New York: Macmillan, 1954), 155.

7. Murray A. Sperber, ed., *Arthur Koestler: A Collection of Critical Essays* (Englewood Cliffs, NJ: Prentice-Hall, 1977), 67, 37.

8. Irving Howe, *Politics and the Novel* (New York: New American Library, 1987) [orig. 1957], 227.

9. David Cesarani, *Arthur Koestler: The Homeless Mind* (New York: Free Press, 1998), 71.

10. Ibid., 397.

11. Koestler, *Arrow in the Blue*, 99.

12. Ibid., 107.

13. Arthur Koestler, *The Yogi and the Commissar* (New York: Macmillan, 1945), v.

14. Mark Levene, *Arthur Koestler* (New York: Frederick Ungar, 1984), 1.

15. Hyam Maccoby, "Koestler's Racism," *Midstream* 23, no. 3 (March 1977): 31.

16. Scammell, *Koestler*, 282, 336.

17. Koestler, *Arrow in the Blue*, 280.

18. Cesarani, *Arthur Koestler*, 12.

19. Scammell, *Koestler*, 24, 42.

20. Cesarani, *Arthur Koestler*, 227.

21. Koestler, *Invisible Writing*, 210.
22. Sperber, ed., *Arthur Koestler: A Collection of Critical Essays*, 107–8.
23. Bernard Avishai, "Koestler and the Zionist Revolution," *Salmagundi*, no. 87 (Summer 1990): 244.
24. Koestler, *Arrow in the Blue*, 95.
25. Ibid., 87, 91.
26. Ibid., 115.
27. Amos Oz, "Meaning of Homeland," *New Outlook*, December 1967.
28. Avishai, "Koestler and the Zionist Revolution," 246.
29. Koestler, *Arrow in the Blue*, 113.
30. W. E. B. Du Bois, *The Souls of Black Folk* (New York: Modern Library, 1996) [orig. 1903], 200, 201.
31. Michael Walzer, *The Paradox of Liberation: Secular Revolutions and Religious Counterrevolutions* (New Haven: Yale University Press, 2015), 2, 3, 8.
32. Koestler, *Promise and Fulfilment*, 194.
33. Walzer, *Paradox of Liberation*, 47.
34. H. N. Bialik, *Complete Poetic Works of Hayyim Nahman Bialik*, vol. 1, ed. Israel Efros (New York: Histadruth Ivrith of America, New York, 1948), 141–42.
35. Yehezkel Kaufmann, "Anti-Semitic Stereotypes in Zionism: The Nationalist Rejection of Diaspora Jewry," trans. Jacob Sloan, *Commentary*, March 1, 1949 [originally published in *Be-Havle Ha-Zeman*, Tel Aviv, 1936], https://www.commentarymagazine.com/articles/anti-semitic-stereotypes-in-zionismthe-nationalist-rejection-of-diaspora-jewry/.
36. Avishai, "Koestler and the Zionist Revolution," 237.
37. Walzer, *Paradox of Liberation*, 38.
38. Arthur Koestler, *The Trail of the Dinosaur* (New York: Macmillan, 1955), 110, 113, 132. Koestler's denial of Jewish cultural accomplishments was a particularly startling claim for a Hungarian Jew to make. Jews constituted only 5 percent of Hungary's population in the early twentieth century but were prominent in the sciences, law, the arts, journalism, finance, and medicine. (In 1905, over half of the country's medical school graduates were Jewish.) The Jewish community set much of Budapest's intellectual and cultural tone.
39. Robert Alter, "Zionism for the 70's," *Commentary*, February 1, 1970, emphasis added.
40. All quotes from Kaufmann, "Anti-Semitic Stereotypes in Zionism: The Nationalist Rejection of Diaspora Jewry," *Commentary*, italics in original.
41. Koestler, *Arrow in the Blue*, 133.
42. Ibid., 138–39.
43. Scammell, *Koestler*, 59.
44. Koestler, *Arrow in the Blue*, 193.
45. Scammell, *Koestler*, 58.
46. Koestler, *Arrow in the Blue*, 198–99.
47. Ibid., 204.

48. Arthur Koestler, "A Sentimental Journey Through Palestine," in *Foreign Correspondent: Personal Adventures Abroad in Search of the News By Twelve British Journalists*, ed. Wilfrid Hindle (London: George G. Harrap, 1939), 52.

49. Ibid., 57, 65, 57, 61.

50. Ibid., 58, 60, 78.

51. "Palestine Royal Commission Report," July 1937, https://palestinianmandate. files.wordpress.com/2014/04/cm-5479.pdf.

52. Koestler, "Sentimental Journey Through Palestine," 79.

53. Koestler, *Yogi and the Commissar*, 89.

54. Cesarani, *Arthur Koestler*, 224.

55. Scammell, *Koestler*, 252.

56. Cesarani, *Arthur Koestler*, 238.

57. Scammell, *Koestler*, 256, 258.

58. Ibid., 281.

59. J. Nedava, *Arthur Koestler* (London: Robert Anscombe, 1948), 49.

60. Scammell, *Koestler*, 328. The insistence that terror was the key factor leading to the British withdrawal used to be a self-serving right-wing claim. Now it is a left-wing claim. For instance, in 2015, a play staged in London called *A Land Without a People* promised to reveal "the story behind the overthrow of British rule in Palestine at the hands of Zionist terrorists."

61. Koestler, *Thieves in the Night*, 330–31.

62. Edmund Wilson, "Books," *New Yorker*, November 16, 1946, 129; Diana Trilling, "Fiction in Review," *Nation*, November 9, 1946, 534; Sperber, ed., *Arthur Koestler: A Collection of Critical Essays*, 51.

63. Cesarani, *Arthur Koestler*, 179.

64. Scammell, *Koestler*, 208.

65. Koestler, *Thieves in the Night*, 54, 9.

66. Ibid., 55, 83, 150.

67. Cesarani, *Arthur Koestler*, 320.

68. Koestler, *Thieves in the Night*, 151.

69. Ibid., 150–51.

70. Ibid., 27–28, 94, 155, 156.

71. Ibid., 27–28, 94, 155, 156, 228.

72. Ibid., 217, 157, 211.

73. Ibid., 310, 313.

74. Ibid., 275.

75. Scammell, *Koestler*, 327.

76. Cesarani, *Arthur Koestler*, 318.

77. Ibid., 317.

78. Ibid., 316, 319, 324. On a 1950 visit to the U.S., Koestler disparaged the Jewish New York intellectuals as "an assembly of anti-Semitic caricatures," and he wondered why there wasn't more anti-Semitism in America. See Cesarani, *Arthur Koestler*, 388, 375.

79. Koestler, *Promise and Fulfilment*, 41.

80. Ibid., 29.
81. Ibid., 74, 178.
82. Tariq Ali, "Notes on Anti-Semitism, Zionism and Palestine," *Counterpunch*, March 4, 2004, https://www.counterpunch.org/2004/03/04/notes-on-anti-semitism-zionism-and-palestine/.
83. Koestler, *Promise and Fulfilment*, 7, 4.
84. Ibid., 9.
85. Ibid., 55, 56, 102.
86. Ibid., 167, 117.
87. Ibid., 120.
88. Ibid., 57, 111, 121.
89. Ibid., 127, emphasis added; 180, 182.
90. Ibid., 330.
91. Ibid., 314, 41; 331, italics in original.
92. Ibid., 335.
93. Koestler, *Trail of the Dinosaur*, 120, 115, 133.
94. Ibid., 113, 108, 111.
95. Ibid., 126, 136.
96. Scammell, *Koestler*, 419.
97. Maccoby, "Koestler's Racism," 36.
98. Arthur Koestler, *The Thirteenth Tribe: The Khazar Empire and Its Heritage* (New York: Random House, 1976), 191, 17.
99. Cesarani, *Arthur Koestler*, 533.
100. Karl Marx, "On the Jewish Question," in Karl Marx, *Early Texts*, ed. and trans. David McLellan (Oxford: Basil Blackwell, 1971), 110.
101. Enzo Traverso, *The Marxists and the Jewish Question: The History of a Debate, 1843–1943*, trans. Bernard Gibbons (Amherst, NY: Humanity Books, 1990), 4, 60.
102. Robert S. Wistrich, *From Ambivalence to Betrayal: The Left, the Jews, and Israel* (Jerusalem and Lincoln, NE: Vidal Sassoon International Center for the Study of Antisemitism, 2012), 278.
103. Robert S. Wistrich, *Revolutionary Jews from Marx to Trotsky* (New York: Harper and Row, 1976), 7.

3. RODINSON

1. Maxime Rodinson, *Cult, Ghetto, and State: The Persistence of the Jewish Question*, trans. Jon Rothschild (London: Al Saqi Books, 1983), 23.
2. I. F. Stone, "Holy War," *New York Review of Books*, August 3, 1967, http://www.nybooks.com/articles/archives/1967/aug/03/holy-war/?pagination=false&printpage=true.
3. Rodinson, *Cult, Ghetto, and State*, 8. Lanzmann wrote in his memoir, "I should never have allowed the issue . . . to open with Rodinson's article. . . . Rodinson's simplifications, though dressed up as 'science,' did much harm." Lanzmann believed that Rodinson influenced Sartre's propensity to justify "the worst," i.e., Palestinian terrorism. But at the time, and for

a few years afterward, Lanzmann added, "I could not imagine Munich or Entebbe." See Claude Lanzmann, *The Patagonian Hare: A Memoir*, trans. Frank Wynne (New York: Farrar, Straus and Giroux, 2012) [orig. 2009], 399–400. In a 1988 interview, Rodinson praised Lanzmann's work in the Resistance and during the Algerian war but implied that he was overly consumed by the Shoah.

4. "Maxime Rodinson," in Nancy Elizabeth Gallagher, ed., *Approaches to the History of the Middle East: Interviews with Leading Middle East Historians* (Reading, UK: Ithaca Press, 1994), 110.

5. Joan Mandell and Joe Stork, "Maxime Rodinson Looks Back," *Middle East Report* 269 (Winter 2013), http://www.merip.org/mer/mer269/maxime-rodinson-looks-back.

6. Gallagher, ed., *Approaches to the History of the Middle East*, 111.

7. Ibid., 124, 113.

8. Ibid., 123, 119.

9. Maxime Rodinson, *Marxism and the Muslim World*, trans. Jean Matthews (New York: Monthly Review Press, 1981) [orig. 1972], 171, 28, 293.

10. Ibid., 114, 116, 119.

11. Ibid., 124.

12. Ibid., 288, 289, 119.

13. Ibid., 43, 42, 150.

14. Ibid., 295.

15. Ibid., 41, 251.

16. Ibid., 27, 130.

17. Gallagher, ed., *Approaches to the History of the Middle East*, 120.

18. Maxime Rodinson, *Israel: A Colonial-Settler State?*, trans. David Thorstad (New York: Monad Press, 1973) [orig. 1967], 28.

19. Ibid., 36–37, 84, 83, 39.

20. Ibid., 94, 65.

21. Ibid., 42.

22. Ibid., 46, 93.

23. Ibid., 83, 69, 86.

24. Ibid., 69, 95.

25. Ibid., 94.

26. Ibid., 92–93.

27. Ibid., 93.

28. Maxime Rodinson, "Why Palestine?," trans. Margaret Chiari, *Journal of Palestine Studies* 13, no. 3 (Spring 1984): 19.

29. Rodinson, *Cult, Ghetto, and State*, 157.

30. Ibid., 169.

31. Maxime Rodinson, *Israel and the Arabs*, trans. Michael Perl (New York: Pantheon, 1968), 236.

32. Ibid., 150.

33. Michel Winock, *Nationalism, Anti-Semitism, and Fascism in France*, trans. Jane Marie Todd (Stanford: Stanford University Press, 1998), 134.

34. Martin Kramer, *The Jewish Discovery of Islam: Studies in Honor of Bernard Lewis* (Tel Aviv: Moshe Dayan Center for Middle Eastern and African Studies, 1999), 3.

35. Rodinson, *Cult, Ghetto, and State*, 110.

36. Rodinson, *Israel and the Arabs*, 10–11.

37. Rodinson, "Why Palestine?," 22.

38. Rodinson, *Cult, Ghetto, and State*, 13. Rodinson apologized for using this phrase, then repeated it elsewhere.

39. Ibid., 111, 149, 212.

40. Maxime Rodinson, "Maxime Rodinson on Zionism and the Palestine Problem Today," *Journal of Palestine Studies* 4, no. 3 (Spring 1975): 25.

41. Rodinson, "Why Palestine?," 21.

42. Ibid., 20.

43. Rodinson, *Cult, Ghetto, and State*, 155.

44. Rodinson, "Maxime Rodinson on Zionism and the Palestine Problem Today," 22.

45. Rodinson, *Marxism and the Muslim World*, 303.

46. Rodinson, *Cult, Ghetto, and State*, 10.

47. Ibid., 223, 228.

48. Isaac Deutscher, *The Non-Jewish Jew and Other Essays* (London: Oxford University Press, 1968), 67.

49. Omar Barghouti, *BDS: Boycott, Divestment, Sanctions: The Global Struggle for Palestinian Rights* (Chicago: Haymarket Books, 2011), 178, italics in original. Though Barghouti advocates the boycott of all Israeli institutions, he has received a master's degree from Tel Aviv University.

50. Rodinson, *Cult, Ghetto, and State*, 111, 165, 166.

51. Ibid., 150; Rodinson, *Israel and the Arabs*, 126.

52. Rodinson, *Cult, Ghetto, and State*, 24, 31–32, 65.

53. Arthur Koestler, *Arrow in the Blue* (New York: Macmillan, 1961) [orig. 1952], 274.

54. Rodinson, *Cult, Ghetto, and State*, 27, 28.

55. Lanzmann, *Patagonian Hare*, 378–79.

56. Rodinson, *Cult, Ghetto, and State*, 33, 34, 40.

57. Rodinson, *Marxism and the Muslim World*, 23, emphasis added. The three Communists were Karl Radek, László Rajk, and Rudolph Slansky.

58. Rodinson, *Cult, Ghetto, and State*, 32.

59. Rodinson, *Israel and the Arabs*, 111.

60. Rodinson, *Islam and Capitalism*, 13.

61. Rodinson, "Why Palestine?," 18; Rodinson, *Marxism and the Muslim World*, 41.

62. Rodinson, *Israel and the Arabs*, 40, 104; Rodinson, *Cult, Ghetto, and State*, 115.

63. Rodinson, *Israel and the Arabs*, 46, emphasis added.

64. Rodinson, *Marxism and the Muslim World*, 200.

65. Rodinson, *Israel and the Arabs*, 228, 220.

66. Lanzmann recalled Sartre's angry speech to his Egyptian hosts: "He spoke about the vastness of the Arab countries, the extraordinary wealth of some of

them, his disbelief that they could leave the people of Jabailya or Dar El Bayla to rot, surviving on handouts from the United Nations Relief and Rehabilitation Administration—the product, he noted, of the very American imperialism they purported to despise—instead of marshalling Arab solidarity and doing something concrete, dealing with this cancer, whatever the eventual outcome of the conflict." Lanzmann, *Patagonian Hare*, 385.

67. Rodinson, *Israel and the Arabs*, 232, italics in original.

68. Y. Harkabi, "Fatah's Doctrine (December 1968)," in Walter Laqueur and Barry Rubin, eds. *The Israel-Arab Reader* (New York: Penguin, 2001) [orig. 1969], 121–22, emphases added.

69. Rodinson, *Cult, Ghetto, and State*, 201.

70. Oriana Fallaci, "Yasir Arafat," in Oriana Fallaci, *Interview with History*, trans. John Shepley (Boston: Houghton Mifflin, 1976), 131.

71. Rodinson, *Cult, Ghetto, and State*, 223.

72. Ibid., 205, 187.

73. Rodinson, *Israel and the Arabs*, 69, 70.

74. Rodinson, *Cult, Ghetto, and State*, 161, 162.

75. Ibid., 162, brackets in original.

76. Ibid., 14–15.

77. Ibid., 160, 224–25.

78. Rodinson, "Maxime Rodinson on Zionism and the Palestine Problem Today," 38.

79. Gallagher, ed., *Approaches to the History of the Middle East*, 114, 116.

80. Rodinson, *Marxism and the Muslim World*, 303.

81. Martin Kramer, "Islamism and Fascism: Dare to Compare," September 20, 2006, http://martinkramer.org/sandbox/2006/09/islamism-and-fascism-dare-to-compare/; see also Walter Laqueur, "The Origins of Fascism: Islamic Fascism, Islamophobia, Antisemitism," *OUPblog*, October 25, 2006, https://blog.oup.com/2006/10/the_origins_of_2/.

82. Gallagher, ed., *Approaches to the History of the Middle East*, 124.

83. Rodinson, *Marxism and the Muslim World*, 148, 190; Maxime Rodinson, *The Arabs*, trans. Arthur Goldhammer (Chicago: University of Chicago Press, 1981) [orig. 1979], 178.

84. Rodinson, *Marxism and the Muslim World*, 305.

85. Fred Halliday, "Maxime Rodinson: In praise of a 'marginal man,' " *openDemocracy.net*, September 8, 2005, https://www.opendemocracy.net/globalization/Rodinson_2819.jsp. Halliday was also referring to Isaac Deutscher.

86. Adam Shatz, "The Interpreters of Maladies," *Nation*, November 24, 2004, http://www.thenation.com/article/interpreters-maladies/.

87. Michael Young, "Some thoughts on the death of 'anti-Marxist' Maxime Rodinson," *Daily Star* (Lebanon), May 27, 2004, http://www.dailystar.com.lb/Opinion/Commentary/2004/May-27/95172-some-thoughts-on-the-death-of-anti-marxist-maxime-rodinson.ashx.

88. Rodinson, *Marxism and the Muslim World*, 34.

89. Gallagher, ed., *Approaches to the History of the Middle East*, 125–26.

4. DEUTSCHER

1. Tamara Deutscher, "Editor's Note," in Isaac Deutscher, *The Non-Jewish Jew and Other Essays* (London: Oxford University Press, 1968), unpaged.

2. Martyn Hudson, "Revisiting Isaac Deutscher," *Fathom*, Winter 2014, http://fathomjournal.org/revisiting-isaac-deutscher.

3. Leopold Labedz, "Deutscher as Historian and Prophet," *Survey: A Journal of Soviet and East European Studies*, April 1962, 132. Labedz points out that Deutscher frequently, and wrongly, detected the emergence of revolutionary democracies in the Soviet Union and China.

4. Isaac Deutscher, *The Prophet Armed: Trotsky, 1879–1921* (London: Oxford University Press, 1954), 326.

5. Labedz, "Deutscher as Historian and Prophet," 120.

6. Tamara Deutscher, "The Education of a Jewish Child," in Deutscher, *Non-Jewish Jew and Other Essays*, 1.

7. Ibid., 19.

8. Ibid., 15.

9. Bernard Wasserstein, *Isaiah Berlin, Isaac Deutscher and Arthur Koestler: Their Jewish Wars* (Amsterdam: Menasseh ben Israel Instituut, 2009), 22.

10. S. J. Goldsmith, *Twenty 20th Century Jews* (Freeport, NY: Books for Libraries Press, 1962), 39.

11. Neal Ascherson, "Victory in Defeat," *London Review of Books* 26, no. 23 (December 2, 2004), http://www.lrb.co.uk/v26/n23/neal-ascherson/victory-in-defeat.

12. Adam Shatz, ed., *Prophets Outcast: A Century of Dissident Jewish Writing about Zionism and Israel* (New York: Nation Books, 2004). The anthology takes its title from the last volume of Deutscher's Trotsky trilogy. Shatz's other "outcast prophets" include Noam Chomsky, Judith Butler, and Tony Judt—all acclaimed, tenured academics. The implied comparison to Trotsky, who was reviled, hounded, exiled, and murdered, is questionable.

13. Roane Carey, "A 'Non-Jewish Jew,' Hitchens Welcomed Finding He Was Jewish—But Not Zionism," *Jewish Daily Forward*, December 21, 2011, http://forward.com/articles/148355/a-non-jewish-jew-hitchens-welcomed-finding-h/.

14. Deutscher, *Non-Jewish Jew and Other Essays*, 26, 27.

15. Ibid., 30.

16. Ibid., 40, 41.

17. Ibid., 39, 41.

18. Ibid., 36, 37.

19. Ibid., 93, 104, 93.

20. Ibid., 99, 100, 102.

21. Ibid., 102–3, 106.

22. Ibid., 114, italics in original.

23. Ibid., 116.

24. Ibid., 113–14.

25. Ibid., 111–12.

26. Ibid., 116, 117.
27. Joseph Nedava, *Trotsky and the Jews* (Philadelphia: Jewish Publication Society of America, 1971), 116, 117.
28. Deutscher, *Prophet Armed*, 74.
29. Nedava, *Trotsky and the Jews*, 49.
30. Robert S. Wistrich, *From Ambivalence to Betrayal: The Left, the Jews, and Israel* (Jerusalem and Lincoln, NE: Vidal Sassoon International Center for the Study of Antisemitism, 2012), 387–88.
31. Nedava, *Trotsky and the Jews*, 56.
32. Ibid., 116.
33. Ibid., 195. Weizmann added that the Marxist revolutionary Georgi Plekhanov "sneered that a Bundist was a Zionist who was afraid of seasickness." See Chaim Weizmann, *Trial and Error* (New York: Harper and Brothers, 1949), 50.
34. Leon Trotsky, *On the Jewish Question* (New York: Pathfinder Press, 1970), 28.
35. Ibid., 30.
36. Ibid., 20, 18.
37. Nedava, *Trotsky and the Jews*, 209.
38. Ibid., 224, italics in original; 225, italics in original.
39. Norman Geras, "Marxists before the Holocaust," *New Left Review* 224 (July–August 1997): 31, 32. "Uncontrolled madness" was a phrase of Primo Levi's.
40. Nedava, *Trotsky and the Jews*, 56.
41. Isaac Deutscher, *The Prophet Outcast: Trotsky, 1929–1940* (London: Oxford University Press, 1970) [orig. 1963], 369.
42. Trotsky, *On the Jewish Question*, 21, 28–29.
43. Wistrich, *From Ambivalence to Betrayal*, 404.
44. Deutscher, *Non-Jewish Jew and Other Essays*, 118.
45. Ibid., 124, 123.
46. Albert Memmi, *Jews and Arabs*, trans. Eleanor Levieux (Chicago: J. Philip O'Hara, 1975), 12.
47. Deutscher, *Non-Jewish Jew and Other Essays*, 120.
48. Ibid., 50, 158, 162.
49. Jon Kimche, "Orwell and Deutscher," *New Middle East*, no. 3 (December 1968): 55.
50. Deutscher, *Non-Jewish Jew and Other Essays*, 46–47.
51. Isaac Deutscher, "On the Israeli-Arab War," *New Left Review* 1, no. 44 (July–August 1967): 43.
52. Goldsmith, *Twenty 20th Century Jews*, 40.
53. Deutscher, *Non-Jewish Jew and Other Essays*, 45.
54. S. J. Goldsmith, "Deutscher in Marxland," *Jewish Observer and Middle East Review*, November 22, 1968, 14.
55. Isaac Deutscher, "Preface to the Yiddish Edition," in Hersh Mendel, *Memoirs of a Jewish Revolutionary*, trans. Robert Michaels (London: Pluto Press, 1989) [orig. 1959], xviii, xxi.

56. Enzo Traverso, *The Marxists and the Jewish Question: The History of a Debate, 1843–1943*, trans. Bernard Gibbons. (Amherst, NY: Humanity Books, 1994), 205.

57. Deutscher, *Non-Jewish Jew and Other Essays*, 49, emphasis added.

58. Ibid., 49–50.

59. Deutscher, "On the Israeli-Arab War," 30.

60. Ibid., 32, 34.

61. Jacob Sonntag, "Deutscher's Tragic Dilemma," *Jewish Vanguard*, January 29, 1969, 8.

62. Deutscher, "On the Israeli-Arab War," 37, 42, 43.

63. Ibid., 45, 44.

64. Isaac Deutscher, *Ironies of History: Essays on Contemporary Communism* (Berkeley, CA: Ramparts Press, 1971), 120.

65. Deutscher, "On the Israeli-Arab War," 37, 38.

66. Ibid., 41, 42, 41, emphasis added; 42.

67. Ibid., 42.

68. Ibid., 43, 42, 38, 39.

69. Ibid., 45.

70. Trotsky, *On the Jewish Question*, 16.

71. Wistrich, *From Ambivalence to Betrayal*, 382.

72. Deutscher, *Non-Jewish Jew and Other Essays*, 57.

73. Ibid., 163.

74. Ibid., 164.

75. Ibid., 51.

5. MEMMI

1. Gary Wilder, "Irreconcilable Differences: A conversation with Albert Memmi," *Transition*, no. 71 (1996): 169.

2. Albert Memmi, *Portrait of a Jew*, trans. Elisabeth Abbott (New York: Viking Press, 1971) [orig. 1962], 30.

3. Wilder, "Irreconcilable Differences," 158.

4. Memmi, *Portrait of a Jew*, 3.

5. Albert Memmi, *Jews and Arabs*, trans. Eleanor Levieux (Chicago: J. Philip O'Hara, 1975), 55.

6. Memmi, *Portrait of a Jew*, 124.

7. Ibid., 289, 303, 287.

8. Ibid., 289, 291–92.

9. Ibid., 289, 175–76.

10. Albert Memmi, *The Liberation of the Jew*, trans. Judy Hyun (New York: Viking Press, 1973) [orig. 1966], 278.

11. Albert Memmi, *The Colonizer and the Colonized*, trans. Howard Greenfeld (Boston: Beacon Press, 1967) [orig. 1957], xvi.

12. Memmi, *Liberation of the Jew*, 126, 19, 20.

13. Ibid., 22.

14. Memmi, *Portrait of a Jew*, 5, 195.

15. Ibid., 5, italics in original.

16. Ibid., 6.

17. Albert Memmi, *Jews and Arabs,* trans. Eleanor Levieux (Chicago: J. Philip O'Hara, 1975), 30.

18. Memmi, *Portrait of a Jew,* 6.

19. Albert Memmi, "Jews, Tunisians, and Frenchmen," *Literary Review* 41, no. 2 (Winter 1998): 223.

20. Memmi, *Portrait of a Jew,* 245.

21. Albert Memmi, "Am I a Traitor?," *Commentary,* October 1962, 291.

22. Ibid., 291.

23. Ibid., 292.

24. Memmi, *Portrait of a Jew,* 200, 246.

25. Memmi, "Jews, Tunisians, and Frenchmen," 223.

26. Albert Memmi, *The Pillar of Salt,* trans. Edouard Roditi (Boston: Beacon Press, 2001) [orig. 1953], 17.

27. Isaac Yetiv, "Albert Memmi: The Syndrome of Self-exile," *International Fiction Review* 1, no. 2 (1974): 125.

28. Memmi, *Pillar of Salt,* 271.

29. Ibid., 95–96.

30. Ibid., 285, 292.

31. Memmi, *Colonizer and the Colonized,* 89.

32. Ibid., 138, 139.

33. Albert Memmi, *Dominated Man: Notes towards a Portrait* (Boston: Beacon Press, 1968), 32.

34. Memmi, *Colonizer and the Colonized,* 91–92.

35. Ibid., 34, emphasis added.

36. Ibid., 30–31.

37. Corey Robin, "Dragon-Slayers," *London Review of Books* 29, no. 1 (January 4, 2007), http://www.lrb.co.uk/v29/n01/corey-robin/dragon-slayers.

38. Albert Memmi, *Decolonization and the Decolonized,* trans. Robert Bononno (Minneapolis: University of Minnesota Press, 2006) [orig. 2004], 63.

39. Memmi, *Colonizer and the Colonized,* 150, 153.

40. Memmi, *Portrait of a Jew,* 208.

41. Memmi, *Liberation of the Jew,* 25.

42. Memmi, *Portrait of a Jew,* ix, 20–21.

43. Ibid., 38, 37–38.

44. Ibid., 263, 75–76.

45. Memmi, *Liberation of the Jew,* 217, 218, 221.

46. Ibid., 150.

47. Ibid., 208.

48. Ibid., 159.

49. Ibid., 275, 278, 284.

50. Ibid., 284, italics in original; 287.

51. Ibid., 303.

52. Ibid., 230.

53. Memmi, *Jews and Arabs*, 212.

54. Memmi, *Liberation of the Jew*, 231, 234.

55. Ibid., 239, italics in original; 244.

56. Ibid., 230, 231.

57. Memmi, *Jews and Arabs*, 203.

58. Memmi, *Dominated Man*, 58.

59. Ibid., 60, italics in original.

60. Ibid., 62.

61. Simcha Flapan, *The Arab-Israeli War of 1967: A Reply to Isaac Deutscher* (Tel Aviv: International Department of the United Workers' Party—MAPAM, 1968), 15.

62. Memmi, *Dominated Man*, 70.

63. Albert Memmi, "Does the Jew Exist?," *Commentary*, November 1966, 76.

64. Memmi, *Dominated Man*, 106.

65. Memmi, *Liberation of the Jew*, 303.

66. Memmi, *Decolonization and the Decolonized*, 132.

67. Memmi, *Jews and Arabs*, 11.

68. Ibid., 21, 12. Memmi refers to the 1969 execution, in front of cheering crowds, of nine Iraqi Jews as alleged "Zionist spies" by the recently installed Saddam Hussein regime. A reign of discrimination and terror against Iraq's already decimated Jewish community followed.

69. Ibid., 20, italics in original.

70. Ibid., 26, italics in original; 28, 27.

71. Ibid., 102, 163.

72. Ibid., 14, 15.

73. Ibid., 35, 13.

74. Ibid., 14, 35, 166.

75. Ibid., 13; 159, italics in original; 144.

76. Ibid., 164–65.

77. Ibid., 211, 216–17.

78. Ibid., 13, 138; 29, italics in original.

79. Ibid., 129; 205, italics in original.

80. Ibid., 210, italics in original; 220.

81. Memmi, *Decolonization and the Decolonized*, ix.

82. Lisa Lieberman, "Albert Memmi's About-Face," *Michigan Quarterly Review* 66, no. 3 (Summer 2007).

83. Memmi, *Decolonization and the Decolonized*, x.

84. Ibid., 128.

85. Ibid., 18, 43.

86. Ibid., xi, xiii, xi, 20.

87. Ibid., 34, 32–33.

88. Ibid., 49, 51.

89. Ibid., 61.

90. Ibid., 119.

91. Ibid., 44, 129.
92. Ibid., 128, 143.

6. HALLIDAY

1. Mohamed Sid-Ahmed, *After the Guns Fall Silent: Peace or Armageddon in the Middle-East*, trans. Maissa Talaat (London: Croom Helm, 1976), 127.
2. Joseph Massad, "Imperialism, Despotism, and Democracy in Syria," *aljazeera.com*, February 6, 2012, http://www.aljazeera.com/indepth/opinion/2012/02/2012269456491274.html. Massad also described the Assad regime in Syria as "an agent of US imperialism."
3. Edward Said, "On Palestinian Identity: A Conversation with Salman Rushdie," *New Left Review* 1, no. 160 (November–December 1986): 74.
4. Fred Halliday, "Imperialism and the Middle East," *MERIP Reports* 117 (September–October 1983).
5. Fred Halliday, *Islam and the Myth of Confrontation: Religion and Politics in the Middle East* (New York: I. B. Tauris, 1995), 198.
6. Fatah in Y. Harkabi, "Fatah's Doctrine (December 1968)," in Walter Laqueur and Barry Rubin, eds., *The Israel-Arab Reader: A Documentary History of the Middle East Conflict* (New York: Penguin Books, 2001), 127; Dutschke in Hans Kundnani, *Utopia or Auschwitz: Germany's 1968 Generation and the Holocaust* (London: Hurst, 2009), 41.
7. Fred Halliday, "Revolutionary Realism and the Struggle for Palestine," *MERIP Reports* 96 (May 1981), http://www.merip.org/mer/mer96/revolutionary-realism-struggle-palestine.
8. Fred Halliday, "1967 and the Consequences of Catastrophe," *MERIP Reports* 146 (May–June 1987), http://www.merip.org/mer/mer146/1967-consequences-catastrophe.
9. Fred Halliday, *Political Journeys: The openDemocracy Essays*, ed. David Hayes (New Haven: Yale University Press, 2012), 105, 140. Halliday was referring to the Arab-Israeli wars of 1967 and 1973 and the Oslo Accords of 1993.
10. Fred Halliday, "Revolutionary Internationalism and its Perils," in John Foran et al., eds., *Revolution in the Making of the Modern World* (New York: Routledge, 2008), 66; Halliday, *Political Journeys*, 53.
11. Stephen Howe, "Introduction," in *Political Journeys*, 17.
12. Halliday, *Islam and the Myth of Confrontation*, 198.
13. Halliday, *Political Journeys*, 22, 28.
14. Adam Roberts, "Simon Frederick Peter Halliday, 1946–2010," *Proceedings of the British Academy* 172 (2011): 146. I have taken much of the information on Halliday's youth and family from this informative essay. Roberts was a colleague and friend of Halliday's for four decades.
15. Ibid., 156, 157.
16. Halliday, *Political Journeys*, 26.
17. Danny Postel, "Remembering Fred Halliday in Chicago," May 3, 2010; dannypostel.homestead.com/Remembering-Fred-Halliday-in-Chicago.html.

18. Halliday, *Political Journeys,* 194.

19. Ibid., 58.

20. Fred Halliday, "The Crisis of the Arab World: The False Answers of Saddam Hussein," *New Left Review* 184 (November–December 1990): 72; Halliday, *Political Journeys,* 224–25.

21. Albert Memmi, "Am I a Traitor?," *Commentary,* October 1, 1962, 292.

22. Halliday, *Political Journeys,* 19–20.

23. E. P. Thompson, *E. P. Thompson and the Making of the New Left,* ed. Cal Winslow (New York: Monthly Review Press, 2014), 237, 218.

24. Halliday, *Political Journeys,* 162.

25. Fred Halliday, *Iran: Dictatorship and Development* (New York: Penguin, 1979), 309.

26. Fred Halliday, "The Coalition Against the Shah: Stories of 'Mad Mullahs' Mask a Wider Public Revolt," *New Statesman,* January 5, 1979, 5.

27. Fred Halliday, "The Revolution Turns to Repression," *New Statesman,* August 24, 1979, 263.

28. Ibid., 264.

29. Fred Halliday, *Two Hours that Shook the World: September 11, 2001: Causes and Consequences* (London: Saqi Books, 2002), 62.

30. "Popular Front for the Liberation of Palestine: Platform (1969)," in Laqueur and Rubin, eds., *Israel-Arab Reader,* 142.

31. The Entebbe hijacking was a joint operation between the PFLP and a far-Left German group called the Revolutionary Cells, and the singling out of Jewish passengers had a profound impact on some members of the West German Left. Joschka Fischer, then a member of a group called Revolutionary Struggle, would later say that Entebbe showed how Germany's New Left had "almost compulsively repeated the crimes of the Nazis." Fischer became Germany's foreign minister in 1998. See Kundnani, *Utopia or Auschwitz,* 136.

32. Fred Halliday, "On the PFLP and the September Crisis: Interview with Ghassan Kannafani," *New Left Review* 1, no. 67 (May–June 1971): 50.

33. Ibid., 56, 57.

34. Halliday, "Revolutionary Realism and the Struggle for Palestine," 9.

35. Ibid., 4, 10, 3, 10, 11.

36. Ibid., 4.

37. Ibid.

38. Ibid., 10.

39. Ibid., 10, 8.

40. Ibid., 8, 9.

41. Ibid., 9, 8, 12.

42. Ibid., 4.

43. Ibid., 11.

44. Fouzi el-Asmar, Uri Davis, and Naim Khadr, eds., *Towards a Socialist Republic of Palestine* (London: Ithaca Press, and Kefar Shmaryahu, Israel: Miftah Publishers, 1978), 63, 55.

45. Halliday, "Revolutionary Realism and the Struggle for Palestine," 12.

46. Ibid., 12.

47. Ibid., 9.

48. Ibid., 9; 11, italics in original.

49. Ibid., 6.

50. Maxine Molyneux and Fred Halliday, "Marxism, the Third World and the Middle East," *MERIP Reports* 120 (January–February 1984), http://www. merip.org/mer/mer120/marxism-third-world-middle-east.

51. Fred Halliday, "The Fate of Solidarity: Uses and Abuses," 1, 2. An earlier version of this essay appeared in Christine Chinkin and David Downes, eds., *Crime, Social Control and Human Rights: Essays in Honour of Stan Cohen* (Oxford: Deer Park Productions, 2007). The later version, which I have used, can be accessed at www.platypus1917.org/wp-content/uploads/readings/ hallidayfred_fateofsolidarity.pdf.

52. Ibid., 9.

53. Fred Halliday, "The Left and War," *New Statesman and Society,* March 8, 1991, 16.

54. Ibid., 15.

55. Halliday, "Fate of Solidarity," 9, 10.

56. Ibid., 11.

57. Ibid., 12.

58. Fred Halliday, *Nation and Religion in the Middle East* (Boulder: Lynne Rienner Publishers, 2000), 72.

59. Ibid., 75.

60. Ibid., 73.

61. Halliday, *Two Hours that Shook the World,* 133, 134, 135.

62. Ibid., 137.

63. Halliday, "Fate of Solidarity," 12.

64. Halliday, *Nation and Religion in the Middle East,* 36.

65. Halliday, *Islam and the Myth of Confrontation,* 211.

66. Edward Said, "The Morning After," *London Review of Books* 15, no. 20, October 21, 1993, http://www.lrb.co.uk/v15/n20/edward-said/the-morning-after.

67. Said, "On Palestinian Identity," 69; Edward Said, *The End of the Peace Process: Oslo and After* (New York: Pantheon, 2000), 77.

68. Graham Usher, "Arafat and the Opposition: An Interview with Marwan Barghouti," *Middle East Report* 191 (November–December 1994), http://www. merip.org/mer/mer191/arafat-opposition.

69. Halliday, *Political Journeys,* 135.

70. Ibid., 139.

71. Ibid., 178.

72. Fred Halliday, "Revolution in Afghanistan," *New Left Review* 1, no. 112 (November–December 1978): 32, 5, 44.

73. Fred Halliday, "War and Revolution in Afghanistan," *New Left Review* 1, no. 119 (January–February 1980): 30, 32, 38.

74. Fred Halliday, "The Jihadism of Fools," *Dissent* 54, no. 1 (Winter 2007): 55.

75. Fred Halliday, "Kabul's Patriarchy with Guns," *Nation*, November 11, 1996, http://www.thenation.com/article/kabuls-patriarchy-guns.

76. Halliday, *Political Journeys*, 105, 106.

77. Ibid., 53.

78. Halliday, *Two Hours that Shook the World*, 50.

79. Halliday, *Political Journeys*, 77, 78.

80. Fred Halliday and Danny Postel, "Who Is Responsible? An Interview with Fred Halliday," *Salmagundi*, nos. 150–51 (Summer 2006): 223.

81. Halliday, *Political Journeys*, 171.

82. Tariq Ali, "Editorial: Mid-Point in the Middle East?," *New Left Review* 38 (March–April 2006): 6.

83. Ibid., 18–19.

84. Perry Anderson, "Editorial: On the Concatenation in the Arab World," *New Left Review* 68 (March–April 2011): 12; 15, emphasis added.

85. Perry Anderson, "Editorial: The House of Zion," *New Left Review* 96 (November–December 2015): 36, 37.

86. Halliday and Postel, "Who Is Responsible?," 222–23, 237.

87. Ari Shavit, "My Right of Return: Edward Said Interviewed by Ari Shavit," *Haaretz*, August 2000. The "my" refers, of course, to Said.

88. Ibid.

89. David Grossman, *The Yellow Wind*, trans. Haim Watzman (New York: Farrar, Straus and Giroux, 1988), 41, 48.

90. Halliday and Postel, "Who Is Responsible?," 240.

91. Fred Halliday, "What Was Communism?," *openDemocracy.net*, October 16, 2009, https://www.opendemocracy.net/article/what-was-communism.

7. STONE

1. I. F. Stone, *Polemics and Prophecies, 1967–1970* (Boston: Little, Brown, 1970), xiii.

2. D. D. Guttenplan, *American Radical: The Life and Times of I. F. Stone* (New York: Farrar, Straus and Giroux, 2009), xi.

3. Stone, *Polemics and Prophecies*, 343.

4. Guttenplan, *American Radical*, 443; Andrew Patner, *I. F. Stone: A Portrait* (New York: Anchor Books, 1990), 107.

5. Myra MacPherson, *"All Governments Lie": The Life and Times of Rebel Journalist I. F. Stone* (New York: Scribner, 2006), 25.

6. Patner, *I. F. Stone: A Portrait*, 118.

7. Ibid., 47; 48–49, italics in original.

8. Guttenplan, *American Radical*, 264–65.

9. Paul Berman, "The Watchdog," *New York Times Book Review*, October 1, 2006, http://www.nytimes.com/2006/10/01/books/review/Berman.t.html.

10. Dan Diner and Jonathan Frankel, "Jews and Communism: The Utopian Temptation," in *Dark Times, Dire Decisions: Jews and Communism: Studies in Contemporary Jewry, An Annual, XX*, ed. Jonathan Frankel (New York: Oxford University Press, 2004), 7.

11. I. F. Stone, *The Haunted Fifties* (London: Merlin Press, 1964), 149, italics in original.

12. MacPherson, *"All Governments Lie,"* 386.

13. Guttenplan, *American Radical,* 105, 237.

14. Neil Middleton, "Introduction," in Neil Middleton, ed., *The Best of "I. F. Stone's Weekly"* (London: Penguin Books, 1973), xi.

15. Guttenplan, *American Radical,* 290, xvii.

16. Bart Barnes, "I. F. Stone, Radical Gadfly, Dies at 81," *Jerusalem Post,* June 20, 1989.

17. Walter Ruby, "I. F. Stone and the Ancient Mystery: Offering a New Perspective on the Death of Socrates," *Washington Post,* March 10, 1988.

18. Guttenplan, *American Radical,* 251–52.

19. I. F. Stone, *The Best of I. F. Stone,* ed. Karl Weber (New York: Public Affairs, 2006), 205; 206, emphasis added.

20. Ibid., 209, 210.

21. Ibid., 215.

22. Ibid., 212.

23. Ibid., 217, 218.

24. I. F. Stone, *The War Years, 1939–1945* (Boston: Little, Brown, 1988), 324, 325, 340.

25. I. F. Stone, *Underground to Palestine and Reflections Thirty Years Later* (London: Hutchinson, 1979) [orig. 1946], 16, 96.

26. Ibid., 3, 4.

27. Ibid., xi, 13.

28. Ibid., 146, 148, 202.

29. Ibid., 47, 155, 48.

30. Ibid., 155.

31. Ibid., 194.

32. Ibid., 214.

33. Ibid., 215–17.

34. Ibid., 218, 219, 223.

35. Ibid., 217; 218, italics in original.

36. Ibid., 48.

37. Ibid., 222–23.

38. I. F. Stone, "Tel Aviv Quiet, But You Know There's a War On," *PM,* May 12, 1948, 12.

39. I. F. Stone, "Born Under Fire," *New Republic,* May 31, 1948.

40. I. F. Stone, *This Is Israel* (New York: Boni and Gaer, 1948), 21.

41. Ibid., 86, 26–27.

42. Ibid., 89.

43. I. F. Stone, "Israel's Hopes and Fears of Russian Intervention," *I. F. Stone's Weekly,* April 30, 1956.

44. Stone, *This Is Israel,* 91, 74, 75.

45. Stone, *Best of "I. F. Stone's Weekly,"* 280.

46. Stone, "Israel's Hopes and Fears of Russian Intervention."

47. I. F. Stone, "Theirs is a Moral Challenge to World Jewry and Israel," *I. F. Stone's Weekly*, April 30, 1956.

48. I. F. Stone, "The Road to Peace Lies Through the Arab Refugee Camps," *I. F. Stone's Weekly*, April 30, 1956.

49. Ibid.

50. I. F. Stone, "America's Satellites Turn Desperate, Too," *I. F. Stone's Weekly*, November 5, 1956.

51. I. F. Stone, "The Terrible Truth About the World Crisis (And Me)," *I. F. Stone's Weekly*, November 12, 1956.

52. Stone, *The Best of "I. F. Stone's Weekly,"* 281, 282, 283, 284.

53. I. F. Stone, "Why Not A Global Settlement Before It's Too Late?," *I. F. Stone's Weekly*, June 5, 1967.

54. I. F. Stone, "On The Pro-Israel Left," *I. F. Stone's Weekly*, June 5, 1967.

55. I. F. Stone, "The Future of Israel," *Ramparts*, July 1967, 44, 41.

56. Stone, *Best of "I. F. Stone's Weekly,"* 288.

57. I. F. Stone, "Suppose Those Were Jewish Refugees From Arab Armies?," *I. F. Stone's Weekly*, July 3, 1967.

58. Stone, "The Future of Israel," 44.

59. Stone, "Suppose Those Were Jewish Refugees From Arab Armies?"

60. Yehoshua Arieli, "Trapped in Vicious Circles," in *Israel, the Arabs and the Middle East*, ed. Irving Howe and Carl Gershman (New York: Bantam Books, 1972), 318.

61. Jonathan Frankel, "Israel: The War and After," *Dissent* 30, no. 1 (Winter 1983): 11.

62. I. F. Stone, "The Need for a Double Vision in the Middle East," *I. F. Stone's Bi-Weekly*, January 13, 1969.

63. Oriana Fallaci, *Interview with History*, trans. John Shepley (Boston: Houghton Mifflin, 1976), 130–31. Arafat added, "If you're so anxious to give a homeland to the Jews, give them yours."

64. Shlomo Avineri, "Modernization and Arab Society: Some Reflections," in *Israel, the Arabs and the Middle East*, ed. Howe and Gershman, 308, 311.

65. I. F. Stone, *Polemics and Prophecies*, 416; see also *New York Review of Books*, August 3, 1967.

66. Nancy Elizabeth Gallagher, ed., *Approaches to the History of the Middle East: Interviews with Leading Middle East Historians* (Reading, UK: Ithaca Press, 1994), 121.

67. Stone, *Polemics and Prophecies*, 420.

68. Ibid., 421.

69. I. F. Stone, "Gangsters or Patriots?," *Nation*, January 12, 1946.

70. Stone, *Polemics and Prophecies*, 425, 423, 425–26.

71. Claude Lanzmann, "From the Holocaust to the *Holocaust*," trans. Simon Srebrny, *Telos* 42 (Winter 1979–80): 137.

72. Robert Alter, "Israel & the Intellectuals," *Commentary*, October 1, 1967, 51.

73. Bartley Crum, "Foreword," in Stone, *This Is Israel*, 10.
74. Stone, "The Need for Double Vision in the Middle East."
75. Stone, "Gangsters or Patriots?"
76. I. F. Stone, "War for Oil?," *New York Review of Books*, February 6, 1975.
77. Michael Blankfort, "War for Oil? An Exchange," *New York Review of Books*, March 6, 1975.
78. I. F. Stone, "The Hope," *New York Review of Books*, October 26, 1978.
79. I. F. Stone, *In a Time of Torment, 1961–1967* (Boston: Little, Brown, 1967), 360.
80. I. F. Stone, "The Pilgrimage of Malcolm X," *New York Review of Books*, November 11, 1965.
81. Stone, *Polemics and Prophecies*, 481.
82. Stone, *In a Time of Torment*, 167.
83. Guttenplan, *American Radical*, 424.
84. Stone, *Polemics and Prophecies*, 466, 467, 468.
85. Stone, "The Hope."
86. Stone, *Polemics and Prophecies*, 411.
87. Saul Friedländer and Mahmoud Hussein, *Arabs & Israelis: A Dialogue*, trans. Paul Auster and Lydia Davis (New York: Holmes and Meier, 1975), 182, 215.
88. Ibid., 184.
89. Jacobo Timerman, *The Longest War: Israel in Lebanon*, trans. Miguel Acoca (New York: Alfred A. Knopf, 1982), 99.
90. Friedländer and Hussein, *Arabs & Israelis*, 216.
91. Ibid., 37, 58.
92. Ibid., 192.
93. Ibid., 170, 171, 186.
94. Ibid., 138, italics in original; 172, 171, 205.
95. Ibid., 213, 221.
96. Stone, *Underground to Palestine and Reflections Thirty Years Later*, 253.
97. Joel Carmichael, "I. F. Stone Reconsiders Israel," *Midstream*, October 1967, 15.
98. Marvin Maurer, "I. F. Stone—Universalist," *Midstream*, February 1979, 12, 5, 4.
99. Marie Syrkin, "Underground to Palestine and Reflections Thirty Years Later," *New Republic*, January 27, 1979, 29.
100. Abba Eban, "I. F. Stone: Gadfly in the Promised Land," *Washington Post*, February 25, 1979.
101. Stone, *Underground to Palestine and Reflections Thirty Years Later*, 232.
102. Eban, "I. F. Stone: Gadfly in the Promised Land."
103. Mark Bruzonsky, "Israel's No. 1 Dove," *Worldview*, January 1978, 7, 8.

8. CHOMSKY

1. Frank Barat, "Interview with Noam Chomsky," *Red Pepper*, May 3, 2011, http://www.redpepper.org.uk/interview-with-noam-chomsky/.
2. Edward Said, "Chomsky and the Question of Palestine," *Journal of Palestine Studies* 4, no. 3 (Spring 1975): 96; Edward Said, "Foreword," in Noam

Chomsky, *Fateful Triangle: The United States, Israel, and the Palestinians,* updated edition (Montreal: Black Rose Books, 1999) [orig. 1983], vii.

3. Mouin Rabbani, "Reflections on a Lifetime of Engagement with Zionism, the Palestine Question, and American Empire: An Interview with Noam Chomsky," *Journal of Palestine Studies* 41, no. 3 (Spring 2012): 92.

4. Said, "Chomsky and the Question of Palestine," 91.

5. David Samuels, "Q&A: Noam Chomsky," *Tablet,* November 12, 2010, http://www.tabletmag.com/jewish-news-and-politics/50260/qa-noam-chomsky.

6. Rabbani, "Reflections on a Lifetime of Engagement with Zionism," 103.

7. Samuels, "Q&A: Noam Chomsky"; Rabbani, "Reflections on a Lifetime of Engagement with Zionism," 94.

8. Samuels, "Q&A: Noam Chomsky."

9. Ann Garrison, " 'Denying' the Srebrenica Genocide Because It's Not True: an Interview with Diana Johnstone," *Counterpunch,* July 16, 2015, http://www.counterpunch.org/2015/07/16/denying-the-srebrenica-genocide-because-its-not-true-an-interview-with-diana-johnstone/.

10. Emanuel Stoakes, "Chomsky and his Critics," *Jacobin,* November 23, 2015, https://www.jacobinmag.com/2015/11/noam-chomsky-interview-isis-syria-intervention-nato/; Andrew Stephen, "NS Interview—Chomsky," *New Statesman,* June 19, 2006, http://www.newstatesman.com/node/164578.

11. Said in Chomsky, *Fateful Triangle,* vii; Emma Brockes, "The Greatest Intellectual? Noam Chomsky Interviewed by Emma Brockes," *Guardian,* October 31, 2005, https://chomsky.info/20051031/.

12. George McLeod, "Noam Chomsky Interview," *Phnom Penh Post,* March 27, 2009, https://chomsky.info/20090327; Tim Sebastian, "On Afghanistan: Noam Chomsky Interviewed by Tim Sebastian," *Hard Talk,* February 2, 2002, https://chomsky.info/20020227/.

13. Noam Chomsky, Address to the United Nations (question and answer session), October 14, 2014, https://www.youtube.com/watch?v=1eGlgOnHOJE&t=0s.

14. Noam Chomsky, *Towards a New Cold War: Essays on the Current Crisis and How We Got There* (New York: Pantheon, 1982), 254; Noam Chomsky, *Middle East Illusions* (Lanham, MD: Rowman and Littlefield, 2004), 30, emphasis added.

15. Chomsky, *Middle East Illusions,* 20; Chomsky, "Nationalism and Conflict in Palestine," *Liberation* 14, no. 8 (November 1969), 10.

16. Chomsky, *Towards a New Cold War,* 264; Chomsky, "Nationalism and Conflict in Palestine," 10.

17. Chomsky, *Towards a New Cold War,* 430, 262.

18. Chomsky, *Middle East Illusions,* 78.

19. Chomsky, *Towards a New Cold War,* 231; Chomsky, *Middle East Illusions,* 31.

20. Chomsky, "Nationalism and Conflict in Palestine," 15.

21. Chomsky, *Fateful Triangle,* xii.

22. Chomsky, *Middle East Illusions,* x.

23. See Alain Gresh, *The PLO: The Struggle Within,* trans. A.M. Berrett (London: Zed Books, 1985), 4; also Rashid Khalidi, *The Iron Cage: The Story of the Palestinian Struggle for Statehood* (Boston: Beacon Press, 2006), 174–75.

24. Chomsky, *Fateful Triangle*, 504, emphases added.
25. Ibid., 504.
26. Chomsky, *World Orders Old and New*, 265; the UN speech transcript is reprinted in Amy Goodman, "In U.N. Speech, Noam Chomsky Blasts United States for Supporting Israel, Blocking Palestinian State," *Democracy Now!*, October 22, 2014, https://www.democracynow.org/2014/10/22/in_un_speech_noam_chomsky_blasts.
27. Khalidi, *Iron Cage*, 179.
28. Rodinson in Gresh, *PLO: The Struggle Within*, 245–46.
29. Eqbal Ahmad, *Confronting Empire: Interviews with David Barsamian* (Cambridge, MA: South End Press, 2000), 35–36. Chomsky and Ahmad were friends; Chomsky also met with PLO leaders in a period he remembered as "the late 1970s, 1980." Chomsky recalled these meetings as "pretty pointless. . . . We would go up to their suite at the Plaza [Hotel], . . . and basically just sit there listening to their speeches about how they were leading the world revolutionary movement, and so on and so forth." However, Chomsky still believed that the PLO leaders were "fundamentally nationalists" who wanted only to end the Occupation and "elect our own mayors." See Rabbani, "Reflections on a Lifetime of Engagement with Zionism," 105.
30. David Kimche, *The Last Option: After Nasser, Arafat, and Saddam Hussein* (New York: Charles Scribner's Sons, 1991), 66–67.
31. Matti Steinberg, *In Search of Modern Palestinian Statehood* (Tel Aviv: Moshe Dayan Center, 2016), 85–86, emphasis added.
32. Noam Chomsky, "Blinded by the Truth," *Al-Ahram Weekly*, November 2–8, 2000, https://chomsky.info/20001102/.
33. See, for instance, Chomsky, *Fateful Triangle*, 68.
34. Ibid., 343; Noam Chomsky, "Introduction," in Roane Carey, ed., *The New Intifada: Resisting Israel's Apartheid* (New York: Verso, 2001), 11.
35. United Nations Security Council Official Records, 1879th Meeting: January 26, 1976, 5, 18, 17.
36. Ibid., 22–23.
37. Ibid., 24–25.
38. Jay Parini, "The Land of Oz," *New York Times Book Review*, April 14, 1991.
39. Noam Chomsky and Ilan Pappé, *Gaza in Crisis: Reflections on Israel's War against the Palestinians* (Chicago: Haymarket Books, 2010), 79; Chomsky, *Towards a New Cold War*, 334.
40. Khalidi, *Iron Cage*, 178.
41. Yezid Sayigh, *Armed Struggle and the Search for State: The Palestinian National Movement, 1949–1993* (Oxford: Oxford University Press, 1999), 664, 687, 23.
42. Hussein Agha and Ahmad Samih Khalidi, "The End of This Road: The Decline of the Palestinian National Movement," *NewYorker.com*, August 6, 2017, http://www.newyorker.com/news/news-desk/the-end-of-this-road-the-decline-of-the-palestinian-national-movement.
43. Chomsky, *Fateful Triangle*, 486, 485.
44. Eric Hobsbawm, *On History* (New York: New Press, 1997), 30.

45. Eugene Genovese, *In Red and Black: Marxian Explorations in Southern and Afro-American History* (New York: Vintage, 1972), 4.
46. Zeev Sternhell, "Israel's Wars: Is Anyone Capable of Setting Policy?," *Haaretz*, March 10, 2017.
47. Chomsky, *Fateful Triangle*, 525.
48. Ibid., 385, emphasis added; 183.
49. Ibid., 317, 277.
50. Hobsbawm, *On History*, 239.
51. Christopher Lydon, "Noam Chomsky: Neoliberalism Is Destroying Our Democracy," *Nation*, June 2, 2017.
52. Avishai Margalit, "Israel: A Partial Indictment," *New York Review of Books*, June 28, 1984.
53. Shlomo Ben-Ami, *Scars of War, Wounds of Peace: The Israeli-Arab Tragedy* (New York: Oxford University Press, 2010), 136.
54. Noam Chomsky and Ilan Pappé, *On Palestine* (Bungay, UK: Penguin, 2015), 164.
55. Chomsky, *World Orders Old and New*, 249; Chomsky and Pappé, *Gaza in Crisis*, 123; Chomsky and Pappé, *On Palestine*, 71.
56. Gresh, *PLO: The Struggle Within*, 218.
57. Eugene Goodheart, "An Interview with Amos Oz," *Partisan Review*, Summer 1982, 355.
58. Joshua Cohen, "A Balkans of the Mind," *New York Times Book Review*, January 1, 2017, 7.
59. *Liberation*, February 1974, 25.
60. Chomsky, *Middle East Illusions*, 134–35, 138, 136, 139.
61. *The Great Berrigan Debate* (New York: Committee on New Alternatives in the Middle East, 1974), 1, 2. There are slight variations in the three published versions of the speech, though each bears Berrigan's byline.
62. Ibid., 3.
63. Ibid., 4, 3, 4.
64. Robert Alter, "Berrigan's Diatribe," *Commentary*, February 1, 1974.
65. *Great Berrigan Debate*, 4–7.
66. Ibid., 5, 3, 5.
67. Ibid., 5, emphasis added; 7.
68. Todd Gitlin, email to the author, February 4, 2017.
69. Noam Chomsky, "Daniel in the Lions' Den: Berrigan & His Critics," *Liberation*, February 1974, 16, 19, 21, 24.
70. Chomsky, *Fateful Triangle*, 504.
71. Chomsky and Pappé, *Gaza in Crisis*, 120.
72. Chomsky, *Fateful Triangle*, 113, 132; Brockes, "Greatest Intellectual?"
73. Samuel Korb, "Chomsky's Allegations Should Be Questioned," *Tech*, December 6, 2002, 4.
74. Noam Chomsky, "Some Tasks for the Left," *Liberation*, August–September 1969, 41, 39.
75. Chomsky, *Fateful Triangle*, 165.

76. Ibid., 380.
77. Ibid., 69.
78. Chomsky, *Middle East Illusions*, 230.
79. See, for instance, Chomsky, *Fateful Triangle*, 49–51.
80. Ibid., 313.
81. Ibid., 500.
82. Ibid., 463.
83. Chomsky and Pappé, *Gaza in Crisis*, 17.
84. Chomsky, *Middle East Illusions*, 91; Chomsky, *World Orders Old and New*, 222.
85. Jon Kimche, *There Could Have Been Peace: The Untold Story of Why We Failed with Palestine and Again with Israel* (New York: Dial Press, 1973), 280.
86. Chomsky, *Fateful Triangle*, x.
87. Chomsky, *World Orders Old and New*, 256.
88. Chomsky and Pappé, *On Palestine*, 202; Chomsky reiterated this claim in his 2014 United Nations speech.
89. "Iran Pulls Palestine from the Margins," *Al-Monitor*, February 26, 2017, http://www.al-monitor.com/pulse/originals/2017/02/iran-conference-palestine-turkey-victory-albab-kurds.html. See also Adnan Abu Amer, "In Eye of Regional Storm, Hamas Pushed Closer to Tehran," *Al-Monitor*, June 2, 2017.
90. For Chomsky's claims on this subject, see Chomsky and Pappé, *Gaza in Crisis*, 6, 85, 195, 225.
91. Agha and Khalidi, "End of This Road."
92. "Hamas hails Iranian military after damaged relations are mended," *New Arab*, August 28, 2017, https://www.alaraby.co.uk/english/news/2017/8/28/hamas-hails-iranian-military-after-damaged-relations-are-mended.
93. Chomsky and Pappé, *Gaza in Crisis*, 85.
94. Chomsky, *Fateful Triangle*, 236, 411, 412.
95. Ibid., 489, 233, 133; *Towards a New Cold War*, 276; *Fateful Triangle*, 499, 474.
96. Chomsky, *Fateful Triangle*, 314.
97. Steinberg, *In Search of Modern Palestinian Statehood*, 89.
98. Chomsky, *Fateful Triangle*, 1.
99. Meron Benvenisti, "The Twilight War," *New Yorker*, March 18, 1996, 10.
100. Chomsky's UN address (question and answer session). Available on YouTube.
101. Chomsky, *Middle East Illusions*, 27; Chomsky, *World Orders Old and New*, 210.
102. Chomsky and Pappé, *Gaza in Crisis*, 116.
103. Chomsky in Goodman, "In UN Speech, Noam Chomsky Blasts United States."
104. Chomsky, *World Orders Old and New*, 211.
105. See Michael Bérubé, *The Left at War* (New York: New York University Press, 2009), 113.
106. Tim Sebastian, "On Afghanistan: Noam Chomsky Interviewed by Tim Sebastian," *Hard Talk*, February 2, 2002, https://chomsky.info/20020227/.
107. Jacobo Timerman, *The Longest War: Israel in Lebanon*, trans. Miguel Acoca (New York: Alfred A. Knopf, 1982), 138, italics in original.

108. Chomsky, *Fateful Triangle*, 211, 354.

109. Ibid., 101.

110. Ibid., 25.

111. Chomsky and Pappé, *Gaza in Crisis*, 109–10.

112. Chomsky and Pappé, *On Palestine*, 52; Chomsky, *World Orders Old and New*, 240.

113. Chomsky and Pappé, *On Palestine*, 52; Chomsky, *Fateful Triangle*, 382; Chomsky and Pappé, *On Palestine*, 67.

114. Hannah Arendt, "On Hannah Arendt," in Melvyn A. Hill, ed., *Hannah Arendt: The Recovery of the Public World* (New York: St. Martin's Press, 1979), 338.

115. Alexander Klein, ed., *Dissent, Power, and Confrontation* (New York: McGraw-Hill, 1971), 107, 123. This contains a transcript of the debate; questioners from the audience included Susan Sontag.

116. Ibid., 111, 112.

117. Chomsky, *Middle East Illusions*, 219.

118. Chomsky and Pappé, *Gaza in Crisis*, 9; Chomsky, *World Orders Old and New*, 250. The belief that Oslo was doomed to failure is shared by leftists such as Chomsky and Edward Said and by the Right in Israel. For perceptive analyses of the accords, including their contradictions and flaws, see Nathan Thrall, *The Only Language They Understand*, chap. 1; Shlomo Ben-Ami, *Scars of War, Wounds of Peace*, chaps. 9 and 10; Ron Pundak, "From Oslo to Taba: What Went Wrong?," *Survival*, Autumn 2001; and Yezid Sayigh, "Who Killed the Oslo Accords?," *aljazeera.com*, October 1, 2015, http://www.aljazeera.com/indepth/opinion/2015/10/killed-oslo-accords-151001072411049.html.

119. Chomsky's UN address (question and answer session).

120. Bernard Avishai, "Confederation: The One Possible Israel-Palestine Solution," *New York Review of Books Daily*, February 2, 2018, http://www.nybooks.com/daily/2018/02/02/confederation-the-one-possible-israel-palestine-solution/

121. Noam Chomsky, "On Israel-Palestine and BDS," *Nation*, July 2, 2014.

122. Ibid.

123. Ibid.

124. Chomsky, Noam and David Barsamian. *Global Discontents: Conversations on the Rising Threats to Democracy* (New York: Metropolitan Books, 2017), 54.

125. Chomsky, "On Israel-Palestine and BDS"; Chomsky and Pappé, *On Palestine*, 91.

126. Rabbani, "Reflections on a Lifetime of Engagement with Zionism," 98, 117.

127. Chomsky and Pappé, *Gaza in Crisis*, 13.

128. Arduous attempts to dissociate Hezbollah's anti-Zionism from anti-Semitism continue. Adam Shatz, an American anti-Zionist journalist who frequently writes about the Middle East and has interviewed Hassan Nasrallah, boasted that the Hezbollah leader had "no problems" with the fact that Shatz is Jewish. Shatz has derided Jeffrey Goldberg's reports on Hezbollah in the *New Yorker* as "lurid," but it may be that Shatz's writings were too sanguine. In 2004, he told readers that Lebanese fears

of Hezbollah "may be exaggerated" because the group had avoided attacks that could lead to a larger conflict; Shatz wrote that Nasrallah would not endanger his people by recklessly attacking Israel. Two years later Nasrallah did just that, initiating a cross-border raid and kidnapping two Israeli soldiers; this led to the 2006 Hezbollah-Israel war in which hundreds of Lebanese civilians were killed. See Adam Shatz, "Patrick Seale: A Remembrance," *Middle East Report Online*, May 1, 2014, http://www.merip. org/mero/mero050114; also Adam Shatz, "In Search of Hezbollah," *New York Review of Books*, April 29 and May 13, 2004, http://www.nybooks.com/ articles/2004/04/29/in-search-of-hezbollah/ and http://www.nybooks.com/ articles/2004/05/13/in-search-of-hezbollah-ii/.

129. Chomsky and Pappé, *On Palestine*, 100; Chomsky and Pappé, *Gaza in Crisis*, 90, 88, 101.

130. Sam Hamad, "How Noam Chomsky Betrayed the Syrian People," *Syria Deeply*, April 14, 2016, https://www.newsdeeply.com/syria/community/2016/04/14/ how-noam-chomsky-betrayed-the-syrian-people.

131. Chomsky, *World Orders Old and New*, 271.

132. Eric Hobsbawm, *The Age of Extremes* (New York: Pantheon, 1994), 5.

133. Barat, "Interview with Noam Chomsky."

134. Chomsky, "On Israel-Palestine and BDS"; Chomsky and Pappé, *On Palestine*, 67.

135. Anne Barnard, "Syria Changed the World," *New York Times*, April 23, 2017, SR2. Al-Haj Saleh has assailed those western leftists for whom "people are invisible, and their lives do not matter. . . . The only one [issue] that matters is the struggle against imperialism." See Yassin Al-Haj Saleh, "The Syrian Cause and Anti-Imperialism," trans. Yaaser Azzayyaat, *Al-Jumhuriya*, May 5, 2017, http:// aljumhuriya.net/en/critical-thought/the-syrian-cause-and-anti-imperialism.

136. Chomsky, *Middle East Illusions*, 73.

137. Publisher's back cover blurb, Chomsky, *World Orders Old and New*.

CONCLUSION

1. Noam Sheizaf, "The 52 words that foretold the future of Israel's occupation in 1967," *Haaretz*, May 26, 2017, http://www.haaretz.com/israel-news/ six-day-war-50-years/.premium-1.791825. The advertisement was placed by members of Matzpen, a Marxist, anti-Zionist party, though Left Zionists such as Amos Oz made similar arguments at the time.

2. Walid Khalidi, "Thinking the Unthinkable: A Sovereign Palestinian State," *Foreign Affairs*, July 1978, 701.

3. Sheizaf, "52 words."

4. Walter Laqueur, "Zionism, the Marxist Critique, and the Left," *Dissent* 18, no. 6 (December 1971): 569.

5. Colin Shindler, *Israel and the European Left: Between Solidarity and Delegitimization* (New York: Continuum, 2012), 176; Laqueur, "Zionism, the Marxist Critique, and the Left," 571.

6. Laqueur, "Zionism, the Marxist Critique, and the Left," 563–64.

7. Yezid Sayigh, *Armed Struggle and the Search for State: The Palestinian National Movement, 1949–1993* (Oxford: Oxford University Press, 1997), 687.

8. Sherene Seikaly, "The Politics of Hope: 1967 and Beyond," *Middle East Report Online,* June 9, 2017, http://merip.org/mero/mero060917.

9. Alain Gresh, "What Does a 'One-State Solution' Really Mean?," trans. George Miller, *Le Monde Diplomatique,* October 2010, emphasis added.

10. The other exception is Ireland, though its partition preceded World War II and, as Halliday pointed out, the fight against it can hardly be considered a positive model. Germany and Yemen were partitioned and reunited, but for a plethora of reasons neither is a conceivable model for Israel-Palestine.

11. For the views on this subject by an array of "ordinary" Palestinians, see Nir Baram's 2015 book *A Land Without Borders: My Journey Around East Jerusalem and the West Bank.* Numerous articles in the *Journal of Palestine Studies* and the *Arab Studies Journal* illuminate the views of a range of Palestinian intellectuals on the one-state/two-state debate.

12. Nathan Thrall, *The Only Language They Understand: Forcing Compromise in Israel and Palestine* (New York: Metropolitan Books, 2017), 69–70.

13. See Shaul Arieli, *Messianism Meets Reality: The Israeli Settlement Project in Judea and Samaria: Vision or Illusion, 1967–2016* (Tel Aviv: Economic Cooperation Foundation, 2017), especially pages 24 and 46. Arieli uses official Israeli government figures.

14. Ibid., 49, 52, 76.

15. Gershon Shafir, *A Half Century of Occupation: Israel, Palestine, and the World's Most Intractable Conflict* (Oakland: University of California Press, 2017), 184, 192. Politically, the question of evacuating the Ariel settlement would be one of the most contentious.

16. Khelil Bouarrouj, "Mouin Rabbani: 'Ignore Palestine At Your Peril,' " *Palestine Square,* May 23, 2016, https://palestinesquare.com/2016/05/23/mouin-rabbani-ignore-palestine-at-your-peril/.

17. Walid Khalidi, "One Century after World War I and the Balfour Declaration: Palestine and Palestine Studies," *openDemocracy.net,* April 2, 2014, https://www.opendemocracy.net/north-africa-west-asia/walid-khalidi/one-century-after-world-war-i-and-balfour-declaration-palestine-and-pal.

18. Shafir, *Half Century of Occupation,* 192.

19. Judith Butler, *Parting Ways: Jewishness and the Critique of Zionism* (New York: Columbia University Press, 2012), 24, 216.

20. Ibid., 215, 214, 208.

21. Ariella Azoulay and Adi Ophir, *The One-State Condition: Occupation and Democracy in Israel/Palestine,* trans. Tal Haran (Stanford: Stanford University Press, 2013), 263.

22. Lama Abu-Odeh, "The Case for Binationalism," *Boston Review,* December 2001–January 2002, http://bostonreview.net/forum/lama-abu-odeh-case-binationalism.

23. Leila Farsakh, "The One-State Solution and the Israeli-Palestinian Conflict: Palestinian Challenges and Prospects," *Middle East Journal* 65, no. 1 (Winter 2011): 70.

24. Janan Bsoul, "What occupation? New generation of Palestinian writers shifts focus from politics to 'life itself,' " *Haaretz*, June 4, 2017.

25. For Bargouti's views, see Rami Younis, "Interview: The Man Behind the BDS Movement," + *972 mag.com*, June 14, 2015, https://972mag.com/interview-the-man-behind-the-bds-movement/107771/.

26. Amos Oz, "50Voices50Years," https://www.50voices50years.com/amos-oz.

27. Uri Avnery, "Rosemary's Baby," *Gush-Shalom.org*, July 24, 2010, http://zope.gush-shalom.org/home/en/channels/avnery/1279969692.

28. Khalidi, "One Century after World War I and the Balfour Declaration."

29. Roger Gaess, "Interview: Hussein Agha," *Middle East Policy Council* 57, no. 2 (Summer 2010), http://www.mepc.org/interview-hussein-agha.

30. Butler, *Parting Ways*, 215, italics in original. Butler is affirmatively discussing Edward Said's *Freud and the Non-European*.

31. Albert Londres, *The Wandering Jew Has Arrived*, trans. Helga Abraham (Jerusalem: Gefen Publishing, 2017) [orig. 1930], 193.

32. George Prochnik, *Stranger in a Strange Land: Searching for Gershom Scholem and Jerusalem* (New York: Other Press, 2016), 16.

33. Londres, *Wandering Jew Has Arrived*, 149–50.

34. Max Horkheimer, *Dawn & Decline: Notes, 1926–1931 and 1950–1969*, trans. Michael Shaw (New York: Seabury Press, 1978) [orig. 1974], 206–7.

35. Robert Alter, "Israel & the Intellectuals," *Commentary*, October 1, 1967, 51.

36. David Grossman, "On hope and despair in the Middle East," *Haaretz*, July 8, 2014.

37. David M. Halbfinger and Isabel Kershner, "Israel Declares the Country the 'Nation-State of the Jewish People,' " *New York Times*, July 19, 2018, A1.

38. Shlomo Ben-Ami, *Scars of War, Wounds of Peace: The Israeli-Arab Tragedy* (New York: Oxford University Press, 2006), 304.

39. Nissim Calderon, email to the author, June 15, 2017.

40. Gaess, "Interview: Hussein Agha."

Abu-Odeh, Lama. "The Case for Binationalism." *Boston Review,* December 2001–January 2002. http://bostonreview.net/forum/lama-abu-odeh-case-binationalism.

Agha, Hussein, and Ahmad Samih Khalidi. "The End of This Road: The Decline of the Palestinian National Movement." *NewYorker.com,* August 6, 2017. http://www.newyorker.com/news/news-desk/the-end-of-this-road-the-decline-of-the-palestinian-national-movement.

Ahmad, Eqbal. *Confronting Empire: Interviews with David Barsamian.* Cambridge, MA: South End Press, 2000.

Ajami, Fouad. *The Dream Palace of the Arabs: A Generation's Odyssey.* New York: Pantheon, 1998.

Al-Haj Saleh, Yassin. "The Syrian Cause and Anti-Imperialism." Translated by Yaaser Azzayyaat. *Al-Jumhuriya,* May 5, 2017. http://aljumhuriya.net/en/critical-thought/the-syrian-cause-and-anti-imperialism.

Ali, Tariq. "Editorial: Mid-Point in the Middle East?" *New Left Review* 38 (March–April 2006): 5–19.

———. "Notes on Anti-Semitism, Zionism and Palestine." *Counterpunch,* March 4, 2004. https://www.counterpunch.org/2004/03/04/notes-on-anti-semitism-zionism-and-palestine/.

Alter, Robert. "Berrigan's Diatribe." *Commentary,* February 1, 1974.

———. "Israel & the Intellectuals." *Commentary,* October 1, 1967.

———. "Zionism for the 70's." *Commentary,* February 1, 1970.

Aly, Götz. *Why the Germans? Why the Jews? Envy, Race Hatred, and the Prehistory of the Holocaust.* Translated by Jefferson S. Chase. New York: Metropolitan, 2014.

Amer, Adnan Abu. "In Eye of Regional Storm, Hamas Pushed Closer to Tehran." *Al-Monitor*, June 2, 2017.

Améry, Jean. "Anti-Semitism on the Left." *Dissent* 29 (January 1982): 41–50. Translated by Sidney and Stella P. Rosenfeld.

Anderson, Perry. "Editorial: The House of Zion." *New Left Review* 96 (November–December 2015): 5–37.

———. "Editorial: On the Concatenation in the Arab World." *New Left Review* 68 (March–April 2011): 5–15.

———. "Editorial: Scurrying Towards Bethlehem." *New Left Review* 10 (July–August 2001): 5–30.

Arendt, Hannah. *Between Past and Future: Eight Exercises in Political Thought.* New York: Penguin, 1993.

———. *Eichmann in Jerusalem: A Report on the Banality of Evil.* New York: Penguin, 1977.

———. *Essays in Understanding.* New York: Harcourt Brace, 1994.

———. *Hannah Arendt: The Recovery of the Public World.* Edited by Melvyn A. Hill. New York: St. Martin's Press, 1979.

———. "A Heroine of Revolution." *New York Review of Books*, October 6, 1996.

———. *The Jew as Pariah: Jewish Identity and Politics in the Modern Age.* New York: Grove Press, 1978.

———. *The Jewish Writings.* Edited by Jerome Kohn and Ron H. Feldman. New York: Schocken Books, 2007.

———. *On Revolution.* London: Penguin, 1990.

———. *The Origins of Totalitarianism.* Cleveland and New York: Meridian Books, 1962.

———. *Rahel Varnhagen: The Life of a Jewess.* Edited by Liliane Weissberg. Translated by Richard and Clara Winston. Baltimore: Johns Hopkins University Press, 1997.

Arieli, Shaul. *Messianism Meets Reality: The Israeli Settlement Project in Judea and Samaria: Vision or Illusion, 1967–2016.* Tel Aviv: Economic Cooperation Foundation, 2017.

Arieli, Yehoshua. "Trapped in Vicious Circles." In *Israel, the Arabs and the Middle East*, edited by Irving Howe and Carl Gershman, 312–20. New York: Bantam Books, 1972.

Aronowitz, Stanley. "Setting the Record Straight: Zionism from the Standpoint of Its Jewish Critics." *Logos* 3, no. 3 (Summer 2004). http://www.logosjournal. com/aronowitz_zionism.htm/.

Ascherson, Neal. "Victory in Defeat." *London Review of Books* 26, no. 3 (December 2, 2004): 3–6.

Aschheim, Steven, ed. *Hannah Arendt in Jerusalem.* Berkeley: University of California Press, 2001.

Avineri, Shlomo. "Modernization and Arab Society: Some Reflections." In *Israel, the Arabs and the Middle East*, edited by Irving Howe and Carl Gershman, 300–11. New York: Bantam Books, 1972.

Avishai, Bernard. "Confederation: The One Possible Israel-Palestine Solution." *New York Review of Books Daily*, February 2, 2018. http://www.nybooks.com/ daily/2018/02/02/confederation-the-one-possible-israel-palestine-solution/.
———. "Koestler and the Zionist Revolution." *Salmagundi*, no. 87 (Summer 1990): 234–59.
Avnery, Uri. "Rosemary's Baby." *Gush-Shalom.org*, July 24, 2010. http://zope. gush-shalom.org/home/en/channels/avnery/1279969692.
Azoulay, Ariella, and Adi Ophir. *The One-State Condition: Occupation and Democracy in Israel/Palestine*. Translated by Tal Haran. Stanford: Stanford University Press, 2013.
Baram, Nir. *A Land Without Borders: My Journey Around East Jerusalem and the West Bank*. Translated by Jessica Cohen. Melbourne, Australia: Text Publishing, 2016.
Barat, Frank. "Interview with Noam Chomsky." *Red Pepper*, May 3, 2011. http:// www.redpepper.org.uk/interview-with-noam-chomsky/.
Barghouti, Omar. *BDS: Boycott, Divestment, Sanctions: The Global Struggle for Palestinian Rights*. Chicago: Haymarket Books, 2011.
Barnard, Anne. "Syria Changed the World." *New York Times*, April 23, 2017.
Barnes, Bart. "I. F. Stone, Radical Gadfly, Dies at 81." *Jerusalem Post*, June 20, 1989.
Barnouw, Dagmar. *Visible Spaces: Hannah Arendt and the German-Jewish Experience*. Baltimore: Johns Hopkins University Press, 1990.
Bauer, Yehuda. *The Jewish Emergence from Powerlessness*. Toronto: University of Toronto Press, 1979.
Bell, J. Bowyer. *The Long War: Israel and the Arabs since 1946*. Englewood Cliffs, NJ: Prentice-Hall, 1969.
Ben-Ami, Shlomo. *Scars of War, Wounds of Peace: The Israeli-Arab Tragedy*. New York: Oxford University Press, 2006.
Benhabib, Seyla. *The Reluctant Modernism of Hannah Arendt*. Thousand Oaks, CA: Sage Publications, 1996.
Benhabib, Seyla, Wolfgang Bonß, and John McCole, eds. *On Max Horkheimer: New Perspectives*. Cambridge: MIT Press, 1993.
Benjamin, Walter. *Illuminations: Essays and Reflections*. Translated by Harry Zohn. New York: Schocken Books, 1969.
Benvenisti, Meron. "The Twilight War." *New Yorker*, March 18, 1996.
Berman, Paul. "The Watchdog." *New York Times Book Review*, October 1, 2006.
Bernstein, Michael André. "A Yes or a No." *New Republic*, September 27, 1999, 35–41.
Bernstein, Richard J. *Hannah Arendt and the Jewish Question*. Cambridge: MIT Press, 1996.
Berrigan, Daniel. "Daniel Berrigan on the Moral Dilemma in the Middle East, 1974." *Progressive*, March 1974. http://progressive.org/magazine/daniel-berrigan-moral-dilemma-middle-east-1974/.
Bérubé, Michael. *The Left at War*. New York: New York University Press, 2009.

Biale, David. *Power and Powerlessness in Jewish History*. New York: Schocken Books, 1986.

Bialik, H. N. "In the City of Slaughter." In *Complete Poetic Works of Hayyim Nahman Bialik*, edited by Israel Efros. Histadruth Ivrith of America, vol. 1. New York, 1948.

Blankfort, Michael. "War for Oil? An Exchange." *New York Review of Books*, March 6, 1975.

Bouarrouj, Khelil. "Mouin Rabbani: 'Ignore Palestine At Your Peril.' " *Palestine Square*, May 23, 2016. https://palestineunbound.wordpress. com/2016/05/23/mouin-rabbani-ignore-palestine-at-your-peril/.

Brightman, Carol, ed. *Between Friends: The Correspondence of Hannah Arendt and Mary McCarthy, 1949–1965*. New York: Harcourt Brace, 1995.

Brockes, Emma. "The Greatest Intellectual? Noam Chomsky Interviewed by Emma Brockes." *Guardian*, October 31, 2005. https://chomsky.info/20051031/.

Bruzonsky, Mark. "Israel's No. 1 Dove." *Worldview*, January 1978.

Bsoul, Janan. "What occupation? New generation of Palestinian writers shifts focus from politics to 'life itself.' " *Haaretz*, June 4, 2017.

Butler, Judith. *Parting Ways: Jewishness and the Critique of Zionism*. New York: Columbia University Press, 2012.

Caplan, Neil. *Futile Diplomacy*. 4 vols. New York: Frank Cass, 1983–1997.

Carey, Roane. "A 'Non-Jewish Jew,' Hitchens Welcomed Finding He Was Jewish— But Not Zionism." *Jewish Daily Forward*, December 21, 2011.

———, ed. *The New Intifada: Resisting Israel's Apartheid*. New York: Verso, 2001.

Carmichael, Joel. "I. F. Stone Reconsiders Israel." *Midstream*, October 1967.

Cesarani, David. *Arthur Koestler: The Homeless Mind*. New York: Free Press, 1998.

Chomsky, Noam. Address to the United Nations, October 14, 2014. Available on YouTube.

———. "Blinded by the Truth." *Al-Ahram Weekly*, November 2–8, 2000. https:// chomsky.info/20001102/.

———. "Daniel in the Lions' Den: Berrigan & His Critics." *Liberation* 18, no. 6 (February 1974): 15–24.

———. *Fateful Triangle: The United States, Israel, and the Palestinians*. Montreal: Black Rose Books, 1999.

———. *Middle East Illusions*. Lanham, MD: Rowman and Littlefield, 2004.

———. "Nationalism and Conflict in Palestine." *Liberation* 14, no. 8 (November 1969): 7–21.

———. "On Israel-Palestine and BDS." *Nation*, July 2, 2014.

———. "Some Tasks for the Left." *Liberation* 14, nos. 5–6 (August–September 1969): 38–43.

———. "A Special Supplement: The Responsibility of Intellectuals." *New York Review of Books*, February 23, 1967.

———. *Towards a New Cold War: Essays on the Current Crisis and How We Got There*. New York: Pantheon, 1982.

———. *World Orders Old and New*. New York: Columbia University Press, 1994.

Chomsky, Noam, and David Barsamian. *Global Discontents: Conversations on the Rising Threats to Democracy*. New York: Metropolitan Books, 2017.

Chomsky, Noam, and Ilan Pappé. *Gaza in Crisis: Reflections on Israel's War against the Palestinians*. Chicago: Haymarket Books, 2010.

———. *On Palestine*. Bungay, UK: Penguin, 2015.

Cohen, Joshua. "A Balkans of the Mind." *New York Times Book Review*, January 1, 2017.

Cooke, Rachel. "David Grossman: 'I cannot afford the luxury of despair.' " *Guardian*, August 29, 2010.

Cox, Michael. "Fred Halliday, Marxism, and the Cold War." *International Affairs* 87, no. 5 (2011): 1107–22.

Darwish, Mahmoud. *La Palestine comme métaphore: entretiens*. Translated by Elias Sanbar and Simone Bitton. Paris: Sindbad/Actes Sud, 1997.

Davis, Mike. "Editorial: Spring Confronts Winter." *New Left Review* 72 (November–December 2011): 5–15.

Deutscher, Isaac. *Ironies of History: Essays on Contemporary Communism*. Berkeley, CA: Ramparts Press, 1971.

———. *The Non-Jewish Jew and Other Essays*. London: Oxford University Press, 1968.

———. "On the Israeli-Arab War." *New Left Review* 44 (July–August 1967): 30–45.

———. *The Prophet Armed: Trotsky, 1879–1921*. London: Oxford University Press, 1954.

———. *The Prophet Outcast: Trotsky, 1929–1940*. London: Oxford University Press, 1970.

Diner, Dan. *Beyond the Conceivable: Studies on Germany, Nazism, and the Holocaust*. Berkeley: University of California Press, 2000.

Diner, Dan, and Jonathan Frankel. "Jews and Communism: The Utopian Temptation." In *Dark Times, Dire Decisions: Jews and Communism: Studies in Contemporary Jewry. An Annual, XX*, edited by Jonathan Frankel. New York: Oxford University Press, 2004.

Du Bois, W. E. B. *The Souls of Black Folk*. New York: Modern Library, 1996.

Eban, Abba. "I. F. Stone: Gadfly in the Promised Land." *Washington Post*, February 25, 1979.

El-Asmar, Fouzi, Uri Davis, and Naim Khadr. *Towards a Socialist Republic of Palestine*. London: Ithaca Press and Kefar Shmaryahu, Israel: Miftah Publishers, 1978.

Fallaci, Oriana. *Interview with History*. Translated by John Shepley. Boston: Houghton Mifflin, 1976.

Farsakh, Leila. "The One-State Solution and the Israeli-Palestinian Conflict: Palestinian Challenges and Prospects." *Middle East Journal* 65, no. 1 (Winter 2011): 55–71.

Feldman, Keith P. *A Shadow over Palestine: The Imperial Life of Race in America*. Minneapolis: University of Minnesota Press, 2015.

Flapan, Simcha. *The Arab-Israeli War of 1967: A Reply to Isaac Deutscher*. Tel Aviv: International Department of the United Workers' Party-MAPAM, 1968.

Frankel, Jonathan. "Israel: The War and After." *Dissent* 30, no. 1 (Winter 1983): 7–10.

Friedländer, Saul, and Mahmoud Hussein. *Arabs & Israelis: A Dialogue.* Translated by Paul Auster and Lydia Davis. New York: Holmes and Meier, 1975.

Gaess, Roger. "Interview: Hussein Agha." *Middle East Policy Council* 17, no. 2 (Summer 2010). http://www.mepc.org/interview-hussein-agha.

Gallagher, Nancy Elizabeth, ed. *Approaches to the History of the Middle East: Interviews with Leading Middle East Historians.* Reading, UK: Ithaca Press, 1994.

Garrison, Ann. " 'Denying' the Srebrenica Genocide Because It's Not True: an Interview with Diana Johnstone." *Counterpunch,* July 16, 2015. http://www.counterpunch.org/2015/07/16/denying-the-srebrenica-genocide-because-its-not-true-an-interview-with-diana-johnstone/.

Gellhorn, Martha. "Eichmann and the Private Conscience." *Atlantic Monthly* 209, no. 2 (February 1962): 52–59.

Genovese, Eugene. *In Red and Black: Marxian Explorations in Southern and Afro-American History.* New York: Vintage, 1972.

Geras, Norman. "Marxists before the Holocaust." *New Left Review* 224 (July–August 1997): 19–38.

Goldsmith, S. J. "Deutscher in Marxland." *Jewish Observer and Middle East Review,* November 22, 1968.

———. *Twenty 20th Century Jews.* Freeport, NY: Books for Libraries Press, 1962.

Goodheart, Eugene. "An Interview with Amos Oz." *Partisan Review* 49, no. 3 (Summer 1982): 351–62.

Goodman, Amy. "In U.N. Speech, Noam Chomsky Blasts United States for Supporting Israel, Blocking Palestinian State." *Democracy Now!,* October 22, 2014. https://www.democracynow.org/2014/10/22/in_un_speech_noam_chomsky_blasts.

Gouri, Haim. *Facing the Glass Booth: The Jerusalem Trial of Adolf Eichmann.* Translated by Michael Swirsky. Detroit: Wayne State University Press, 2004.

Graetz, Heinrich. *The Structure of Jewish History and Other Essays.* Edited and translated by Ismar Schorsch. New York: Jewish Theological Seminary of America, 1975.

The Great Berrigan Debate. New York: Committee on New Alternatives in the Middle East, 1974.

Gresh, Alain. *The PLO: The Struggle Within.* Translated by A. M. Berrett. London: Zed Books, 1985.

———. "What Does a 'One-State Solution' Really Mean?" Translated by George Miller. *Le Monde Diplomatique,* October 2010.

Grossman, David. "On hope and despair in the Middle East." *Haaretz,* July 8, 2014.

———. *The Yellow Wind.* Translated by Haim Watzman. New York: Farrar, Straus and Giroux, 1988.

Guttenplan, D. D. *American Radical: The Life and Times of I. F. Stone.* New York: Farrar, Straus and Giroux, 2009.

Halbfinger, David M. and Isabel Kershner. "Israel Declares the Country the 'Nation-State of the Jewish People.' " *New York Times,* July 19, 2018.

Halliday, Fred. "The Coalition Against the Shah: Stories of 'Mad Mullahs' Mask a Wider Public Revolt." *New Statesman,* January 5, 1979.

———. "The Crisis of the Arab World: The False Answers of Saddam Hussein." *New Left Review* 184 (November–December 1990): 9–19.

———. "The Fate of Solidarity." Undated. www.platypus1917.org/wp-content/uploads/readings /hallidayfred_fateofsolidarity.pdf.

———. "Imperialism and the Middle East." *MERIP Reports* 117 (September–October 1983): 19–23.

———. *Iran: Dictatorship and Development.* New York: Penguin, 1979.

———. *Islam and the Myth of Confrontation: Religion and Politics in the Middle East.* New York: I. B. Tauris, 1995.

———. "The Islamic Republic of Iran After 30 Years," London School of Economics, February 23, 2009.

———. "The Jihadism of Fools." *Dissent* 54, no. 1 (Winter 2007): 53–56.

———. "Kabul's Patriarchy with Guns." *Nation,* November 11, 1996. http://www.thenation.com/article/kabuls-patriarchy-guns.

———. "The Left and War." *New Statesman and Society,* March 8, 1991.

———. "Maxime Rodinson: in praise of a 'marginal man.' " *openDemocracy.* September 8, 2005. https://www.opendemocracy.net/globalization/Rodinson_2819.jsp.

———. *Nation and Religion in the Middle East.* Boulder, CO: Lynne Rienner Publishers, 2000.

———. "1967 and the Consequences of Catastrophe." *MERIP Reports* 146 (May–June 1987). http://www.merip.org/mer/mer146/1967-consequences-catastrophe.

———. "On the PFLP and the September Crisis: Interview with Ghassan Kannafani," *New Left Review* 67 (May–June 1971): 50–57.

———. *Political Journeys: The openDemocracy Essays.* Edited by David Hayes. New Haven: Yale University Press, 2012.

———. "Revolution in Afghanistan." *New Left Review* 112 (November–December 1978): 3–44.

———. "The Revolution Turns to Repression." *New Statesman,* August 24, 1979.

———. "Revolutionary Internationalism and its Perils." In *Revolution in the Making of the Modern World,* edited by John Foran et al., 65–80. New York: Routledge, 2008.

———. "Revolutionary Realism and the Struggle for Palestine." *MERIP Reports* 96 (May 1981). http://www.merip.org/mer/mer96/revolutionary-realism-struggle-palestine.

———. "Right-Wingers on the Rampage." *New Statesman,* August 17, 1979.

———. *Two Hours that Shook the World: September 11, 2011: Causes and Consequences.* London: Saqi Books, 2002.

———. "War and Revolution in Afghanistan." *New Left Review* 119 (January–February 1980): 20–41.

———. "What Was Communism?" *openDemocracy.net,* October 16, 2009. https://www.opendemocracy.net/article/what-was-communism.

Halliday, Fred, and Danny Postel. "Who Is Responsible? An Interview with Fred Halliday." *Salmagundi*, nos. 150–51 (Summer 2006).

Hamad, Sam. "How Noam Chomsky Betrayed the Syrian People." *Syria Deeply*, April 14, 2016. https://www.newsdeeply.com/syria/community/2016/04/14/how-noam-chomsky-betrayed-the-syrian-people.

"Hamas hails Iranian military after damaged relations are mended." *New Arab*, August 28, 2017. https://www.alaraby.co.uk/english/news/2017/8/28/hamas-hails-iranian-military-after-damaged-relations-are-mended.

Hanson, Harry. "Britain and the Arabs." *New Reasoner*, no. 6 (Autumn 1958): 3–14.

Harkabi, Y. "Fatah's Doctrine (December 1968)." In *The Israel-Arab Reader*, edited by Walter Laqueur and Barry Rubin, 121–30. New York: Penguin, 2001.

Hasson, Nir. "A Fight to the Death, and Betrayal by the Arab World: The Most Disastrous 24 Hours in Palestinian History." *Haaretz*, January 25, 2018. https://www.haaretz.com/middle-east-news/palestinians/.premium-1.833130.

Hicks, Granville. "Arthur Koestler and the Future of the Left." *Antioch Review* 5, no. 2 (Summer 1945).

Hobsbawm, Eric. *The Age of Extremes*. New York: Pantheon, 1994.

———. *On History*. New York: The New Press, 1997.

———. *Revolutionaries*. New York: The New Press, 2001.

Horkheimer, Max. *Dawn & Decline: Notes 1926–1931 and 1950–1969*. Translated by Michael Shaw. New York: Seabury Press, 1978.

———. "The Jews and Europe." In *Critical Theory and Society: A Reader*, edited by Stephen Bronner and Douglas Kellner, 77–94. New York: Routledge, 1989.

Howe, Irving. *Politics and the Novel*. New York: New American Library, 1987.

Hudson, Martyn. "Revisiting Isaac Deutscher." *Fathom* (Winter 2014).

"Iran Pulls Palestine from the Margins." *Al-Monitor*, February 26, 2017.

Isaac, Jeffrey. *Arendt, Camus, and Modern Rebellion*. New Haven: Yale University Press, 1992.

Jay, Martin. *Permanent Exiles*. New York: Columbia University Press, 1985.

Jewish Virtual Library. "Hannah Arendt, 1906–1975." http://www.jewishvirtuallibrary.org/hannah-arendt.

Jonas, Hans. "Hannah Arendt, 1906–1975." *Social Research* 43, no. 1 (1976): 3–5.

———. *Hans Jonas: Memoirs*. Edited by Christian Wiese. Translated by Krishna Winston. Lebanon, NH: Brandeis University Press, 2008.

Jones, Mervyn. "Israel, Palestine and Socialism." *Socialist Register* 7 (1970): 63–87.

Judis, John B. *Genesis: Truman, American Jews, and the Origins of the Arab/Israeli Conflict*. New York: Farrar, Straus and Giroux, 2014.

Kaufmann, Yehezkel. "Anti-Semitic Stereotypes in Zionism: The Nationalist Rejection of Diaspora Jewry." Translated by Jacob Sloan. *Commentary*, March 1, 1949.

Khalidi, Rashid. *The Iron Cage: The Story of the Palestinian Struggle for Statehood*. Boston: Beacon Press, 2006.

Khalidi, Walid. "One Century after World War I and the Balfour Declaration: Palestine and Palestine Studies." *openDemocracy.net*, April 2, 2014. https://

www.opendemocracy.net/north-africa-west-asia/walid-khalidi/one-century-after-world-war-i-and-balfour-declaration-palestine-and-pal.

———. "Thinking the Unthinkable: A Sovereign Palestinian State." *Foreign Affairs*, July 1978, 695–713.

Kimche, David. *The Last Option: After Nasser, Arafat, and Saddam Hussein*. New York: Charles Scribner's Sons, 1991.

Kimche, Jon. "Orwell and Deutscher." *New Middle East* 3 (December 1968).

———. *There Could Have Been Peace: The Untold Story of Why We Failed with Palestine and Again with Israel*. New York: Dial Press, 1973.

Klein, Alexander, ed. *Dissent, Power, and Confrontation*. New York: McGraw-Hill, 1971.

Koestler, Arthur. *Arrow in the Blue: An Autobiography*. New York: Macmillan, 1961.

———. *The Invisible Writing: An Autobiography*. New York: Macmillan, 1954.

———. *Promise and Fulfilment: Palestine, 1917–1949*. London: Macmillan, 1949.

———. "A Sentimental Journey Through Palestine." In *Foreign Correspondent: Personal Adventures Abroad in Search of the News by Twelve British Journalists*, edited by Wilfrid Hindle, 51–79. London: George G. Harrap, 1939.

———. *Thieves in the Night: Chronicle of an Experiment*. London: Macmillan, 1961.

———. *The Thirteenth Tribe: The Khazar Empire and Its Heritage*. New York: Random House, 1976.

———. *The Trail of the Dinosaur*. New York: Macmillan, 1955.

———. *The Yogi and the Commissar*. New York: Macmillan, 1945.

Kohler, Lotte, ed. *Within Four Walls: The Correspondence between Hannah Arendt and Heinrich Blücher, 1936–1968*. Translated by Peter Constantine. New York: Harcourt, 2000.

Kohler, Lotte, and Hans Saner, eds. *Hannah Arendt/Karl Jaspers Correspondence, 1926–1969*. Translated by Robert and Rita Kimber. New York: Harcourt Brace, 1992.

Korb, Samuel. "Chomsky's Allegations Should Be Questioned." *Tech*, December 6, 2002.

Kramer, Martin. "Islamism and Fascism: Dare to Compare." *MartinKramer.org*. September 20, 2006. http://martinkramer.org/sandbox/2006/09/islamism-and-fascism-dare-to-compare/.

———. *The Jewish Discovery of Islam: Studies in Honor of Bernard Lewis*. Tel Aviv: Moshe Dayan Center for Middle Eastern and African Studies, 1999.

Kundnani, Hans. *Utopia or Auschwitz: Germany's 1968 Generation and the Holocaust*. London: Hurst, 2009.

Labedz, Leopold. "Deutscher as Historian and Prophet." *Survey: A Journal of European and East European Studies* 41 (April 1962): 120–44.

Lanzmann, Claude. "From the Holocaust to the *Holocaust*." Translated by Simon Srebrny. *Telos* 42 (Winter 1979–80): 137–43.

———. *The Patagonian Hare: A Memoir*. Translated by Frank Wynne. New York: Farrar, Straus and Giroux, 2012.

Laqueur, Walter. *A History of Zionism*. New York: Holt, Rinehart and Winston, 1972.

————. "The Origins of Fascism: Islamic Fascism, Islamophobia, Antisemitism."
  OUPblog. October 25, 2006. https://blog.oup.com/2006/10/the_origins_of_2/.
————. "Zionism, the Marxist Critique, and the Left." *Dissent* 18, no. 6
  (December 1971): 560–74.
Lazare, Bernard. *Antisemitism: Its History and Causes.* Edited by Robert Wistrich.
  Lincoln: University of Nebraska Press, 1995.
————. *Job's Dungheap.* New York: Schocken Books, 1948.
Levene, Mark. *Arthur Koestler.* New York: Frederick Ungar, 1984.
Levi, Primo. *The Drowned and the Saved.* Translated by Raymond Rosenthal. New
  York: Vintage International, 1989.
————. *Survival in Auschwitz.* Translated by Stuart Woolf. New York: Simon and
  Schuster, 1996.
Lichtheim, George. *The Concept of Ideology and Other Essays.* New York: Random
  House, 1967.
Lieberman, Lisa. "Albert Memmi's About-Face." *Michigan Quarterly Review* 46,
  no. 3 (Summer 2007). http://hdl.handle.net/2027/spo.act2080.0046.326.
Lipstadt, Deborah E. *The Eichmann Trial.* New York: Schocken Books, 2011.
Londres, Albert. *The Wandering Jew Has Arrived.* Translated by Helga Abraham.
  Jerusalem: Gefen Publishing, 2017.
Lydon, Christopher. "Noam Chomsky: Neoliberalism Is Destroying Our Democ-
  racy." *Nation*, June 2, 2017.
Maccoby, Hyam. "Koestler's Racism." *Midstream* 23, no. 3 (March 1977).
MacFarquhar, Larissa. "The Devil's Accountant." *New Yorker*, March 31, 2003.
MacPherson, Myra. *"All Governments Lie": The Life and Times of Rebel Journalist
  I. F. Stone.* New York: Scribner, 2006.
Mandell, Joan, and Joe Stork. "Maxime Rodinson Looks Back." *Middle East Report*
  269 (Winter 2013).
Margalit, Avishai. "Israel: A Partial Indictment." *New York Review of Books*, June
  28, 1984.
Marx, Karl. *Early Texts.* Edited and translated by David McLellan. Oxford: Basil
  Blackwell, 1971.
Massad, Joseph. "Imperialism, Despotism, and Democracy in Syria." *aljazeera.
  com*, February 6, 2012. http://www.aljazeera.com/indepth/opinion/2012/02/
  2012269456491274.html.
Maurer, Marvin. "I. F. Stone—Universalist." *Midstream*, February 1979.
McCarthy, Mary. "The Hue and Cry." *Partisan Review* 31, no. 1 (1964): 82–94.
McLeod, George. "Noam Chomsky Interview." *Phnom Penh Post*, March 27, 2009.
  https://chomsky.info/20090327/.
Memmi, Albert. "Am I a Traitor?" *Commentary*, October 1962.
————. *The Colonizer and the Colonized.* Translated by Howard Greenfeld. Boston:
  Beacon Press, 1967.
————. *Decolonization and the Decolonized.* Translated by Robert Bononno.
  Minneapolis: University of Minnesota Press, 2004.
————. "Does the Jew Exist?" *Commentary*, November 1966.
————. *Dominated Man: Notes towards a Portrait.* Boston: Beacon Press, 1968.

———. *Jews and Arabs*. Translated by Eleanor Levieux. Chicago: J. Philip O'Hara, 1975.

———. "Jews, Tunisians, and Frenchmen." *Literary Review* 41, no. 2 (Winter 1998): 223–27.

———. *The Liberation of the Jew*. Translated by Judy Hyun. New York: Viking Press, 1973.

———. *The Pillar of Salt*. Translated by Edouard Roditi. Boston: Beacon Press, 2001.

———. *Portrait of a Jew*. Translated by Elisabeth Abbott. New York: Viking Press, 1971.

Mendel, Hersh. *Memoirs of a Jewish Revolutionary*. Translated by Robert Michaels. London: Pluto Press, 1989.

Molyneux, Maxine, and Fred Halliday. "Marxism, the Third World and the Middle East." *MERIP Reports* 120 (January–February 1984): 18–21.

Morris, Benny. *One State, Two States*. New Haven: Yale University Press, 2009.

———. *Righteous Victims: A History of the Zionist-Arab Conflict, 1881–2001*. New York: Vintage, 2001.

Nedava, Joseph. *Arthur Koestler*. London: Robert Anscombe, 1948.

———. *Trotsky and the Jews*. Philadelphia: Jewish Publication Society of America, 1971.

Oz, Amos. "50Voices50Years." https://www.50voices50years.com/amos-oz.

———. *Israel, Palestine and Peace*. New York: Harvest, 1994.

———. "Meaning of Homeland." *New Outlook*, December 1967.

"Palestine Royal Commission Report." July 1937. https://palestinianmandate.files.wordpress.com/2014/04/cm-5479.pdf.

Parini, Jay. "The Land of Oz." *New York Times Book Review*, April 14, 1991.

Patner, Andrew. *I. F. Stone: A Portrait*. New York: Anchor Books, 1990.

Peled, Yoav. "Zionist Realities." *New Left Review* 38 (March–April 2006): 21–36.

Piterberg, Gabriel. "Zion's Rebel Daughter." *New Left Review* 48 (2007): 39–57.

"Popular Front for the Liberation of Palestine: Platform (1969)." In *The Israel-Arab Reader*, edited by Walter Laqueur and Barry Rubin, 139–42. New York: Penguin, 2001.

Postel, Danny. "Remembering Fred Halliday in Chicago." May 3, 2010. dannypostel.homestead.com/Remembering-Fred-Halliday-in-Chicago.html.

Prochnik, George. *Stranger in a Strange Land: Searching for Gershom Scholem and Jerusalem*. New York: Other Press, 2016.

Pundak, Ron. "From Oslo to Taba: What Went Wrong?" *Survival* 43, no. 3 (Autumn 2001): 31–45.

Rabbani, Mouin. "Reflections on a Lifetime of Engagement with Zionism, the Palestine Question, and American Empire: An Interview with Noam Chomsky." *Journal of Palestine Studies* 41, no. 3 (Spring 2012): 92–120.

Raz-Krakotzkin, Amnon. "Jewish Peoplehood, 'Jewish Politics,' and Political Responsibility: Arendt on Zionism and Partitions." *College Literature* 38, no. 1 (Winter 2011): 57–74.

Roberts, Adam. "Simon Frederick Peter Halliday, 1946–2010." *Proceedings of the British Academy* 172 (2011): 143–69.

Robin, Corey. "Dragon-Slayers." *London Review of Books* 29, no. 1 (January 4, 2007). http://www.lrb.co.uk/v29/no1/corey-robin/dragon-slayers.

Rodinson, Maxime. *The Arabs.* Translated by Arthur Goldhammer. Chicago: University of Chicago Press, 1981.

———. *Cult, Ghetto, and State: The Persistence of the Jewish Question.* Translated by Jon Rothschild. London: Al Saqi Books, 1983.

———. *Israel: A Colonial-Settler State?* Translated by David Thorstad. New York: Monad Press, 1973.

———. *Israel and the Arabs.* Translated by Michael Perl. New York: Pantheon, 1968.

———. *Marxism and the Muslim World.* Translated by Jean Matthews. New York: Monthly Review Press, 1981.

———. "Maxime Rodinson on Zionism and the Palestine Problem Today." *Journal of Palestine Studies* 4, no. 3 (Spring 1975): 21–45.

———. "Why Palestine?" Translated by Margaret Chiari. *Journal of Palestine Studies* 13, no. 3, (Spring 1984): 16–26.

Rose, Jacqueline. *The Question of Zion.* Princeton: Princeton University Press, 2005.

Ruby, Walter. "I. F. Stone and the Ancient Mystery: Offering a New Perspective on the Death of Socrates." *Washington Post,* March 10, 1988.

Said, Edward. "Chomsky and the Question of Palestine." *Journal of Palestine Studies* 4, no. 3 (Spring 1975): 91–104.

———. *The End of the Peace Process: Oslo and After.* New York: Pantheon, 2000.

———. "The Morning After." *London Review of Books* 15, no. 20 (October 21, 1993): 3–5. https://www.lrb.co.uk/v15/n20/edward-said/the-morning-after.

———. "On Palestinian Identity: A Conversation with Salman Rushdie." *New Left Review* 1, no. 160 (November–December 1986): 63–80.

Samuels, David. "Q&A: Noam Chomsky." *Tablet,* November 12, 2010.

Sayigh, Yezid. *Armed Struggle and the Search for State: The Palestinian National Movement, 1949–1993.* Oxford: Oxford University Press, 1999.

———. "Who Killed the Oslo Accords?" *aljazeera.com.* October 1, 2015. http://www.aljazeera.com/indepth/opinion/2015/10/killed-oslo-accords-151001072411049.html.

Scammell, Michael. *Koestler: The Literary and Political Odyssey of a Twentieth-Century Skeptic.* New York: Random House, 2009.

Schalit, Joel. *Israel vs. Utopia.* New York: Akashi Books, 2009.

Scholem, Gershom. *A Life in Letters, 1914–1982.* Translated by Anthony David Skinner. Cambridge: Harvard University Press, 2002.

Sebastian, Tim. "On Afghanistan: Noam Chomsky Interviewed by Tim Sebastian." *Hard Talk,* February 2, 2002. https://chomsky.info/20020227/.

Segev, Tom. *One Palestine, Complete: Jews and Arabs Under the British Mandate.* Translated by Haim Watzman. New York: Henry Holt, 2000.

———. *The Seventh Million: The Israelis and the Holocaust.* Translated by Haim Watzman. New York: Hill and Wang, 1993.

Seikaly, Sherene. "The Politics of Hope: 1967 and Beyond." *Middle East Report Online*, June 9, 2017. http://merip.org/mero/mero060917.

Shafir, Gershon. *A Half Century of Occupation: Israel, Palestine, and the World's Most Intractable Conflict*. Oakland: University of California Press, 2017.

Shatz, Adam. "In Search of Hezbollah." *New York Review of Books*, April 29 and May 13, 2004. http://www.nybooks.com/articles/2004/04/29/in-search-of-hezbollah/ and http://www.nybooks.com/articles/2004/05/13/in-search-of-hezbollah-ii/.

———. "The Interpreters of Maladies." *Nation*, November 24, 2004. http://www.thenation.com/article/interpreters-maladies/.

———. "Patrick Seale: A Remembrance." *Middle East Report Online*, May 1, 2014. http://www.merip.org/mero/mero050114.

———. *Prophets Outcast: A Century of Dissident Writings about Zionism and Israel*. New York: Nation Books, 2004.

Shavit, Ari. "My Right of Return: Edward Said Interviewed by Ari Shavit." *Haaretz*, August 18, 2000.

Sheizaf, Noam. "The 52 words that foretold the future of Israel's occupation in 1967." *Haaretz*, May 26, 2017. http://www.haaretz.com/israel-news/six-day-war-50-years/.premium-1.791825.

Shindler, Colin. *Israel and the European Left: Between Solidarity and Delegitimization*. New York: Continuum, 2012.

Shklar, Judith N. *Political Thought and Political Thinkers*. Chicago: University of Chicago Press, 1998.

Sid-Ahmed, Mohamed. *After the Guns Fall Silent: Peace or Armageddon in the Middle-East*. Translated by Maissa Talaat. London: Croom Helm, 1976.

Slezkine, Yuri. *The Jewish Century*. Princeton: Princeton University Press, 2004.

Sonntag, Jacob. "Deutscher's Tragic Dilemma." *Jewish Vanguard*, January 29, 1969.

Sperber, Murray A., ed. *Arthur Koestler: A Collection of Critical Essays*. Englewood Cliffs, NJ: Prentice-Hall, 1977.

Steinberg, Matti. *In Search of Modern Palestinian Statehood*. Tel Aviv: Moshe Dayan Center, 2016.

Stephen, Andrew. "NS Interview—Chomsky." *New Statesman*, June 19, 2006. http://www.newstatesman.com/node/164578.

Stern, Sol. "Hannah Arendt and the Origins of Israelophobia." *City Journal* 22, no. 1 (2012): 92–103.

Sternhell, Zeev. *The Founding Myths of Israel: Nationalism, Socialism, and the Making of the Jewish State*. Translated by David Maisel. Princeton: Princeton University Press, 1998.

———. "Israel's Wars: Is Anyone Capable of Setting Policy?" *Haaretz*, March 10, 2017.

Stoakes, Emanuel. "Chomsky and his Critics." *Jacobin*, November 23, 2015. https://www.jacobinmag.com/2015/11/noam-chomsky-interview-isis-syria-intervention-nato/.

Stone, I. F. "America's Satellites Turn Desperate, Too." *I. F. Stone's Weekly*, November 5, 1956.

———. *The Best of I. F. Stone*. Edited by Karl Weber. New York: Public Affairs, 2006.

———. *The Best of "I. F. Stone's Weekly."* Edited by Neil Middleton. London: Penguin Books, 1973.

———. "Born Under Fire." *New Republic*, May 31, 1948.

———. "The Future of Israel." *Ramparts*, July 1967.

———. "Gangsters or Patriots?" *Nation*, January 12, 1946.

———. *The Haunted Fifties*. London: Merlin Press, 1964.

———. "Holy War." *New York Review of Books*, August 3, 1967.

———. "The Hope." *New York Review of Books*, October 26, 1978.

———. *In a Time of Torment, 1961–1967*. Boston: Little, Brown, 1967.

———. "Israel's Hopes and Fears of Russian Intervention." *I. F. Stone's Weekly*, April 30, 1956.

———. "Izzy on Izzy." *New York Times Magazine*, January 22, 1978.

———. "The Need for Double Vision in the Middle East." *I. F. Stone's Weekly*, January 13, 1969.

———. "On The Pro-Israel Left." *I. F. Stone's Weekly*, June 5, 1967.

———. "The Pilgrimage of Malcolm X." *New York Review of Books*, November 11, 1965.

———. *Polemics and Prophecies, 1967–1970*. Boston: Little, Brown, 1970.

———. "The Road to Peace Lies Through the Arab Refugee Camps." *I. F. Stone's Weekly*, April 30, 1956.

———. "Suppose Those Were Jewish Refugees From Arab Armies?" *I. F. Stone's Weekly*, July 3, 1967.

———. "Tel Aviv Quiet, But You Know There's a War On." *PM*, May 12, 1948.

———. "The Terrible Truth About the World Crisis (And Me)." *I. F. Stone's Weekly*, November 12, 1956.

———. "Theirs Is a Moral Challenge to World Jewry and Israel." *I. F. Stone's Weekly*, April 30, 1956.

———. *This Is Israel*. New York: Boni and Gaer, 1948.

———. *Underground to Palestine and Reflections Thirty Years Later*. London: Hutchinson, 1979.

———. "War for Oil?" *New York Review of Books*, February 6, 1975.

———. *The War Years, 1939–1945*. Boston: Little, Brown, 1988.

———. "Why Not A Global Settlement Before It's Too Late?" *I. F. Stone's Weekly*, June 5, 1967.

Syrkin, Marie. "Underground to Palestine and Reflections Thirty Years Later." *New Republic*, January 27, 1979.

Thompson, E. P. *E. P. Thompson and the Making of the New Left*. Edited by Cal Winslow. New York: Monthly Review Press, 2014.

Thrall, Nathan. *The Only Language They Understand: Forcing Compromise in Israel and Palestine*. New York: Metropolitan Books, 2017.

Timerman, Jacobo. *The Longest War: Israel in Lebanon*. Translated by Miguel Acoca. New York: Alfred A. Knopf, 1982.

Traverso, Enzo. *The End of Jewish Modernity*. Translated by David Fernbach. London: Pluto Press, 2016.

————. *The Marxists and the Jewish Question: The History of a Debate, 1843–1943*. Translated by Bernard Gibbons. Amherst, NY: Humanity Books, 1994.

Trilling, Diana. "Fiction in Review." *Nation*, November 9, 1946.

Trotsky, Leon. *On the Jewish Question*. New York: Pathfinder Press, 1970.

United Nations Security Council Draft Resolution S/11940, January 23, 1976.

United Nations Security Council Official Records, 1879th Meeting: January 26, 1976.

Usher, Graham. "Arafat and the Opposition: An Interview with Marwan Barghouti." *Middle East Report* 191 (November–December 1994): 22–25. http://www.merip.org/mer/mer191/arafat-opposition.

Walzer, Michael. *The Company of Critics: Social Criticism and Political Commitment in the Twentieth Century*. New York: Basic Books, 2002.

————. *The Paradox of Liberation: Secular Revolutions and Religious Counterrevolutions*. New Haven: Yale University Press, 2015.

Wasserstein, Bernard. *Isaiah Berlin, Isaac Deutscher and Arthur Koestler: Their Jewish Wars*. Amsterdam: Menasseh ben Israel Instituut, 2009.

Wilder, Gary. "Irreconcilable Differences: A conversation with Albert Memmi." *Transition*, no. 71 (1996): 158–77.

Wilson, Edmund. "Books." *New Yorker*, November 16, 1946.

Winock, Michel. *Nationalism, Anti-Semitism, and Fascism in France*. Translated by Jane Marie Todd. Stanford: Stanford University Press, 1998.

Wistrich, Robert S. *From Ambivalence to Betrayal: The Left, the Jews, and Israel*. Jerusalem: Vidal Sassoon International Center for the Study of Antisemitism, 2012.

————. *Revolutionary Jews from Marx to Trotsky*. New York: Harper and Row, 1976.

Yakira, Elhanan. *Post-Zionism, Post-Holocaust: Three Essays on Denial, Forgetting, and the Delegitimation of Israel*. Translated by Michael Swirsky. Cambridge: Cambridge University Press, 2010.

Yetiv, Isaac. "Albert Memmi: The Syndrome of Self-exile." *International Fiction Review* 1, no. 2 (1974): 125–34.

Young, Michael. "Some thoughts on the death of 'anti-Marxist' Maxime Rodinson." *Daily Star* (Beirut), May 27, 2004. http://www.dailystar.com.lb/Opinion/Commentary/2004/May-27/95172-some-thoughts-on-the-death-of-anti-marxist-maxime-rodinson.ashx.

Young-Bruehl, Elisabeth. *Hannah Arendt: For Love of the World*. New Haven: Yale University Press, 1982.

Younis, Rami. "Interview: The Man Behind the BDS Movement." *+972 mag.com*. June 14, 2015. https://972mag.com/interview-the-man-behind-the-bds-movement/107771/.

ACKNOWLEDGMENTS

Many people helped me with this book, though I am pretty sure that none of them agree with everything in it.

During several trips to Israel over the past few years, I spoke with writers, journalists, academics, activists, and others who generously took time to answer my questions. Though they are not quoted directly, they were extremely helpful in providing background information and context. Thank you to Aluf Benn, Bradley Burston, Eyal Chowers, Gershom Gorenberg, Ilan Greilsammer, Amal Jamal (interviewed in New York), Benny Morris, Danny Rubinstein, Shlomo Sand, Anita Shapira, Noam Sheizaf, David Shulman, Zeev Sternhell, Yerri and Shoshana Yovel, and to the activists of MachsomWatch and Peace Now in Tel Aviv.

In the West Bank, and in Israel, I greatly benefited from meeting, and listening to, representatives of the Palestinian Authority and members (or former members) of the PLO.

In Berlin, speaking with Dan Diner was an illumination.

Back home, friends and colleagues read chapters and helpfully commented on them. Thank you to Kaavya Asoka, Michael Bérubé, Omri Boehm, Bob Boyers, Shimon Dotan, Todd Gitlin, Michael Kazin, Naomi Kleinberg, and Ann Martin (as wonderful an editor as she is a friend). Michael Walzer encouraged me early on in my writing, which meant a lot.

Lara Zarum—who stuck with this from the beginning, and for whom no fact or comma is too unimportant to check—was a superb researcher. She is a talented young journalist in her own right.

I began this book at the American Academy in Berlin, and (almost) finished it at NYU's Center in Paris. Many thanks to the staffs of each, who provided peaceful places to write and excellent library services.

My agent, Stephanie Steiker, immediately understood this book and knew how to represent it—and, equally important, how to comment on it wisely.

I envisioned this book with Steve Wasserman in mind, and I feel lucky that he took it on as editor. I have benefited, for years, from working with Steve. The breadth of his erudition never ceases to impress me, as does his passion for ideas; he has been absolutely crucial to this project. I also thank John Donatich, Seth Ditchik, Dan Heaton, Jenya Weinreb, Eliza Childs, and the rest of the team at Yale University Press for their knowledge, support, and enthusiasm; it was a pleasure to work with them.

Two people, in particular, read everything, sometimes more than once, and were immeasurably helpful. Nissim Calderon of Tel Aviv is a keen observer of the Left and of Israel, and of the follies of each; he offered sharp insights and saved me from innumerable mistakes. Jay Bernstein kept on (re)reading and, amazingly, never tired of discussing all this.

Of course, the ideas in this book, and any errors it may have, are solely my responsibility.

This book is dedicated to my father, Jordan L. Linfield, a proud leftist and proud Jew. It is also for Jay Bernstein. Ever since I met him, he has demanded, "Give me an argument!" This is my attempt to do so.